More praise for *The Antagonist*

"This book is a must read."   Pamela Wallin

"This book, as the saying goes, is more than its cover. . . . A commendable job."   Jeffrey Simpson, *The Globe and Mail*

"Martin's book . . . may be an eye opener to most Canadians. Fortunately, it is also so well written that readers will have a hard time putting it down."   *The Leader Post* (Regina)

"One of the most penetrating political biographies of recent memory. . . . Lucien Bouchard is like an automobile accident: we don't want to look, but we can't bring ourselves to look away."
See Magazine

"Anyone with the slightest interest in the future of Canada must read this excellent biography of one of the greatest opportunists in a profession—politics—that has always attracted more than its fair share of them."   *The Daily News*

"An intriguing book . . . a page-turner peppered with surprises."
London Free Press

"Martin . . . has brought a much-needed psychological dimension to political biography in this country. With *The Antagonist*, he has set a new standard. Bravo!"   *The Calgary Herald*

PENGUIN BOOKS
THE ANTAGONIST

Lawrence Martin is the critically acclaimed author of seven previous books on politics and sport. His most recent bestselling biography, *Chrétien: The Will to Win*, won widespread praise from critics for it insight and scholarship. Raised in Hamilton, Ontario, and educated at McMaster University and Harvard, Martin worked at *The Hamilton Spectator* before joining *The Globe and Mail* where he reported for fourteen years and served as the newspaper's correspondent in Montreal, Washington and Moscow. He currently lives in Ottawa with his wife Maureen and daughters Katie and Kristina.

Merry Christmas, 1998
To Dad from
Richard & Catharine

THE ANTAGONIST

Lucien Bouchard and the Politics of Delusion

LAWRENCE MARTIN

Penguin Books

PENGUIN BOOKS
Published by the Penguin Group
Penguin Books Canada Ltd, 10 Alcorn Avenue, Toronto, Ontario,
Canada M4V 3B2
Penguin Books Ltd, 27 Wrights Lane, London W8 5TZ, England
Penguin Putnam Inc., 375 Hudson Street, New York, New York 10014, U.S.A.
Penguin Books Australia Ltd, Ringwood, Victoria, Australia
Penguin Books (NZ) Ltd, cnr Rosedale and Airborne Roads, Albany,
Auckland 1310, New Zealand

Penguin Books Ltd, Registered Offices: Harmondsworth,
Middlesex, England

First published in Viking by Penguin Books Canada Limited, 1997
Published in Penguin Books, 1998

1 3 5 7 9 10 8 6 4 2

Copyright © Lawrence Martin, 1997

All rights reserved.

Manufactured in Canada.

Canadian Cataloguing in Publication Data

Martin, Lawrence, 1947–
The antagonist: Lucien Bouchard and the politics of delusion

ISBN 0-14-026427-2

1. Bouchard, Lucien, 1938– . 2. Canada—Politics and government—
1984–1993.* 3. Quebec (Province)—Politics and government—1994– .*
4. Prime ministers—Quebec (Province)—Biography. 5. Politicians—Canada—
Biography. 6. Politicians—Quebec (Province)—Biography.
I. Title.

FC631.B68M37 1998   971.064'7'092   C97-930166-1
F1034.3.B68M37 1998

Visit Penguin Canada's web site at **www.penguin.ca**

AUTHOR NOTE

Could it be that he will change banners once again? When the hardcover edition of *The Antagonist* was published in the fall of 1997 Lucien Bouchard was firmly committed to another referendum on sovereignty. His brilliant platform performance in the referendum of October 1995 had taken the country to the brink. It remained for him to nudge just one percent of Quebec voters into the separatist camp to realize his dream. Or was it his dream?

Over the course of his career Lucien Bouchard alternated between federalism and separatism no less than six times. He was three times a federalist—as a student editorialist at Le College de Jonquiere, as a campaigner in the 1960s for Pierre Trudeau, and as Canada's Secretary of State and Minister of the Environment under Brian Mulroney. He was a sovereignist three times—in his toughly-worded declarations at Laval law school, as a campaigner for René Lévesque, as head of the Bloc Quebecois and Parti Quebecois.

While his astonishing reversals might have sparked enough ridicule and accusations of hypocrisy to destroy any normal politician, Lucien Bouchard was no ordinary politician. His animal magnetism and his capacity as a grievance-bearer—'I will bear your crown of thorns'—were unparalleled. To start 1998 he was riding high, well ahead in the polls, ready for an easy election triumph in his province to be followed by a referendum call. But then came another Quebecker of charisma and overnight the bets were off. Conservative party leader Jean Charest had been in Ottawa 13 years and had little record of accomplishment and little new to say on the unity issue. But if the image is right, substance doesn't mean much in politics. Charest was new generation. He was 'Spice Boy.' He instantly propelled the federalists well into the forefront.

Charest made Bouchard look old and he immediately tapped into Bouchard's history of backflips, alleging that Bouchard was preparing yet another "virage" for the population of Quebec. He would, predicted Charest, back off on his pledge for another referendum. Indeed within days of his statement, that's what Bouchard appeared to be doing. Whenever the tide of opinion had swayed in his province, Bouchard, it seemed, had swayed with it. When Trudeaumania was the rage, he turned to Trudeau. When Mulroney took flight, he turned to Mulroney. Now the nation was faced with the fantastic possibility that the same man, the former Secretary of State—as such the tribune of Canadian Unity—who had then turned and led a campaign for its break-up would reincarnate once again and re-issue his unity soundtrack.

With Bouchard all was possible. An intellectual, a dreamer, a schemer, an emotional inferno, a man of Cartesian logic, a stranger to his own country, he was nothing if not complex. Since he had come the closest of anyone in Canadian history to splitting up the country, the Liberals of Jean Chrétien had good reason to want to know more about him. A Liberal MP sought the advice of one of Canada's top psychiatrists, Vivian Rakoff. The psychiatrist produced a report on Bouchard which made its way through the offices of the prime minister. When the contents of the report were revealed in the first edition of this book, they produced some understandable sympathy for Bouchard. The scrutiny politicians have to endure is tough to begin with and this seemed to be taking it to a new level. It was ironic however to hear the views of some who suggested that since the psychiatrist had not sat down and interviewed Bouchard he had no right to offer his opinion. Journalists annually write dozens of analyses of Bouchard without ever sitting down with him. They are less qualified to analyze human character than those, like Dr. Rakoff, from the psychology and psychiatry profession.

While some of his conclusions were dubious, others coincided with the impressions I gained from spending hundreds of hours researching this book. His insights offered a possible explanation for the astounding number of zig zags, reversals, and contradictions that dot Lucien Bouchard's career path.

While Bouchard himself did not agree to be interviewed specifically for this book, I am thankful to two of his brothers, Gérard and Roch, for giving hours of their time in responding to my questions. My thanks also to many of his closest friends and associates who were among the more than one hundred who were kind enough to be interviewed for the story. With only a couple of exceptions all interviews for the book were on the record.

The book was written over a period of two years and I wish to thank my family for their patience and support during this time as well as the highly professional staff at Penguin Canada.

CONTENTS

1. BURNING INSIDE

Looking back, the brother who was closest in age to Lucien thought there was something unnatural about growing up in the Bouchard home. The word Roch Bouchard used to describe the experience was *de-réel*. Abnormal. This was not to be taken in the Hitchcockian sense, he cautioned, but there was an inveiglement of some kind. "Our family was transported along by a type of mystique…In effect, there was a Bouchard mythology." Life inside the home, Roch unhappily noted, was unreal in comparison to the outside world.

He didn't like to think back. It brought him stress and psychological pain. Myth and reality had competed in such a way in the early years he spent with Lucien and the others that it was hard to get a clear picture of things. Later in life, when he suffered bouts of manic depression, Roch couldn't help but look back in anger. He suspected that the strange conditions he lived under were a source of his affliction.

He was one of five Bouchard children. They were raised in the 1940s and 1950s in the faraway town of Jonquière in northern Quebec. Lying in back of the Laurentian Mountains, Jonquière was cut off from the rest of Quebec and of Canada by the great barrier. Next door to Jonquière was a company town called Arvida, which was operated by Anglos who tended to view the French as an inferior breed—like peasants.

Along with Lucien and Roch were Claude, Claudette and the youngest and perhaps most conventional sibling, Gérard. The father, Philippe, delivered lumber supplies from his pick-up truck. He worked fourteen-hour days, leaving the running of the household to his intensely spiritual wife, Alice.

Alice Simard, who played organ at the church, had a forbidding, God-fearing look which intimidated friends of the Bouchard boys who visited. To them she was chilling. To Roch Bouchard, she was almost devoid of joy. Though she had the capacity for happiness, her worries over family security as well as her intense religiosity seized her with consternation. She tended to view events in traumatic terms, as if Armageddon were around the corner. Her attitude weighed heavily on the children. Earthly joy had to be suppressed if salvation were to be found. "We felt guilt in the simple fact of trying to enjoy life," recalled Roch. "We couldn't laugh much."

Each day was viewed as critical. Time could not be squandered. When Roch thought back, he remembered the regimentation. "There was the piano. Every one of us knew what we were supposed to do as soon as the piano began to play."

The father, too, came under Alice's hawkish glare. On Saturday nights he wanted to relax with friends and have a few drinks. But the moment that the beer started to flow in any kind of abundance, the moment Philippe Bouchard felt a little mirth bubbling up, Alice would send forth thunderbolts, creating a scene. How dare he have a good time!

Her rigid disposition was "very important to understanding our mentality," thought Roch. The mother was "a misfit," he said. "She didn't belong to the world we lived in." His older brother, Lucien, never put it in such bald terms, but one day when he would write the story of his life, there would be a rather startling omission. In a book of several hundred pages there was barely a mention of Alice Simard.

If the mother was a misfit, the father was a saint. He was a tall, lean character with a cigarette dangling from the side of his mouth and the charisma of a motion picture star. He was honest and he was warm, and the children thought that, despite his lowly station, he was the repository of all the wisdom the world contained. They knew he was poor and uneducated, but they knew also that this wasn't his fault, that rather it was probably the people in places like Arvida next door who had seen to it.

The father bore his lot with dignity, the dignity of a martyr. All the boys vied for his attention, particularly the two eldest. Not finding much love from their mother, it became especially important. Unfortunately for Roch, when the father took one of them on his rounds on the truck route, it was usually Lucien. Lucien was the senior son, the favoured son, the good son.

Unlike Roch, who started to rebel against the constraints of the extreme puritanism his mother favoured, Lucien remained virtuous and conservative. Life was serious business. The stakes were enormous. There was no time for frivolity.

While parochial and immersed in the traditional family culture, the brothers found that another part of Lucien looked far beyond his piece of compartmentalized Quebec that was the Saguenay. Lucien had a wondrous imagination, a conqueror's imagination. Roch saw him in his young years as being "already on the world stage." Gérard got the same impression. Though nobody got too close to the detached senior brother with the sombre true-believer eyes, Gérard had the most immediate sense of him. He shared a room with Lucien on the second floor of their sparsely furnished working-class home.

He found him intellectual, resolute and brilliant. His depth was readily apparent from the way he devoured books and retained their contents. At a very young age Lucien was poring over histories of Alexander, Hannibal, Napoleon and Julius Caesar. Lucien didn't only read books, Gérald recalled, he lived them. He got so caught up in the drama of these gigantic figures of history that he imagined himself in the role—a prince! a pope! a king!—up there on the world stage directing great armies, leading empires.

To say he had an appointment with destiny was perhaps an overstatement, thought Roch and Gérard. But there was no doubting his obsession. "He would read the history of the Roman Empire," recalled Gérard, "and then he would live through that for one year and he would almost be making the decisions. And he would read *Remembrance of Things Past*, and then he would know everything about this novel and live with it and grow with it, and then he would turn to something else and [it would be] the same thing."

The books pushed his imagination to new horizons, which he expanded upon with great fervour at the dinner table, holding the attention of the others for an hour at a time. "And then after dinner we would go and read this damn book," recalled Gérard, "because he was so convincing and made things so vivid."

These were hardly passions of an ordinary kind, Gérard concluded. It was a zeal one could hardly imagine. "He was burning!" he said of Lucien. "He's always been burning!"

Behind Lucien's eyes there was what Roch described as "a force of will that was indestructible." Indestructible, and, judging at times from his behaviour, uncontainable. Sometimes the boy Lucien would lose control. He'd go through long stretches in which he was cool, reasoned, steady, but then the fires would leap from him and he would explode. While hot Latin tempers were not so unusual where Lucien came from, what struck Gérard was that there was no seeming basis in reason for his outbursts. Lucien was "very impulsive, very choleric," Gérald said. "He would very easily get in a bad mood—for nothing! He had difficulty keeping control over himself in that sense."

The tendency was not easily explained, nor were the less conventional ways of others in the family. There were the psychological difficulties experienced by Roch, who became a philosophy professor. He traced them to the conflict of positive and negative sentiments, as written about by Spinoza, whom he regarded as the real inventor of psychoanalysis. There was the enigma of another exceptionally bright brother, Claude. He would get a batch of impressive university degrees but would drop out of the mainstream, becoming a reclusive writer and poet.

Their mother's proclivities certainly weighed on them, contributing to a sense of the *de-réel*. As well there was a host of other unusual influences, some having to do with the mystique of family lineage. The Bouchard boys were raised in a contrasting culture, one which seemingly alternated between deprivation and ennoblement. The deprivation was the poverty of their circumstances; ennoblement was the family lineage. To hear them tell it, they were part of a special breed. The Bouchard clan—or cult as the brothers sometimes referred to it—extended back through the ages. Their forefathers had settled in this faraway corner of Quebec with the dream of building a distinct new region, a French kingdom on the continent. They had carved out from the rugged forest a special place which was the family farm but which, in the vocabulary of the Bouchards, was more like an oratory or a shrine. "A high temple of spirituality," Roch called it. A sanctuary of "human values, of excellence, of mysticism."

The boys were taken to it, in a village called Saint-Coeur-de-Marie, on weekends. The 100-kilometre pilgrimage was made in the prosaic majesty of the father's pick-up truck. Aunts, uncles, curés and nuns from the extended family all congregated at the white frame house where Lucien had been rocked as a baby on the encircling verandah and where the air hung like incense and where the atmosphere was more exalted than at Sunday church itself.

The ancestors, so many from the clergy, were God's chosen people and they counted themselves as missionaries to God's chosen land. The boys would kneel before them and join them in hymns and prayer, chanting the glories of God and of the Bouchard line and of the old country, which was France. Here, as Lucien recalled, "the cult of family and all its myths so nurtured our imagination."

The boys were young. They were impressionable. They heard of their moral and spiritual duty, of how they had to surpass others, of how they had to carry the torch forward and become, as Roch put it, the pioneers of a country, founders of a people.

Not all of them took it so seriously. Gérard, for one, didn't buy into the cult stuff. But for the eldest boy, the one who was burning inside, the benedictions had grand meaning. They fired his imagination and embedded in his mind. They would return to haunt both him and his country.

2. THE MYTHS OF THE KINGDOM

The moment in the Laurentide forest in the labour camp owned and operated by the Anglos was a humiliation not easily forgotten. Lucien was in his mid-teens when he was sent up there to work for the summer. He was an intellectual youth who cherished self-esteem, dignity and now he was working with illiterate brutes, living in shanties, hauling out stumps, beating his way through sheets of mosquitoes.

Roch had his taste of the same. He was sent there as a teen too, the family needing the money. He worked an eleven-hour shift, daily, and it was hellish. "I had to work with bums, tough guys who beat me, who threw knives."

Roch was home in the summer of 1953 when he received a phone call from his brother. Lucien was in a state of revulsion. The debasement he had experienced was too much. He had stepped out of the camp in the darkness and as he told Roch, he suddenly found himself in a bog of human excrement. Standing in shit! Up to his ankles in it.

Roch's voice heightened in indignation as he recounted the incident. How could they have been expected to tolerate this? The shame! Of course, none of the Anglos of the area were subjected to this kind of treatment. They were the bosses who set the conditions and the wages. They constituted a tiny 2 percent of the population of 300,000 in the Saguenay-Lac-Saint-Jean region, but they ran one hundred percent of the major industries—pulp and paper and chemicals.

Having scraped the dung from his shoes, Lucien Bouchard could see how well this other side lived in comparison to his own people because he travelled with his father, the humble trucker, to neighbouring Arvida. Founded in 1926 by the Aluminum Company of Canada, the town was the residential base for its huge smelter works. It was divided, as if along racial lines, with railway tracks running through it, denoting the barrier between the haves and the have-nots. The Anglos didn't talk much to the "Frenchies" because it wasn't good for their reputations. It was a matter of pride that they spoke no French—even if they had lived in Arvida for decades. However, for young Francophones like Lucien Bouchard, it was important to know some English to get a job.

The housing in Arvida was all owned by Alcan and the French normally could not rent in the high-class district, even if they had the means. "The Anglophones considered the French to be second-class citizens, like Negroes in the South," said Joan Bell, who lived in the town and later wrote a report on the conditions. "They were bigots." The town "epitomized the two solitudes because there was no mixing between the Anglophones and the Francophones. There's emotional baggage being carried around from this time. Bouchard's was the last group to carry it around."

Lucien Bouchard's close-up view of this and other Anglophone pockets of privilege left a lasting memory. "Very early in my life," he recalled, "money and authority were English." It was a major factor, he would reason, in the emergence of his region's nationalism.

Much would change with the Quiet Revolution that began in the 1960s. Quebec wrested itself free of the control by a clergy whose politics had actually encouraged discriminatory stratification. With a new education system, French Canadians became competent in engineering and business and began replacing the English in executive positions and gradually took charge of their own economy. Arvida would disappear, formally incorporated into the city of Jonquière in the 1980s. But to Bouchard and thousands of others in the Saguenay-Lac-Saint-Jean region, it didn't matter much. The wrong had already been inflicted.

His youth, and so much of his later life, was a story of isolation in the French solitude. He was born on a strip of geography as remote and ethnically pure as could be found anywhere in the country. His home region was a cocooned collectivity, one with a segregated history and a segregated soul. It even had a name which set it apart. The territory where he was raised was called the Kingdom of the Saguenay.

Its location in north-eastern Quebec was not so far north of the provincial capital, Quebec City—only 200 kilometres. But the mountains made the divide momentous. No decent road to get through the highlands to the Saguenay region was built until the 1950s. The territory was bordered on the east side by the St. Lawrence and on the west by the glittering Lac Saint-Jean. Cutting crosswise and linking the two bodies of water ran the deep, dark Saguenay River, along which were located the three cities where Lucien Bouchard spent much of his life—Alma, Jonquière and Chicoutimi.

The Saguenay, majestic and intimidating, was formed, as legend had it, with a fantastic wrenching of the earth's crust which lacerated a divide in the mountains, leaving great fjords and rock cliffs at the river's edge. The native peoples who first inhabited the land spoke of the waterway in terms of awe and gloom. It had no bottom! When Jacques Cartier came and claimed the land for France, he was told wild tales of a magic kingdom of rubies and emeralds and a white race at the far end of the river which supposedly did not eat.

Cartier turned the area into a reserve of France, which formed an alliance with the natives for the purpose of exploiting the principal economic activity—the fur trade. The native peoples were given the run of the region, so long as they delivered the pelts. The French called the territory *Le Domain du Roi* and, as well, the more august appellation, *Le Royaume du Saguenay*—the Kingdom of the Saguenay.

For two centuries, while the fur trade flourished under the French—and later the English—white settlers were not allowed in the kingdom. But in 1842, the Hudson's Bay land lease was renewed only on condition that agricultural settlement be permitted. The migration north to Saguenay-Lac-Saint-Jean from other regions of Quebec began. It carried with it far more significance than any ordinary settlement. To hear the folklore, this was a Hegira of sorts—the birth of a holy land.

Gérard Bouchard became an eminent social historian, an expert on demographics whose views certainly informed Lucien. He reasoned that in crossing the Laurentides to this new territory of the Saguenay, Francophones were creating a new dream. The failed rebellions of 1837 in Lower Canada against British dominion brought an end to the hope of a new French republic. "But when Quebeckers saw settlements spreading over the Laurentides," Gérard Bouchard analysed, "a dream was born according to which the land in the north could be an opportunity to start all over again. They saw this land as a sort of paradise, a promise for the future of a nation."

The Kingdom of the Saguenay was to be a new all-French province, or even state. Among its first settlers were the grandparents of Lucien Bouchard. They came from Charlevoix and Trois-Rivières and eventually they settled in little Saint-Coeur-de-Marie where they cleared out a thousand acres of timber and built the family home—the shrine. Lucien Bouchard's great-grandfather, Sixte, erected a cross in the front yard. The young man's grandfather, Joseph, knelt and boomed out rosaries before meals.

The dreams of the settlers of the kingdom did not die easily. According to Gérard Bouchard, a few dynamic entrepreneurs in Chicoutimi, the big city in the region, looked at the riches of their land, the natural resources and the outlet to the St. Lawrence, and filled themselves with delusions of grandeur. They envisaged a Chicago of the north. They reasoned that via the Saguenay and the St. Lawrence, Chicoutimi was closer to Europe than New York. It would be the major seaport of the continent.

Alas, no Chicago of Quebec came into being. For the longest time the region remained a fiefdom of an English entrepreneur, William Price and his family. Beginning in the middle of the nineteenth century, they exploited the land for its forest resource and developed successful pulp and paper enterprises. They ran a daunting monopoly with the complicity of governments, which took a hands-off approach. The Francophones fended for themselves without the benefits of government services and programs. They carved out a living from a landscape that was cold, inhospitable and arable only at great pains. A spirit of independence developed in the Saguenay-Lac-Saint-Jean area. Politicians were remembered only for having bestowed timber grants to Mr. Price or giving other rights to the English at the expense of the population that constituted the vast majority.

Industrial development in the twentieth century brought hydroelectric power projects and the aluminum works of Alcan. The economy was highly Americanized, dependent on exports south of the border. Transportation out of the region to Quebec City and other main centres was terribly awkward owing to the absence of highways and a slow rail system. Inhabitants travelled rarely, remaining wedged behind the mountains. This, as analysed by historian Camil Girard, was another factor in fostering a mentality of self-sufficiency, a sense among the Francophones that their fate was in their own hands. The people of the Saguenay did not need or want government. Some of them, the Bouchard grandparents included, showed their disdain during the Great Depression by refusing the dole or by returning their old-age pension cheques.

The sense of pride and independence of the people was rooted in literature as well. The quintessential novel written about Saguenay-Lac-Saint-Jean, Louis Hémon's *Maria Chapdelaine*, was first published in 1913. It was a celebration of the pioneers who moved north to hack out a living from the dense forests and hard terrain. Maria, the daughter of one such trailblazer, ultimately faced the choice of remaining on the new frontier and marrying a local farmer, or going off to a comfortable life in Boston with another suitor. She wrestled with the dilemma but ultimately a voice came to her. "We bore overseas our prayers and our songs; they are ever the same...We traced the boundaries of a new continent...Within these limits all we brought with us, our faith, our tongue, our virtues, our very weaknesses are henceforth hallowed things which no hand may touch, which shall endure to the end."

She endured, as did the sense of uniqueness and separation of her region. In 1988 when the Saguenay celebrated its 150th anniversary, the Quebec magazine *L'Actualité* entitled its article "150 Years of Solitude."

The people were still alone, and still thinking big. They talked of themselves as the Texans of the north. Just as in Texas, everything was bigger in the Saguenay—including the spirit of independence.

"It is not a society that behaves like a dependent society," observed Gérard Bouchard, summarizing the history. "It is quite a confident people. They want to assert themselves. This is a strange mentality... Culturally it is very different. It's not like Newfoundland. It's not the loser mentality."

Demographically, it is one of the few areas of Canada which has not changed since Confederation. Benoît Bouchard (no relation), a native of the region who would carve out a career in federal politics, noted how it remained frozen in time. It didn't have immigrants and the Anglophones, after decades of proprietorship, were eventually assimilated. Understanding Lucien Bouchard, he explained, required understanding the homogeneity of his home-land. "These people are independent, period."

Born in the region in 1905, Philippe Bouchard, Lucien's father, would live seventy years but step out of the province of Quebec only twice—each time to the United States. Once he went to a hockey game at Boston Garden and on another occasion he jour-neyed to the racetrack at Saratoga Springs, New York. By compar-ison to Alice, however, he was an inveterate traveller. Her seques-tration could hardly be surpassed. At nearly ninety, she gave an interview to an American magazine. Asked about her impressions of English Canadians, she explained that she couldn't say because she didn't know any. She had never met them.

A contemporary, five years older than Lucien Bouchard, was Jean Chrétien. Like the Bouchards, the working-class Chrétiens lived in a small town, Shawinigan, where the great majority spoke French and where the bosses who dominated the industries were English. They had a father who had to work at several jobs to keep the family fed and who was determined, like Philippe Bouchard, to have his children educated. The Chrétiens, however, were not located in a remote kingdom hidden behind mountains. Jean Chré-tien's parents travelled into the English-speaking world. Wellie, the taciturn father, made annual treks to New Hampshire to the head-quarters of the life insurance company for which he worked part-time. New Hampshire had a large French settlement and over his two decades of visits there, Wellie Chrétien witnessed the rapid rate of assimilation into the American melting pot. He grew to appreciate how, by contrast, the French fact survived inside the Canadian federation. Significant also were the excursions of Jean's mother, Marie Chrétien, whose father had moved his family west to Alberta. Mrs. Chrétien visited him, returning from trips to the Rockies to regale her sons with stories of the beauty of the vast Canadian landscape and the spectacular mountains. She was a warm, outgoing woman, in many ways the direct opposite of Alice Bouchard. While the Bouchard boys were being filled with stories of the wonders of France, Marie Chrétien's accounts of a different land captured the imagination of the youngest boys, Michel and Jean. They became pan-Canadians.

Lucien Bouchard's parents never had the opportunity to

appreciate a broader perspective. Philippe led a life which was at times desperate, leaving him almost a broken man. Philippe had stayed on the family farm in Saint-Coeur-de-Marie, helping out until well beyond the time that sons were supposed to leave. He had planned to have his own farm, but as his boys told it, he found there was no more arable land to cultivate and he moved to Montreal and found work installing furnaces. But life didn't work out for him in the metropolis and he returned home again, where he was idle for long periods. With a grade four education, only semi-literate, no skills other than farmhand, he had few prospects. A proud man, he was humiliated, hungry, haunted by failure. Finally, in his mid-thirties, he moved out, down the road to Jonquière where his brother Abélard, who had opened a small lumber operation, hired him at a subsistence-level wage.

In the meantime, however, Philippe was producing children. Lucien, the first to arrive, was born in 1938 when war was about to break out in Europe, and he was followed by four more in the next four years. Five kids were a lot for a man of few means, though by no means a lot by Quebec standards of the time. The children had a roof over their heads and just enough food and clothing to get by. But life wasn't easy. When grown up, Lucien would often speak of his poverty as a youth, praising his father for surviving it and seeing to it that the children received top educations. For his part, Roch felt the stresses of youth so much that he would be led to a dire conclusion later in life. "My father shouldn't have had children," he said. "He was too poor. He shouldn't have."

Roch had an experience unlike the others. At age twelve he was sent off for a year of schooling at a chillingly religious institution in Ste.-Anne-de-Beaupré. "You're twelve, a very young twelve, and it was a terrible place, full of sins and culpability and the devil and homosexuality, and very dangerous for a boy to be there." Then he was home again and praying every morning, and being made to confess his sins. "It was a frantically religious environment. Irrational."

He saw Lucien as having it easier because he was the eldest and because he had a special bond with his father. "There were five infants in five years in a family where the parents were very busy, very stressed. We lived in a religious and cultural climate that was extremely tense. And so you had the personalities of the children who tried to find some space in there. Lucien was older, stronger, and he took up more space."

Despite his dire past, Philippe Bouchard earned the reputation in Jonquière as a strong citizen, a man to be admired, one who was raising a good family. He had a special charisma. Paul-André Gauthier, who would be a classmate and close friend of Lucien's, recalled meeting Philippe on a few occasions in the lumber yard where he collected wood for his route. "I lived near the house where the Bouchards lived in Jonquière. I didn't know Lucien at the time and I didn't know who this man was at first. But I remember him very well. He stood out from the rest. I remember him in the lumber yard. He was lean. He didn't look strong necessarily, but at the same time you knew he was very powerful. He had a radiant presence. There was a special warmth about him, a bearing that could much impress the younger generation like myself."

The sons respected their father's every gesture. In the evenings near bedtime when they were creating a ruckus upstairs, it would take only the sound of his footsteps on the stairway to silence them. Often he came home late from work when the children were already in bed. He would make a tour of the rooms, kiss the boys in their sleep and return downstairs to Alice, weeping.

One of the only negative things said against him was that he was an overly exuberant drinker. It was a criticism his wife certainly appeared to agree with, but one which incensed Lucien. His pride was such that he could not stand to hear a negative word about his father or, for that matter, any aspect of his family. It was the likely explanation for why he did not speak of his mother in his autobiography and why he painted a rosier picture of the years growing up than was evidently the case.

One of his long-time school friends was André Tremblay whose family was one who got their wood supplies delivered by Philippe Bouchard. The drinking rumour spread, he suggested, because Bouchard made some of his deliveries smelling of beer. "Lucien's father knew his job was no good. He had a large family and the guy is looking for some form of compensation, fun in his life—two or three or four beers with the guys." It was understandable, said Tremblay, and if he went a little overboard at times, it was not a true reflection of his character. "The guy was always there. The guy never missed a day's work. He was beautiful, happy, strong. He was giving everything to his family. He was a strong man and at the same time a weak man. But he was honest."

That Philippe had such a difficult life, that he wasn't a success, became a great motivating factor for Lucien at an early age, thought Tremblay. He detected a permanent undercurrent of bitterness in his friend. If, for Gérard Bouchard, it was the fire inside that marked his brother, for Tremblay it was the anger, an anger that was always there, simmering, ready to burst, an anger likely born of the conditions his family had to face. "We were coming from a social milieu which was low, almost non-educated, a milieu that was not on the map," recalled Tremblay, "we were coming from nowhere...Lucien's father had no status. Don't forget that." Lucien's life, he suggested, could be seen in part as a quest to rehabilitate his father and his people, deprived of their just standing by conditions forced upon them by outsiders. But so many complex factors went into the shaping of Lucien Bouchard that he did not want to venture far with any particular theory. "It could be the explanation. But I am not the dean of the school of psychology."

The hardships left Philippe a very insecure man. Their father "would not trust the future because of the past," noted Gérard. He detected a similar insecurity in Lucien. Lucien was doing well in school, he was popular enough, and competitive in sports—all qualities that might normally give a young man confidence. But like his parents, he was drowned in doubts. "It is something that I have always known about Lucien," said Gérard. "He was raised very close to my parents and he shared their very deep concern of everyday life."

In a rare commentary on his mother, whose traumatic ways appeared to mark him, Lucien would say that she imposed a heavy discipline "in an atmosphere almost Jansenist." High standards were demanded of the boys. They may have looked poor, but they were not allowed to act that way. They could not be typical of the milieu from which they came. Any habit that was suggestive of being superficial, or coarse, or tilting towards hayseed stock was frowned upon. Though their father was only semi-literate, he wanted the boys to speak the French language with sophistication. One night, when Lucien was speaking coarse street French at the dinner table, Philippe lashed out at him. He told him he couldn't even understand what he was saying. He threw down his fork in disgust and ordered Lucien to speak properly. The image of it, of the uneducated father in grimy work clothes demanding such high quality, fixed itself in Lucien's mind. He never forgot the moment.

The entire Bouchard clan emphasized the importance of speaking high-quality French and for Lucien it became a significant priority, a symbol of pride. Those who spoke the language badly, those who spoke *joual*, were frowned upon. Books being his treasures, he developed a broad vocabulary. At the family shrine there was the once-beautiful and highly articulate grandmother. Never having fulfilled her dream of becoming a nun, she divided her time between milking cows, writing poetry and collecting a stash of great books, one hundred of them. "They were huge tomes," recalled Lucien, "many of them gilt-edged, with hard covers and bright colours, mostly red and blue." They included an illustrated biography of Napoleon and Dickens's *David Copperfield*. Lucien feasted on them. He read them all.

Often he was engaged in church activity. The Bouchards expected one of their sons, all altar boys, to become a priest. On Sundays, Lucien and Roch attended mass three times. They sang the grand mass as members of the choir at 10:45 a.m. To receive the sacrament of communion, church regulations stipulated that no food be eaten from midnight Saturday. Not wanting to see the boys go hungry, Mrs. Bouchard devised a plan to have them eat before the high mass. She had them get up in time to go to 7 a.m. mass. They received communion there, returned home for breakfast and went back to church for the big ceremony. Just for good measure, Alice Bouchard also had them go to the seven o'clock service in the evening.

Lucien was the one the parents had slotted for the holy robes. He was the moralist among the bunch, more like his mother in this regard, and he set an austere model for his brothers and sister. In their teens, when the father had a little money, he gave them weekly allowances. Lucien and Roch got three dollars a week each, Claude and Gérard two. Three of the four of them went into town Friday nights to spend the money. The one who stayed behind—he had books to read—was Lucien. "He never smoked. He never drank. He didn't want us to have a beer, to fool around," recalled Gérard. "He hated that. He wanted us to hate that. He was not that successful. My father was a smoker and he taught us to smoke."

All was not deadly serious and rife with religion and trying circumstances in the Bouchard home. The family loved to sing,
Philippe's rich voice often leading the way, and Lucien was not such
a terrible tenor himself. Humour was often of the dry sort, and the
boys, when time allowed, were avid amateur sportsmen. Competition among them on the playfields was serious business. Their parents couldn't afford bicycles or sports equipment for them, so they
invented games that didn't require much.

In keeping with his historical mindset, Lucien preferred the old
sports of ancient Greece like wrestling and weightlifting. He once
organized a mini-Olympic Games in his neigbourhood with
wrestling, weightlifting and running as the featured events. In the
first two disciplines he had a role model of sorts, a fabled figure
who could be found at the family shrine on the weekends.

Uncle Romeo was six feet five inches tall with a pinched mous-
tache. He was a dandy dresser and a champion wrestler, and there
was no man in the land as strong as him. They called him *armoire-
à-glace*—the icebox—and according to André Tremblay, who
attended school with Lucien for twelve years, it was a well-merited
moniker. "Once I came with my friend to the garage where Romeo
was. We had heard of his reputation. We were in the garage and we
challenged him to lift a V-8 motor engine. He did it! He did it!"

On those Sundays when the Bouchard boys attended mass
three times, the afternoons were free for sports. On one such day
Lucien's Jonquière football team went up against hated Chicoutimi. For the game, the Jonquière coach needed a lineman to take
on the toughest man on the Chicoutimi squad, a horrendous bar-
barian named Paul Charest. Charest made mincemeat of all his
opponents. For some reason the coach chose Lucien Bouchard to
face him.

Bouchard was strong enough, but at this time of his life, still
rather short. Despite being the eldest he was the smallest of all his
brothers, and it bothered him, though not as much as it did another
future political leader of the time, Jean Chrétien. Almost apoplectic
about his diminutive size as a teen, Chrétien once demanded that
his brother, a doctor, give him something "to make me grow."
What he got was vitamin pills.

Against Chicoutimi, Lucien Bouchard bravely took on the
assignment of facing the giant Charest. He suffered the

consequences, emerging black and blue at game's end, but his brothers were proud of him. He had lasted the entire match.

So too were they proud when he stood in front of them to defend the family honour in the face of neighbourhood toughs who ridiculed the Bouchards. Two fights in particular were remembered. Lucien, recalled Roch, got beaten up each time, suffering the blows to self-esteem which such defeats incur.

His forte was not the physical arena. The battlefields Lucien would shine on were the battlefields of the mind. His heroes could be found not so much in the sports leagues, but in the books he treasured and in his own family line. They were people like Uncle Rivard, who had been crushed by a tractor as a boy and crippled for life and who moved about the shrine with an air of reverence, a respect for humanity, an understated grandiloquence. Just the sight of him made the Bouchard brothers feel they were in glorified company. There was the grandfather Joseph who sang the religious hymns with such a venerable, classic air. On special days of the year when the boys would arrive, they would fall to their knees and he would bless them and they would sing the religious songs. There was the fabled great-grandfather Sixte, the prosperous farmer whose honesty was never challenged. His word was "as straight as the king's sword." The boys were born too late to get to know him, but the stories of his legendary status were passed down to them. All of the Bouchard clan talked knowingly and with great appreciation of France, even though they had never been there. Sixte had been there—which made him extraordinary.

They had all come to build this special territory called the kingdom. English Canadians, Roch Bouchard explained, couldn't hope to understand the attachment the Bouchard family could have to their "national collectivity." They had no clue. Nor, he said, could Francophones in other parts of Quebec have the same sense of belonging. They hadn't been part of the grand experiment—as the Bouchard forefathers had been—of moving across the mountains to build a new land.

3. THE CLASSICS STUDENT

It has long been thought—and research appears to support the theory—that the first-born child tends to be more like the parents. He or she will be more inclined to share their conservative attitudes. More dissonant behaviour will show up in later siblings.

Lucien Bouchard appeared to fit the stereotype—certainly his younger brothers thought so—and it revealed a lot about him. Lucien was more morally rigid and authoritarian than the others. He was more prepared to believe not only what Philippe and Alice believed, but also the extended family. Being closer to the lineage made him more like the lineage. If not the mind, then the mindset was parental. He appeared to have the great pride and sense of dignity and social conscience of his father. From his mother, he took the regime of harsh personal discipline and her penchant for traumatizing. No one would ever accuse Lucien Bouchard of being easygoing. He was a man on the edge, on the edge of landmines. As Gérard noted, he found it difficult to stay calm, even while reading. His insides churned. Potential crises lay around every corner.

His buddy André Tremblay, sensing Lucien's delicate and mercurial nature, was always very cautious in his presence lest the balance be tilted. Tremblay could tease others, but not Bouchard. "Thin-skinned. Very thin-skinned," recalled Tremblay. "Lucien had an unpredictable character. An unpredictable character means difficult to manage, difficult to live with. Explosive!"

Bouchard's sensitivity increased his susceptibility. The rich romantic firmament that was his mindset was hesitant to dismiss the fantasy and folklore of territory and family. "I'm the historian in the family," said Gérard Bouchard, "and I might be the most distant to this cult. I had an interest, but not at the same level as Lucien and Roch. They were very, very much impressed by this idea, this vision, this feeling. This would be the difference between Lucien and I. We always knew we were different on this ground."

How many myths could one mind take? There was the mythol-

ogy of the Kingdom of the Saguenay and of the Bouchard cult, and
of the mother, Alice. Then, as Lucien Bouchard waded into his
classical college years, there was yet another layer of illusion to add
to the pile. This was the conception he was given of the history of
Canada. The teaching of it, as Bouchard himself would later testify,
was a surfeit of distortion: English as villains, French as heroes and
martyrs.

At the college in Jonquière, the instruction focused on the history of New France up to the defeat at the hands of the English on
the Plains of Abraham. The treatment given this early period was a
glorious one, as if it were a golden age, recalled Bouchard. "The
French were here. They were building things. They were convert-
ing the natives. There were good natives and bad natives: the good
ones who supported the French, the bad ones who supported the
English. It was a very simplistic view, but that was the way it was."

"The rest of the country," Bouchard told Jeffrey Simpson, "was
presented as only a blur. It was another country, a country we
didn't know. We studied a lot of history of France, Great Britain,
Germany, Europe, the United States, and Quebec. But what happened in the rest of Canada after Confederation, we didn't know.
We were terribly ignorant about English Canada." He had already
received many a tutorial on the glories of France from grandparents at the shrine. All was now reaffirmed. "For me and for those
of us who went to the college, the history we learned was French
history. The heroes were French heroes: Napoleon, Jeanne d'Arc,
Louis XIV, the great writers. We were in awe…"

The clergymen teachers did everything to make the students
loathe Great Britain, whereas the United States, which had successfully rebelled against Britain, was accorded a luminous
appraisal. As Bouchard's teachers spoke, and as Wellie Chrétien
witnessed, the French were being assimilated at a precipitous rate
in America, particularly in the north-eastern states. President
Franklin Delano Roosevelt heartily approved of this trend. In letters, he advised Canadian prime minister Mackenzie King that he
should undertake a similar assimilation policy in Canada. Ottawa
did no such thing, but Bouchard and his classmates never learned
this kind of history.

On Western Canada about the only news came from relatives
who reported, with some accuracy, that it was difficult for

Francophones to maintain their language there. Yves Villeneuve, a classmate of Lucien's, said that "we knew more about Rome than Western Canada." Of English Canada, he said, "We knew it existed. That was about it."

Lucien had done splendidly in primary school, and it was a proud day for his parents when he received the note that he had passed the entrance exams and made it into Quebec's scholastic big leagues—the classical college system. Any Quebec youth hoping to enjoy a career in a prestigious profession had little choice but to spend eight years in these clergy-controlled boot camps which steeped their students in ancient languages, philosophy, science, discipline and God. They took the boys, aged twelve and thirteen, sequestered them within their forbidding concrete barracks and drummed the basics into them. For many of the inmates, it was pure purgatory—the isolation, the discipline, the absence of female companionship. But when it was done and many had gone on to prosper, they could appreciate the rigour, the depth, the cultural treasure of languages and philosophy these institutions had provided. Wrestling for years with the likes of Horace and Virgil, noted René Lévesque, who like most of Quebec's great politicians had gone the classical college route, was fine fruit indeed. "A bridge had been thrown between Greece and Rome, and we could begin to guess how a civilization is constructed."

Fortune smiled upon Lucien Bouchard in several respects. He came of age to go to a classical college just as one was opening in his town of Jonquière (in 1951). This meant that his parents would not have to pay the room and board to send him away. They couldn't have afforded it, and it is well possible that had the college in Jonquière not opened, he may never have pursued higher education. Another advantage was that he could get his elite education without the pain of confinement, the most dreaded aspect of the classical college system. Having *externe* status meant Lucien had the liberty to come and go. He didn't have to suffer the quarantine experienced by Roch at Ste.-Anne-de-Beaupré or Jean Chrétien at Joliette. Chrétien became so desperate for freedom that he faked appendicitis to get out. Intent on keeping up the pretense, he endured an appendectomy at a Shawinigan hospital.

Bouchard's first four years of the eight-year program were at the Externat St.-Michel, run by the Order of the Brothers of the

Sacred Heart. Then, in 1955, the order known as the Oblate Fathers took over, founding Le Collège de Jonquière in a new yellow-brick, three-storey building with all the modern amenities. Compared to other orders, like the Jesuits who schooled Pierre Trudeau, the Oblates were non-elitist. Much to Bouchard's favour, they had a working-class orientation and were considerably more liberal in both curriculum and disciplinary standards.

Bouchard was part of an inaugural class of thirty, most from poorer families like his own who could not afford the elite Séminaire de Chicoutimi. If he had a sense of purpose about his life, enrolling in this school at this time did nothing to diminish it. The students harboured a drive to establish credibility for themselves and their new institution. They wanted to prove themselves as worthy as the advantaged ones in Chicoutimi. "It seemed like we had a mission," said class member Gaston Arseneault, who lived in the French section of Arvida. "It was a pretty serious group. We were the first ones. We felt we were kind of privileged to be going. We were all hoping to do something special in life."

Bouchard took the rivalry with Chicoutimi very seriously. Chicoutimi was sometimes called the city of Cadillacs because so many residents drove them. They were a manifestation, among other things, of Saguenay pride. One Cadillac driver, a man who would soon play an important role in Lucien Bouchard's life, was the town's most highly reputed lawyer, Roland Fradette. Fradette was not normally an ostentatious man, but as he told his partners at the law firm, to lure potential clients in Chicoutimi you had to give the impression you were well-heeled. On his trips into the big city as a teenager in the back of his father's pick-up truck, Bouchard couldn't help noticing the better cars and clothes of the other boys. He felt somewhat embarrassed by this, but at the same time it provided him with further incentive to show the Cadillac people they were no better.

His upbringing had imbued in Lucien a sensitivity to the hardships and suffering of the people. He was well aware of the experiences of his father. Philippe Bouchard had sometimes had to attend school barefoot so that he would not wear out his only pair of shoes. On his father's delivery route, Lucien saw the poverty some endured and he saw the social conscience of his dad at work. Philippe sold woodchips and strips for home heating in the winter.

Even though he was just scraping by himself, he extended credit to his customers. At the start of each winter, he would cut up a load of wood with his own hands and deliver it free of charge to one of the poor families in the town. Lucien remembered.

At the college, Lucien's reading habits, developed since age five, served him well. Some days he read from four in the afternoon until midnight, getting through two books. As a member of the local reading club, he had guidance on what to choose and covered the likes of Jules Verne, Dickens, Balzac and Victor Hugo. He steeped himself in histories such as that of Hannibal, the Carthaginian conqueror whose brilliant campaigns against the Romans almost undid the empire. Young Lucien committed these campaigns to memory, and decades later, when a family member who fancied himself as well-read in this area raised the subject, Lucien corrected him, providing a detailed account of the Punic Wars.

Father Lionel Lamonde, one of the only teachers left at the college to recall Lucien's school days at Jonquière, recognized Bouchard's superior quality. "I classified the students into two groups—those who didn't grow, who remained as almost mechanical thinkers who simply memorized, and those who opened their minds." Bouchard, he said, was in the latter category. Pausing to consider him, a smile crossed the philosophy professor's face. "In the case of Lucien, it was a matter of not getting in the way of his development." Lamonde, who thought Lucien "an ardent, fiery defender of Jonquière," knew he had a gift horse. He opened the gates to let him gallop.

His brilliance lay particularly in the humanities, less so in mathematics and science. Learning Greek and Latin for Bouchard was like inhaling air. One glance down a vocabulary chart and the list was forever imprinted, ready for recall. A member of his class, Guy Aubin, recalled sitting next to Bouchard in a Greek exam. The students were allowed to use their dictionaries to help in the translation of passages. Aubin could hear book pages flapping all around him, but in looking over at Bouchard he was struck to see no such activity. His dictionary lay closed for the exam. He didn't need it. Of his studies in these subjects, Bouchard recalled, "I cherished Greek and Latin and the access they provided to the treasures of antiquity. I would have been ready to pay for the privilege of translating Latin texts."

He absorbed Sophocles, Horace, Euripides and Plato. He loved the ancient Olympic sports. Though nobody can recall him saying it in so many words, he seemed to be using the ancient Greeks as his model in life: their kind of valour, their kind of intellect, philosophy, athleticism—their representation of life's ennobling elements. For him, the man of knowledge, the erudite man, was the most worthy.

His ability in languages was never more evident than in his mother tongue. No one at the college wished to go up against Lucien Bouchard in debates. "He had the stuff of a tribune," recalled another classmate, Gérard Sénéchal. "He had a mind which allowed him to say things exactly as they were." He argued his case trenchantly and with crisp logic, and given his range of reading, he could buttress his points with a wide range of source material. Camille Thivièrge recalled going up against Bouchard on the question of the new medium, television, and whether it was a negative or positive instrument of communication. Bouchard's parents had warned the boys that watching TV was a waste of time and Lucien certainly agreed. Shallow stuff when sitting on your shelf was Horace, Corneille, Proust and Racine. Thivièrge was unable to counter him. "I must tell you that he won. It was clear he had a culture superior to the rest of us."

The debates were big shows with outside juries brought in, halls rented, the public invited. Bouchard's physical presence gave him an immediate advantage. The young man's look exuded a sense of conviction. The brows were bushy and dark, shading sensitive, melancholy eyes. The nose was boldly symmetrical, the chin rock-solid, the demeanour classical and strong. In response to his evident need for more physical strength, he had put himself on a strenuous exercise regime. There were no barbells or exercise equipment in his home, so Lucien lifted concrete blocks used in the building of houses.

His voice lacked a full swell of confidence at this early age, but listeners took note of a passionate, harsh edge. The words cascaded quickly with natural force like water from a spring, or, in more intense moments, like blood. His sentences ended with a pronounced thud.

Another topic he debated was whether girls should be entitled to higher education. On this one he could lament the example of his sister, Claudette, who was then experiencing the trials of trying to get a good education in 1950s Quebec. Her parents did not have the means to send her to Chicoutimi, one of the few classical colleges that admitted females. She was hurt by it since all her brothers were attending classical colleges. She would eventually marry and settle in France.

The only time anyone can remember Lucien losing a debate was at Jonquière's old city hall on a subject dear to his heart—the question of maintaining the teaching of the ancient languages of Latin and Greek, versus modern ones. He naturally argued the pro-side but was beaten by his academic arch-rival, Yves Villeneuve.

He always had a running battle with the wily Villeneuve for top honours in the class and a debate still goes on among the students as to which of the two was best. Villeneuve maintained there should be no confusion. "He [Bouchard] was always losing. In fact, most of the time he was third."

They were a curious duo. They were friends but different in too many ways to be really close. Villeneuve admired Bouchard's range of mind but found him overly serious and aggressive. "He was always more like the bull in a china shop. He was pushy. He was not somebody I would have thought would have become an ambassador." The two challenged one another, engaging in long discussions, philosophical seminars on the meaning of the humanities and where the world was going.

At a college where the ambiance was quiet, religious and austere, Villeneuve was a bit of a rebel. He was a heavy drinker before dropping it altogether, and was always ready to take on the gods of religion and he was sometimes put off by Bouchard's somber, holier-than-thou ways. When Villeneuve and the other students headed downtown for a beer, they could always count on Lucien not being there. As part of the Catholic rite of confirmation, he had taken a vow not to drink. Most who took this vow didn't take it seriously, but Bouchard did. Not until age twenty-one did he taste his first drop of liquor.

Unlike the other students, Bouchard rarely dated girls. It was a result, he would say, of his shyness. Others would say it was a result of the fact that he preferred Latin, Greek, Homer and Horace. Vice, any kind of vice, was Lucien Bouchard's enemy. He wanted to conquer them all. It was like he kept tabs, measuring himself against improbably high standards of excellence. Villeneuve found that Bouchard just couldn't lighten up enough. "He was serious all the time. I would say he probably didn't know how to have fun— he was afraid to have fun." Not knowing Alice Bouchard, Villeneuve didn't know the likely source of this aspect of Bouchard's character.

Adamantly opposed to the primacy of religion in the lives of the students, Villeneuve had a hard time believing someone as bright as Bouchard could be so gullible on this subject. "Villeneuve hated religion, priests, all that goes with it," recalled classmate Arseneault. "One night we had gone out to take a few beers and we went back to the school. We went to chapel, and I'll never forget what happened. Villeneuve spit in the chalice. I saw him. He wanted to show us how much he hated religion—especially the symbols."

Bouchard wasn't present for that spectacle. At this time he was being yanked from two different directions—from one, by the likes of the dark angel Villeneuve, from the other, by the likes of his mother and the clerical establishment—all pushing him hard to don the robes. In the latter group was none other than the head of the diocese, Monsignor Morin. He had watched young Lucien as an altar boy, took note of his devout progress and was enormously impressed. One day at church, in the presence of Lucien's parents, the monsignor placed his red biretta on Lucien Bouchard's head and issued a prophecy. Some day, the monsignor solemnly declared, "Lucien will be our cardinal."

The episode generated some excitement around the household but it was not, according to Gérard Bouchard, an exceptional event. The monsignor was just one of many who were predicting a prominent future for Lucien Bouchard. "Everybody who had known Lucien for years," recalled Gérard, "even the teachers who worked at primary school, had the same feeling—that he was going to do something great in life. Everybody had this feeling and I remember, when he was young, close friends would kid him and tell him, 'You know that someday you are going to become premier of Quebec.' I could tell you a hundred stories like that."

In the summer of 1958, while working for Price Brothers in the forests, Bouchard determined he would make a decision on whether he had a religious calling. He immersed himself in the

writings of George Bernanos and his rather stringent philosophy—
reject materialism, reject ambition, follow the path of the Lord;
life's goodness lies in sacrifice. But neither Bernanos nor his mother
nor the words of the monsignor could move Lucien enough. He
decided to pass on the priesthood.

His friends and classmates thought him best suited for a career
as an academic, a writer or a lawyer. Twenty of the thirty students
in his class who were contacted for their memories of Bouchard
spoke largely in praise of his qualities—his intelligence, his dedication to work and his command of the French language. Back then
most could see he was headed for great success. Hardly any, however, thought of him as having the right stuff for a political career.
They thought, like Paul-André Gauthier, who considered him
almost a perfect student, that he was too sensitive a person to sustain the low blows of politics—either that or too emotionally
volatile.

At the college, he occasionally exhibited the rushes into fury he
did at home. There was an aspect to Lucien and his anger that distinguished him from others, recalled Louis Noël, another member
of his class. "When he got mad, he turned white! His body changed
colour." Noël noticed both the character of his anger and the
degrees of it. "He was someone who could get more angry than
anyone else."

At the same time, he was not without humour and a mischie-
vous side. There was the occasion of the birthday of one of the
balding clerics who taught him. For a gift, Lucien removed the
teeth from a comb and slid it under the professor's door.

His most notable act of provocation came in the form of a
clever challenge to the age-old curriculum. The Oblate Fathers
who ran the institution favoured a modernization of some of the
courses, but were constrained by the educational authorities in
Quebec City. In the major discipline of philosophy, the overseers
prescribed an enormous dose of Thomas Aquinas. The thirteenth-
century theologian whose opus, *Summa Theologica*, sought to reconcile all previous philosophical thinking with his version of Chris-
tianity, had always been a staple of the classical colleges. Wilfrid
Laurier had been swamped with Aquinas a century earlier at Collège de l'Assomption and wasn't thrilled either. Bouchard's philosophy professor, Lionel Lamonde, tried to veer somewhat from the

standardization. He turned a blind eye to students reading works on the infamous forbidden list known as the Index—works by Teilhard de Chardin, Camus and Sartre, many of Bouchard's favourites. Nevertheless, Bouchard and others were fed up with being put in the Aquinas straitjacket. They were expected to memorize badly written summaries of his work and regurgitate them.

Taking their cue from *Hamlet*—"The play's the thing/wherein I'll catch the conscience of the king"—Bouchard and friends decided they'd stage a mock piece of theatre satirizing St. Thomas and the slavishness of the educational system towards him. Bouchard was deemed the best writer in the class. As well as a golden tongue, he had a golden pen. One year when Louis Noël had to make a commencement speech, he was very nervous and mentioned his wariness to the school's authorities. They told him to get Lucien Bouchard to write the speech.

For the play, Bouchard was designated principal author and chose to re-create St. Thomas's life in a most unflattering manner. One scene presented Thomas's father ushering in sexy girls to try to dissuade his son from becoming a priest. Another portrayed Aquinas as a man of less than average intelligence who simply plagiarized the works of the great thinkers Plato and Aristotle. Rehearsals were carried out in secret so as not to alert the curés to their nefarious intent.

At the debut, the audience of 150 included all the unsuspecting clergymen nestled in the front rows. As the play progressed, and as Bouchard's telling broadsides hit home, and as the students lapped it up, the curés could take it no longer. They got up from their seats and fled the auditorium. It was just as the students had hoped. Their gambit worked.

"We were for the first time rebelling," recalled Paul-André Gauthier, the producer of the show. "I think it was the beginning of something." Bouchard, he recalled, had shown steely determination in carrying the project through, and this was typical of him. "When it came to something he really believed, he'd go to great lengths to have his point of view accepted. He was very serious, well organized, very decisive."

In any other classical college, Lucien Bouchard and the other perpetrators of the satire would probably have been thrown out. These establishments had exacting disciplinary standards, expelling students for the slightest infractions of the rules. But true to its liberal standards, Le Collège de Jonquière did not take action. Deep down, Lamonde and some of the others did not disagree with the message of the play, and Lucien Bouchard was a favoured son of all the faculty. Though he had stepped out of line on this occasion, it was an unrepresentative act.

In a sense, however, the old guard did get a measure of revenge. The only exam Bouchard failed in college was the one on philosophy and the teachings of Thomas Aquinas. Almost the entire class went down with him. In spending more time on Plato, Cicero and others, Lamonde hadn't prepared his students for such a test. The only student who passed it was a recent transfer from Chicoutimi, where they memorized Aquinas letter by letter.

In the summer, when the marks came in, Lamonde had to track down the students to write a make-up exam. Bouchard was then toiling in the lumber camp in the Laurentian forest, the same one from which, years earlier, he had telephoned Roch to complain about being marooned in a swamp of excrement. He returned home, boned up and passed with ease on his second run at the test.

Given his writing talents, Bouchard was interested in newspapers. Villeneuve, whose father was a newspaperman, came up with the idea of starting a college paper. He took the plan to Bouchard and together they launched Le Collège de Jonquière's first student journal, Le Cran. It appeared initially as a small insert in the local Jonquière paper before becoming a separate newspaper.

Le Cran was hardly a radical sharp-edged sheet, but Bouchard's editorials, some co-written with Villeneuve, offered a taste of his early thinking. They showed Lucien Bouchard as a young moralist with a pressing social conscience. He wrote of wasted human potential, targeting the provincial school system as the culprit: Why the lack of public funding? Why the lack of universal access to higher education? Why policies which left so many idle? He was perhaps thinking about his father as well as his sister, Claudette, when he wrote this editorial. To illustrate the point of his editorial, he quoted from Thomas Gray's English poem Elegy Written in a Country Churchyard: "Full many a flower is born to blush unseen,/And waste its sweetness on the desert air." Though not able to speak any English at this time, Bouchard could read it. He had subscribed for many years to Time magazine and learned the vocabulary from it with the speed he learned Greek and Latin.

At this time (1958), university students across Quebec were demanding greater access to university. At the Laval law school an upstart, Jean Chrétien, was leading fellow collegians in marches on the offices of Premier Duplessis. Bouchard editorialized that he thought their demands a little excessive, but saluted the courage and perseverance manifested by the students.

These were the years when the Russians were taking the lead in the space race with the successful launch of *Sputnik*. Drawing on his religious nature, Bouchard tried to calm readers, suggesting there was no need to despair. He wrote that while the development had to be taken seriously, the Russians were without spirituality, without liberty, and were therefore an empty monolith. They had won the first match, but there were many more to come in which the enemies of church and state would be defeated.

Bouchard the moralist attacked the yellow journalism at local radio stations, demanding higher standards and less kowtowing to American values. Free markets, Bouchard suggested, tended to give too much vent to the tastes of society's lowest common denominator. Of the increasing dissemination of lowbrow literature, he wrote, "In this sanctuary of culture, it will be praiseworthy for each to frequent the greatest of humanity's thinkers."

He and his brothers were highly active in campus sport—Roch being a star quarterback—and Lucien castigated those who wanted to commercialize athletics. He argued that the classic Greeks should be honoured as an example, citing their equating of a healthy body with a healthy mind. Capitalistic tendencies were stripping athletics of their purity. "Return sport to its primitive nature and you will have in it an indispensable element of human growth," he advised, quoting Bishop Fulton J. Sheen.

For Lucien and all the Bouchard brothers, time constraints soon narrowed sporting opportunities. More important things, namely work, took precedence, and Lucien tended to overburden himself. His mother was concerned that even at this young age he was pushing too hard. She started worrying about his health and his general state of fatigue and never stopped. "He overworked himself often," noted Roch. "He worked harder than the rest of us. We allowed ourselves to have a good time occasionally." It wouldn't surprise Roch when, later in life, he became physically vulnerable.

"I think he had already developed in himself a state of fatigue that made him vulnerable to the virus." He was warned many times that he should slow down, but, as the brothers had noted, this was someone who had an indestructible will.

Gaston Arseneault saw in Lucien Bouchard a classmate who was poor, very poor, and who was gripped by a raw ambition to succeed. It was hard for anyone to know what was in his head, said Arseneault, because he didn't like to mix with people. It was an assessment Bouchard tended to share. Reflecting on his years growing up, he would say, "I have the impression of having spent my youth very much alone." Arseneault would come to regard Bouchard as "scary, someone who wanted to be God and King at the same time." He was too attached, he thought, to his own sheltered little corner of the world. For the entire duration of his eight years at the college, Bouchard left the Saguenay only once when his teachers took the class to Quebec City to see a production of Molière's play *Le Bourgeois Gentilhomme*.

Neither Canadian nor Quebec politics were important matters of discussion. Bouchard became class president and enjoyed giving speeches on behalf of the students, but there wasn't much for him to get fiery about. For the most part, the students were proud of their school and their teachers. The Oblate Fathers steered clear of any criticism of Duplessis and the Union Nationale government for the obvious reason that it was paying the freight. "This non-committal attitude hardly contributed to our politicization," recalled Bouchard. His parents also supported Duplessis and the status quo, even though the economic domination of their region by the small Anglo minority was part of that status quo. Neither the students nor their parents liked it, but it was an accepted fact of life and they did not rail against it. The Anglos had the jobs as captains of industry because they were qualified for them.

Philippe Bouchard could not be shaken from his faith in Duplessis and his inward vision of religious retrenchment. After all, he told his sons, Duplessis was the one who brought electricity to the countryside. His sons, however, were part of an emerging consensus among the students that Duplessis was a corrupt manipulator with a backward view of the province. It was one of the few disagreements they had with their father.

There was no indication at this time that Lucien Bouchard was headed down a sovereignist path. In a 1957 edition of the student paper, he laid bare his political attitudes. He issued a ringing endorsement of bilingualism and coupled it with a call for a closer economic union and increased harmony with English Canada. Among his ancestors, he noted, it was considered almost treasonous to learn English. But "our beautiful country," Bouchard wrote, "at the dawn of an extraordinary prosperity, requires the collective efforts of all its citizens, and bilingualism could well turn out to be one of the better means of realizing this new unity between the two races, so necessary to our future expansion." In contradiction of the Duplessis philosophy, he wrote that it was time for the Province of Quebec to involve itself more deeply with English Canada, "not via interminable debates but by tangible achievement: an active contribution to the development of Canada."

The young Bouchard also believed that Canada would realize its economic power more readily with a stronger unity between its two ethnic groups. Population density was a major factor in a country's developing prosperity, and Quebec was too underpopulated to pursue with impunity a policy of isolationism. Such a policy would "inhibit the efforts of almost five million French Canadians in the contribution to the building of a big and great Canada." Sounding as federalist as a Quebecker could be, Bouchard then declared, "We do not have the right to do such a thing!"

A bridge had to be built between the leading elites of the two races, Bouchard wrote, and bilingualism would be that bridge. The harmony between the language groups in Belgium was an example that should be followed. Canada's prestige would double, he continued, when throughout the world it was made clear that close and warm relations existed between its two groups. English-language courses had to be increased throughout the Quebec school system. Of course, it was of paramount importance to maintain the primacy of French. But according to the student editor, a policy of bilingualism would only strengthen the French language. "It is quite simply a new weapon we are introducing in the struggle," a new weapon which would help knock down economic barriers and create the type of strong Quebec economy which would ensure the maintenance of a strong French culture.

Bouchard was nineteen when he wrote that editorial. Talk of sovereignty was not yet in the air, but two years later, his last at the

college, he got his first taste of it. The Quebec nationalist organization, the Saint-Jean-Baptiste Society, made an appearance in
Jonquière and held a public meeting to attract interest. Only two
students from the college attended the meeting. One of them was
Bouchard. The producer of the Aquinas satire, Paul-André Gauthier, had been contacted about the meeting and took Bouchard
along with him.

Gauthier recalled the day. "We were invited because we were
the younger generation and they wanted to get in touch and possibly recruit us. I remember we came back from that meeting completely pissed off. The only thing they talked about that night was
being against the Anglos. It was just a bunch of sour old people."

Bouchard and Gauthier had been expecting to hear talk of ways
to achieve a bigger role for Quebec in Canada, larger visions for the
province. Rants about the misdeeds of English Canadians did not
impress them much. Not yet.

4. Cultural Transformation

The moderate, rather federalist view of Canada that Lucien Bouchard penned as a student at Jonquière was much in keeping with the prevailing wisdom of the day. The Saint-Jean-Baptiste Society was peripheral. The Quiet Revolution was still in the future. The sovereignty movement had yet to take wing.

Bouchard was not then—nor would he be—one to confront the prevailing intellectual trend of the time. He preferred to jump on board trains that were already at a good speed, as opposed to charting a new course. As his brother Gérard testified, he was a man marked by caution and insecurity. These types needed ballast.

Many of his Jonquière classmates noted that while Lucien had a brilliant and intellectual mind, it was not an innovative one. New ideas weren't percolating in his inner caverns. Instead he was inclined to ruminate on what was already out there. He took what was in front of him, the notions of others, the histories of others, the books of others, and absorbed the knowledge like a sponge. He massaged it, groomed it, slotted it into frameworks. He had vast, computer-like powers of recall which allowed him to impress interlocutors with precise historical analogy, rendered always with fine, forceful articulation.

He was undecided about what to do upon graduating from Jonquière at age twenty. He had already considered and rejected the vocation of the priesthood. It had been declining in fashion and the lack of presssure coming from the Oblates of Jonquière was also a consideration. Other such religious establishments exercised heavier influence upon students, churning out clerics at a rate of 30 percent of their graduating numbers. Jonquière produced far fewer.

Among classmates and teachers, Bouchard's future was a keen topic of conversation. Given his degree of passion and ability, there was a feeling that he wouldn't be stopped. He would become the cardinal's equivalent, no matter what the profession. While some saw craven ambition in him, Gérard demurred. "Ambition was not

the right word." It had more to do, he said, with the traumas their
parents had lived through, experiences that he swore would not be
repeated. "We were so much convinced, persuaded of the importance to our parents to do well—I would say the sense of pride
accounted for much more than ambition."

Having rejected the clergy, Bouchard visited Laval University
in Quebec City on a scouting mission. Paul-André Gauthier, the
bon vivant of the Jonquière class who could not entice Bouchard to
the wonders of wine, women and song, was one of two students
who owned a car. He piled Lucien and a few others in his big Ford
and drove over the mountains to Quebec City.

At Laval, they chose the medical school as the first stop, but the
timing was bad. It was the day of the guillotine. "We happened to
come at the time they were killing animals—a bunch of rats,"
recalled Gauthier. "They had some kind of contraption, a little
guillotine of sorts, and they placed the rats in there one by one and
chopped their little heads off." Lucien and his friends were also
ushered past some disfigured humans. That was enough for
Bouchard. He told Gauthier that he preferred the living to the
dying and he would not be going into medicine.

Leaving options open, he decided to enrol in a general program
in the social sciences. It was September 1959, and it was in this
year—the year when de Gaulle was proclaimed president of the
French Fifth Republic, when Castro came to power in Cuba, when
Kennedy was nearing the presidency, when Duplessis had passed
from the scene—that it could be said Lucien Bouchard entered the
real world. The car trip to Laval was only his second time out of
the Kingdom of the Saguenay. He had never been to English
Canada. He had never had a drink or a smoke or, as far as friends
could attest, a close relationship with a girl.

In his first week at Laval, a week of festivals for freshmen, a
breakthrough of sorts took place. Bouchard attended a dance and
cracked open the first beer of his life. With coaxing from Normand
Simard, a good friend from Jonquière, he decided that he could
forgo the abstinence pledge he had taken as a Catholic youth.
Simard had taken a blind date to the dance, a pretty girl, Jocelyne
Côté, who caught Lucien's eye. Simard took note of his friend's
interest. He had another girl in mind for himself. "So I told Lucien
that if he wanted to continue the night with my date, it was okay

with me." Bouchard took Simard up on the offer, spending the rest of the dance with his friend's blind date. It was the beginning of a tempestuous twenty-five-year relationship.

Quebec City, as another young law student named Brian Mulroney was discovering, teemed with stylish big-city girls, the likes of which the boys from the country had never seen. But in Jocelyne Côté, the handsome Lucien had chosen one of his own. She was a *bleuet* (blueberry). In Saguenay-Lac-Saint-Jean, the residents believed they grew the biggest blueberries in the world. They were thus known as *les bleuets*.

Bouchard could feel more secure with a girl from his home region. To the classy girls of the capital, he and his like were seen as country hicks. "For us it was like these people were from the boonies," recalled Nicole Arseneault, a contemporary at Laval. "You could tell them right away when you saw one of them—by the way they dressed and looked and behaved. They got all excited about going to a restaurant or bar. They were not used to that. We thought they needed to come out of the country and get some culture." Nicole had visited the Saguenay. "Jonquière was backward. I couldn't believe it—people still lived like that. The stores didn't have much, and the houses were so far apart. For me it was worse than the country. It was primitive."

Bouchard's new surroundings were right in the heart of the magnificent old quarter of the city. He was awed by the imperious majesty of the Château Frontenac, by the sweep of the Plains of Abraham, by the quaint bistros of the narrow cobblestoned streets. The cultural transformation he was making was sumptuous. It was as if overnight he was passing from medieval times to the Renaissance, from Aquinas to the Medicis.

However, the academic side soon disappointed him. Bouchard found the lectures in the social sciences courses to be largely a repetition of material he had already mastered. His room-mate, André Tremblay, had enrolled in law and Lucien was finding himself more interested in the books Tremblay was bringing home than his own statistical texts on sociology, economics and political science. First-year law sped Tremblay back to the judicial debates of ancient times, those times, those words, those giants of history—Demosthenes, Cicero, Philip of Macedonia—Bouchard revelled in.

In his first year at Laval, one of his heroes, French president Charles de Gaulle, came to Quebec City. For Bouchard, his excitement barely containable, it was a wrenching experience. The parade route, which took the general to city hall, was lined four and five deep and Lucien, desperate to get close, could barely see over the people. As the great man came into view, his unrestrained passion hurled Bouchard forward. He burrowed through the spectators as if he were playing lineman for Jonquière. But his momentum was such that it carried him too far. He careened face first into the taut steel wire guarding the parade route. The wire cut deep into his mouth, bringing instant agony and embarrassment. De Gaulle noticed this and, moved by the young man's ardour, reached out his long arm. Lucien clutched his hand as if it were God's and felt how regal it was.

Midway through his first year, Bouchard was tired of being taught what he already knew and decided he would follow Tremblay into law. However, by the end of his year in social sciences, he began to wonder about his decision. Better professors had appeared in the second term and he was scoring high grades and being urged by his economics professor to stay on. As opposed to law, the social sciences were a ground-breaking discipline in Quebec. The province's education system churned out vast numbers of doctors, lawyers and priests, but few experts in social sciences, particularly in the vitally important area of economics in which Bouchard was on his way to a prize of excellence. Social science departments such as the one at Laval, which was founded by the revered Dominican from Lac Saint-Jean, Georges-Henri Lévesque, would play a leading role in the rapid modernization of the province.

Blaming his timidity, Bouchard never talked to his social science professors about the exciting programs of years two and three. He had already transferred to law and it was too late to reconsider. However, once ensconced in law, he never regretted the change. It brought him a discipline he loved. Moreover, it introduced him to a classmate who would change his life, one who would give him the breaks he needed to capitalize on talents that were formidable but which, owing to his insecurities, might never have flourished.

It was a long while after entering law school that he got to know Brian Mulroney well. At first he surveyed the boy from Baie-Comeau's immense charm from a distance. On the surface they were two very different Canadians with little to draw them into one another's orbit.

More important in his initial years of law than new friends were the new ideas percolating in Quebec. Now out of his closeted kingdom he could savour a slice of the modern, and realize how confined his old world had been. Before his bloody but joyous encounter with de Gaulle, he had attended Duplessis's funeral at the Basilica of Quebec and watched the passing of an era. His beloved grandfather, Joseph, had gotten up from his deathbed to cast one last ballot for Duplessis in 1956 and his father had continued to be a believer. But in Quebec City, Lucien was discovering just how backward the Union Nationale government of Duplessis had been. It was like an advertisement for rear-view mirrors.

Lucien was having his ears bent on politics by his brothers. They had come to the view that Quebec had been frozen in time and they saw two landlords responsible—the Union Nationale and Les Anglais. The culpability of the English was forever branded in the minds of Roch and Claude Bouchard after their first visit to Montreal. They had moved on from Jonquière as well, selecting the University of Ottawa in the nation's capital. Ottawa was a far more Anglicized city in those times. The federal government, as Pierre Trudeau had discovered during a stint in the Privy Council Office in the early 1950s, spoke only English. This bias was egregious enough for young students like the Bouchards who believed that Confederation was about two equal partners and two equal languages. But, as Roch would attest, they were even more appalled by what they witnessed in Montreal.

In the city, which was three-quarters French, they saw streets plastered with only English signs. They were humiliated. It was, Roch said, a "desecration." The province that was theirs was covered in the language of outsiders. Language was culture, and their language was hidden.

Before the Montreal trip, they could be broadly classified as nationalists. Now they were so bitter that they joined the sovereignty movement. Since it was only finding its feet and its members were viewed as insurgents, it was a radical undertaking.

But they went further than just pinning on the new label. Their newfound hostility to English Canada led them to an act of defilement that the family would keep silent for many years. In the autumn of 1961, Roch and Claude went out in the Ottawa night, paint and brushes in hand, and smeared the Confederation monument with *Québec Libre* slogans. Two or three other Quebeckers, who would later become prominent figures, accompanied them. It was a full six years before Lucien's hero, de Gaulle, would come back to Quebec to issue a similar *cri de coeur.*

Roch and Claude realized that their act was "disgraceful." Their parents had tutored them on dignified comportment, but the apparent inferior status being forced on them was too much to take. They began to pressure Lucien to take a similar hardline stance. Gérard Bouchard was also moving quickly into the sovereignist camp and he joined in the campaign to recruit his elder brother. Lucien wasn't easily persuaded, noted Gérard. "But he was very excited by what was cooking... He was certainly listening and taking notice of our excitement."

The realization had set in, as Roch and Gérard explained, that the Confederation ideal had been shattered. In their schools, they had been taught that the French were Canadians from the year 1608; that with the British Conquest and the Quebec Act, the English had become Canadians too; and that the Confederation of 1867 was a good pact between the two peoples because they were coming together to form one great country. In the analysis of the Bouchards it was only now, however, in the early 1960s that Quebeckers were beginning to see how things had gone awry. For English Canadians, the French were no longer one half of the duality. They were merely one of the ten provinces.

The original interpretation of the Confederation agreement—a country of two peoples, two nations and two territories—was one to which many Quebeckers subscribed, having been taught it in their schools. However, no consensus among constitutional experts suggested it was as clear as that. Four cultural nations—English, French, Scots and Irish (but none for the native peoples)—were discussed during Confederation. History following the 1860s only served to cloud the issue further.

The Bouchard brothers returned from the universities to spend their summers in Jonquière. They debated the problem of Quebec's status, and a consensus, if not yet shared entirely by Lucien, emerged. Reparation had to be made. English Canada had to give judicial recognition that Confederation was between two peoples.

Without such recognition the only other possible route was the sovereignty option.

Lucien was becoming caught up in law and journalism. He quickly established himself as one of the very best students in his law class, one which included a segment of Canadian society that, to all intents and purposes, he was meeting for the first time. The Anglos in Bouchard's class were a small minority of just eight students, but they were a rather impressive introduction to the other solitude. All were bright, ambitious, bilingual. They were, with the exception of Brian Mulroney and Sonny Mass, from reasonably well-to-do families. They were a congenial group of young men who looked on the Francophones not with suspicion, but with respect. In addition to Mulroney, there was Michael Meighen, the grandson of Prime Minister Arthur Meighen. There was Peter Kilburn, fresh from a year in India. There was the astute and purposeful Peter White, later an important fixture in the Conrad Black empire.

At first Bouchard viewed the outsiders with a degree of distrust. Why had they come to study at Laval when they had their own prestigious centres of high learning such as McGill? But Bouchard was soon impressed by this heady group, finding them, as he put it, restless, brilliant and ambitious. In him, they found similar qualities. "Quiet, restrained, extremely bright," recalled one of the eight, the future judge, Sonny Mass. "But it never occurred to me that he would be a politician one day."

Though Bouchard would speak highly of Laval, the law school was rather undistinguished academically. The faculty, except for two, were all part-timers, practising law most of the day, then rushing over to deliver standardized lectures. Sometimes, recalled Kilburn, they didn't even bother to show up. In this respect they shared a habit with some of the students. Peter White found he could do well on an absentee basis. In one course, criminal law, he hardly attended a lecture. On the eve of the exam, he borrowed a classmate's notes, committed them to memory, and ended up getting a higher grade than the lender, the somewhat nonplussed Peter Baker.

Compared to other law schools, Laval was, in fact, mainly a memory exercise. At McGill or the University of Montreal, they were really *learning* the law, explained Peter Kilburn. "Well, we didn't." Types like Lucien Bouchard, however, took it upon them-

selves to learn the law anyway, never missing a lecture and studying
full-time.

Bouchard steered clear of the social whirl of Mulroney, White
and others. He lived on rue Claire-Fontaine, in an apartment with
Bernard Angers and André Tremblay. They were treated warmly by
the landlady, Madame Saint-Pierre, who could not have asked for
more responsible tenants.

Tremblay soon noticed a change in Bouchard. Out of his mother's purview, out of the narrow spiritual confines of the Saguenay,
he freed himself of religious shackles. He not only gave up attending church every Sunday, he now turned to mocking the fidelity of
those who did, such as his room-mate Angers, also a Jonquière
graduate.

As a measure of how seriously they took the learning process,
the three room-mates formed an intellectual cell which met
nightly in the apartment at 10 p.m. For two or three hours,
Bouchard, Tremblay and Angers sat with bad wine and sparred with
one another on the woes of the world. As Tremblay put it, they
looked at every piece of rock in the forest. While other students
were out boozing in the bistros with *les belles*, the three cell members talked Sophocles, Sartre and the Soviets. Being from the
boonies, they felt energized, fortunate to be among the privileged
in Quebec. They weren't about to waste their time on idle chatter.

In the presence of André Tremblay, who became president of
the law-school student body, Lucien fell under the influence of a
hardline radical. "I was intellectually close, I must confess, to the
FLQ [Front de Libération du Québec]," recalled Tremblay.
"Angers was a soft nationalist, always difficult to know. I was a ter-
rorist. I spoke that language. I was the militant who had no fear of
being violent to attain the cause of separation." A trenchant presence, he gave force to his thoughts and, because he spent so much
time with Bouchard, they couldn't help but register. Bouchard
described himself in this period as "a socialist and a nationalist."
Fashionable on campus for the high-minded was the newly formed
New Democratic Party which, proceeding from the wisdom of
McGill philosopher Charles Taylor, became a proponent of the
two-nations concept. Bouchard attended meetings of the party, taking a serious interest. Tremblay saw him more as a thinker than an
action-oriented type. He was more Greek than Roman, and his

intellectualism, noted his room-mate, came with a seigneurial edge. There was a certain haughtiness to Bouchard. It was as if the world owed him something. He could well mock and tease others and get a hearty laugh out of it, noted Tremblay. But Bouchard could not tolerate being the target of such jibes himself. To criticize him was to inflame the embers that burned within.

The attitude was evident in the treatment of the staff at the rooming house. He was occasionally brusque to Madame Saint-Pierre and intolerant of Madame Blanchette, who cooked the meals. He demanded high quality of others, but especially of himself. His friends recalled that Bouchard attended maybe two dances during his entire law-school tenure. Beers with the boys were not on the agenda. Jean Chrétien had passed through this law school in the four years before Bouchard's arrival and followed a similar non-social regimen. He never missed a class, and on rare social outings he allowed himself one beer. But Bouchard's commitment was even more fierce. He felt the tension of having to do well, to do better than the others. His force of character impressed André Tremblay as it had Lucien's brothers at home in Jonquière.

Recalling the days, Tremblay leaned forward in his chair and his face heightened in colour. It was clear then that nothing was about to stop Lucien Bouchard, he declared. "He had a force of will that I have never seen before in a human being." He summed up the Bouchard attitude in three crisp sentences. "Nobody will resist me. Nobody will interrupt me. Nobody will block my way."

Bouchard could survive on very little sleep. Time, as he had been taught by his mother, was too precious. Put four books in front of him and if it was important, he would devour them in one sitting. "Understand this," said Tremblay. "Lucien will not lose time. He will not lose time. Lucien is an angry man. Born unsatisfied."

As he did at Jonquière with top student Yves Villeneuve, Bouchard befriended Yvon Marcoux, the best student at Laval. From modest origins in the beautiful part of the province known as the Beauce, Marcoux had more in common with Bouchard than the others. They spent a good deal of their time comparing notes on legal questions. To Marcoux, Bouchard was passionately close to his own people and had "a very good legal mind, disciplined, rigorous." He concurred with an aspect of Tremblay's assessment of him. "Once he took on a cause," noted Marcoux, "he would never let go. He never does something half-heartedly. You could see this at that age, in his early twenties. You don't change after that."

Bouchard and his two room-mates, Tremblay and Angers, spent twelve to fifteen hours a day on their studies and in their weighty seminars. Then, on Friday afternoons, they would speed across the Laurentians in Lucien's Volkswagen to see their girlfriends in the Saguenay. Bouchard's girl was still the other guy's blind date, Jocelyne Côté, who had returned to her home region. As they got to know her, Tremblay and Angers became sceptical of the relationship. They didn't think she was right for Lucien. He was an intellectual; she was not. Where was the meeting of the minds, they wondered. Where was the substance in the relationship?

Bouchard's interest in females at this stage, remembered Tremblay, was limited to their esthetic appeal. "Lucien was looking for the curves, the legs of young women. He was very talkative about the beauty of the legs of young women. In Jocelyne Côté, Lucien was cultivating a rose, but a rose does not last, and maybe Lucien did not realize this."

Tremblay and Angers felt they dare not raise questions about her. Bouchard was so proud that he would not tolerate anyone questioning his capacity to decide, they thought. In the end, it would be left to another close student friend of Bouchard's to doubt his choice of female companion. Bouchard's reaction would confirm Tremblay's suspicion. The friend would regret bringing up the matter.

Because of the writing talents he demonstrated as editor of the Jonquière paper, Bouchard had been able to land a job as a stringer for the Montreal newspaper *La Presse* during the summer before he enrolled at Laval. He was an extremely active and efficient correspondent, sending *La Presse* more stories than it could possibly handle. At Laval he wished to pursue his journalistic interests at the student journal, *Le Carabin*. Pierre DeBané, the future Liberal Cabinet minister and senator, had turned down the position of director of the paper and the job went to Denis de Belleval. He barely knew Bouchard but, informed of his marvellous mind and pen, hired him as editor in his second year at the law school.

Teaming with de Belleval, Bouchard came under the influence of yet another strong sovereignist. De Belleval aggressively supported René Lévesque, the budding *indépendantiste* in the heavily reformist Liberal government of Jean Lesage. De Belleval, raised in the elite of Quebec City, and educated at the London School of Economics and other fine institutions, was well-travelled in Canada and elsewhere. While impressed by Bouchard's literary base and overall depth, he found the new editor terribly uninformed about English Canada. He also learned before too long of another negative—his hypersensitivity.

De Belleval chuckled when recalling it. "Everybody knows this is his weakness," he said. It was so easy to get under his skin. Touch the wrong button and Lucien detonated. The Bouchard personality, analysed de Belleval, was a curious mix of the calm charmer and seething temperament. He found him dominating at meetings and shrewd at cultivating allies. "I would look at him and see how he would operate in a group and he would remind me more of a Latin cardinal or a Renaissance philosopher or a Florentine political practitioner." His personality was a paradox, partly explained—but only partly—by the fact that he came from a region where "they don't bow to anybody, where they think they are on top anyway."

The contrast between Bouchard's tame political writing in the Jonquière student paper and his output in Laval's was striking. It marked the first in a long series of severe political swerves that would characterize his political ascendancy. Bouchard was not yet prepared to defile monuments with liberation slogans, but he was now clearly advancing down the nationalist road. He was barely in the chair as *Le Carabin*'s editor before writing one of the most foreboding of analyses on the subject of Ottawa-Quebec relations. For a youth his age, the piece displayed a strategic political eye.

On October 5, 1961, under the headline "Separatism—Two Versions," Lucien Bouchard gave his. It wasn't a question for the moment, he observed, of judging whether separatism was a good or bad idea. But what had to be recognized, he counselled, was that by promoting the separatist agenda, Quebec could force English Canada into a corner and wrench favours.

His strategy, if one was to choose a tough word for it, was blackmail. English Canadians "know full well," he wrote "that Canada without Quebec would no longer be Canada." The province therefore had the ace in the deck. He suggested it could employ a brinkmanship strategy similar to that of arch-American

cold warrior Secretary of State John Foster Dulles in his dealings
with the Soviet Union. The strategy? Make the enemy believe you
are ready to declare war, even if you're not, in order to force them
to be flexible at the bargaining table.

The name Bouchard employed for it was *rapport de forces*.
Demands by Quebec would "create a state of tension," he wrote.
"Fearing that French Canadians will create a separate state, there is
no doubt that Canadians at large will do what is necessary to keep
them in the family, in giving them what they've demanded for so
long: the respect of their provincial autonomy, their language and
a greater participation in the economic and political direction of
the country."

Bouchard put his signature to this editorial at the very time his
brothers were painting the Confederation monument in Ottawa.
Thirty-five years later, Lucien Bouchard would still be using the
same strategy to win concessions and the same words for it—
rapport de forces.

The student editor explained his thoughts on the country further in an article subtitled "The Phantom Nation." It was another
harbinger of his attitude towards the other solitude. "Several facts
appear like living proofs of the impossibility of this ethnic marriage," Bouchard wrote. "We don't act and think the same way.
There is no such thing as a true national conscience in Canada...
Most of the English Canadians ignore our culture and vice versa."

The pessimism continued. "The only thing we know about the
other group is that it represents a nation absolutely distinct from
ours... So let's call a spade a spade. We form two nations... Why
maintain hope in a communion between English and French Canadians when most of their relations consist of a mix-up of grievances,
pressures, and frictions—if not open hostility?"

In taking these positions, Bouchard was by no means going out
on a limb. They were in vogue on the campus, just as were his far
more temperate positions at Laval.

His outpourings in "The Phantom Nation" came during the
Congress of Canadians, a conference organized during the autumn
of 1961 by Mulroney, White and others to deliberate on the direction of the country. A sensation was created as the colloquium proceeded. A featured speaker, Marcel Chaput, who was a declared
sovereignist but who nonetheless worked in Ottawa's department

of defence, issued his separatist credo and was promptly fired. Peter Kilburn, who worked with Bouchard as a co-editor of *Le Carabin*, recalled that Bouchard, who used to kid Kilburn about his silver-spoon upbringing, was one of the few who felt the Chaput affair had more than temporary significance. The Rassemblement pour l'Indépendance Nationale (RIN), of which Chaput was a member, was looked upon as a marginal group. "Most people in our law class didn't believe in that sort of stuff," said Kilburn, who himself at the time leaned towards sovereignty. "Lucien was one who sensed there might be more to it."

The conference pleased Bouchard because "for the first time in my life I saw a group of English Canadians on the defensive over relations between the two nations." For readers of the campus paper, for those involved in the conference such as Mulroney and the other Anglos, Bouchard's thinking must have been clear. A degree of ambiguity was present, however, because in conversation, particularly with the Anglos, he was more conciliatory. They did not see him as a hardliner.

In future editions of *Le Carabin*, he continued to dish out the invective. He called Confederation "*un fourre-tout*"—a cupboard of junk. French Canadians, he said, were at a dead end. Quebec was, in its present form, "a marginal civilization." He cheered in an article when the law school chose more *indépendantistes* in campus elections than representatives of other political stripes. "The student intelligentsia wants independence...and who can blame them for it?"

For a man of Bouchard's decidedly parochial upbringing, he chose to draw broad conclusions. He had never really met the other partner, but was saying the ethnic marriage was impossible. Those taking a different view included the worldly Pierre Trudeau and Jean Chrétien, who was still burrowed in La Belle Province. At the very time Bouchard was laying down his beliefs in *Le Carabin*, Chrétien was coming to a crossroads. As a young lawyer in Shawinigan not long out of Laval, he began sounding sympathetic to Chaput and new hot nationalists like Lévesque. It seemed he was having a change of heart, moving away from the views of his pan-Canadian parents.

It was then that a friend of Chrétien's, lawyer Guy Lebrun, in a bitter exchange over lunch in Trois-Rivières, accused Chrétien of having views formed in ignorance—knowing nothing of English

Canada, the language, the people, the geography and the spectacular potential of the country. Lebrun told him, "Educate yourself
before leaping to conclusions." Chrétien was steaming, almost
jumping out of his seat on the drive back to Shawinigan, but he
later decided that Lebrun's views deserved reflection. He would
count the episode as one of the turning points on his road to
becoming a confirmed federalist. When he began to explore the
country, there was no doubt in his mind.

Bouchard was not prepared to lay all the blame for the back-
wardness of Quebec at the feet of the Anglophones. Since the English conquest, the province, he wrote, had buried itself in a hole—
like "an ostrich"—instead of engaging in cultural and economic
expansion. He could see, particularly as a result of the teachings in
Quebec schools, that a measure of xenophobia had resulted.
"Indeed we came to consider a foreign country everything that
wasn't the province of Quebec." The attitude had to be overcome.
The province was in desperate need of idealists to take the imagination of Quebeckers to new and stirring heights. Quebeckers now
had to impose themselves on the rest of the country, instead of
avoiding it "like the plague."

On this aspect of the dynamic, as noted by the Quebec journalist Michel Vastel, he was in agreement with Trudeau, who was
then teaching law at the University of Montreal and urging French
Canadians to stop enclosing themselves in the Quebec box. Where
the two men differed was on a vital element, however. Trudeau was
not inclined towards a strategy of brinkmanship. Quebec, he felt,
did not have to rely on favours from Ottawa for its development. It
could flourish, as the Quiet Revolution was to suggest, under the
existing construct.

In addition to the unity dilemma, Bouchard took to the pulpit
on other issues. While avidly opposing censorship, he condemned,
as he had in *Le Cran*, man's plunge into base materialism and his
overemphasis on sensual satisfaction. Many students complained
about his highbrow musings, feeling the newspaper was overly serious and intellectual. They sent letters advising Lucien to lighten
up. But in his estimation, these students were philistines. Culture
could not be ennobled by a continual catering to the lowest common denominator. Ignoring the pleas for a student paper of
fun-filled frolic, he enhanced *Le Carabin*'s erudite standards. He

wanted it to be an "*élite de pensée*" and he generally succeeded. Under his stewardship, it won the award as best student paper in Quebec.

Not all his attitudes were progressive. Opening one editorial on the subject of women, Bouchard wrote, "University students are like pretty girls: we spend a lot of money on them, but we don't expect that they'll say anything intelligent." But more characteristic was a humanist sensitivity, as evidenced in a movingly eloquent passage on the meaning of Christmas—"a night in which the human condition reverberates with hope...a night in which love and understanding warm hearts..." Man, he wrote, is not made to suffer, but to love. But it is because he loves that he suffers. "Our happiness, the one which Christmas symbolizes, lies in faith and acceptance." Well aware of his fortune, it was at Christmas when he thought of those he had left behind. Later, in reflecting on his experience at Laval, he would write, "I thought with indignant sadness rather than hurt pride of my father, my mother, my ancestors and all the others who had never been allowed to shine."

His class was filled with those who, like him, were allowed to shine. None of them was more radiant than Brian Mulroney. Bouchard was struck, almost intimidated, by his Irish charm and sociability. Mulroney's personality was as smooth as gold. He made everyone around him feel at ease and warm and important. His voice, with its rolling deep timbre, coated his words with honey, and his smile was rich, mellow and inviting.

In the fourth and final year at Laval, the two of them came together, becoming special friends. The law school had two lives: the first three years of regular studies, and the last year concentrating on articling and preparing for the all-important bar exams. Many friends of both Mulroney and Bouchard left to do their articling in Montreal and elsewhere, but the two of them remained in Quebec. For the first three years, they had been regular classmates. When Bouchard ran for a position on the students' association, Mulroney and other Anglos supported another candidate and Bouchard was defeated. Mulroney never once visited Bouchard's apartment in those years.

Their differences were readily discernible. Bouchard was a bookish intellectual, a brilliant student, a private type, determinedly Francophone and not terribly interested in the social whirl. But people were attracted to him, said classmate Bernard Roy, who was carving out a close relationship with Mulroney himself, because of his knowledge and intellect. "It sort of oozed in class."

Mulroney was an average student, spoke poor French and was far more interested in action—social, political and female—than ideas. Bouchard would later give the classic definition of him. Mulroney, he said, "saw the world as something to conquer rather than to change." In his defiant Irishness, said Bouchard, Mulroney was like a French-speaking Québécois who'd lost his language and his country. "Deprived of primary loyalties, he stood alone to realize his dreams and aspirations."

Besides being smooth, savvy and streetwise, thought Denis de Belleval, Mulroney was courageous. He stood by himself under the banner of the Conservative Party when it would have been much easier for him to join a more popular political formation.

Nicole Arseneault, the Quebec City girl who at first looked upon the blueberries as country bumpkins, was a room-mate of a friend who dated Mulroney. Arseneault was awed at how, at such a young age, Mulroney moved so comfortably in high society. "Mulroney was a partyer. I remember the girl with him. She was always dressed up and he was taking her to the best places." Mulroney may have been from backwoods Baie-Comeau, Arseneault said, but he sure didn't look it. It was apparent in her view that he was picking his people, lining up the deckchairs for the big show.

Although Mulroney certainly didn't look working class, it was this aspect of him that secured the tie with Lucien Bouchard. There was a sociological bonding. They both came from modest, working-class, small-town Quebec families. The other Anglophones in the law class were more upper crust, but Mulroney, the son of a mere electrician, stood out above them all. The sight of him stirred Bouchard's heart. Mulroney had come from outside the ruling class and yet he was cracking it. This, said a woman who would later work for Bouchard, appealed greatly to the conquering spirit in him. Starting low gave upward mobility special meaning.

For Mulroney, many aspects of Bouchard had appeal. Mulroney was always impressed by intellectuals and wished to be accepted by them. Besides being editor of the newspaper, Bouchard took charge for a time of the legal journal *Cahiers de Droit*, where he published learned legal commentaries. Bouchard's presence could lend Mulroney more intellectual clout and it could certainly polish his underdeveloped skills in the French language.

They were the thinker and the doer, their chemistry not entirely different from that of the pair which would eventually lead the Liberal party—Trudeau's mind, and Chrétien's heart. Mulroney was the player. He exhibited none of Bouchard's timidity and insecurity. As president of the law students, André Tremblay enlisted Mulroney's support in a protest against the quality of teaching by the law faculty. "Mulroney backed me but Lucien was not there," he said. "Mulroney was a man on the move. Lucien didn't yet possess the fight that Mulroney possessed." Bouchard wanted to become somebody, said Tremblay, but it was not defined at the time.

Bouchard was astonished at Mulroney's connections. What power the boy from Baie-Comeau wielded, he thought. From his college days in St. Francis Xavier University, where he had been introduced to the Tory party by classmate Sam Wakim, Mulroney had carved out a friendship with The Chief himself—Prime Minister John Diefenbaker. At one point, he got on the phone and chatted with the PM and arranged for him to visit the Laval campus. On the Quebec political side, he cultivated a close friendship with Daniel Johnson, the suave leader of the party of Bouchard's parents, the Union Nationale. Mulroney met Johnson regularly at the main-floor bar of the Château Frontenac. Bouchard was not around for these sessions, but as Peter C. Newman has analysed, the Johnson link was of foremost importance to Mulroney's development.

Johnson, who would soon become premier, exhibited so many of the dominant qualities that would be seen in the future Mulroney. He was immaculately dressed (three shirt changes per day). He had a love affair with most everything American. He placed exceptional importance on keeping his party caucus happy and, above all, he was pragmatic. He didn't like being pigeon-holed.

In politics, Johnson said, you had to be free to fly, to move with the winds of the public mood. "In politics," Johnson informed Newman, in an observation that would be most telling in the careers of both Mulroney and Bouchard, "it's very dangerous to have a philosophy."

Bouchard wasn't yet thinking of politics. Before leaving law school, he gave his first major public address. At a boisterous out-door student rally, he launched into a vigorous defence of Jean Lesage's reforms, only to be followed by a strong orator, Pierre Marois, who ringingly rebutted Bouchard's arguments and left him disappointed.

Denis de Belleval witnessed the moment. "There were maybe two thousand there and Lucien decided he would address the crowd. I remember him vividly, standing on the pedestal. He was not very efficient because he had no experience, not the experience of a Mulroney, for example. But he was eager and he was not bad and I said to myself. 'My god, he has the bug. Sooner of later he will take up the political challenge.'"

5. THE YOUNG LAWYER

He had scored near-top grades in his law class. He had been editor of the legal journal. Upon graduation he had a luxury of choice. Some of the biggest and the best Quebec law firms sought him. The plush carpets of Montreal beckoned. Instead, Lucien Bouchard chose to return to his cloistered kingdom to practise small-town law in anonymity.

The decision astonished his Laval classmates. They pressed him hard to go to Montreal. They told him he was crazy to sell himself short. "We all thought it was a tremendous waste," recalled Bernard Roy. As a lawyer in Chicoutimi, how could he exercise his potential? He'd be stuck with the assignment shared by so many lawyers in these places—the car-crash beat. Accident claims.

Bouchard had his reasons. Home was home. Kingdom, roots, family shrine. "In a way our father never left the old family homestead," he would later say. "And neither did the rest of us." He was also planning to marry the local girl, Jocelyne Côté, who liked the Saguenay. Most important, he had an offer to join the firm of Chicoutimi's Roland Fradette, the most highly respected lawyer in the region.

Friends like Roy heard him out, but they knew there was another reason. Bouchard couldn't speak English. To shine in Montreal, he realized—if not from his own experience then certainly from that of his brothers—that he would have to speak the other tongue. While Brian Mulroney had profited from the Bouchard friendship to greatly enhance his French, Bouchard had not done likewise with English. Even though he had a good vocabulary base in the language from which to build, even though he had editorialized in *Le Cran* on the vital importance of Quebeckers learning the other language, he had stuck to his native voice.

Bouchard suffered from a Hamlet-like hesitance in several areas. The English language was one of them. To speak faulty English would expose weakness. To return to his all-French home was his safest option. He piled his books into his Volkswagen and turned his back on the big-city lights. In his editorials in *Le Carabin* he had admonished young Quebeckers for their inward-looking nature, for their refusal to beat a path for their province into the English stronghold. Now he was turning a deaf ear to his own sermon.

Mulroney did not return to his native Baie-Comeau to practise law. He headed straight for Montreal, to the big firm of Ogilvie, Cope. Unfortunately he flunked his bar admission exams twice in succession, thereby delaying his entry to the firm. From Laval, four years earlier, Jean Chrétien had returned home to Shawinigan. But this was with the express purpose of developing a base for an early run at politics. Chrétien had already formed a club back home, the Sixties Club, to spearhead the drive. He spent three years in Shawinigan, developing a successful law practice, and then in 1963, at age twenty-nine, defeated a heavily favoured Créditiste incumbent and took his seat in Parliament.

Bouchard had no such early ambitions. The only other option he seriously pondered—and he might in fact have chosen it had he not had debts—was going off to France like his brothers to get a doctorate degree and then pursuing an academic career.

Despite the reservations of his Laval pals, teaming with a barrister of the prestige of Roland Fradette was nothing to scoff at, small town or not. Fradette enjoyed a reputation in the Saguenay-Lac-Saint-Jean region as a legal deity. To be sought out by him was high tribute. Fradette saw so much promise in Bouchard that he chose him over another candidate for the firm—his own son. Paul Fradette and Lucien Bouchard had worked as summer students at the firm Fradette, Bergeron and Cain. As soon as the other lawyers saw the chemistry between Fradette and Bouchard, they knew what the hiring decision would be. There was a bond between the much older Fradette and the newly minted Bouchard which passed well beyond the business of law. It extended to intellect, literature and, most of all, language. Michael Cain, the tall Irish partner in the firm, a tennis player of championship calibre, recalled the fusion. "I have never met any two people who had such a marvellous, exceptional command of the French language and who delighted in speaking it most correctly." They each spoke a sophisticated French, one of grammatical perfection. Fradette was astonished to meet a young man of such scholarly expression. The admonition Lucien had received from his father for using street language around the table had been scrupulously heeded.

Fradette was a short man with a fox-like demeanour and an air of supreme confidence. Bouchard saw him as a model. As well as a master of the courtroom who mowed down adversaries with witheringly eloquent precision, Fradette was a reader, a man who bathed in the magnificent literature of France and a lawyer with a social conscience who tried, noted Cain, to instil an idealism in employees of the firm. "He would finance, out of his own pockets, cases he thought worth it." If a client with a good case didn't have the funds to take it to appeal, Fradette instructed his law partners to "pay it yourself."

Similarities aside, there was one glaring difference between Fradette and Bouchard. Fradette detested Quebec nationalists. If Bouchard was in fact the quasi-sovereignist his editorials in *Le Carabin* indicated, he was a lone wolf in this Liberal law firm. The old master did not try to hide his disdain for the nationalist radicals, recalled Cain. "I can still see him at a little restaurant next to the office expounding on that. He would point out all the evils which flowed from it."

Fradette had soured on the whole idea of politics. In 1935, as a young man, he had run federally for the Liberal party and was demolished by his opponents through contemptible campaign tactics. Afterwards, he stayed away. Many law firms profited from political connections, but Fradette took the view that his firm could do just fine without such meddling.

Bouchard lamented the fact that Fradette had been denied wider fame. Few knew of his superiority. Outside Quebec, no one had heard of him. In speaking of him, and other Quebeckers who never achieved what they might have, Bouchard often sounded wounded. He appeared to place such a high degree of importance on status—as if a man was to be measured by public reputation alone, as if other earthly satisfactions were not enough. He lumped Fradette with other unfulfilled Quebeckers and hinted that somehow the Canadian system was responsible.

Bouchard had wrestled from time to time with the idea of being a writer. He dreamed of doing a history of Saguenay-Lac-Saint-Jean in which he would expose it all—the colonization, the suffering and the degree to which his people's dreams had been thwarted. He was proud that his three brothers were now embarked on serious, prestigious studies. They were off in the old country—France—getting their doctorates, and the family wouldn't have wanted it any other way.

Lucien took special pride in Gérard. They were like professor and favourite pupil, like father and favourite son. "Lucien was always trying to set an example for us," observed Gérard. "I remember when he had begun as a lawyer and I was still a student at Laval and I bought a car which was a Volkswagen. It was winter and I arrived Friday night in Jonquière and Lucien was having dinner at our family home and saw my car and saw that it did not have the new type of winter tires with the spikes in them...The day after, Lucien took my car to the garage and had the best winter tires with the nails in them put on and paid the bill. He did that sort of thing. He was a very generous person."

For the first couple of years, like many lawyers starting out, Bouchard toiled through many assignments involving automobile accidents while occasionally thinking of Laval friends who were in the big leagues. It took some time before he felt comfortable in a courtroom. Though articulate, his shyness proved to be an impediment. During his first forays, he was so nervous that he wouldn't let family members come to see him perform. One day he suffered a piercing humiliation. Overly eager, too meddlesome in trying to put his case forcefully, he incurred the wrath of a veteran judge. "You, young man, remain seated," the judge told Bouchard. "You have a good case. Don't spoil it."

Fradette put high priority on courtroom skills, instructing his employees on the art of pleading a case. He wanted a stage actor's presence and a surgeon's precision. Michael Cain appeared with him before the Supreme Court of Canada, where the lawyers made their pitches standing behind podiums. After watching Cain, Fradette took him aside and tore into him. Cain was almost six-foot-two and, in making his delivery, had leaned forward like Ichabod Crane. "Don't let me ever catch you doing that again," scolded Fradette. "You've got that height. Use it! Stand as tall as you can. Me, I've got to reach up to even get to the microphone."

Fradette was nearing retirement, scaling back his workload. He had the time to take Lucien under his wing. Pleading case after case, often spending all day in the courtroom, Bouchard soon found his feet. Thanks in part to Fradette, he learned how to marshall arguments with reverberating force. Confidence gradually came. He worked long hours mastering the files and impressing superiors. Pierre Bergeron, the pear-shaped senior partner, had thought the firm would surely lose him to Montreal. Now he delighted in the young man's potential. He saw Bouchard as "aiming for perfection," dedicated to pure law. One of the few problems Bouchard had, noted Bergeron, was that he didn't know how good he really was.

Socially, he remained the abstainer. With his thick black hair, smart suits and intense romantic air, he looked more like a European nobleman than the son of a Jonquière trucker. He likely could have had his choice of the women in the kingdom, but he had no interest in playing the field. His girl was Jocelyne Côté. In 1966, two years out of law school, he married her. As far as anyone could tell, she was the only girl he had ever seriously dated.

The bride was from a working-class family in Alma, not far from the Bouchard family farm. Bouchard's friends from Jonquière found her tough, not terribly career-oriented and moody. Doubts about her suitability for him endured. The friend who had the nerve to tell Bouchard to his face was de Belleval. "He knew I was not very fond of this marriage," recalled de Belleval. "I did not dislike her, but she was not right for him." As could be imagined, Bouchard did not respond kindly to the rather gratuitous assessment. He preferred the type of support he received from Brian Mulroney, who made the long trip from Montreal to attend the nuptials. As for de Belleval, Bouchard put the friendship on ice—for two years.

Bouchard was keen on making a good living, but he was not the blatant buck chaser many new lawyers were. Shakespeare's neatly worded philosophy of greed—"Where the bee sucks, there suck I"— was not one to which he subscribed. Financial security, yes. Ostentatious trappings, no. After the workday, other lawyers congregated at George's Steak House on Racine Street. For Bouchard, it was usually straight home. He tried taking up tennis with his wife but, as Cain recalled, they were quite hopeless at it. He hadn't learned to swim as a youth, as the family life did not include beaches. He finally did learn, but sport was now an afterthought. His chief entertainment, as it had always been, was books. On weeknights he went home to read. On weekends, he read some more.

His clear favourite among his hundreds of books was the Marcel Proust classic, *À la recherche du temps perdu* (*Remembrance of Things Past*). The French author's massive opus was a multi-volume work of more than 3,000 pages of kaleidoscopic introspection. Plot and drama were sacrificed in the early-century tome, the reader carried along instead by the promise of the illumination of the human condition. Proust distilled moods, memories, sensations in greatly prolonged word symphonies of breathtaking detail. One publisher rejected the two-ton manuscript, explaining that he had difficulty understanding how any writer could spend thirty pages on an analysis of how someone rolled over to go to sleep.

Neither the extended roll-over passages nor any other bothered Bouchard. He read *Remembrance* several times. His mind kept returning to it. That it captivated him so much, that his imagination could be transported so readily into Proust's deep labyrinth, spoke to his own ruminatory, introspective patterns. Did the great work hold clues as to how the mind of Bouchard functioned? It would be said of him, as the years went by and contradictions and severe changes of mood marked his passage, that he viewed the world through quite a different lens than conventional types did.

One of the dominant themes of *Remembrance*, which is full of examples of hyper-selective recall, and no recall at all, is that memory is but the servant of the imagination. Images come flooding back to overwhelm the senses and all other considerations. A testimony to cool Cartesian logic, the great novel was not. Julia Kristeva, one of the leading authorities on Proust, noted how his "psychic universe," his exploration of memory, established a completely new form of temporality. Proust's learning process involved a journey from the past to the present and back again.

Marcel Proust was an asthmatic who holed himself up in a cork-sealed bedroom for years to complete the epic. Like Bouchard himself, he was an extremely sensitive man, a voracious reader, a humanist and an explorer of the language. As a matter of further coincidence, Bouchard showed a notable physical likeness to Proust around the eyes.

In absorbing himself in the work, the young lawyer from Chicoutimi could find other interesting parallels. The grandmother of the book's central character, Marcel, was in some respects reminiscent of his own grandmother, the one who kept the chest of great works for Lucien to revel in. In one scene, Marcel's grandmother brings to him a parcel of intellectual works, all heavy fare. "She considered light reading as unwholesome as sweets and cakes," wrote Proust. She didn't pause, he added, to consider how the strong breath of genius might have impacted on the child. "The truth was that she could never permit herself to buy anything from which no intellectual profit was to be derived."

In Kristeva's analysis, Proust comes across as many described Bouchard—an esthetic and a moralist: "A moralist of outrage." Pleasure weighed heavily on the Proustian conscience, Kristeva observes. "At times when pleasure overtakes him, the narrator feels that he 'makes his mother's soul weep.'"

The character Marcel, full of human sensitivity, undergoes great traumas with childhood memories coming back to harry and haunt him time and time again. *Remembrance*, noted another critic, is about the power and the truth of involuntary memory. It is, said Harold Bloom, a visionary romance. "Aesthetic salvation is the enterprise of his vast novel." For Proust, so much was fleeting. "The bonds that unite another person to ourself exist only in our mind," he wrote. Memory will grow faint, the bonds are shed and in the end, "we exist alone." In 1994, after Bouchard had shed many a friend, an interviewer took this quote from the masterpiece and asked Bouchard, who had the reputation of being a solitary man, for his reaction. "We are alone," Bouchard explained. "We are alone with our obligations, with the urges we feel to be faithful to what we are."

Given Lucien Bouchard's intellectual nature, it was easy to imagine how the appearance in his early legal years of the philosopher king, Pierre Trudeau, would enthral him. Trudeau had made the trek from Collège Jean-de-Brébeuf through the world's finest universities. He had spent some years as a labour lawyer and law professor at the University of Montreal, specializing in the Constitution. He read the texts on the Vatican's Index of banned books, he edited the journal *Cité Libre*, he challenged Duplessis and was inclined towards the socialists, having supported NDP candidates in elections.

This was a pedigree that impressed Bouchard mightily, though the thinkers influencing Trudeau were of considerably different orientations. One favourite, as noted by Christina McCall-Newman and Stephen Clarkson in their study of Trudeau, was Michel de Montaigne, with his emphasis on "the thoughtful man's need to master emotion, and his egotistical dismissal of self-doubt." These were traits which Trudeau exhibited in abundance but which, to be sure, ran wholly contrary to the hot-blooded psyche of Bouchard. Other writers Trudeau favoured, Robert Berner and François Hertel, railed against forms of chauvinism and nationalism which were rife in the history of the Kingdom of the Saguenay.

Bouchard was not only excited by Trudeau. The Liberal Party, at both the federal and provincial levels, held appeal for him. He endorsed the assertive steps taken by Lesage in his home province—the nationalization of the hydro industry, the educational reforms and the stripping away of clerical powers. At the Ottawa end, Lester Pearson impressed him as being open to Quebec's aspirations, giving prominence in the Cabinet to Quebec ministers, creating the Royal Commission on Bilingualism and Biculturalism, and acceding to Quebec's wish to preside over its own pension plan. "Pearson," said Bouchard, "was prepared to make compromises." Pearson had recruited not only Trudeau to the federal team, but also the powerful union leader Jean Marchand. Bouchard was a fan of Marchand's, and was "very proud of Trudeau. I was so proud to hear Trudeau speak such marvellous English, even if I didn't understand what he said." With the new entrants on the federal scene, Ottawa would know "what extraordinary people we can produce."

So while Bouchard was a Quebec nationalist, while he had produced those steamy sovereignty-sounding editorials at Laval, he found himself contented with the federalist party. That his law firm, while not terribly politically active, was Liberal, made this decision a more comfortable one. His family, however, continued its march in the other direction. Bouchard's four siblings had all become sovereignists and with Duplessis gone, his father chose this side as well. His wife, Jocelyne, was also a hardliner, looking to René Lévesque to press his nascent sovereignist movement further.

Lucien Bouchard became a Liberal not just in name. He was active, agreeing to take on the vice-presidency of the party's Quebec wing. He campaigned for the party's candidates in the 1968 federal election, touring the small towns of Saguenay-Lac-Saint-Jean under the Trudeau banner. Following the Trudeau victory that year, he considered an offer from André Ouellet, who had been a law-school classmate, to come to Ottawa and work in the Cabinet office of Transport Minister Paul Hellier. He turned that down and also rejected lucrative contract offers of federal government work in his region. Neither he nor Fradette were inclined towards such patronage.

In 1970, when the young Robert Bourassa captured the provincial leadership of the Liberal Party, Bouchard was considered to be of high enough standing to be approached by the team to run. He turned that down. Though he appreciated the enormous power politicians wielded, he did not, as he noted, "have it in the guts." He was enamoured, far too enamoured, of the law.

While officially a Grit, Bouchard had also been working the other side of the tracks. Through the late 1960s he was forming a good friendship with Marc-André Bedard, a criminal lawyer who worked in a firm next door. Bedard, a chain-smoker in the Lévesque mould, was one of the first of the new breed of secessionists in Quebec. Several years earlier he had joined the separatist RIN. In meetings in the corridors of Chicoutimi's Palais de Justice or at La Tabagerie Royale on rue Racine, Bedard put forward his arguments for sovereignty and sensed Bouchard's profound attachment to the ascendancy of Quebec. "I noticed Lucien was positive when I brought it up," recalled Bedard. "He worked for the Liberals but it didn't affect our relations, because we had a lot of respect for one another and our convictions."

By now Bouchard was graduating from accident-claim cases to more interesting fare. Pierre Bergeron, who was working for the firm in Montreal, turned over many dossiers to Bouchard, in whom he held burgeoning confidence. Just as he could absorb and retain large books in one sitting, so he was with legal files. His mental space seemed inexhaustible. Bergeron thought maybe he had piled too much work on him, but there was never a complaint from Bouchard.

There was another aspect the senior partner appreciated in him. The morally upright Bouchard never stole a client from him then or in the future when they parted ways. All the files were returned to his desk.

Under Bergeron's eye, Bouchard undertook assignments that moved him towards his specialty—labour law. The young Trudeau had been a labour lawyer. Brian Mulroney was then, in the mid-sixties, building a successful labour-law practice in Montreal, and in Shawinigan, another future prime minister, Jean Chrétien, had held labour dossiers as a mainstay of his practice. Bouchard's cases involved the Quebec government's purchase of the Chicoutimi Hospital and the Chicoutimi Seminary, as well as the rental of an orphanage. These experiences led him to larger assignments as a negotiator between the public and private sector in Quebec. One was as president of the arbitration tribunals for grievances arising out of a province-wide agreement on uniform working conditions for teachers. In this capacity, Bouchard repeatedly travelled the length and width of the province learning the land, its educational system, and developing important contacts—with Robert Cliche, who had been one of the law professors he admired, and with union men Guy Chevrette and Jean-Roch Boivin.

His contacts with Liberals expanded also. Although he did not enter the 1970 provincial race as a candidate, he was a high-profile campaigner for Bourassa against the Union Nationale and the new independence party, René Lévesque's Parti Québécois. In the Chicoutimi constituency the Liberal candidate lost, but Bouchard celebrated anyway because the Liberals swept 78 of the 108 seats. Bouchard held a reception at his home for all the big-time Grits of the area and toasted the achievement. The only damper on the soirée came from the adjoining chamber when Bouchard's wife broke into audible sobs when she heard that PQ candidates René Lévesque and Marc-André Bedard were defeated. Her conduct raised a few eyebrows from the partyers, many of them members of Bouchard's firm.

At the law firm they had some sense, as Michael Cain recalled, that despite formal allegiances, despite hosting parties for the Grits, Bouchard's nationalism had been hardening over the years. But they were not very concerned with Bouchard's political orientation. Pierre Bergeron, like so many others, felt that Bouchard was far too sensitive a man for politics. Another young partner in the firm, François Lamarre, had campaigned with Bouchard for the Liberal candidates. "It was mainly Trudeau," Lamarre remembered. "Trudeau for us was a little bit like the remake of a Kennedy." He didn't see Bouchard as profoundly attached to the Liberals, or to the sovereignists.

But then, as Lamarre recalled, came Bouchard's big change of mind. Sometime in 1971 he disappeared, not telling Lamarre where he was headed. In fact the destination was the land which had captivated him since childhood and stirred his historical imagination—Ancient Greece. It was where Bouchard's heroes lay, the civilization he cherished, the first great democracy, the jewel of men of learning, the paramount philosophers. Bouchard stood atop the Acropolis, the citadel of Athens, and imagined the great orators of the day. He had studied their speeches—in their own language, which he still knew. They had built, in a land a fraction the size of Quebec, the model of future civilizations.

What great visions stirred the young lawyer's dreams. Lamarre remembered that when he returned from Greece and sat down with the others, it was all he could talk about—the exalted society these men had fashioned. His soul awakened, he concluded that this was a dream to follow. He told his partners that he was becoming an *indépendantiste*, that he was casting his lot with René Lévesque and the Parti Québécois. There had been no Péquistes at the firm—until now. But there was no problem in Bouchard's remaining—so long as he didn't flaunt his new political views.

He explained to partners that he could no longer tolerate the Liberals. He'd been in a stew since the October Crisis of 1970, reasoning that Trudeau had responded with unnecessary and undemocratic severity to the kidnapping of a British diplomat and the murder of provincial Cabinet minister Pierre Laporte by the separatist FLQ. To bring the crisis to an end, Trudeau had employed the War Measures Act, suspending civil liberties. Left-leaning Quebeckers were arrested on the basis of reputation alone. The army was sent in and soldiers patrolled the streets of Montreal. Bouchard happened to be in the city, on an arbitration assignment. "I saw the army. I didn't recognize my country." He recalled going through "a personal trauma"—for Lucien Bouchard there would be many of these—and he decided he could no longer support the prime minister. Trudeau, Bouchard reasoned, had turned the powers of Canada against Quebec. Officially, at least, it was the Quebec government which had asked Ottawa to send in the army. In fact, three Quebeckers—Trudeau, Bourassa and Montreal mayor Jean Drapeau—were the principals behind the decision.

But Bouchard didn't see it this way. "I realized," he would later explain, "that Trudeau was not in Ottawa to bring about the blossoming of Quebec. He was there to screw us." Trudeau had revealed "once and for all, with a persistence that bordered on provocation, his determination to keep Quebec a province, a simple module." Bouchard further concluded that the Quiet Revolution was over. It was "condemned to immutability by English Canada's intransigence."

While appalled, with some legitimacy, by Trudeau's repressive measures, Bouchard showed little interest in condemning the separatist terrorists who had kidnapped and murdered on behalf of their cause. Opinion polls suggested Quebeckers, in huge majorities, backed Trudeau's measures. But the longer-term impact showed a surge of nationalist sentiment in the province.

Denis de Belleval, who was by now on speaking terms with Bouchard again, recalled Bouchard sharing his own disgust over the War Measures Act. Their theory was that it was a pretext used by Trudeau in an attempt to crush the independence movement. "To a democrat like Lucien Bouchard, this was the turning point," de Belleval said. Drapeau and Bourassa may have asked for the army, but they were just pawns. "Trudeau was not an imbecile. He knew damn well how revolutions and political movements start. At first there are just a little bunch of guys, a prophet and twelve guys, and a few years later you have a church with millions of people. He knew the story of the Communist party in various parts of the world, of the Algerian movement, of the anti-colonial movements." In the independence movement, said de Belleval, "Trudeau saw the root of something dangerous and he thought he could crush it in the egg. That's what Lucien Bouchard thought."

Bouchard had been pleased enough with the Liberals to campaign for Bourassa in 1970, and it seemed that he was also satisfied with the federal party. He had hoped that Quebec's estimable newcomers to federal politics—Trudeau, Marchand and Gérard Pelletier—would have a big impact in Ottawa. In fact, French power descended on the capital like it never had before. Trudeau made a quantum leap virtually unprecedented in Canadian politics. Within three years, he was catapulted from backbencher to Liberal Party leader and prime minister of the country. In large part, he and his Quebec colleagues—Marchand, Pelletier, Michael Pitfield and Marc Lalonde—assumed the running of the government.

Trudeau introduced reforms allowing far greater numbers of Quebeckers to occupy top federal government posts. He took steps to bilingualize the public service so that all Quebeckers could be dealt with in their own language at the federal level. His Official Languages Act sought to spread bilingualism across the country. He reopened the constitutional question with the intent of giving a veto on changes to Quebec and more spending powers for La Belle Province and the other provinces.

In some respects the cultural revolution that had come to Quebec was being extended to the rest of Canada. The ascendancy of a new French-Canadian power elite—Jean Chrétien being a prominent member—had set about transforming the Canada of two solitudes into a bicultural entity. All the steps were taken in the early years of Trudeau's stewardship. For many in the country, French power had gone far enough. Trudeau was decried in the West for showing too much favouritism to his own province, and the Grits lost substantial support.

The reforms didn't nearly begin to satisfy the demands of Quebec's hardline nationalists and secessionists. Nor were they expected to. If the agenda was secession, there could be no satisfaction with renewed and reformed federalism. But judging by polls, Trudeau appeared to be on the right track. The people of Lucien Bouchard's province greatly favoured his changes. From his school days, Bouchard himself had been a keen proponent of bilingualism of the very type Trudeau had introduced. And the new prime minister had seemingly advanced the agenda of which Bouchard was proud—the Pearson record.

Bouchard's initial faith in Trudeau could not have been rooted in any notion that Trudeau was a strong nationalist. He clearly wasn't. When Bouchard's hero de Gaulle came to Montreal in 1967 and shocked the country with the declaration "*Vive le Québec Libre*," Bouchard had not been moved enough to switch sides. He stuck with the Grits. His decision to abandon them, it seemed, was based less on Trudeau and the Liberal Paty changing than on Bouchard himself changing.

In the wake of the October Crisis, Trudeau sped up his bid for a constitutional reform which would satisfy some of the nationalists' demands. In electing the provincial Liberals, Quebeckers had chosen Bourassa's more federalist approach, turning their backs on

Union Nationale leader Jean-Jacques Bertrand's special status as well as Lévesque's sovereignty agenda. Trudeau now asked Bourassa for a proposed package of reforms which would persuade voters to accept a new Constitution. With Bourassa's recommendations, he developed a plan to try to accommodate Quebec's desire for greater control of social policy. This was taken, along with proposals for repatriating the Constitution, to the premiers' conference in Victoria in June 1971. A tentative agreement was reached on an amending formula. Ottawa compromised to some extent on demands for provincial primacy in allowing Quebec and other provinces to set up their own social programs affecting old-age pensions and family and youth allowances. Bourassa wanted broader change, but even if Trudeau or any prime minister wanted to accommodate him, there was the formidable problem of opposition in many of the other nine provinces.

Nonetheless, a compromise was reached and the premiers went home to mull it over. All were prepared to go ahead. But, responding to pressures in his restive province, Bourassa now decided that he could not accept the Victoria formula. He called Trudeau to tell him he was rejecting the package.

In his later commentaries on Trudeau's first years in power, Bouchard would argue that Trudeau had betrayed the interests of Quebec. Given the reforms the PM had introduced, given the surge of French power, given Bourassa's repudiation of the Victoria package, it wasn't an easy case to make, even for an advocate as strong as Bouchard.

Bouchard would later describe his joining the Péquistes as "an unconscious process of maturation." There was the pressure from his brothers, there was Greece and there was Proust. There were the myths of land, parents, lineage and schooling—myths he could never escape.

In late 1971, one of the high priests of the PQ, the London-schooled, moustachioed economist Jacques Parizeau, arrived on rue Racine, the main street of old Chicoutimi. Marc-André Bedard escorted him to the Hotel Chicoutimi. In the main-floor dining room they met Lucien Bouchard, who had only to look across the street to see the law offices of his old mentor Roland Fradette. The three men chatted for a short time whereupon Parizeau presented Bouchard with a membership card for the Parti Québécois.

6. FLEEING THE FIRM

With Fradette in semi-retirement, Bergeron and Cain were the senior partners at the firm. They strongly opposed the sovereignty movement, but as long as Bouchard was a silent separatist, it was tolerable.

In 1973, Bouchard dropped his silence. In the provincial election of that year, Marc-André Bedard was again seeking the local seat for the Parti Québécois. Bouchard admired Bedard. He liked the way he had stood his ground in the face of semi-ostracization from the legal community for his radical politics and regretted having worked against him in the 1970 election. Now, as a Péquiste himself, he wanted to make amends.

Giving up his vacation, Bouchard worked as communications director in the Bedard campaign. He gave speeches, appeared on television and was quoted in the newspapers. He was particularly helpful in establishing warm relations between the candidate and the religious community, with which Bouchard had excellent contacts, having done legal work on its behalf.

He must have known his behaviour would raise the ire of his law partners. While it was fine to do some modest work for Liberals, politicking was regarded as off-limits. Pierre Bergeron was adamant about this. The division between sovereignists and Liberals in Chicoutimi was pronounced, more so than in many other areas of the province where the secessionist presence was meagre. Bergeron had many well-to-do clients who were snooty federalists. He knew how they would look upon a member of the firm becoming a flag-waving Péquiste.

In the face of Bouchard's action, he and Cain did not sit quietly. They struck back, openly campaigning for the Liberal candidate. The fight was on, the political peace of the old law firm shattered by a headstrong young man. Working full-time, Bouchard poured more effort into the Bedard campaign than his colleagues could for their man. Bedard won the election, becoming only one of six PQ members elected. Bourassa's Liberals swept the province, winning an astonishing 102 of 110 seats, but the PQ could take some solace from the popular vote. There it fared well with 30.2 percent.

Bouchard's role in the Bedard triumph sharpened divisions within the firm to the point where a decision had to be made on a policy regarding future political conduct. Discussions began immediately after election day with Bouchard being the obvious focal point. Many of the lawyers favoured a compromise which would allow for freedom of political allegiance and some campaigning activity. But Bergeron, the most senior partner, wanted none of it. The law practice had to remain pure.

At a luncheon meeting at a restaurant at La Place Saguenay on boulevard Talbot, "all hell broke loose," recalled Michael Cain. It had been obvious for months that relations between Bergeron and Bouchard had become terribly strained. Colleagues said they had comparable egos—each the size of Mount Olympus. Neither was of a mind to back down.

The luncheon proceeded smoothly enough until Bergeron, whose face reddened noticeably in moments of high tension, rumbled in and stoked the coals. He levelled several broadsides at Bouchard, suggesting the firm could get along fine without him. "That lit the fire," recalled François Lamarre. "Bergeron wanted to show he was boss." The air of compromise was now replaced by rancour. Bergeron didn't have majority support at the table, but held fast to his position. Bouchard, not one to hold his tongue in such circumstances, became more heated and abusive as the meeting progressed. No one was going to tell him what to do.

Then came the snap decision. He told his colleagues he couldn't tolerate any decision infringing on his democratic liberties. He was leaving the firm.

In the days following, the other lawyers tried to dissuade him. They thought he was overreacting. "I used all my skills as a pleading attorney," said Cain. "I remember saying to him to forget about Bergeron. 'You know Pierre, he's a hard guy to get along with. He always has been. Look, I want you to stay. Lamarre and Guy Wells want you to stay. Don't go off on a tangent. You're better off here. We're better off with you.' "

The stakes were higher than personal allegiances and friendships. The lawyers all knew Bouchard's departure could have a significant impact on their incomes. "We realized if Lucien left and opened his own firm, it would only be a matter of time before our main opposition in this neck of the woods would come from him," said Cain. "He would siphon away clients. You'd have to be crazy to let go of such a talented guy."

The lobbying effort to keep Bouchard failed. The personal conflict between Bergeron and Bouchard had become too deep to heal and Bouchard no longer wanted to work alongside him. He had had enough. He wanted to be his own boss. After nine years at the law firm of his archetype, Roland Fradette, he announced he was setting up his own shop down the street. He would go it alone and establish a fine practice and support the independence ticket in whatever way he chose. He would show Bergeron and the others who was tops.

The news hit hard. Fradette, at home in his retirement, playing a lot of chess, at which he was a master, wasn't directly involved in the dispute. But he was hurt, badly hurt, to see one of the best recruits he had ever made leave the firm in this way. Lamarre felt the wrong man had gone. "Between Bergeron the Liberal and Bouchard the separatist," he said, "I preferred the separatist, even though I was a Liberal myself."

The lawyers had sensed that Bouchard was a proud type who marched to his own drummer. But they hadn't thought he was this impulsive. His leaving, they said, resulted from his excessive pride. It wasn't just that his liberties were infringed; there was the matter of his ego. As André Tremblay had noticed at Laval, Bouchard couldn't tolerate anyone encroaching on his ability to decide.

The way the event played out left the impression that his leaving was very hard for Bouchard: that for the sake of principle, he was putting his career at risk. "My brother had to pay the price of his convictions," recalled Gérard Bouchard. "This was a very painful part of his personal story." Gérard suggested that it took great courage to leave the firm. "He was building a very good labour practice within his firm, but then he left everything. It really was everything." Lucien Bouchard himself did not discourage this type of martyrdom-tinged playback.

But there was another interpretation. There was suspicion that Bouchard had been wanting to leave for some time, but he needed a pretext. Flagrant support for the Péquistes provided it.

His friend and partner François Lamarre, who had attended Laval ahead of him, felt his leaving was Bouchard's best career move at the time. Once having established their credentials, lawyers like Bouchard were striking out on their own all the time, Lamarre pointed out. Bouchard, he added, was in an excellent position to do so. He was young, superbly talented, had money and no children. He knew the legal landscape well and had a long client list, some of whom would naturally stick with him.

In Lamarre's view, the advantages outweighed the risks. Why answer to someone else when you can run your own firm? It was the dream of many lawyers. "Lucien was very much conscious of his ability as a lawyer to open his own bureau and start his own business. He was a brilliant lawyer. He wasn't really dependent on anyone."

In striking out on one's own, financial security was a paramount consideration. Bouchard had no such worries. According to his friend de Belleval, he was a millionaire. Nine years of hard work at the firm had allowed him to salt that much away. Lamarre wasn't sure of his total accumulation, but he was doing "very, very well."

If Bouchard wanted to leave the firm, he certainly needed an alibi. To just get up and leave the top firm in town, one that had treated him so well, and open an office in competition would have been seen as perfidious. But by bringing the matter of political affiliation to a crisis point in actively supporting the Péquistes, he could give himself cause. He could engineer a dénouement in which he could be viewed as the victim, one who sacrificed his own personal interests for the sake of high democratic standards.

Years earlier in the 1960s, when his family members were pressuring him to cut with federalism and put on the separatist badge, Bouchard could not realistically have done so—even if in his heart he had badly wanted to make the move. At that time, he was cutting his teeth as a lawyer with Fradette, the staunch anti-nationalist, and did not yet have a financial footing. To declare himself a sovereignist could have been suicidal. He could only do so when the conditions were right—when Fradette had left, when he had money in the bank, when he could make it look like he was the wounded party.

His departure and his retreat to his own citadel, whether premeditated or not, was a story which with time would become familiar. There would be other friends of Bouchard's who would find themselves in similar positions as his law partners. They would find themselves trying to harness his impulsive instincts, aware that they couldn't afford to lose him, that he might take too much power with him, then wondering whether it was his principles that were motivating his departure, or whether it was ego—a skin too thin to be anyone's subordinate.

This would be a question Bouchard would leave hanging throughout his career. Was he a man of principle or a schemer with a martyr complex? A man of honour or a glory seeker whose hubris ruled him?

In his memoir, Bouchard skipped quickly over his departure from the law firm. His account did not even mention the pivotal dispute with Bergeron. He later told a former law colleague about how, in the writing of this stage of his life, he had been able to finesse the whole story for public consumption so as not to offend any of the law partners.

He had withdrawn his support for Trudeau and the Liberals ostensibly because of the PM's violation of his democratic rights and principles in invoking the War Measures Act. But it was far from that simple. As with leaving the law firm, as with other drastic turns he would take, there were always ostensible motivations and there were always ones more camouflaged.

At the time of his leaving, his wealth wasn't known to many. He had saved and invested much of it. His only expenditures apart from the basics were on books, European travel and one luxury item he allowed himself—an impressive car. As a teenager visiting the city of Cadillacs, he was embarrassed to look so poor. As a lawyer he could show them he was not a cut below. He did so, wheeling out one of the most expensive automobiles on the market—a brand new Citroën. It was his symbol of success. He loved driving it through the streets of Chicoutimi and he loved taking it to Montreal, where many of his former classmates were with the big firms. When Lucien showed up in his Citroën, recalled Bernard Roy, the old law-school boys were mightily impressed.

With his money, he could help his parents live more comfortably. He could get good medical care for his father, who had serious cardiovascular problems. He could afford holidays in France and Greece. He could work for destitute clients without pay. Most importantly, the financial base allowed him to open his new firm without any undue pressure.

To begin in 1974, Bouchard, thirty-five, was a free man. He had cleared himself of old burdens—political, legal, financial—and he was on his own. He hung up his shingle on rue Racine, just down the street from the old partners. He brought in his wife as secretary and bookkeeper and began again.

The new beginning didn't last long. Business was slow for a few weeks but some of his former clients, unoffended by his political turn, returned to him and new ones appeared. Before too long Bouchard was setting up plans for expansion. But all this was interrupted by a phone call from Brian Mulroney.

After the failed attempts at the bar-admission exams, Mulroney had succeeded on the third try and landed on his feet at the highly regarded firm of Ogilvie, Cope. With his dashing, gleaming presence, with his mastery of the social arts and aptitude for making political connections, he was soon a high-flyer, on a first-name basis with the business and political establishment. Though a Tory, the boy from Baie-Comeau was also cosy with the big Grits, including Robert Bourassa. In 1974 Bourassa recruited him to serve on a commission to investigate violence in the construction industry brought on by labour unions warring for the spoils from the premier's massive James Bay hydroelectric development. Bourassa dipped deeply into the Laval network, choosing Robert Cliche, who had taught Mulroney and Bouchard a course in legal interrogation and pleading at the university, to head up the inquiry.

Mulroney had heard about Bouchard's break with the law firm. It sounded to him as if his old friend was down on his luck. As a staunch federalist, he had looked dimly upon Bouchard's political change, but it wasn't enough to badly harm the friendship. Needing an associate counsel for the commission, Bouchard's name was one of the first that crossed his mind. He had to lobby hard with the premier because Bourassa wasn't keen on having Péquistes on the commission.

Bouchard didn't hesitate in accepting Mulroney's invitation. The position gave him a chance to shine in the big city. He could renew his friendship with Brian, and the coincidence that saw Robert Cliche in charge was indeed fortunate. He greatly admired

Cliche as a teacher and as a man. Bouchard didn't speak English yet. Michael Cain had given him the odd lesson at the firm, but time rarely permitted and, curiously, learning the language was still not high on Bouchard's priority list. On the Cliche Commission, however, all he needed was his immaculate French.

While excited, neither Bouchard nor Mulroney realized what a gold mine they had fallen upon. The Cliche Commission became Quebec's version of the McClelland Commission in the United States, which had tackled labour union corruption almost two decades earlier. Robert Kennedy was the aggressive counsellor, John Kennedy was on the panel, and powerhouses such as Jimmy Hoffa were the targets.

By Canadian standards the media attention the Cliche Commission received was comparable to its U.S. counterpart. The parade of union heavies and foul-mouthed thugs included a pimp with a diamond-studded tooth and hitmen who had wielded baseball bats. The fantastic tales of bribery rings, protection rackets and blackmailers provided captivating television drama.

It was dangerous business. Bouchard, Mulroney and the others were moved around under heavy police protection. Once Bouchard was awakened in the middle of the night to be told that a man had been found dead in the trunk of a car at a shopping mall. Someone had apparently not wanted the chap to testify. He was found with his lips sewn shut with steel wire. The task of viewing the body fortunately did not fall on Bouchard, who had seen all he wished to see of dead bodies when he visited the medical school at Laval. Another commissioner, a pale-faced Guy Chevrette, got the honour. For the rest of the day, he had the dry heaves.

The home of Bouchard's neighbour in Chicoutimi was ransacked by vandals. While it was never proven who did the deed, it was assumed to be a warning to Bouchard to go easy at the hearings. But Bouchard did not go easy. His black thatch of hair shook with anger, his dark eyes glowered, and his voice counter-attacked witnesses with crisp, unrelenting conviction. It took little to incite his rhetorical outrage, recalled Chevrette. He was a man easily convinced of the truth of what he was stating. Sometimes he went overboard, insisting that everyone be brought forward to testify, including Premier Robert Bourassa, who had backed his appointment. Mulroney and the others convinced Bouchard not to go that far.

Like Robert Kennedy at the McClelland Commission, Bouchard came across as a man of moral passion and searing commitment. It would strike some that the Mulroney-Bouchard mix was not so different from that of the Kennedy brothers. Bouchard was the tough idealistic Robert, while Mulroney had John's polished veneer, smooth charm and ambition to go all the way.

Two factors played heavily on the success of the commission. One was the role of the Quebec provincial police, La Sûreté du Quebec. After a long period of sizing up the commission counsels, its investigators began to cooperate with the commissioners, supplying key evidence to nail suspects. The results of their wiretapping operations proved invaluable. Having heard witnesses deny allegations, Bouchard was able to roll tapes which contradicted what they had just testified.

Not only did the commissioners have the cops on their side, the media were there too. Though Bouchard had worked for *La Presse* and *Le Carabin* and had handled communications in Bedard's campaign, he still didn't know how to operate in the big leagues. Mulroney soon fixed that. Mulroney had had a handle on the importance of working the media since his student days at St. Francis Xavier University. He knew that if it wasn't reported, it hadn't happened. He knew if you didn't get your news out before the TV and press deadlines, it wouldn't appear. He knew that if you got along well with the reporters on a personal basis, they treated you well. He was the player. He knew the game.

This in mind, most everything was orchestrated with an eye for media maximization. Star witnesses and crucial elements of testimony were scheduled to coincide with press deadlines. Bouchard was instructed to end his interrogations in time to keep the reporters happy. Mulroney had worked his long list of media contacts, most of whom he knew on a first-name basis, to make sure they turned out. He bumped into L. Ian MacDonald, a columnist for *The Montreal Gazette*. "Ian," he said, "We have a seat ready for you at the Cliche Commission."

Mulroney had a political eye cocked to the big sky. Following three straight defeats to Pierre Trudeau, Robert Stanfield's days as head of the federal Conservative Party were finished. Mulroney had never run for a seat for the Tories, and he was only in his midthirties, but he was contemplating a leadership bid. He needed a booster shot to propel him onto the front pages. The Cliche Commission did the trick.

Bouchard's reputation benefited enormously from the proceedings as well. He had made the leap from obscure Chicoutimi lawyer to the front pages of the Montreal dailies. He proved to himself that he could succeed in the big leagues and he had fun doing it. His marriage was becoming more difficult, and he enjoyed being away and tasting some of the high life in Montreal.

Most importantly, the experience at the commission sealed his friendship with Brian Mulroney. They faced a big test together and seized the opportunity. Mulroney had gambled in recruiting a relatively unknown Péquiste, but Bouchard had vindicated his judgment. Mulroney boasted to all his friends about what a splendid job Lucien had done. Now the two of them had not only the days at law school to bind them but a big career success. At Laval they had developed a close friendship, but their geographical separation and political differences subsequently threatened to dilute it. The commission had reunited them, more tightly than ever.

It had also united Bouchard with Robert Cliche. Mulroney was a source of deep friendship. Cliche was a source of inspiration. Watching from a distance from Chicoutimi, Michael Cain could understand how the two would come together. Cliche, he said, had similarities to Fradette. "They were both imbued with a sense of their roots," said Cain, and were therefore much like Lucien in that regard. All his life Bouchard would have a special place for those who, like himself, like Mulroney, like Fradette, like his father, had risen from humble station. Cliche was a union sympathizer and leftist politician from the Beauce who became one of the finer legal minds in the province. Bouchard held Cliche in reverence, finding him soft-hearted, learned and wise, gentle but demanding. So many of the things he said about Cliche could be said about Bouchard himself. Cliche revered his land and his father. Cliche went through several different mood swings in a given day. Cliche was a man of deep complexity "who never resolved his ambivalent feelings."

Cliche had been a lifelong federalist, but Bouchard sensed in these years he was moving towards the sovereignty option. Lévesque visited Cliche to try to get him to run in the 1976 election. Cliche turned him down, saying that his health was failing. He would die two years later, never having officially made the conversion that Bouchard thought he was on the verge of undertaking.

Bouchard included Cliche among those such as Fradette and his father who had not attained the renown in life they merited. Speaking of his province, he said, "We can no longer count the number of people whose lives have ended without realizing their ideals."

The supreme importance he placed on status and fulfilment suggested that Bouchard was a man with no small ambition of his own. Cliche spurred it. Like a father figure, he filled his two young counsels with visions of grandiose futures. He told Bouchard not to worry about making money, that politics and public service were the more honourable path. He saw big things for him, but even bigger ones for Mulroney. Mulroney would go to Ottawa, Cliche predicted, and become prime minister. That was precisely what Mulroney had been telling Bouchard and others since his college days.

Cliche, Fradette and Philippe Bouchard, the brightest stars in Bouchard's galaxy, all died within a few years of one another, between 1975 and 1978. Lucien's father, aged sixty-nine, passed away in 1975, when the Cliche Commission had finished its work and Lucien had returned home to his law practice. The funeral, which Mulroney attended, naturally brought with it a lot of emotion. Gérard, Roch and Lucien regarded their father as the finest man they had ever encountered in their lives. They formally drew this conclusion one day after the funeral when they met and talked about the impressive people who had crossed their paths. There had been many inspiring ones but none, they decided, had the sensitivity and humanity of their father.

Gérard recalled the day of the funeral: "It was the first experience for us of a loss of a very close person. I was living in Chicoutimi and I got the phone call from the hospital and Lucien got the same phone call and we went together. When we got to the hospital, he had just died." They took their saintly dad to Saint-Coeur-de-Marie, where he was buried at the family homestead. "Everybody controlled their emotions," said Gérard. "We were not the types to display that sort of thing. But inside we were just destroyed."

To cushion the pain and the emptiness, the siblings could be comforted in the thought that, though some had career difficulties, they had fulfilled their father's first commandment of not being simpletons. They knew that he had drawn much pride from their superior educations.

Lucien's big strides were evident. Gérard, based in Chicoutimi, was becoming a leading historian, specializing in demographic studies. When his thesis was published in France, Lucien was so pleased he offered to pay Gérard's plane fare to go there for the occasion. Roch was moving towards professorial status in philosophy, but Lucien was not impressed—at this time or in later years. Lucien's old room-mate André Tremblay spent several years with Roch at the University of Ottawa and regarded him as the brainiest of the Bouchards—"one of the brightest men in this world I ever met." But Roch was also the most frustrating in that he was an underachiever, not producing up to the level Lucien and Tremblay expected. They thought Roch should have become president of the university or something similar. But Roch didn't have the moral strength and work discipline of Lucien. Roch was a bon vivant. He liked to drink and go out with beautiful women, and these indulgences, recalled Tremblay, held him back. In Tremblay's analysis, Lucien also had such cravings, but he had the discipline to overcome them. He didn't drink and always put work before other pleasures.

Soon after Lucien returned home from the Cliche Commission, the Conservative Party began preparations for its leadership convention to replace Robert Stanfield. In November 1975, Brian Mulroney entered the race. His platform was rather Trudeauvian. He was a loud federalist, opposing the two nations theory, speaking proudly of one Canada, indivisible. Bouchard was a full-blown Péquiste at this stage. He was being courted by Lévesque and others to run for the PQ in the next provincial election. But, just as he had kept one foot in both camps in the 1960s, he did so in the '70s.

While breaking bread with Lévesque, he climbed on board the Mulroney team and began writing speeches for him. Other candidates, such as Joe Clark, espoused a more decentralized vision of the country and appeared far more accommodating of the aspirations of Quebec and therefore of Bouchard. But even if Bouchard liked to think of himself as a man of principle, there were times when principles could be sacrificed. Just as he had apparently left his law firm because he felt so deeply about campaigning for the PQ, just as he ostensibly left the Liberals because Trudeau had not been supportive enough of Quebec, now he could campaign for a Tory federalist with a Trudeau vision and leave many to wonder where he really stood.

What camp was Lucien Bouchard in? At a young age, he had already made a goodly number of leaps: federalist at Jonquière, fervent nationalist at Laval, federalist under Trudeau, secessionist after Greece, and now federalist with Mulroney. Denis de Belleval offered a rationale for his Tory turn. While certainly aware that the Tory's Canadian vision ran counter to the PQ's, de Belleval recalled that he and Bouchard felt it was harmless to work for Mulroney because they didn't feel he had a chance of winning. "We had our own agenda," said de Belleval in reference to the Péquiste platform. "We couldn't care less about the substance [of the Mulroney campaign]. It was merely a matter of helping a friend." There was also the realization that, win or lose, Mulroney was a man on the move.

He proceeded to run a spirited and effective early leadership campaign and, within a couple of weeks of the convention, had a clear chance of winning. Bouchard increased his activity for him. He went to the Mulroney retreat at Lake Memphremagog, where he spent a week huddled with the candidate and his closest advisers. There he worked primarily on Mulroney's major speech to the convention, helping him pen his federalist pitch. In the final days, the speech was discarded in favour of a high-minded text of butterfly prose and vapid philosophy. It bombed, and so did Mulroney's candidacy. In a shocker, Joe Clark carried the day.

Bouchard's federal man had lost, and now Bouchard turned to his other mentor—Lévesque. The Bourassa Liberals called the election for the fall of 1976. Keen on recruiting Bouchard as a candidate, Lévesque arranged a meeting with him at a Montreal restaurant. Having seen Bouchard perform at the Cliche Commission, he knew what a prize catch he would be. In addition, many PQ members such as Marc-André Bedard were singing his praises. The first meeting between the two was stilted. Not even a fashion show, which was in full swing at the restaurant and featured a platoon of tall models gliding by the premier's table, could relax them. But the session was not a harbinger of their relationship.

Bouchard knew the PQ was in an excellent position to make a breakthrough. He had predicted to his disbelieving colleagues on the Cliche Commission that Lévesque could even form a government. But after much prodding by the PQ, Bouchard, while willing to campaign for them, backed away from a candidacy. As he said, he was afraid of what politics did to people. Great men lost. Fradette had lost. Cliche had taken a couple of runs for the NDP and lost. Was it really a test of merit? And wasn't politics, in its essence, too unseemly a craft for him?

The decision to stay on the sidelines wasn't made out of a lack of ambition. de Belleval, who won a seat and entered the first Lévesque Cabinet after the historic PQ victory in the 1976 provincial election, could see, along with Bouchard's brothers, that a big prize was in store for him and that he wanted it. But it was a matter of time, and the time wasn't yet ripe.

"He was a man who was waiting for the right occasion." Since the 1960s, in de Belleval's judgment, he had been waiting. "It was so obvious to everybody, even to himself. But he wasn't going to go the ordinary route."

Along with de Belleval, his friend Marc-André Bedard joined the PQ Cabinet. Several job offers, such as deputy minister of labour, came to Bouchard just as they had come from the Liberals in the late 1960s. He turned them down this time as well. He was building up his law practice at home, and as his former colleagues had predicted, siphoning off some of their business. There were, however, many moments of remorse and self-reproach for not having had the fortitude to run in the election. The new PQ group of ministers struck Bouchard as an exceptionally erudite group on a historic mission. He wished he was a part of it. Instead, he was in the shadows, waiting for his moment.

He had outgrown Chicoutimi and Jonquière. He was too grand for such a small stage. An offer set up by de Belleval and Bouchard's other friends in the capital came his way to head up a commission to study labour negotiating procedures with the Quebec public service. Quebec had experienced its fill of illegal strikes in hospitals and schools as well as shutdowns of government operations. Bouchard was well-seasoned in these areas, having negotiated contracts as part of his law practice. He took the post.

The Martin-Bouchard Commission, as it was called, held

public hearings for several months during 1977. Though Bouchard felt that Lévesque was anticipating radical proposals, such as the abolition of the right to strike in the public service, none were forthcoming. Bouchard reasoned the government was not in a position to change the integrity of the collective-bargaining process. The report proposed giving the unions a key role in defining essential services and advocated more effective bargaining timetables.

Bouchard was disappointed in Lévesque's reaction. But according to Jocelyne Ouellette, who was minister of public works and supplies, it was a wrong read. Lévesque, whom she knew well, rarely told anyone to their face that they had done a good job, she said. Lévesque was comfortable with the report, and the more he saw of Bouchard, the more he liked him. "Lévesque found him intellectual, cultured and organized. What he liked about him was that he was intellectually rigorous." The premier quickly separated real people from the phonies, and he found Bouchard authentic. "Lévesque was a great humanist of the heart and the mind," said Ouellette, who became a very close companion of his wife, Corinne Côté-Lévesque. "It was in this respect, the humanist side, that Bouchard appealed to him."

As proof he was keen on Bouchard, the premier was soon back with another offer, one which flowed from the report Bouchard had tabled. He appointed him as the government's chief negotiator for contract talks with the public-sector unions. It was a weighty responsibility requiring close coordination with Lévesque's minister of everything, Jacques Parizeau. Parizeau oversaw all financial dealings of the government. After signing his PQ membership card in his presence, Bouchard had met Parizeau again when he came to the Saguenay looking for money to save the Parti Québécois's newspaper, Le Jour. He had been impressed by Parizeau's singular dedication to the cause. With his outstanding training in economics, Bouchard thought Parizeau could have been governor of the Bank of Canada had he gone to Ottawa. Instead he chose to bus the backroads of Quebec looking for converts to the cause of independence.

Parizeau's background in the civil service of Quebec had familiarized him deeply with public-sector negotiations, which he now wanted to control. That the appointment of Bouchard was handed down to him from above did not sit well. Bouchard could soon feel a slight chill from this rather pompous master of the treasury. Concerned, he asked Jean-Roch Boivin, Lévesque's chief of staff, whether he should speak to the premier to get some clearer directions. Boivin pelted Bouchard with a flurry of expletives suggesting it was crazy to contemplate going over Parizeau's head. He told him he had better learn to get along with him.

The government's goal was to draw back public service wage increases so that they paralleled increases in the cost of living and were more in line with private-sector wages. In Ottawa, Jean Chrétien was embarked on similar work, presiding over cutbacks in wage settlements in these years, first as secretary of the Treasury Board, then as minister of finance, where he warred with Parizeau.

Bouchard immersed himself totally in the task, as he did with any assignment that came his way. It was intriguing work, high drama, and again his thoughts turned back to Hellenistic times. The scale of the operation was akin, he noted, to a Greek tragedy in four acts. The grievances were stated, then the arguments elaborated. Denunciations, threats and strikes ensued before the final stage of resolution. His description of the process exhibited the reach and the richness of the Bouchard mind, as well as the eloquence of his pen.

The dealings, he wrote, never achieved the heights of dialogues of Aeschylus. "The actors gesticulate on forty different stages at the same time, while the real action takes place behind the scenes. Cacophony replaces the music of the strophe. Journalists in jeans take the place of the chorus. Victims do not cry out in pain on stage but meet their fate in the silence of everyday life. They sit in bleachers, deprived of public services and of any voice in the matter."

Bouchard was more than just a student of Greek and of Aeschylus and the like. He could cast himself, as Gérard once noted, inside the characters, adopting their thoughts, their view of humanity, their arrogant pride, their ancestral curses.

The hard bargaining presided over by him brought rancour, threat, counter-threat and illegal strikes by hospital employees. In the end, just before Christmas 1979, an agreement was forged. The Lévesque government came up with generous terms, caving in to many of the unions' demands.

At the head of the negotiating table, Bouchard met for the first time a namesake from Lac Saint-Jean—Benoît Bouchard. This

Bouchard was executive director of a college, or CEGEP as they were known. He recalled the final moments of the negotiating process. "We were five on the negotiating team. We had an agreement not to move. And we got up one morning and Lucien gave up everything to the unions. Totally."

Lucien Bouchard, in this instance, was acting at the behest of his political bosses. He had major input but the final decisions were not all his own. Benoît Bouchard was fascinated, however, by the twists and turns of the man he faced at the head of the table. One moment he surged with emotion; the next he was cool, hard and logical. For the college director the way the resolution came about, with a fabulous eleventh-hour backflip, would prove characteristic. He would find in Lucien Bouchard a man who alternated moods and mindsets at a startling rate. At times, said Benoît Bouchard, he was "totally blinded by his emotions."

7. Long Knives or Long Lies

It was no secret that one of the reasons the Bouchard-led negotiations came to a generous conclusion was the coming referendum on Quebec's future. The 300,000 employees benefiting from the new arrangement, along with their families, represented a good swath of the Quebec population. The PQ tilted to the left, to the unions. It would need them for the vote on sovereignty-association.

Given his newfound prominence in the party, Bouchard played a rather modest role in the referendum. Under the direction of Marc-André Bedard, the PQ's strongman in Saguenay-Lac-Saint-Jean, he did some campaigning on his home turf for the Yes side. But he wasn't the fiery, passionate fighter, working day and night for the cause. One reason was complacency. The sovereignists were faring remarkably well in the kingdom. They would carry the day there with or without Bouchard's assistance. In the rest of the province, Bouchard's name wasn't yet big enough to be a pivotal force. In any case, Bouchard looked at the mood of the people and at the polling and felt confident victory was on the way.

This was to be the culmination of the twenty-year march. For all his apparent despair over the politics of the Liberals, Bouchard felt his province had done very well under them. In his assessment, he could hardly have been more categorical. "From June 22nd, 1960, to May 20, 1980, it had been a beautiful trip," he would write. He listed the new educational system, social programs, a modern public service and a state organization with the proper tools for economic development. "Quebec had made enormous progress since 1960," he said. Many of the changes were forged by the Liberals who, under Lesage and Bourassa, were in power through most of the twenty years. At the federal level, the Liberals ruled every year between 1963 and 1979. Bouchard often spoke highly of Trudeau's bilingualism program and of Pearson's great social programs. For the Bouchard family, social security meant a lot. While growing up, they worried so much about what would happen if their father lost his health or his job or if his delivery truck broke down. There was no unemployment insurance, good pensions or protection for disabled workers.

Bouchard's words seemed peculiar. If it had been such a "beautiful trip" and the Liberals had been the ones leading the way, why had he jumped ship? Why was he alleging that Trudeau, who enjoyed the constant blessings of Quebec voters, was such a disaster for the province? If the progress was "enormous," how had he kept it, as Bouchard alleged, "a simple module"?

Because of his confidence in a referendum victory, the heavy beating inflicted upon the sovereignist forces brought with it a profound sense of disillusionment. Much like his mother, Bouchard tended to rush towards alarmist interpretations. He said the defeat made him feel ostracized and turned him sour on politics, so sour that he determined he would end his flirtations with it. The battle had been lost. "It was necessary to turn the page. I was hurt. At forty-two, when you normally begin to live, I thought I was finished."

These feelings proved decidedly temporary. For a while he remained in the Saguenay practising law and pondering the future of his declining marriage. Under his direction, the little firm he started with his wife had continued to grow and prosper. He also sat on corporate boards where he was joined on occasion by his Laval classmate Peter White, now a major apparatchik in the Conrad Black empire. "I thought he was very effective as a board member," recalled White. "He was well prepared and certainly knew his files."

During the referendum Trudeau had promised a new constitutional deal for Quebec. He tried to forge a consensus with the provinces on a method of bringing home the Canadian Constitution from Britain. Failing, he decided to proceed unilaterally, thus raising the ire of the premiers. He proposed an amending formula for a new Constitution as set out at the failed Victoria Conference a decade earlier. It gave Quebec the right to a veto of any amendment. In addition, the prime minister wanted a Charter of Rights and Freedoms, one which entrenched minority language rights. Quebec was opposed. This clause could override Lévesque's prized Bill 101, the language law seen as the great protector of French culture.

Bouchard joined Lévesque in opposing the language provisions.

He virulently opposed Trudeau's brinkmanship in proceeding alone with the repatriation plan. When the province formally challenged the legality of Trudeau's action in the Quebec Court of Appeal, Bouchard gladly came on board as one of a group of four lawyers to argue Quebec's case. He was appointed by his friend Marc-André Bedard, now justice minister. A decision on the case was still pending as Lévesque fought an election in the spring of 1981 against Claude Ryan's Liberals. Voters were concerned about the economy, not the Constitution. Though Lévesque did go after the language decrees in the Charter of Rights, the repatriation controversy was not a subject of priority. Quebeckers had just rejected Lévesque's form of nationalism and were tremendously loyal to Trudeau, as demonstrated by opinion polls. They were also loyal, despite the repudiation of his sovereignist vision, to Lévesque. They still wanted a secure Quebec, they still liked the man and they couldn't warm to the austere demeanour of the new Liberal leader, Claude Ryan. They re-elected the PQ in convincing fashion.

Surprisingly enough, Bouchard greeted Lévesque's triumph sceptically. In retrospect, he would say it was Lévesque's "passport to hell." He felt that the victory put in place a dynamic that could not work. How could a party dedicated to sovereignty have credibility in trying to negotiate a new unity pact with Pierre Trudeau?

Bouchard's analysis of this dynamic was stark, frank and of historical significance. He would write in his book that "A party that had tried to 'destroy' Canada held little credibility in negotiating seriously or repelling the federal offensive." He added that "the Parti Québécois existed for the sake of Quebec independence. It was not at ease in this new role that went against its very nature: negotiating the 'renewal' of Canadian federalism."

While coming many years after the fact, it was an astonishing admission. In essence Bouchard was conceding a vital point to his arch-foes Trudeau and Chrétien. The two federalists believed that Lévesque was not interested in signing on to a new unity agreement. Chrétien liked to cite a remark from a leading PQ member, Claude Charron. When Chrétien suggested to him that the time was right to make music with Ottawa, Charron responded, "Jean, you know we are separatists. So how can we sign up for a new Confederation?" Chrétien wondered how, in the light of such attitudes, Ottawa could be charged with isolating Quebec in forging a constitutional package. Wasn't isolation what the Quebec government wanted?

Bouchard's words seemingly placed him in the Charron camp. But while believing that Lévesque lacked credibility in the negotiations, he also tried to make the case that the federalists were undermining Lévesque. For this period of his life, the historical record would show one remarkable contradiction following another.

His good friend Mulroney wasn't making it any easier for him in this regard. As president of the Iron Ore Company of Canada, Mulroney was a vigorous supporter of the federal side in the referendum. He again took opposite sides to Bouchard in supporting Trudeau and Chrétien on their repatriation plans.

Tory leader Joe Clark, who was much more in sync with Bouchard in opposing Trudeau's constitutional politics, was the recipient of Mulroney's scorn. In early 1981, Peter Blaikie, president of the Conservative Party, attended a meeting with Clark and Mulroney and senior Quebec Tories in Montreal. "Joe opened the meeting by explaining his position," recalled Blaikie. "Mulroney was sitting on the edge of his chair. He could hardly contain himself. And the minute Joe finished, Mulroney launched himself into it and basically took the position, 'Joe, you're wrong. You couldn't be more wrong. Trudeau's got the country behind him. He's got Quebec behind him. We have to support him 100 percent on this. He's totally right in terms of vision.' "

Mulroney's crowning argument on that night, recalled Blaikie, was to say that in his capacity as president of the Iron Ore Company, he had just toured the mines of northern Quebec and heard from working-class Quebeckers. Far from being upset or feeling betrayed by Trudeau's Charter and his unilateralism, they told Mulroney—at least as he recounted it—that Trudeau was right and the Tories should support him.

But despite these views, Mulroney would emerge shiningly in Bouchard's eyes. So too would René Lévesque.

The well-documented events of the repatriation drama provided Bouchard with ammunition that he would later put to spectacular use. Dissenting provincial premiers developed a counter-proposal to Trudeau's repatriation plan and Lévesque joined with them to form what was called the gang of eight. In doing so, Lévesque surprisingly gave up Quebec's de facto claim to a veto to any change in the

Constitution. The package he signed with the dissenters provided for a formula in which constitutional amendment required the support of seven provinces containing at least half the population of Canada. Provinces could also opt out or choose not to adhere to the provisions of any amendment and receive financial compensation from Ottawa.

By teaming with the provinces, Lévesque felt he could either scuttle Trudeau's ambitions or force him into signing a package which was acceptable to Quebec. At the federal-provincial conference of November 1981, the Quebec premier appeared well on his way to realizing his ambitions. No compromise on a repatriation deal seemed possible. The provinces still opposed aspects of the Charter and Trudeau's amending formula. Trudeau was now considering going over their heads and directly to the people. He'd hold two referendums, one on the amending formula, another on the Charter. His proposal succeeded in cracking the unity of the gang of eight.

René Lévesque, for one, liked the idea of referendums. It appealed to his democratic spirit. Other premiers became concerned. They could well lose in such a test. The disaccord helped open the door to a compromise that had been cobbled together by Chrétien, Roy Romanow of Saskatchewan and Ontario's Roy McMurtry. In general terms it featured a trade-off. The provinces would accept the Charter in return for Trudeau's acceding to their amending formula. Late in the evening of November 4th, 1981, last-minute bargaining in the absence of Lévesque led to an agreement on the compromise.

Bouchard found the modus operandi in reaching the pact offensive. He and many on the sovereignist side alleged that the provincial premiers, with Chrétien acting as ringleader, purposely schemed through the night because Lévesque was absent, then presented him with a fait accompli in the morning. It was, as Bouchard and the others labelled it, the dreaded "night of the long knives."

The interpretation was met with derision by the federal side. As the premiers attested, Chrétien, in fact, went home at 11 p.m. and made a couple of phone calls before going to bed. Some of the other premiers, attorneys-general and aides continued discussions in various groups in various places until one and two in the morning. No one was coordinating the random process from the top.

Since Lévesque and his people were at a hotel on the other side of the river in Hull and since negotiations would be continuing in the morning anyway, no one thought it imperative to try and get Lévesque's views at this time.

The negotiations did proceed in the morning at breakfast, but Lévesque wasn't there for the early part. Despite the critical juncture in the proceedings, he showed up almost half an hour late for the breakfast meeting. Lévesque was a veteran of so many of these bargaining sessions. In many instances they lasted well into the night. Indeed it was then that crucial business was often done. That he wasn't around the night before, that he wasn't around early in the morning only fuelled suspicion that perhaps Charron, Chrétien, Bouchard and others were correct in saying that his secessionist party wasn't keenly looking for a unity package. If Lévesque agreed to something, what would be the reaction when he went home? Would he have to renege on it as other Quebec premiers had done in the past?

After arriving late, Lévesque was soon briefed on the new set of proposals being put together to take to Trudeau. Lévesque was aghast. Newfoundland Premier Brian Peckford explained that some blocks had been built, one at a time, and "Now, it's your turn." An incensed Lévesque didn't want a turn and the breakfast meeting was adjourned.

An anxious negotiating session with all the premiers and Trudeau ensued. Disputes were ironed out one by one. At one point Trudeau asked Lévesque if he would accept entrenched minority language obligations. "No," Lévesque replied, "there would be riots in the streets of Montreal." The Quebec leader opposed the premiers' new plan on two other grounds. The financial compensation clause in the amending formula had been removed; and job creation programs in Quebec would be hindered by labour mobility clauses in the new deal.

In a side chamber, Lévesque pressed his objections with Trudeau, warning that if the new package was approved, the consequences could be incalculable. He challenged the prime minister to see if he had backing for his deal by calling a referendum in Quebec. Trudeau suggested that Lévesque hold a referendum on the items he disagreed with and if he won, Trudeau would ask the others to reopen the accord.

When Lévesque asked if the veto could be returned, Trudeau was non-committal. Shortly thereafter, Lévesque and the Quebec delegation left. Lévesque looked shaken. He told reporters that as usual Quebec had been isolated and that there could be dire consequences.

Much of the evidence, however, seemed to suggest that Bouchard's later interpretation was correct, that the problem came down to the fact that a sovereignist party could not in good conscience sign a new unity pact. In the view of Hugh Segal, a member of the Ontario delegation, "The notion that there was some 'night of the long knives' is one of the great convenient nationalist fictions for which there is absolutely no substantiation. Those who argue that Quebec was knifed in the back were either not there or incapable of seeing reality."

The burden of proof was on the accusers, and none of the Péquistes, including Bouchard, produced evidence of any deliberate plotting to keep Lévesque to the side.

The final agreement that Lévesque would not sign contained the Charter, which was highly popular in Quebec. If Lévesque—who had bargained away a Quebec veto himself—had reservations about it, the deal handed him a notwithstanding clause to sweep away those reservations. Any decision taken by a judge under the Charter which infringed upon Quebec's culture or language rights could be overturned by the Quebec legislature. In fact the Quebec government would turn around and make wholesale use of this clause.

That Lévesque, added Segal, "could have gone away from the table with far more than Quebec had ever before had, yet chose to leave with nothing, was an act of PQ negligence, almost criminal negligence in the political sense... This was a poker game in which Quebec left all kinds of chips on the table, solely because its representatives were so caught up in the Kafkaesque burden of being sovereignists among the federalists."

The performance of the Péquistes aside, Trudeau could not be said to have the cleanest of hands in all this. His long record of stubbornness towards any special status for Quebec was well known. In the late 1970s, when the Pépin-Robarts task force brought in sweeping recommendations recognizing Quebec's distinct qualities, he had turned up his nose at it. In 1995, in one of the last interviews he gave before his death, Jean-Luc Pépin recalled presenting his report to Trudeau. He remembered sadly how Trudeau had relegated it to the shelves right in front of him, saying, in effect, he would have none of it. Trudeau had then pledged in the 1980 referendum to bring about a new deal for Quebec. In the final analysis, despite the repatriation effort, he did not have one.

Trudeau was not one to sulk over this, however. On the matter of not holding to pledges, he could and would point out that Quebec's hands were hardly unbloodied either. Bourassa had walked away from the Victoria agreement in 1971. Moreover, in the early 1960s, Quebec premier Lesage agreed to the Fulton-Favreau formula for constitutional patriation and amendment. It stipulated that no change to the Constitution in fundamental areas would be possible without the agreement of all eleven governments. The formula was supported initially not only by Lesage, but also by Lévesque, who felt it would protect Quebec against any major federalist initiatives. But, as would be the case with Bourassa, once back home and once submitted to pressure from naysayers, Lesage backed off on his agreement.

In his analysis of history, Bouchard preferred to focus only on the 1981–82 negotiation. It was the ultimate betrayal, he said, the historical turning point. It was "the key event triggering all that happened and will happen, the breach through which Québécois democracy will escape from a regime that violated its moral commitments."

Bouchard was filled with self-pity. "I was furious and even somewhat humiliated. And humiliation, that is a chord that resonates often in me." But the humiliation wasn't shared by his people. They were in favour of Trudeau's initiatives, both the repatriation and the Charter of Rights. A Gallup poll in June 1982 showed that Quebeckers, by a three to one margin (49 percent to 16 percent), supported the new Constitution. Polls also showed that Quebeckers, by an even greater margin, wanted a Charter of Rights and Freedoms in the new Constitution. As well, they favoured the guarantee of minority language rights. The months and years after repatriation appeared to confirm the message of the polls. Support for sovereignty in the province dropped and remained low.

But despite the polls, despite Quebec's reneging on previous constitutional deals, despite evidence the night of the long knives was hype, despite the admitted credibility gap in the PQ's seeking a unity accord, it didn't matter. The repatriation drama, once wrapped in his apocalyptic terminology, would become Lucien Bouchard's great political meal ticket in the years to come.

For now, however, the times were tough on Lucien Bouchard. He was in the course of losing his marriage. His side lost the referendum battle. During the repatriation proceedings, he had lost the court challenge to Trudeau's unilateralism when the Quebec Court of Appeal beat down his team's bid. And the blue streak was by no means over. Bouchard accepted another appointment as the government's chief negotiator with the public service unions. When he began the assignment, there were clear indications that, primarily because of the recession, the government would be hard-pressed to meet the salary commitments Bouchard had negotiated with the unions in 1979. It was likely that it would even have to renege on its contract. Bouchard could see the hailstorm on the horizon, but accepted the appointment anyway. Having already negotiated the first contract, he was in a difficult position to say no to Premier Lévesque's request that he do the follow-up. He was now living apart from his wife Jocelyne, and it was more comfortable to be away from Chicoutimi. As well, the position of chief negotiator was one of enormous power, power which he enjoyed. There were the words from his brother Roch. "*Il ne peut pas rester dans les choses ordinaires.*" He couldn't be happy with an ordinary role in life.

Embarking on the task of conducting the new round, Bouchard helped prepare an analysis of the government's financial dilemma for the Treasury Board. He calculated that the scheduled salary increases he had negotiated in 1979 would heighten the government's deficit—which was at $3 billion—by another $275 million. Meeting such salary commitments was normally a matter of course for the government. One method was by increasing taxes, another simply by absorbing the cost and borrowing more money to cope with the increasing deficit. Parizeau, the proud purse master, had raised taxes enough and didn't wish to go that route. Nor was he willing to increase borrowing for fear it would lead to a downgrading of the government's credit rating.

There remained other, decidedly unsavoury, alternatives. The government could demand from the unions a voluntary roll-back. Failing that, it could issue an edict, legislating a default on the old contract.

Lévesque appeared to be spoiling for a fight with the unions. His love-hate relationship with them had turned more to the latter in recent years. He didn't like the union tactics—threats, blackmail, force. Their role in the referendum was another sore point. Despite the handsome contract settlement of 1979, the unions hadn't come through for him on voting day the way he had hoped. Though half expecting it, he was nonetheless angered.

With Parizeau not wanting to mess with his books and with Lévesque in a foul mood, the decision was made to roll back. Bouchard did not contest this plan. He approached the unions to reopen the contract and renegotiate substantial cuts. He laid out a catastrophic picture of the government's finances and pleaded for compromise. But the unions were not prepared to budge.

The government then debated bringing in special legislation to cancel the pay increase, which was scheduled for July 1, 1982. Parizeau opposed such a decisive breaking of the contract terms. After long debate, Bouchard and the other principals chose a different tack. The higher wages would be paid until the end of the year when the contract expired. Then, draconian pay cuts, a result of special legislation, would begin.

As Bouchard himself would note, the ploy didn't fool or placate anyone. The wage increase was being given as scheduled, then withdrawn six months later. The unions came away, as Bouchard conceded, feeling as if they were "victims of a hoax."

Whatever his sense of unease, he went to war in defence of the government's plan. He made strong arguments that public-sector salaries, as indexed to inflation, far exceeded those of the private sector, and that it was only fair they be brought back into line. It appeared to be a realistic argument—though a study dismissed his statistics as exaggerated—but it still left a gaping hole in his reasoning. The press was outraged. Columnist Lysiane Gagnon of *La Presse* reflected the mood. "What a farce it is to hear Messieurs Parizeau, Lévesque and Bouchard denounce the privileged salaries of state employees when it was they themselves who granted these salaries," she wrote. This is a government "that doesn't respect its own signature."

Bouchard was stung by the criticism, taking it personally. As friends pointed out, his mandate was to present a case on behalf of the government. In a sense, it was like acting for a client, doing the bidding of others. On the other hand, however, Bouchard was a central player in decisions on government strategy. He didn't appear to challenge the course strongly. Moreover, he always had before him an option he never chose to take. Having negotiated in good faith the first contract with the unions in 1979, he could have taken the position that he was not prepared to renege on it and resign.

Having professed to be embittered by Ottawa's alleged reneging on its referendum pledge to bring about a better deal for Quebec, Bouchard himself now faced charges of betraying a commitment to the people. Adversaries such as Marc-Yvan Côté of the provincial Liberals were on the attack. "It was he who took the lead with the government's strategies," recalled Côté. "In this type of situation he has a very large mandate." But he "tore up the agreement." In Côté's analysis it was all motivated by the failure of the unions to deliver the referendum vote after getting the first salary increase. After watching Bouchard through this crisis, after watching him change parties and change fundamental positions with remarkable regularity, Côté would label him "the most odious politician" in the province.

The Lévesque government's actions spawned outrage and uproar: illegal work stoppages, a strike in the schools, vicious name-calling, allegations of a return to the Duplessis era. Cabinet minister Camille Laurin was punched in the face and other ministers of the Crown were manhandled. Bouchard was confronted by a functionary who, with dripping sarcasm, looked him in the eye and said, "Thanks for the great social climate." PQ member Louise Harel broke ranks on the issue, saying there was no indication the money saved by the government would go to help those most in need. "What I refuse to countenance is the idea that only brutal methods can make the employees and their unions listen to reason." To make matters worse, at the same time as the cuts were coming into force, Péquistes were proposing a 6 percent raise in their own salaries. In the previous six years they had realized a 33 percent hike.

In ramming through its legislation, the government presented 35,000 pages of decrees detailing their decisions as they affected various unions. They gave opposition parties only a few hours to study them. *Le Devoir*'s Lise Bissonnette called it "the most enormous and most odious special law that the National Assembly has ever adopted." Columnist Marcel Adam of *La Presse* said it was "a parliamentary parody worthy of a banana republic." Employing a phrase which may have particularly stung Bouchard, L. Ian Mac-Donald of *The Montreal Gazette* called the bill "nothing less than the moral equivalent of the War Measures Act."

Even harder to take for Bouchard were accusations impugning his personal honour. He was accused, while taking back money from public servants in the contract negotiations, of abusing the public purse himself. Leaks to the media revealed he had paid $470 for a taxi between Montreal and Quebec City. In fact, as Bouchard explained, he and several other officials took the cab, and compared to what they would have been charged for plane flights, it was a big saving. But critics alleged that a private car trip would have been an even bigger saving. In another leak, he was accused of using public money to rent a formal pair of trousers to make a plea on behalf of Quebec before Newfoundland's Court of Appeal. Such formal wear was required attire in these chambers, but critics compared the matter to that of the Vautrin affair. Vautrin was a minister in the Tâschereau government who was mocked by Duplessis for spending taxpayers' money on spiffy new trousers.

Though the charges were far-fetched, they cut deep because Bouchard did not have the thick skin of many politicians. He was devastated, his honour and pride were shattered as his family name was dragged through the mud. A colleague from Chicoutimi, who had known him closely for twenty years, visited him shortly after the stories went public. He walked into his office and was shocked at the sight. He'd never seen Bouchard like this. Tears streamed down his face.

"I was stung and humiliated as never before in my life," Bouchard recalled. He made another personal pledge that would be contradicted in the years ahead. He resolved never again to accept a government appointment with an honorarium. After spending a depressed Christmas, he was asked to return to negotiate the application of the government decrees. It took three months of volunteer work on Bouchard's part and it was work he performed most ably. "You are more persuasive when we do not pay you," Lévesque joked.

Through the painful negotiations, the one thing no one ever

called into question was Bouchard's talent as a superior advocate. One who negotiated at length with Bouchard was social affairs minister Pierre-Marc Johnson. The animal magnetism Bouchard brandished at the negotiations captivated Johnson and most everyone else. At the bargaining table he worked with brash, inexhaustible conviction, retaining enormous amounts of information and marshalling it with precise logic. At four in the morning, recalled Johnson, when everyone was dog-tired and wanting to go home, Bouchard was barnstorming ahead, feeding off his immense reserve of untapped resources.

Johnson was one of those who got an early sense that this was a man of destiny. Bouchard was profound, articulate and energetic. He could walk into a room and fill it. The key to standing up to him, Johnson felt, was to master the detail of your brief and articulate it with force. In dealing with health issues, Johnson had the special advantage of having been a physician in an earlier career. He knew the situation at the hospitals, let Bouchard know it and didn't back down. Other government officials got caught in a blizzard.

Though the times were trying, Johnson sensed a developing closeness between Lévesque and Bouchard. The two shared passions—French culture and literature and the evolution of thought in modern societies—that went beyond the business at hand. Working under Parizeau, however, continued to be a burden. de Belleval, who served as an adviser to the finance minister during the negotiations, found Parizeau to be overly suspicious, always looking over his shoulder. Even at this stage he worried that the unelected Bouchard was a comer, perhaps a threat to him in the longer term. Their working relationship, which had started on a tough note in 1979, was up and down, depending on Parizeau's mood. "With Parizeau there was always something mysterious in the air, plots, and all kinds of innuendo," recalled de Belleval. "He always loved the dramatic gestures. He was very, very difficult, for everybody, not just Bouchard."

As a hardline secessionist, Parizeau had other reasons to doubt Bouchard. No one was quite sure where he stood. He had not joined the Parti Québécois until age thirty-three. He had then been too cautious to run for office. There was never the degree of strong commitment from him for outright independence that, for example, his brothers shared. As Roch Bouchard pointed out, many

94   THE ANTAGONIST

things about the idea of secession bothered Lucien. He thought
"there was something small there. He didn't like that." Much more
comfortable for him, and aligning him closer to Lévesque, was the
umbrella term of sovereignty-association. It covered a vast geography on the political spectrum. It was a safe haven for many public
figures, allowing them, depending on the public mood, to slide
more closely to the federalist side one week and the sovereignist
camp the next.

Whether on the unity issue or others, Bouchard had few fixed
political positions. While he had defined himself as a social democrat through his school years, in the negotiations with the labour
unions, as noted by Quebec chronicler Benoît Aubin, he had more
the look of a latter-day neo-liberal. He was denouncing overstuffed
bureaucracies, he was dubious of eternal job security for public servants when others in society did not enjoy such guarantees, and he
could be antagonistic to the power brandished by trade union
leaders.

He had already drunk from many political cups. The contradictions were piling up, and he had yet to enter the political arena.

8. BRIAN AND LUCIEN

Back home in Chicoutimi, another crisis was unfolding. Denis de Belleval's audacious advice—don't marry this woman—had come to have resonance. Bouchard's long-troubled marriage to Jocelyne Côté had continued to founder to the point where divorce beckoned. Given his family's deep Catholic wellsprings, the matter weighed heavily on his conscience. He enjoyed a reputation in the Saguenay as a highly ethical man, "*un homme moralement distingué*," who continued well into adulthood to be shy and somewhat formal with women and who found brother Roch lax in his standards.

Lucien Bouchard would later confide to a political assistant that he never really discovered the joys of women until age forty. Then, according to de Belleval and other friends, he really began to make up for lost time.

He had been living away from his wife for some time. Intellectually, friends never found them a good match. They were both high-strung and there was also the problem of children. Lucien badly wanted a family, but Jocelyne either didn't want to have children or couldn't have them. Close friends suggested it was the former. To a journalistic attempt to clear up the ambiguity, she reacted testily, dispatching a threatening legal letter. In this respect she shared the extreme sensitivity of her husband regarding family business. In his book, Bouchard did not mention Jocelyne, his wife of twenty years, by name. There were only three or four scant references to her, all totalling less than a paragraph. She got the same treatment in the volume as Bouchard's mother. The book was perhaps a first of sorts—an autobiography which left out the two principal female forces in the subject's life.

After living apart for a substantial period of time, Bouchard's heavy conscience led him to an unusual step for a man his age. He decided to seek help in the spiritual realm. In the spring of 1982, age forty-three, he went on a religious retreat to the Capuchin monastery at Lake Bouchette in his home region. At college in

Jonquière, he had gone on closed retreats with other students at the end of each school year at a Jesuit home. Now, the man once tagged as a future cardinal was returning to the flock for moral reinvigoration.

The Capuchin retreat was not a place where one knelt in prayer around the clock, but rather a hideaway for reflection—with or without clergy and sacraments. Given the depth of Bouchard, recalled Bertrand Vallaincourt, a Jonquière classmate who became a priest, it wasn't so surprising to find him there.

At the retreat, he buried himself in books, taking with him two sets of confessions: the *Confessions* of St. Augustine and the *Confessions* of one of the philosophers he admired the most, Jean-Jacques Rousseau. As in Proust, though markedly different in style, both works were remembrances of things past. They allowed Bouchard to delve deeply into the lives of their subjects to ascertain what guided them in periods of torment. In his 1600-year-old work, Augustine wrote of his fight to free himself from pride and sensuality. He confessed his sins and described his conversion to Godly faith. Bouchard's appreciation of the work reflected his spiritual side, the idea that man is more than material and flesh, that he must be preoccupied also with the eternal.

In Rousseau's *Confessions* (1784), one of the most-read autobiographies of world literature, the author wrote passionately of affairs and mistresses, of faults and ambition, of discovering, like Bouchard, a great chest of books in the home of his grandparents. Rousseau laid his life before the sovereign judge for verdict. "Thus have I acted: These were my thoughts: Such was I."

Bouchard enjoyed Rousseau, not so much for his espousal of the joys of primitive living, but for his sense, in the Jeffersonian context, of civic virtue. Bouchard was not, his philosopher brother Roch revealed, a man enraptured by the complexities of metaphysics. Impatient with the details, he wanted to know the general message of the great thinkers on the big questions: the existence of God, the origins of the world, human destiny. Discussions among Roch, Gérard and Lucien on philosophy often dissolved into loud disputes. They couldn't agree on much.

The religious retreat appeared to have the intended purifying impact. "I acknowledged my faults, returned to live with my wife and resumed my law practice." But faults acknowledged weren't faults repaired. There were more problems in the marriage and the hopes of salvaging the relationship dimmed. Bouchard ranked this period of the early 1980s, replete as it was with the political defeats, as the most dismal of his life.

The man who came to his aid, as he had done a decade earlier with the Cliche Commission, was Brian Mulroney. Mulroney had surfaced from his own blue period—the depression, heavy boozing and domestic upsets that had followed his loss of the Conservative Party leadership in 1976 to Joe Clark. Feeling Clark was the lesser man, Mulroney's ego couldn't handle the anguish. Clark became prime minister in 1979, winning a minority, which only chafed Mulroney all the more. He felt—and polls pointing to Clark's lack of popularity supported his belief—that a more credible leader could have romped to a majority victory. A half-year into his stewardship, Clark squandered his minority by mismanaging a vote of non-confidence in the Commons. It brought down his government. Trudeau then clobbered him in a general election to begin the new decade.

While continuing in his role as president of the Iron Ore Company of Canada, Mulroney, though ostensibly supporting Clark, worked to undermine his leadership. Forces loyal to Mulroney were highly instrumental in building enough opposition to Clark to have him call a leadership convention. In the campaign, which both Mulroney and Clark entered, Clark continued to appear much closer to Bouchard on Quebec issues. Mulroney attacked him at an all-candidates forum in Toronto for being too soft on Quebec nationalism. The Iron Ore president hammered the PQ government of Lévesque as socialist and separatist, adding, "Before I give away a nickel of Canada's money, I want to know what Lévesque's going to do with it."

Mulroney not only supported Chrétien and Trudeau in the referendum and on repatriation, but he had gone so far as to tell a black-tie dinner at the Mount Royal Club in Montreal that Chrétien was the saviour of the country for his work on each. There were few words that could have come as a greater affront to Bouchard than these. But since it was Mulroney, the heresies didn't seem to matter much. Bouchard would soon come to his side—this before Mulroney had a change of heart and began denigrating Trudeau and Chrétien's positions.

When, to begin 1983, Mulroney launched his leadership bid

against Clark, Bouchard wrote a letter to Mulroney describing him as "my unforgettable friend." During the leadership campaign Bouchard was quiet, but he began actively supporting the boy from Baie-Comeau after his victory.

Mulroney, who was generous with friends and had an exceptional gift for making and maintaining them, had made a gesture that touched Bouchard deeply during the bombardment he faced during the public service negotiations. In the heat of them, Mulroney sent Bouchard a strongly worded telegram praising the work he was doing. His well-publicized words of support were among the few the beleaguered Bouchard was receiving. Mulroney had no ostensible benefit to gain from publicly choosing sides on the issue. Politically it probably would have been better to stay neutral.

After Mulroney defeated Clark in the leadership fight, Bouchard was delighted to appear in the House of Commons on the day of his friend's debut. A general election approached and the new Tory leader was desperate to crack the Liberal stronghold in Quebec. In the run-up to the campaign, he told potential Quebec Tory candidates that, given the defeat of the separatist option in the referendum, they should try to realize their ambitions within Canada. Under him, he added, a much better deal for Quebec was possible.

A student of his party's history, Mulroney knew that Tories formed governments in Canada when they had Quebec nationalists on their side. This had been the case under John A. Macdonald, Robert Borden and John Diefenbaker. Despite Mulroney's rather Trudeauvian record on Quebec, he had to try to reach out to nationalists to run for him. The big one he wanted was Lucien Bouchard.

The Chicoutimi lawyer was being courted by his own party, the PQ. It faced declining polls and tough times and it needed the likes of Bouchard to resurrect its hopes. The party was, of course, much closer to his philosophy than the Tories. Bouchard was a friend of both the fading star in the party, René Lévesque, and the new star, Pierre-Marc Johnson, the son of the last Union Nationale premier, Daniel Johnson. He was an even closer friend of the PQ's regional minister for the Saguenay, Marc-André Bedard. Bedard, who had served Lévesque loyally as justice minister, was stepping down. He had planned to anoint Bouchard as his successor in the riding—one of the safest seats for a PQ candidate. Bedard knew of Bouchard's earlier hesitancies, but this time he was quite confident he was ready.

From the Tory side, Bernard Roy, the Laval classmate who was heading up the Quebec campaign for Mulroney, lobbied Bouchard hard to enter the federal race. Brian and Mila Mulroney paid a personal visit to win over Bouchard's wife to the idea. But Bouchard resisted the pressure. PQ friends told him he would be put in a blatantly hypocritical position in running for the federalist Tories. Moreover, the Conservatives were barely on the map in Quebec in the months before the election. Poll after poll put the Liberals well out front. It was almost three years after the so-called night of the long knives and, far from it being the Armageddon that Bouchard talked about, there was hardly a whimper of protest. Trudeau was still heavily favoured in Quebec. No one was predicting, even when John Turner took over from Trudeau, that the Tories could win more than a dozen of the 75 seats available in La Belle Province.

Bouchard had backed off from running for the provincial Liberals under Bourassa in 1970. He had rejected an offer to run for the PQ under Lévesque in 1976. Now he said no again—both to the Tories and to the PQ.

Though not becoming a candidate for either, he threw in his lot with the Conservatives, signing up with the Mulroney team as a full-bodied campaigner. This was remarkable enough. Rather than devote his time and energies to rebuild the PQ, the party supposedly dearest to his dreams, he was pushing a federalist party with a leader with Chrétien-type attitudes on sovereignty and the Constitution. Bedard and the Péquistes were taken aback. Did friendship extend that far? Did it mean root principles could be hurled to the winds? Were not Lévesque and Pierre-Marc Johnson and Marc-André Bedard friends as well?

Bouchard made the move to the Conservatives while still harbouring doubts as to Mulroney's intentions towards Quebec. "In spite of what Mulroney was telling me in private, the party had made no formal commitments in this respect." But he felt that his friend was worth the risk. It may have looked like he had no principles, said de Belleval, but both he and Bouchard knew that Mulroney was amenable to a change of course. It was obvious since law school, explained de Belleval, that Mulroney knew the route to success for his party in Quebec was through a greater appeal to nationalism. They knew that despite Mulroney's oft-repeated admiration for Trudeau, he would sooner or later have to adopt policies that ran counter to that of the philosopher king.

The other consideration, said Bouchard's friend, was that there was really little alternative. In Quebec, the PQ was on the way out and the provincial Liberals on the way in. The federal Liberals meanwhile offered nothing to nationalists. The Tories remained. "We were like France after the defeat of Napoleon," said de Belleval. "What did Talleyrand do? He said who are my former enemies who can be my future friends. I'll go to those people and they'll become my friends so that I won't be alone anymore in this strange world."

According to de Belleval, Bouchard had spoken to René Lévesque about an alignment of sorts with Mulroney and won his tacit approval. "Lévesque knew that the only way out of the desert was this camel called the Conservative Party on the federal side." In Quebec, Jacques Parizeau was leading the segment of the party whose sovereignty was purer away from Lévesque. "Instead of teaming with Parizeau's band," said de Belleval, "Bouchard was finding a new boat."

Mulroney had attracted some other candidates of nationalist persuasion to his fold, such as Benoît Bouchard. Despairing over Quebec's place under Trudeau, Benoît Bouchard thought Mulroney was worth the gamble. It was not so much, he noted, that Mulroney had offered the moon, but there was a spirit of reconciliation that blessed his words—at least in private conversation.

Bouchard's primary role in the 1988 federal election campaign was that of speech-writer. To Mulroney, his pen was second only to Molière's. But as the campaign kicked off in June, there was little in the Tory platform on Quebec that Bouchard could have liked writing about. Mulroney's themes of "jobs, jobs, jobs," national unity and enhanced relations with the United States applied across the board. There was little on special status for Quebec. In Trudeau's absence, with Turner making gaffe after gaffe, Mulroney began building a lead. In the Quebec ridings, Tory momentum appeared to be growing without the need of bold nationalist promises. It was as if Turner had planted explosives under his own Grit fortress. It was self-destructing.

Nonetheless, for several reasons, not all electoral, Mulroney made a turn to the nationalists midway through the campaign. Whatever his words in the leadership campaign, they were changing now. Now he began taking the line that Trudeau had in fact bludgeoned Quebec in the repatriation process and that amends had to be made. Quebec, he asserted, had to be brought back into the Constitution "with honour and enthusiasm."

Mulroney first made the assertion during the campaign debates. Bouchard had helped him in the preparations. But the major policy announcement on the new direction came during a trip to Sept-Isles in the Tory leader's northern Quebec riding of Manicouagan on Sunday, August 6, 1984, a month before the vote. For this occasion, Mulroney had asked Bouchard to prepare a speech on economic policy for the province. Since Bouchard's background in economics was meagre, he was given names of economists to contact. They did not offer much assistance, so Bouchard came back with a suggestion. Why not speak on the Constitution instead?

Mulroney agreed, and now Bouchard had his opportunity. His text proposed an Ottawa-Quebec reconciliation which would effectively undo the damage of the 1981–82 repatriation, allowing Quebec to become part of a new constitutional accord with, among other things, full veto power over any changes. Bouchard's text was radical in another way. It called for a sweeping decentralization of powers from Ottawa to the provinces. But that segment didn't survive the cuts. The speech was substantially altered—without Bouchard's knowledge—before Mulroney delivered it.

Bouchard had first shown the address to Mulroney in a room at the Chicoutimi Hotel—the same hotel where Bouchard had signed his PQ membership card with Parizeau. While changing shirts, the Tory leader looked it over and pronounced it fine. But when Charlie McMillan, Mulroney's economic adviser, saw the text, he went, as he put it, ballistic. Bouchard, McMillan determined, was trying to change the country in one fell swoop. The day before the speech was to be delivered, a meeting took place at a poolside table at a Sept-Isles hotel. There, McMillan began what he termed "a hell of a fight to get that shit out of there."

"I see this stuff on decentralization. Basically it's eclipsing Ottawa and I say no fucking way. Jean Bazin was there and

Mulroney and a fourth." Following some histrionics, the fast-talk-
ing McMillan was able to effect the deletions he wanted. The federal government would not be serving as headwaiter to the
provinces.

In the address, Mulroney hammered Trudeau for his treatment
of Quebec. "One thing is certain. Not one Quebecker authorized
the federal Liberals to take advantage of the confusion that prevailed in Quebec following the referendum in order to ostracize the
province constitutionally." A year earlier, Mulroney had told
Maclean's magazine: "Trudeau did what had to be done and it serves
no purpose to fight him on it. Let's face it, Trudeau is one of the
most impressive political figures in the world."

The day after the Sept-Isles speech, Graham Fraser, a leading
journalistic authority on Quebec, noted in *The Globe and Mail* that
the address was full of code words that would appeal to Quebec
nationalists.

What it did, noted McMillan, was solidify and build on the
momentum already apparent for the Tories in the province that the
general campaign themes had mustered.

There were other motivations behind the speech, observed
Mulroney biographer Ian MacDonald. "Beyond electoralism, this
had something to do with Mulroney's privately held hopes of winning over the intelligentsia—the nationalist intellectuals in Quebec
and the Red Tories in English-speaking Canada." Macdonald cited
Bouchard as having said that Mulroney's "secret dream is to have
the approval of the intellectuals." The turn in policy was intended
to get him more Quebec seats, win him favour from intellectuals
and get Lucien Bouchard firmly in his camp.

Almost everyone on the campaign team, including a top Mulroney adviser, the Laval gang's Peter White, could see through the
act. "This was Mulroney's classic opportunism," White explained.
"Mulroney's a great opportunist. He always has been, and I think
he was perhaps less concerned about the rightness or wrongness of
events than he was about the political capital he could make out of
it. Because it certainly suited his political purpose at that point."

Though Bouchard has been pegged as the one who triggered
Mulroney's Quebec policy, it wasn't as straightforward as that,
observed White. "Lucien may have been an agent of this, but I
would not portray him as the Machiavellian figure who turned

Mulroney around. Not at all. Mulroney could see it with his own eyes. What Lucien did was give it voice in that speech he wrote."

(Niccolò Machiavelli was, in fact, among Bouchard's favourite authors. Catherine de Médici, a contemporary of the Florentine statesman and political theorist, fascinated Bouchard as well. He could discuss her for hours. Machiavelli's masterwork on political cunning and amorality, *The Prince*, is what people identify him with. But as noted by Luc Lavoie, a Tory insider who became a good friend of Bouchard's, he was just as taken by Machiavelli's other works which demonstrated opposite strains, such as his honouring of virtue and liberty.)

According to McMillan, Bouchard's role in the campaign and in Mulroney's first year as prime minister risked being overstated: "Quebec issues that year weren't big issues. We were always having trouble writing flowery speeches. So Bouchard wrote speeches. But I can tell you ten guys who wrote speeches." Bouchard was important enough in the campaign, however, to write the address on victory night. McMillan also was asked to write one, and the two versions were combined.

That night Bouchard was with the Mulroney party of close friends and aides at the bungalow next to Le Manoir in Baie-Comeau. When, at 9 p.m., the television stations, seeing a Tory sweep in the making, announced a Conservative victory, Mulroney came immediately to Bouchard's side. He had thought at length about how Bouchard might serve in his government. Whether he pondered the problem of how difficult it is in a relationship between two close friends to have one suddenly the undisputed boss was another question. What could make the chemistry even more difficult was the unstated reality of the relationship—that of the two, Bouchard was the intellectual strongman.

Mulroney sat next to his friend as the news of the victory flashed. "Lucien," he said. "As you know, this is my dream come true." Then he added, "I want you in Paris as my ambassador."

Bouchard knew offers would be coming his way from Mulroney, just as they had come before. For a card-carrying PQ member, possibilities were limited. But France seemed a logical possibility. Such an appointment would please nationalists. It would please many of Quebec's intellectuals to have such an eloquent and educated man there. It would please the Paris establishment. What a fine fit Bouchard, with his immaculate French, would be.

Bouchard, however, didn't respond immediately to Mulroney's offer. After the victory-night partying, he was awakened by a call from a Mulroney staffer. The new prime minister wanted to see him at the breakfast table. Of all the priorities facing a newly elected PM, the placement of ambassadors ranked very low. But Mulroney, who had just received a congratulatory call from Ronald Reagan, had Lucien Bouchard at the top of his list. Over breakfast he repeated his proposal: "I want you in Paris." Bouchard replied that he needed time to think it over.

He professed to be totally surprised by the offer, but few believed him. When later he phoned to tell Pierre-Marc Johnson what the PM was planning, Johnson responded, "You're going to tell me Mulroney wants to appoint you ambassador to Paris."

"How did you know that?" asked Bouchard. "Did Mulroney tell you?"

"No, but it is so damned obvious, Lucien."

A Quebecker couldn't dream of a better diplomatic posting. To Bouchard, there was no city greater than Paris—its history, its literary tradition, its beauty, its place in the hearts of his family and ancestors who had dreamed of going there. Yet while no one thought he would turn it down, he played it coy. There were some things to think about. He wondered about his PQ credentials and how accepting such an appointment would look. He worried about leaving behind the healthy law practice he had built in Chicoutimi for the insecure world of politics. His wife, Jocelyne, with whom he was living again, wasn't enthused. She knew, said a Bouchard friend, that the surest way to lose him to another woman was to put him in Paris. Finally, Bouchard knew that by accepting this prize he would by tying himself into the Mulroney web.

Paris was the ultimate lure. There had been the Cliche Commission, the public telegram of support during the labour negotiations, moral support in dealing with his difficult marriage situation, help with the business community in plugging Bouchard for seats on corporate boards. Now, by accepting the big one—France—Bouchard would be in no position to turn down the follow-up: the request to become a full-fledged Tory MP and the party's standard-bearer in Quebec.

Mulroney was thinking ahead. He and Peter White had read

Blair Neatby's book *Laurier and a Liberal Quebec*. It had become something of a bible for them. It made the case that Laurier's major preoccupation was in making sure he dominated Quebec politics and kept it solidly in the Liberal fold. It was a policy, noted White, that had paid off for the Grits almost ever since. Mulroney now wanted to do the same for the Progressive Conservatives. He wanted to build a château fort in Quebec with Bouchard as the cornerstone.

Bouchard knew Mulroney was dreaming big dreams, that he would not content himself with being an ordinary leader of Canada. "Brian doesn't want to be just prime minister," he told a writer. "He wants to live in history."

Bouchard's primary allegiance to the PQ didn't worry Mulroney. The PM had brought other PQ members and hard nationalists under the Tory umbrella. White, who was heading up Mulroney's transition team, said there was no hesitation in doing so. "I think the key is that Lucien incarnated a very broad stream of political thought in Quebec. You can't say a federal party shouldn't have anything to do with that kind of thing. That's absolute nonsense. What has to be understood about Lucien and those like him was that their first choice was always to try and make Canada work well for Francophones. And that it was only after many long attempts and rebuffs and failures that a lot of them concluded it was simply not possible and there's nothing left to do but take Quebec out of Confederation. So we felt damned lucky to have Lucien in the Conservative Party."

Mulroney wanted not only a rapprochement between Quebec and English Canada, but one among Quebec, Canada and France. Relations had been sour and tense since de Gaulle's spectacularly brazen call for Quebec independence in 1967. Quebec had wanted a closer partnership with France, but it was not forthcoming. Though some esteemed French Canadians had been appointed to the embassy in Paris, Bouchard believed that English-Canadian hawks back home dominated the overall policy. In Mulroney, a great admirer of France, he could see a desire to establish a lasting triangular relationship, with Quebec setting much of the agenda.

Bouchard took a month's holiday in Europe after the federal election. Near the end of it, Bernard Roy, Mulroney's chief of staff, informed him that Laurent Fabius, the prime minister of France,

was coming to Canada in November and he asked him to write
Mulroney's speech. Bouchard accepted, but he placed a condition
on that acceptance. His writing was not to be vetted by bureaucrats
in the external affairs department. It wasn't an outlandish request,
but it was an indication of the clout Bouchard expected to carry if
he joined the Tory team. As such, it was a harbinger of some of the
hard times to come.

The speech advocated the establishment of a direct, special
relationship between Quebec and France. The French were
delighted. Bouchard, working on law in Chicoutimi by day and on
speeches for Mulroney by night, began liaising between Quebec
and Paris. Mulroney brought him in to write the words for
Reagan's historic visit to Quebec City. It was the celebrated
singalong summit where the president and the prime minister,
while Canadian nationalists groaned, took to the stage for a rendi-
tion of "When Irish Eyes Are Smiling." The Gipper was a president who, as one wag noted, owned more horses than books. But
he was the leader of the world's most powerful country and it was a
proud moment for Bouchard when Mulroney introduced him as
"the most eloquent French Canadian I know."

After the summit, Bouchard finally gave his formal agreement
to go to Paris. Mulroney had demonstrated his seriousness of intent
in overhauling relations with France. Bouchard knew he would be
doing more than attending cocktail parties.

The announcement was greeted positively by the Quebec
media, but critics in the rest of Canada were of a different mind. A
patronage appointment! A personal friend of the PM! A man
devoid of diplomatic experience! A Péquiste, out to dismember
Canada! Bouchard may well have seen these criticisms coming, but
took great offence. His pride was so stung that he was ready to drop
the whole idea, to quit before he had even started. Mulroney's
entourage sought to cool him down, telling him that his recourse
was to go over there, do an excellent job and prove the critics
wrong. He finally decided on that—but not without carrying the
bitterness with him.

The scepticism of the critics was not without foundation. Not
only was he without experience, he didn't know the land he was to
represent. Bouchard was forty-six years old when he was appointed
and still had never been west of Ontario. In a mind which was deep,

penetrating and imaginative, the greater part of Canada was a blank space. Other prominent Quebeckers—Trudeau, Chrétien and Mulroney—had travelled the country countless times, gaining at least a sense of its variety, its kindnesses, its biases, its beauty, its scope, its potential, its needs. Bouchard had neither seen nor, given the nature of his Quebec education, been schooled in it. English-Canadian history and literature had never been on his intellectual radar screen. He could wax eloquently for hours on Catherine de Médici, Napoleon or Flaubert, but on John A. Macdonald, Robertson Davies or George Grant, the cupboard was bare. If it was true that prejudices were most easily formed in a vacuum, if it was true that divisions in the country were easily augmented by isolation, Bouchard was hardly a ripe candidate for bridge-building. He was an educated man except on the subject of the country he lived in.

As part of his ambassadorial preparations, some amends were made. In the summer of 1985, he set off on a tour of all the provincial capitals for briefings on how the Canadian elite viewed relations with France. His stops included the office of Conrad Black, who had warned Mulroney that in bringing secessionists like Bouchard and Marcel Masse into the party, he was taking a big gamble. Bouchard eased the newspaper magnate's concerns somewhat, coming across as intent on giving federalism a try. "He was exquisitely courteous and purportedly wanted to know whether I had any advice for him."

The tour took the new ambassador to Vancouver. There, the mountains, the sea, the surging beauty of the landscape sent him into raptures. He was finally seeing first-hand the vistas that had been presented to the Chrétien boys and others who had been brought up in a less secluded environment.

Shortly after he arrived in Paris, Bouchard would meet with Adrienne Clarkson, the illustrious agent-general for Ontario in France. Bouchard was part of Team Mulroney now and was expected to show the right colours. He talked as he had done in recent months about his new commitment to federalism and he talked of the moving impact of seeing parts of Canada he had never seen before. Then he astonished Clarkson. British Columbia was so stunning, Bouchard exclaimed. "Had I ever seen Vancouver before I would never have been able to be committed to taking Quebec out of Confederation."

He was received warmly on his tour through the Canadian provinces by all except the committed Péquistes of Quebec City. His brethren were not happy. They saw Bouchard as selling out to the federalists, as going the easy route of the big salary, diplomatic receptions, limousines and kingly residences, instead of staying home to renew the PQ and the sovereignist movement. So rather than being ushered into the highest party chambers, he was sent down for briefings to the lower echelons of the bureaucracy.

Bernard Landry, the Quebec minister responsible for international affairs, snubbed him. Landry had received a memo from functionaries saying that his appointment augured nothing positive for Québec. The province had its own diplomatic representative in Paris—Louise Beaudoin. She was speculating pejoratively in newspaper reports on the role Bouchard might have in mind.

Bouchard was saved from further embarrassment when Louis Bernard, Lévesque's right-hand man, whom Bouchard knew well, called and invited him to meet with the premier at his Laurentian hideaway at Lac-à-l'Épaule. Lévesque had a different view of the appointment than the hardliners in the PQ. He thought it was worthwhile to explore possibilities at the federal level under the Tories. It was a chance worth taking, a *"beau risque."*

Bouchard spent much of the day on the shoreline with a premier who was in the twilight of his power and who regaled him with stories from his meetings with great men. They had dinner and then, during a long walk, Lévesque told Bouchard, "Your mission is La Francophonie." By this he meant the further development of a commonwealth of French nations to protect the language, to forge cultural links, to provide for the endurance of the French fact throughout the world. Bouchard had received a similar message from Mulroney. Now he had the blessings not only of the PM, but also of the premier of Quebec.

Before he left, he had some business to finish in Chicoutimi. His law practice had grown, though not quite at a rate to eclipse the old Fradette firm, which numbered thirteen lawyers. Bouchard's was a good, competent firm of six or seven and Bouchard, recalled Michael Cain, was the one who made it work. Bouchard had even recruited for his practice the same man, Pierre Bergeron, whose obstinacy had led to his leaving Fradette. The old partners at the Fradette firm were surprised by this. It suggested to them that perhaps Bouchard was not one who held grudges.

On preparing to go to Paris, Bouchard merged his firm with Fradette's. Partners in each firm thought it would be beneficial. Surprisingly, said Cain, Bouchard didn't seek or receive a financial settlement in return for the merger. Lawyers estimated his salary on leaving to become ambassador at roughly $200,000 annually.

He was assisted in his leaving by the unlikely figure of Raymond Chrétien, Jean's nephew. Raymond had gone to work for external affairs in the mid-sixties when few Quebeckers did, and was now Canada's inspector-general of embassies. If any enmity was felt towards Bouchard and his ilk, he didn't show it, going out of his way to assist Bouchard's passage and gaining the Quebecker's lasting gratitude for it. Bouchard would remain on good terms with Raymond while calling his distinguished uncle every name in the book.

Two other members of the Bouchard and Chrétien families were also establishing close relations. Bouchard's youngest brother, Gérard, and Jean Chrétien's youngest brother, Michel, had the opportunity to meet one another due to their excellence in their respective professional fields: Gérard as the leading demographer, Michel as a renowned medical researcher.

Though Raymond Chrétien and Lucien Bouchard became friends, their views differed substantially. Raymond had come to Ottawa feeling that the promise of French power was not myth. He rose through the ranks quickly enough, as did many Quebeckers who followed him, changing the culture of the power structure.

Jean Chrétien saw himself as an architect of this change and was proud of his work in decentralizing the federal bureaucracy so that Quebeckers benefited. Though Bouchard could hardly deny these advances, he had nonetheless come to detest Chrétien, considering him a political hack. Chrétien had become popular throughout English Canada, in part because of his lowbrow style in assuming the role of the French-Canadian pea souper. For English Canadians he was folksy and non-threatening. But Quebec elites, including many in the media, detested him for what they saw as an Uncle Tom act. As well, they would never forgive him for the strong federalist biases he displayed in the referendum campaign and the repatriation process.

Bouchard had recently turned down the PQ for a federalist

party. Ironically, Jean Chrétien had once done the same when Lévesque had tried to recruit him for his nationalism drive in the early 1960s. Chrétien felt there were bigger fish to fry—as apparently Lucien Bouchard now did—at the federal level.

9. THE AMBASSADOR

On the day he left for Paris, Bouchard, who had appeared rarely in the Quebec media, granted an interview to the editors of *Le Devoir*. Not far into it, he was going on again about the night of the long knives. The repatriation business was almost four years old but still weighed heavily on him. It was "explosive," he said. "For the time being, the people don't see so much in it. I know that the Charter of Rights satisfies the intellectuals and that everyone is happy. But let me say one thing: It was all shoved down our throats… It was done in the night in a hotel: the others were sleeping, they didn't say a word to them. You don't make constitutions like that."

Amends had to be made. It was absolutely necessary that the two sides sit down and renegotiate, he told the newspaper editors. With Bouchard's encouragement, Mulroney was already making plans to do this. While neither of the populations in English Canada or Quebec were agitated, while the sovereignty option was far down in the Quebec polls, he and Mulroney were set to stir the pot. Rather than letting sleeping dogs lie, the prime minister would enter into protracted negotiations on what would become known as the Meech Lake Accord. Mulroney was a big game hunter with an eye on the history books. He was seeking to reunify the country, to nail down nationalist support in Quebec, to build a château fort. Bouchard could become the cornerstone and more. In Mulroney's mind, his potential was limitless. Bouchard as his successor, at the top of the Tory party, at the top of Canada, was even in the realm of the possible.

Their partnership was tightening. Mulroney could pick up his copy of *Le Devoir* in that week of September 1985 and could read how his friend Bouchard was adorning him with praise—astonishing praise. Bouchard had seemingly already forgotten all of his friend's fulsome backing of Jean Chrétien's positions on Quebec in recent years. Mulroney, he told the editors, "has an extraordinary sensitivity for understanding what is happening in Quebec."

Through Quebec history, Bouchard added, very few others had ever understood Quebec as well as Brian Mulroney.

As he demonstrated in this interview, the new ambassador to France almost defied definition. Was he a federalist, a strong Quebec nationalist or was he trying to sell himself as both? "I am going to Paris firstly because I think that we are in the federation for a long time and perhaps forever." Sovereignty "has been turned down by Quebec. In my mind it's settled for a very long period of time." At the same time, Bouchard could add that because of that dark night in 1981, Quebec was on its knees and could not remain there, and if something wasn't done within five or ten years, Canada would pay a heavy price. He was still, he said, "very nationalist." In fact, he told a journalist, he was still wrestling with the idea of keeping his PQ membership card.

As he approached the shores of France, his thoughts were with the first Bouchard—the one who had left that country to come to the new continent 350 years earlier in the century of Galileo, Bacon, Louis XIV, Cromwell, Peter the Great and John Locke. He was a craftsman named Claude, one who figured prominently in the Bouchard family mystique, in the notion of being pioneer of a country. Bouchard also thought of his father, who was never far from his mind but who was especially close now. Philippe Bouchard, who had become a sovereignist in his late years, regretted never getting a chance to see the old country. Now his son was arriving in the role of Canada's official representative.

The ambiguity of Lucien Bouchard's position was strikingly clear on his first big day, the presentation of credentials to French president François Mitterrand. While not sympathetic to the Quebec sovereignty movement, Mitterrand was an intellectual, a writer, a man of august stature. Captivated by the makers of history, Bouchard's enthusiasm for meeting him had an adolescent's edge. He brought along a book of Mitterrand's—*Ma Part de Verité*—and asked the president to sign it for him. He was especially pleased at the length of time—thirty minutes—he got to spend with the president, Bouchard knew that many in the diplomatic set placed great stock in this rather juvenile reading of things. Had he been only in there a few minutes, it may have touched off gossip that Mitterrand was not pleased with Canada's sending a Péquiste.

Content with the meeting, Bouchard returned to the embassy

where a big reception was being held by the staff and the Quebec delegation. Bouchard had been advised that it wasn't necessary to make a speech but chose to do so. At its termination came the traditional toast to the strengthening of ties between Canada and France. In a slip of mind and tongue rife with unseemly connotations, Bouchard gave a toast to the flourishing of relations between France and Quebec!

A hush fell over the room. In one of the last services she would render him, his wife, Jocelyne, saved the day by immediately alerting Bouchard to his faux pas. Displaying no outward sign of embarrassment, Bouchard corrected himself and moved forward into a quite lengthy explanation, saying he was used to thinking in Quebec terms but was now making a new federal turn, a risk many in Quebec were prepared to take. He thus eased much of the tension in the room.

He soon made it clear to everyone in the embassy and in the French government that he was not a traditional diplomat but a hand-picked friend of the prime minister's and that this meant unusual access and power. Many on the Canadian side knew that for Bouchard, the Paris appointment was a likely stepping stone to Ottawa and a central role in a Mulroney cabinet. It soon became obvious that they had a politician in their midst. There were standing instructions to staff that if anyone from the Saguenay-Lac-Saint-Jean region came by, they were to have an audience with the ambassador.

In order to graduate to Ottawa politics, Bouchard would need to speak English. Finally, at age forty-eight, he now began taking lessons in the language—in France of all places. Several times a week he was tutored by Eva Bild, a trained instructor in English. Her husband, Fred Bild, was the minister plenipotentiary at the embassy, the number-two man and as such, a vital figure in Bouchard's success or failure. Bild had served with distinction no less than five previous Canadian ambassadors in Paris. He knew the dossiers and their history like few others. He knew the city and the inner working of the French bureaucratic machine. He knew what Bouchard could get away with, and what he could not.

Eva Bild came to the embassy early in the mornings to take Bouchard through his drills. He was one of her best students because he was already very proficient in reading the language, thanks to his subscription to magazines beginning as a teenager. With this base, all he needed was vocal practice and pronunciation exercises. Soon he was making excellent headway.

While many career ambassadors were wary of the press, Bild noticed that Bouchard, the politician, sought to cultivate the media. When he was talking to Quebec journalists he would adopt the persona of a Quebec nationalist, but while in the presence of the Anglos it was an all-Canada pitch. "It became very clear to me after a while," recalled Bild, "that he was playing a very interesting game. He was leaving all his options open. Although he was prepared to be Mr. Federal Canada and do the best he could in that job, he kept all his ties to the PQ. He made sure he kept his credibility with the militants in the party. He'd be on the phone till two and three in the morning talking to Quebec and people around there."

These conversations could not have topped the trans-Atlantic telephone bills run up by Bouchard and Mulroney. They talked several times a week on subjects far more varied than Canada-France relations. In Paris, Bouchard continued in his function as an adviser on Quebec and as Mulroney's speech-writer. "A good speech," Bouchard told an interviewer at the embassy, "unites passion with sincerity." He worked late into the night on texts touching on issues back home. Bild was increasingly impressed by the staggering workload Bouchard could take on, and by the opulence of his intellectual capacity. Of all the ambassadors he served, he had never seen one more skilled and more political than Bouchard. "He truly is a person of superior intelligence. He was incredibly astute and a quick learner. He made it very clear to us that he was the kind of person who set his sights on what he wanted and went after it."

Bouchard was all business. While certainly enchanted by his new hallowed halls, he was not one to indulge himself in the trappings of power. The Canadian ambassadorial residence, a nineteenth-century masterpiece of French elegance, was situated on a street called Faubourg Saint-Honoré just off the Champs-Élysées. It was one of the splendours of the diplomatic circuit. With its crystal and marble, high ceilings and heavy drapes, period furnishings and butlers, it took its occupant back to the previous century and the affluence of the Duchess of Rochefoucauld. It was then her sumptuous domain.

Though this might have appeared all the more appropriate for

Bouchard and his volumes of Balzac, Proust and Rousseau, he had trouble feeling comfortable in his surroundings. He tried to move the furniture around to give it some Jonquière hominess, a process which was akin to trying to touch up a Rembrandt. His mother, Alice, was even more ill at ease. She came for a visit, took one look inside, ordered a taxi, and sped off to the more humble quarters of her daughter Claudette, who had married a European and had been living in Paris for many years. Claudette was not terribly close to Lucien or, for that matter, the other brothers, and was never a fixture around the embassy. Lucien would take pride in telling the story of how his mother wouldn't stay in the marvellous residence, this being an anecdote obviously suggestive of his more modest genesis.

At the residence, there was Pascal, a superior butler, but Bouchard was more content with soup and a sandwich. Though he hosted lavish dinners, as was his duty, the new ambassador frequently left the food on his plate untouched. Entertaining was more of a chore for him, small talk being a waste of his time. One perk he did enjoy was the chauffeured car, because it meant he could get work done going to and from his destinations.

Though such an aficionado of French literature and history, embassy staff couldn't get him to explore the city and all its cultural treasures. They pressed him on this, saying it was too fine an opportunity to be missed, but aside from visits to a few of Proust's haunts in his early days in Paris, Bouchard abstained, too consumed by the task at hand.

He was a man who always put work and responsibility before pleasure. It was part of the religious culture he grew up in. In the youth of the time, recalled Bernard Angers, who spent eleven years at school with him, the notion of sacrifice was woven into their minds. "Lucien was someone who was capable of making sacrifices to fill his needs. It was in the nature of the time. Today it is a notion that has almost disappeared."

In his early days at the embassy, he pumped Bild for information on his predecessors and what had gone on in the previous three decades. He was fascinated by what Bild told him and often asked him for supporting documents. Bild saw little harm in this and dutifully went about tracking them down. He didn't realize that, as he would later discover, Bouchard was writing it all down in a diary for later use. This was something Bild wouldn't have minded, especially if Bouchard had been faithful to what he had been told. But years later, when he picked up Bouchard's autobiography, Bild would be shocked. He would discover that much of the information had been distorted to suit the political agenda upon which Bouchard was then embarked.

In the Bouchard account of the embassy's history, the Francophone ambassadors who were sent to Paris were victims of an Ottawa-directed policy prohibiting a flowering of Quebec-France relations. The ambassadors were Jules Léger and Pierre Dupuy. Another Francophone, Marcel Cadieux, directed policy from external affairs in Ottawa. When Jules Léger presented his credentials in Paris in 1964, Bouchard claimed that he was outfitted with words from his Anglophone bosses that offended Charles de Gaulle. In fact, noted Bild, the opposite had happened. Léger had chosen his own words.

Cadieux was under-secretary of state for external affairs in the 1960s. Far from being dictated a tough line on France by Anglophone superiors, said Bild, Cadieux was the architect of Canada's policy against de Gaulle. "He was a de Gaulle basher of a virulent type. There was no arm-twisting whatsoever."

Bild felt that this should have been clear to Bouchard from all the briefings he gave him. "It was specious of Bouchard and calculated to put a spin on the way French-Canadian officers dealing with French matters behaved." To make it look like there was a split on the policy towards France, Bild said, was "sheer nonsense."

Bouchard's handling of this was symptomatic, according to many who dealt with him, of one of his more dominant and dismal tendencies. It was his inclination to invent history as he went along, shaping it to whatever political end he had in mind. Though hardly unique among politicians, this strain in Bouchard was made more extraordinary by his depth of commitment—at the given moment—to whatever interpretation he was rendering. No one got the sense that Bouchard was being deliberately duplicitous—not even in suggesting to Adrienne Clarkson that had he seen British Columbia he could never have become a sovereignist, not even in all the contradictions in his views on repatriation and Mulroney's role.

As Ontario's representative, Clarkson enjoyed fine relations with Bouchard and found him very helpful in regard to her responsibilities as they affected her province. But she was one of many who, then and in future years, came to see him "as a man of successive sincerities." She said that "he mines what he wants out of history, not looking at what is real history, but taking from it what he wants—what is emotionally acceptable." For her it was a very worrisome aspect of his character. She felt that Bouchard was "emotionally on a wavelength that is not rational."

In Paris, any talk of the ambassador's ulterior motives or private agendas was secondary to the day-to-day business at hand. Bouchard had settled in impressively, eased all fears about his diplomatic experience and set the place buzzing with activity and purpose. His intimate rapport with the Canadian prime minister gave him an authority previous ambassadors never had. Gérard Pelletier, ambassador in the late 1970s, was a long-time friend of Pierre Trudeau's, but their communications had been far less frequent.

Bouchard did not have to submit himself to commands from senior bureaucrats back home in the department of external affairs, nor, for that matter, to the external affairs minister himself. A first test arose in the planning for the first summit of the Francophone nations. This was a matter which, under normal circumstances, would clearly fall under the purview of the minister. A great many countries were involved and it was not the job of an ambassador in the field to bring them together. But the creation of a functioning Francophonie was at the heart of Bouchard's mission in Paris. He wanted this trophy himself, which meant easing Joe Clark, the minister of external affairs, out of the picture.

For his part, Clark wanted to appoint a special ambassador to La Francophonie to take charge. He prepared a strategy letter for the prime minister which would effectively sideline Ambassador Bouchard from his master chef's role. When Bouchard caught wind of the letter, he arranged, through Bernard Roy, Mulroney's top aide, to have it short-circuited. Bouchard then put his case to the prime minister and got the assignment.

While negotiations towards the first Francophone summit proceeded, Mulroney began planning for a visit to Paris. The prime minister, who had always been impressed by the grandeur of France and who revelled in the glorification of power, wanted all France to share in his newfound eminence. This became all too clear one day when Bouchard received word from the PM that he wished to have the Champs-Élysées cleared of traffic so he and Mila could motorcade along it just as John F. Kennedy and Jackie had done in 1961. The prime minister's reference point on the public's adulation of political leaders was unfortunately from a bygone era. Bouchard knew how much the ostentatious displays meant to his friend, however, and determined to do his utmost. Since the prime minister was not officially a head of state (in Canada it's the Queen, or her representative, the governor-general), he would have to do without a twenty-one-gun salute and a state dinner. But through Bouchard's efforts, Mulroney got all the other privileges imaginable—the trip up the Champs-Élysées, creating huge traffic jams of irate Parisians in adjoining streets, lodgings for part of his stay in the deluxe Hotel Marigny, the preserve of princes and kings, a magnificent dinner hosted by Prime Minister Laurent Fabius and several audiences with Mitterrand.

Virtually everything proceeded smoothly, Mulroney pushing the concept of La Francophonie at every stop. Bouchard listened in while Mitterrand gave a succinct endorsement of Canadian unity. The federal system, he said, served Quebec. It was the best way for the maintenance of a distinct French culture and language on the North American continent. Mulroney, Bouchard quietly noted, appeared to draw deep satisfaction from the declaration.

While the PM was most pleased, Mila Mulroney, with whom Bouchard's relations were not as warm, took offence at the behaviour of one of the embassy officials. At the opening of a cultural event, a diplomat escorting Mila informed her that it was time to declare the opening of festivities. In so doing, he took her by the arm to guide her to the podium. Mila was offended by the intrusion on her elbow. The official would hear about it later—and Bouchard would have to intervene to save him.

The same diplomat was tied up in another brouhaha which surfaced later. It involved the prime minister's expenses for the trip. Taking advantage of the laws on access to information, reporters revealed expense accounts which sounded extravagant for the portion of the visit during which the Mulroneys resided at the Plaza-Athenée. Because of his big-money, boardroom style, the prime minister, pilloried for it during his first leadership run for the Tories, was vulnerable on these questions. In the House of

Commons, the Opposition ranted on like children about his hotel bills. Mulroney didn't know at the time, nor did the Opposition, that France was paying the bill and that it was therefore a non-story. Though Bouchard's staff had informed the appropriate authorities in Ottawa about the hotel arrangements, the notice was lost.

Some of the embassy staff, however, including Mila's offender, were called up on the carpet. They had apparently run up big bills at top-rated restaurants while preparing for Mulroney's visit. Looking for a scapegoat, the Prime Minister's Office (PMO) moved to recall the diplomat who had escorted Mila. Bouchard, whose staff had to submit to an RCMP investigation over the whole hyped-up affair, angrily intervened. Again displaying his unusual degree of power, he succeeded in having the call-back order rescinded.

Bouchard, Bild recalled, handled the bureaucratic infighting over pomp and protocol admirably. He was tough in dealing with Ottawa and could be just as tough in dealing with snooty French bureaucrats. With their condescending ways, they sometimes gave the impression they were doing Canada a favour in even listening to the ambassador. Bouchard wouldn't stand for this. Bild recalled instances in which Canada was trying to sell high-tech equipment to France. When the bureaucrats held their Napoleonic noses high, giving Canada the colonial treatment, Bouchard was at his seigneurial best. With a hauteur that could outdo any Frenchman and with his withering command of the language, he pinned them coweringly against the wall. "Well, I don't understand why, being from France, would you not expect something of the highest quality and therefore be naturally interested in Canada's superior product?" Sometimes Bild wished he would put others in their place as well. He found that Ambassador Bouchard allowed Mulroney's cronies to impose on him perhaps a little too much when they came to town.

Small bones of contention aside, at the professional level all was going well for him. This was in contrast to the turmoil that greeted Bouchard's personal life, and that pained him. From the outside it appeared as though Jocelyne Bouchard was enjoying life as the ambassador's wife. She had left a good impression in political circles back home, particularly with Mila Mulroney, and was getting along well enough in the Parisian diplomatic whirl.

But the long-standing problems of the marriage had not disappeared. Jocelyne and Lucien made a decision to part for good. Jocelyne returned home to start a new life which, she soon decided, would be in the same field as that of her husband. In her forties she enrolled in law school. Her husband shared the news of the split with family members, some of whom had long seen it coming and thought it perhaps overdue. Then he rebounded in spectacular fashion.

On one of his visits to Canada, where he was returning every couple of months for consultations, Bouchard struck up an affair with the celebrated Radio-Canada hostess Denise Bombardier. Her star quality impressed Bouchard. She was a brassy, brainy writer-interviewer whose emotions, much like his, could gather hurricane force and dissipate just as quickly. Their romance was a *coup de foudre*. The appropriately named Bombardier dropped home and family to bunk down with the just-as-smitten ambassador at La Maison de la Rochefoucauld. Their affair became the subject of tabloid speculation in Europe and Quebec.

Bouchard appeared to be won over. He phoned friends back home to tell them he was going to marry Denise Bombardier. The loyal Denis de Belleval, who had had a brief affair with Bombardier, didn't have the nerve this time to tell him that he didn't think it would work out. He had been through this with him once before.

For many months, the romance progressed. Bombardier had many friends in French cultural circles and introduced her impressive partner to them. She was struck, in spending so much time with Bouchard, by how he was so tied to the emotions of his past. In the City of Light, in the whirl of his exciting new responsibilities, he talked so much of his early life in Jonquière. So much of his personality, his drive, his strengths, his sorrows, were dictated by the humble, low-status nature of his background. In conversations he kept coming back to his early poverty and to his relationship with his father—his father, the great man no one knew about, the great man who didn't get a chance to shine, but who gave his all so that his boys could. The senior son would rehabilitate him and make up for all the hurt pride.

That he carried his bitterness this far into life, that he still walked around with a two-ton chip on his shoulder and his insides knotted, spoke of how meaningful his early life—as myth-laden as it was—had been.

Before too long, the affair was in trouble. They were both so tempestuous, friends joked, that the bills for hurled and broken dishes alone would be enough to make them reconsider. After almost a year together, Bouchard asked Bombardier to move out of the embassy residence into an apartment. When he didn't continue to see her, as promised, she became very upset. At one point she phoned a friend to explain how he had misled and mistreated her. At first she had thought the world of him, she explained that day. He knew all the classics, he spoke the ancient languages, he was a superman. But then she began to consider him a man she could not trust, a man with ulterior motives, a separate agenda.

Stories surfaced that Bombardier had grown incensed that Bouchard, wanting to be discreet, wouldn't let her attend cocktail parties and diplomatic functions with him. This, Bombardier recalled, was absolutely false. "He didn't curb my movements anywhere." Bouchard, however, was obviously sensitive to repercussions that his affair might have—not in France, where the attitude towards this kind of thing was easygoing, but back home in Canada.

In this respect, his mother's side of him began to show. He had a tendency, some who saw him at the embassy recalled, to take everything as a life-and-death issue. "*Il prenait tout au tragique*," said one. "It was as if the fate of humanity was at stake. It was like nuclear submarines were always passing under him." Another associate in Paris said he sometimes gave the impression of bearing a crown of thorns. He likened Bouchard to a modern-day Savonarola, the fifteenth-century Dominican monk who became the moral overlord of Florence, the city-state for which the ambassador held a passionate interest.

Bombardier returned to Canada and Bouchard receded into one of his wounded-animal phases. He was quiet, licking his wounds, not sharing his thoughts with anyone, not even with de Belleval and another very close friend, Gaston Ouellet, with whom he practised journalism as a youth. "It was very bad," recalled de Belleval. "He has lost his wife and then he was left alone in Paris after going through this very stormy affair with Bombardier. And you could tell that there was a change in the man. He was not sad, but you could see that he had not the same energy."

Of his marriage, Bouchard would only say that it had ended

"for reasons and circumstances for which I felt myself responsible."
To help soften any feeling of guilt, he gave Jocelyne the most generous of divorce settlements—practically everything he owned—
house, chalet, furniture, car. de Belleval explained his actions. "We
are not the kind of guys who will run away with the money and
leave our wives in dire straits. We have a sense of duty, obligation,
responsibility. We are those kind of guys and it has cost us a lot of
money."

The break-up of his marriage, along with the Bombardier
affair, ended the friendship between Bouchard and one half of the
Mulroney team. Mila Mulroney sided with Jocelyne. She didn't like
the idea of anyone getting a divorce and was particularly stung by
the nature of this one. She made it clear that she didn't want to see
or talk to Lucien Bouchard again.

Following the Bombardier drama, a new romance was soon to
begin. In the spring of 1987, Bouchard took his seat in business
class on a flight from Paris to London. In a few minutes in walked
a pretty blonde young woman with eyes the size of saucers. She was
born in Nice and had spent much of her youth travelling with her
father, an officer with the US Marines. The twenty-seven-year-old
had worked at McDonnell-Douglas, was recently divorced and was
staying with her grandmother in Paris studying literature. She sat
down in an empty seat next to Bouchard. They didn't chat right
away, but a magazine that dropped to the floor proved to be the ice-
breaker.

Small talk on the plane continued in the airport lounge where
they had a bite to eat and exchanged addresses before going their
separate ways. Bouchard, who had told the young woman, Audrey
Best, that he was a Canadian diplomat, sent a letter a week later on
his ambassador's stationery. A very warm correspondence soon
developed. That Bouchard was unusually attracted to Ms. Best was
evident to everyone around the PMO. When he returned to
Ottawa he didn't hang around the external affairs department, but
headed straight to the Langevin Block where the Prime Minister's
Office was located. At lunch time he'd go up to the fourth floor
cafeteria and eat the woeful food with the PMO staff. One day he
excitedly told L. Ian MacDonald, "*Ian, j'ai poignée une belle.*" (Ian, I
picked up a beauty.)

He was a little concerned about her very young age, raising the matter once with Camille Guilbault, a "*belle*" in her own right who worked for the prime minister overseeing relations with the Quebec caucus. "You'd hear all the stories about him and the women—especially younger women," recalled Guilbault. One day he told her about Best and how she was so great and how he loved her and all that. Then he added, "But Camille, there is just one problem. She is very young."

"Well, Lucien," Guilbault replied. "When did that ever stop you?"

There was a second portentous event in Bouchard's life in this spring of 1987. It was an agreement on a constitutional accord carved out between Mulroney and the premiers at Meech Lake in the Gatineau Mountains outside Ottawa. In the negotiations, Quebec had presented Ottawa with five conditions in order for the province to sign on to the repatriated Constitution: recognition of Quebec as a distinct society, participation in the naming of Supreme Court judges, a veto for Quebec on constitutional changes, limitations on federal spending powers and more power for Quebec over immigration. These were met and now a three-year ratification process began.

Bouchard's position was curious. He appeared to be both strongly opposed to the accord and strongly in favour of it. On a flight between Montreal and Paris, he told Jean-Louis Roy, Quebec's delegate-general in Paris, that the five conditions were "far too weak. Bourassa is squandering the small advantage we now have for peanuts, for trifles." Roy reported this conversation to Quebec's minister of intergovernmental affairs, Gil Rémillard, and the news was also relayed to Ottawa.

Rémillard talked to Bouchard about the agreement. Bouchard repeated his opposition. The accord didn't go far enough. What about a redistribution and decentralization of Ottawa's powers? Bouchard had first proposed this, according to Charlie McMillan, the Mulroney adviser, in the original Sept-Iles speech he wrote for Mulroney. Rémillard told him that decentralization was on the agenda of many premiers and would be the next step—after the Meech Lake Accord was ratified. Bouchard, Rémillard recalled, was still not convinced. "He was reluctant to support Meech because his concern was for the next negotiation for the redistribution of powers." Rémillard argued that to try for everything at once would be to risk getting nothing.

Bouchard was hearing from his close friends and associates in the PQ, as well as from his brothers, that Meech wasn't enough; that, as one friend told him, it was a trap, a final deal to lock Quebec into Confederation with no follow-up.

But if Bouchard was telling Roy and Rémillard and his friends one thing, he was telling his employer, Brian Mulroney, quite another. He had conversations with his chief of staff, Bernard Roy. No opposition was stated.

More emphatic was Bouchard's comportment in a high-level PMO meeting on Meech Lake. Roy was there along with Tory senator Lowell Murray, Norman Spector of the Privy Council Office and others. They discussed the question of more demands from Quebec for concessions in the agreement. Bouchard asked questions about these proposals, but was satisfied with the explanations the PMO officials provided. He was in a position to give a big push to Quebec's demands. But he agreed, recalled Spector, that they should be rejected. It was no mild rejection. Concluding the meeting, Bouchard said, "Screw them!"

On May 1st, the day after Meech was signed, L. Ian MacDonald went into the prime minister's office and said, "You should call Bouchard." Bouchard was in Africa doing routine work for the upcoming Francophone summit. The PM had a brief telephone conversation with him and Bouchard seemed well satisfied. Two weeks later Mulroney made a speech in the House of Commons, his first major address since the signing of the accord. Bouchard contributed to the writing of the speech. From Paris, he faxed the line, "*Le rêve des Québécois est en train de se réaliser.*" (The dream of Quebeckers is being realized.)

It looked as though, as Fred Bild had noticed, Lucien Bouchard was playing a double game. One day his "screw them" message was aimed at the federal side, the next at the sovereignists. In keeping both paths open, he was continuing the habit of alternating allegiances he had begun in the 1960s. He left everyone guessing about who he was and what he wanted. Many wondered if he himself knew. Friends as well as adversaries wondered. Bouchard, said his ally Marc-André Bedard, was a man "rather tormented."

In Paris, Bouchard didn't speak much to embassy officials about Meech Lake. More immediate was the business of arranging summits and setting up La Francophonie. Its establishment was something nobody in English Canada really cared much about, and it was therefore rarely mentioned in the media. But it was a significant achievement. No modern period in Canada-France relations saw so much accomplished as under Mulroney, Bouchard and Robert Bourassa. Mitterrand came to Canada. It was the first visit by a French head of state since de Gaulle in 1967. There was the official visit of Governor-General Jeanne Sauvé to Paris, also a first. Bouchard was a key player in the organization of La Francophonie's first two summits, the first in Paris in 1986, the second in Quebec City the following year. Jean Chrétien was among those who scorned the appointment of Bouchard to Paris as pure patronage. In this matter, Jean Chrétien and the other naysayers had crow on their plates.

The summits required delicate negotiations by Bouchard with the Province of Quebec over what its powers vis-à-vis Ottawa's would be in this new assembly of French nations. He handled these with aplomb as he did most of the business with Quebec's delegates-general in Paris, Louise Beaudoin and Jean-Louis Roy. Under Bouchard, a change transpired. Quebec officials and visitors arriving in Paris went not to the offices of the Quebec delegation, but to the Canadian embassy. Bouchard held dinners twice for René Lévesque and his wife Corinne Côté-Lévesque. When Roy was Quebec's representative, embassy officials delighted in seeing how Bouchard ran circles around a provincial office which had successfully competed for attention with the embassy in the past.

In many ways Bouchard was a perfectionist. Everything had to be just right. When Mitterrand visited Ottawa, Bouchard stayed up until midnight with Ian MacDonald writing the speech of introduction to him that Mulroney would give in the House of Commons. In similar situations other ambassadors might throw in some points to be made in a PM's speech. They wouldn't stay up sweating over every word. "The problem that time," noted MacDonald, "was that we got trapped by Mitterrand. He spoke for forty-five minutes without notes and was brilliant. And we'd worked so hard on this twelve-minute introduction."

At the Quebec summit on La Francophonie, Bouchard fretted over every detail of protocol. He kept checking with Camille Guilbault. "Lucien, don't worry," she repeatedly told him. "Everything is okay." The Quebec City summit in September of 1987 was a special moment for Bouchard and Mulroney because it took place in the city where, as law students, they had looked to the future with wide eyes and boundless dreams. Now they were reassembled and they were hosting presidents, princes and kings.

They had lunch in the Garrison Club. They met the press in the garden and they were beaming. It seemed the country had rarely been so united. "I remember it being kind of a high water mark," recalled MacDonald. "Meech was going well and it looked like all these issues were going to be closed and we could move on. I remember them walking over from the Hilton to the Garrison Club with Bernard Roy. You could see the joy. Quebec City was their kind of town. Brian, in particular, was always much more comfortable when he was on the road there than anywhere else."

The friendship between Brian Mulroney and Lucien Bouchard may have reached its peak at this time. It's rare that the overreaching aspirations of youth come to find such princely fruition. Mulroney, whom Bouchard had spotted early as a well-connected charmer, an action guy determined to go all the way, had made it— to the very top. If at Laval they had imagined a peak for Brian Mulroney, it could only have been PM. And if they had imagined a place for his eloquent intellectual friend, what would have been more appropriate than ambassador to Paris, charting a new organization of French nations?

International organizations of the grandeur of a French Commonwealth were not easy to get up and moving. Without Mulroney and Bouchard, it likely wouldn't have come about. They had given the French-speaking world a focus, the means to come together and do things, such as ensure the survival of the language. It was an example, as the Mulroney people saw it, of how the federal system could work for Quebec. The province could not have spearheaded such a venture alone. "If it had not been for the Canadian federation," said Fred Bild, "I'm sure the whole Francophonie would never have been born. The French had been very happy to have all the French-African countries get together around the French president once a year, which was what they did. They didn't have to have all the other players like Canada which diluted their power."

Bild took note of how the whole process of building La Francophonie was close to Bouchard's heart. After working long hours side by side with this ambassador in Paris, he came to certain realizations. "He's a very emotional person. He's a person with great passion. The way I see him—he's someone who needs to have his mind constantly stimulated, but he also has to have his passions alive. I think Québécois nationalism is the only thing that can do that."

10. A PSYCHIATRIC PERSPECTIVE

André Tremblay talked of how Bouchard carried an inner anger around with him from his earliest days. Denise Bombardier always found him going back to the humbled state of his youth. Bernard Roy recalled him in tears when he talked of his father. Gérard Bouchard found him burning inside as a boy, overcome by a searing intensity that never left him. Almost everyone who met Lucien Bouchard was struck by how much his mind was buried in the past. He could never wipe the slate clean and move on. He could never rid himself of old afflictions.

John Ralston Saul, who was in Paris with Adrienne Clarkson in the Bouchard years, observed with some bemusement, having studied his speeches, that Bouchard's intellectual terms of reference were nineteenth century and earlier. He rarely alluded to French-Canadian novelists or philosophers. "It's very odd," said the author of *Voltaire's Bastards*, "that he has this dream of a new modern Quebec but doesn't seem to have any intellectual references to it. He reminds me in many ways of a nineteenth-century Canadian colonial figure whose references are all external."

Ralston Saul found him to be "a man driven by forces which he himself doesn't seem to understand." He saw in Bouchard an unusually strong psychological component. And "the stronger the psychological, the more unconscious the actor." To understand him, it was necessary, he said, to have a psychological portrait. Bouchard's old friend, Tremblay, came to a similar conclusion. It was necessary to go to the school of psychiatry, he said.

By coincidence, the Chrétien Liberals in Ottawa would come to the same conclusion. Following the 1995 referendum, the Prime Minister's Office would obtain a psychiatrist's study of Bouchard which painted a disturbing portrait.

Liberal MP John Godfrey had developed a fascination and fear of Bouchard ever since seeing him for the first time in the Commons. "Every once in a while there would be these islands of passion, self-transport." He wanted a psychiatric profile done on Bouchard because, as he said in a memo to the Prime Minister's Office, twentieth-century history had produced many dangerous examples of charismatic leaders who discover within their "own personality feelings and desires which resonate exactly with those of an entire population." Logic loses out in a debate with them and "the Big Lie flourishes."

Godfrey approached one of Canada's leading psychiatrists, Dr. Vivian Rakoff, to do the analysis. Rakoff had studied in Cape Town, London and Montreal's McGill University. He was head of the Clarke Institute in Toronto from 1980 to 1990, chairman of the psychiatry department at the University of Toronto for the same period, and head of psychiatry at Sunnybrook Health and Sciences Centre.

After studying Bouchard's career, his writings, his biography, his family background, Rakoff submitted two reports to Godfrey. Godfrey then turned them over to the Prime Minister's Office. Rakoff later met with Chaviva Hošek, a top official in the PMO, to discuss his findings. Eddie Goldenberg, Chrétien's closest adviser, also saw the studies, as did others.

Aspects of the profiles, which totalled 5,000 words, were pertinent to Bouchard's early carreer.

In summary (see later chapters for detail), the psychiatrist found a man with impressive talents but abiding character flaws. Bouchard displayed a core sense of insecurity and great vanity. His nourishment, Dr. Rakoff concluded, was humiliation. Without spelling out names, Rakoff reported that Bouchard was clearly "in the line of political poets of the blood." His goal, he said, was the creation of a nineteenth-century ethnic state, but Rakoff sensed Bouchard was motivated more by ego than anything else. "The true loyalty of Bouchard is to himself."

The most troubling of the psychiatrist's findings was his conclusion that Bouchard appeared to demonstrate a profound discontinuity of thought. "He is like an actor who dedicates himself to a particular role, but leaves it behind when the curtain falls," Rakoff wrote for the Liberals. "The visage at any moment seems absolutely convincing to the outside and, I suspect, subjectively; but it can be sloughed and changed."

For the psychiatrist, Bouchard brought to mind patients who

had what Rakoff described in an interview as the "esthetic character disorder." He described it as a form of emotional zoning. The
actor shuts out the past and becomes totally committed to the scene
of the moment. He is blinded by the light. Actions, declarations can
severely contradict past patterns. No sense of guilt is involved.

The analysis offered a possible explanation for some of the fantastic contradictions and about-faces (see Appendix) which would
mark Bouchard's career; these and Bouchard's shock and indignation when anyone brought them to his attention.

The psychiatrist raised a most frightening prospect. If in fact
Bouchard suffered from such a character disorder, the possibilities
were "alarming," Rakoff said in an interview. It meant that
Bouchard could convince himself in moments of fixation of a reality that bore no resemblance to previously established facts. It
meant he could base important judgments on emotion-charged,
ephemeral imagery.

In analysing Bouchard's early career, Rakoff was fascinated by
Bouchard's years in Paris as ambassador. For Bouchard and his
province, Dr. Rakoff wrote, a re-bonding with France represented
a way out of orphaned status.

"There is a cumulative impression that what Bouchard wants is
not Quebec with its distinct history, but Quebec as France," the
psychiatrist wrote. "In his writing he seems to fuse Quebec and
France, as if he wants to heal the 200-year separation from the
mother country...He doesn't seem to be aware that at some level
he is rejecting what is—modern Quebec—in favour of a romantic,
tormenting and ultimately reactionary dream—reactionary in the
sense that it yearns for a fantasized past in which cultures could be
separate and complete, where one preserves pure lineage."

In Bouchard, the psychiatrist saw a yearning for the lost patrimony of a giant culture. Hence his adoration of French literature
and his seeming lack of interest, as Ralston Saul noted, in his own
country's. Bouchard's superb facility with the French language
became his passport to the wider world of Frenchness and, noted
the report, "in the great patrimony of French literature he could
define himself away from the hard reality of provincial Quebec,
into a shared identity with Boileau, Proust, Voltaire." It is through
the preservation of the cultural tie with France, in Rakoff's analysis, that Bouchard can rehabilitate his father. "His father was poor,

uncultivated—a truck driver. But Bouchard places him in the cultural patrimony as he remembers that his father despised *joual*, and instructed his sons not to speak simple. The respect for the language elevates the memory of a not particularly cultivated man."

In this sense the father is "the guardian of the race," said Rakoff, a preserver of great cultural tradition, as was his grandmother with her hundred books.

With Bouchard, two forces were constantly in play in his public and personal life—pragmatism and emotionalism. "He is smart, hard working and has a lawyer's taste for dispute," Rakoff wrote. "He is not just a windy dreamer. But he is easily wounded, vain about his capacities. And though he is devoted to his ambitions, and, he believes, to his people, he is only too ready to justify himself under all circumstances; his various loyalties all come disguised as defence of principles."

A split which haunted his character, the psychiatrist analysed, was revealed in the choice of reading Bouchard took on the retreat when he was living apart from his wife. In reading St. Augustine, he could dwell on the discovery of original sin, and in Rousseau, on the peculiarly modern virtue of declaring one's indiscretions. A profound struggle resulted: between the severe ethics of the Catholic Fathers on the one hand, and the self-involved, self-indulgent man on the other. Bouchard showed signs of careening between the two.

As Bouchard's term as ambassador in Paris drew to a close in 1988, he was about to turn fifty and a decision had to be made. As he had expected since the beginning of his Paris assignment, Mulroney now came knocking on his door. He wanted Bouchard to become a politician in the real sense of the word.

Bouchard had gone through a long soul-searching phase over the question of making the leap. He discussed it with countless friends and associates, always giving the impression that he was very torn. Most colleagues in Paris, however, sensed his mind had been made up for some time. They could see the ambition and ego within. "I said to him when I was leaving Paris," recalled Adrienne Clarkson, "that I could see that one day he would be premier of Quebec." Bouchard tried to laugh it off. "Oh no, don't be silly," he replied.

"Oh yes," replied Clarkson. "That's where your heart is."

Mulroney had been sending over emissaries like his old Laval classmate Peter White, who kept the pressure on. Bernard Roy had maintained close relations with Bouchard while working on La Francophonie. The Tories had become doubly anxious to recruit him because their Quebec caucus had been blackened with the image of scandal and quasi-scandal. Because the party was considered such a long shot in Quebec in 1984, it had found it difficult to recruit high-quality candidates. The fifty-seven who came to Ottawa featured some who appeared more bent on profiteering than politicking. An election was around the corner, and the Conservatives needed fresh new leadership in Quebec. They needed integrity, prestige and clout. Bouchard was clearly their man.

The argument put to him to come home and run was blunt, as Bernard Roy remembered. "The prime minister needs you and you owe him." The owing part was hard for the ambassador to dismiss. If Bouchard was a friend, he couldn't turn his back on Mulroney now. So, having rejected offers to seek election over a span of almost two decades, Bouchard, now past the age when most enter the game, finally crossed the line.

He had been hedging, cautious, waiting for the right moment, hesitant to put himself to the test that history books demand. If it was true that he saw life in heroic, idealistic terms, he could no longer wait. Now the drama—with markings of the Greek tragedies he tended to favour—was about to begin.

His skin was still thin. He still bled all over the place. He was defensive and wary, his antennae particularly sensitive to reports over his past political affiliations. Newspaper stories, particularly in English Canada, were not focusing on the fine work he had done as ambassador, but instead, given his PQ credentials, tended to raise questions over his legitimacy. Bouchard lamented this. His attitude, recalled Roy, was, "I do all this good work and yet I get these pieces in the newspapers." Those articles "really hurt him. He would be ranting and raving and then he would suddenly calm down, as if to say, 'you understand, you understand why I am like this.'"

Though still emotionally fragile, his success in Paris had outfitted him with an enhanced sense of confidence, power and hauteur. The attitude "don't mess with the seigneur" was evident on occasion. In making his arrangements for his return from Paris, he met with Ian MacDonald and Bernard Roy in a Quebec City hotel suite. Among other things, they discussed the problem of getting his car shipped back from France. There were too many delays, Bouchard complained. This could not be tolerated. He picked up the telephone and got a bureaucrat on the line. Then, as MacDonald recalled, he was suddenly overcome by fury. "Don't you know who I am! I am the ambassador to France! Don't you have any respect? I want this done!!" The fierce tantrum, which Macdonald found alarming, didn't last long. Then, there was a pause and Bouchard was perfectly calm again.

Beyond the question of whether he was temperamentally suited for politics was the more immediate question of whether he was ideologically capable of being a federal Tory. From the socialist and sovereignist Parti Québécois to the Bay Street federalism of the Conservative Party was a quantum leap. Upon his return from Paris in March 1988, he sought to assuage doubts. "I am a Canadian," he told reporters. "Who can doubt it? I was born Canadian and we have been Canadians since 1636 in Quebec. I am very proud to be a Canadian."

Away from the media lights, however, there were signs he was confronting an identity crisis. Once during lunch with MacDonald, they were discussing the prospect of his joining the Mulroney Cabinet and how this was all very exciting. But then Bouchard stopped and asked, "*Oui, mais comment est-ce que je peux traverser la rivière Péquiste?*" That question, how he could make such a transfer of primal loyalties from sovereignist to federalist, still vexed him. MacDonald didn't say anything, but he thought, "Well Lucien, if you haven't figured that by now..."

Instead of calling a by-election right away so that Bouchard could seek a Commons seat, Mulroney brought him directly into the government. The by-election could come later, the prime minister decided. He wanted Bouchard—now.

The question of what Cabinet portfolio to give him was a delicate one. Not one to underestimate his own capacities, Bouchard was looking for the justice ministry as well as some responsibility for Meech Lake. Mulroney, however, though otherwise. He wanted Meech for himself. Big portfolios like justice weren't available unless he was prepared to make a significant Cabinet shuffle. Bouchard was new in Ottawa. It would be risky to load him up with a sprawling department right away.

One position coming open, however, was secretary of state. David Crombie, the former tiny perfect mayor of Toronto, who never felt at home with the Mulroneyites, was abandoning federal politics. His portfolio required the minister to bring in the new Canadian Citizenship Act, to manage the official languages policy and preside over Canada Day. On the face of it, secretary of state seemed wholly unsuitable for Bouchard. How could a Péquiste who was still playing footsie with the party be appointed the country's pre-eminent cheerleader?

Mulroney had a different way of seeing the situation. What better way of convincing all the doubters out there of Bouchard's bona fides as a Canadian patriot? What better way of convincing Bouchard himself? It wasn't a terribly onerous portfolio and it was the one available. Without much debate, and without much fore-sight, Lucien Bouchard was named Mr. Canada.

He knew next to nothing about the department. On the day he was sworn in, he was driving back to his office with Roy and Mac-Donald. The car was pulling in to park at the East Block when Bouchard asked, "What does a secretary of state do?" MacDonald responded in a jesting tone of voice. "Well, among other things, Lucien," he said, pointing to the Peace Tower, "do you see that building up there? On the first of July there will be about 50,000 people there and you will preside over Canada Day and lead them in the singing of the national anthem."

Within a week of the appointment, suspicions arose that a mistake had been made. Nobody at the PMO had looked into the pipeline to see what was coming. "At the time, I don't think it had dawned on us," said Bernard Roy, who consulted Mulroney on the choice, "that this was not the right appointment. I guess we should have known that the Supreme Court was going to rule on sticky issues—the Manitoba and Alberta cases on the official languages, then the bilingual sign thing. I guess it was seen by the PM as a no-problem sort of department where you could travel and give cheques and be seen."

One of Bouchard's first priorities was staff. On his first day back from Paris, he met the national media. Luc Lavoie, the senior communications adviser in the PMO, was assigned to take him through the day. Lavoie, a sandy-haired bilingual tough guy with a young face but a seasoned mind, had been a solid Quebec TV journalist.

He had never met the new minister, but they got along well, and Bouchard returned home to spend the weekend in Chicoutimi.

The following Tuesday Bouchard was being briefed by officials of his department across the river in Hull. Bouchard picked up the phone and got Lavoie on the line. "What are you doing?" he asked. "I'm working," said Lavoie at his desk in the PMO, "trying to earn a living."

"Well, come over here. We've got to talk." Lavoie went to Hull and sat in on the briefing. As the meeting adjourned, he asked Bouchard why he had wanted him. "Well," came the response, "I told them you're my new chief of staff." Lavoie was taken aback. He informed Bouchard of his responsibilities with the prime minister. "Don't worry about that," came the response. "I'll take care of Brian."

Mulroney was vacationing in Florida. Bouchard picked up the phone, called the switchboard, got the PM on the line and said he had Lavoie with him and wanted him as his chief of staff. Mulroney wanted to know what Lavoie thought of the idea. "I'm sure he doesn't have a problem," Bouchard replied. The next day Lavoie began working for his new boss.

In his first week as minister, the Supreme Court brought in a ruling affecting Francophones in Saskatchewan. It said that statutes enacted when the province joined Confederation effectively guaranteed minority language rights. The ruling's impact meant, among other things, that all provincial laws would have to be available in the French language. Grant Devine's Conservative government wasn't amused. It immediately introduced legislation repealing the original statutes. A similar development later took place in Alberta.

The story triggered little reaction in English Canada, but it was big news for Quebec and for Bouchard. "He was absolutely shocked," recalled Lavoie, "that Saskatchewan could do what it did without even picking up the phone and saying maybe we should wait a week and try and work out some kind of compromise. But no, it was just like an automatic reaction that everybody in English Canada thought very normal."

Bouchard pressed Saskatchewan to reconsider. Mulroney made public a critical response he sent to Devine. Eventually a compromise was worked out whereby Ottawa would spend $50 million over five years to allow French-language services to be provided to the Fransaskois. But the episode was not soon to be forgotten. Bouchard was irate not only over the Devine gambit but also by the response at the Cabinet table in Ottawa. Excepting Mulroney, hardly anyone cared. French language rights in the West? They all wondered what Bouchard was talking about.

Prior to his return from Paris, Mulroney already had legislation in the pipeline, Bill C-72, to strengthen minority language rights across the country. As secretary of state, Bouchard would have the responsibility for administering the new bill. But before its passage, Bouchard began displaying some of the brinkmanship for which he would become notorious. Taking matters into his own hands, Bouchard gave a speech in Quebec exempting his own province from a key provision of the bill. The legislation would give Ottawa the right to protect and promote the French language in English Canada and the English language in Quebec. In the case of Quebec, however, Bouchard asserted that the federal government would promote English only after receiving permission from the provincial government. He seemed intent on applying the new law to the other nine provinces and not his own. His words were categorical. "Never will the federal government…wish to or attempt to intervene in the language of work, the language of communications and so forth. Never will it do such a thing. Never! Never! It is contrary to the whole philosophy of the government. It is contrary to the intention of the law. It is contrary to the Meech Lake Accord." Bouchard had only been a Cabinet minister two months, yet already he was challenging the prime minister.

He soon felt uncomfortable sitting in Cabinet without a seat in the House of Commons. He wanted to represent his region, Saguenay-Lac-Saint-Jean, preferably the Chicoutimi riding. The prime minister thought André Harvie, the sitting member, would be willing to give up the seat for a patronage appointment, but Harvie baulked. Bouchard's second priority was the neighbouring riding in his home town of Jonquière, but the Tory MP there wouldn't budge. Bouchard's frustration grew. With a general election scheduled for the fall, Mulroney now thought it better to avoid the by-election altogether and let Bouchard run with everyone else at that time. But his friend was unwilling to do this. He wanted democratic legitimacy for his Cabinet rank as soon as possible.

Finally Clément Côté gave up his seat in the Lac Saint-Jean riding and a by-election was scheduled for June 20th.

This wasn't Bouchard's favoured constituency. While he had been born and spent the first year of his life in this riding, he was by no means viewed as a local. Though the riding was little more than an hour's drive from Chicoutimi, where he had spent most of the previous twenty-five years, internal rivalries were strong in the Saguenay-Lac-Saint-Jean region. In the lake district, people tended to view those coming from Chicoutimi as snobs. So although Bouchard was the big-name candidate, he was an outsider. He was also a novice politician and his party was down in the polls. It would be a tough test, and it would be a humbling experience. Bouchard, who always had dire second thoughts about entering active politics, would come to find out why.

In the 1984 election, Côté, the Mulroney candidate, clobbered his Liberal rival, Pierre Gimaiel, by nearly 13,000 votes. Because the Conservatives swept the province, the myth of the Tory machine took root. In fact, there was no Tory machine in Quebec. Bouchard's riding organization was in disarray, full of internal rivalries and, as green as he was, Bouchard was unable to forge order out of the chaos.

In the initial weeks, no top hand was there to direct him. He appeared on the working-class hustings in glum ambassadorial suits and polished wing tips. As if still drinking champagne at receptions on the Champs-Élysées, he talked of national issues like Meech Lake, free trade and national reconciliation. But what the folks at Mario Tremblay's tavern in Alma, the principal town in the riding, worried about were jobs, roads and local infrastructure. The Liberal Gimaiel, who had represented Lac Saint-Jean twice provincially, hit Bouchard hard on the outsider charge. He argued that if you want an MP for Lake Meech, vote Bouchard, but if you want one for Lac Saint-Jean, vote Gimaiel.

Gimaiel had a powerful one-word campaign slogan: "Fidelity." It stung Bouchard in more ways than one. It suggested that while Gimaiel was faithful to wife, party and riding, Bouchard was disloyal on every count. Gimaiel took his family everywhere with him on the campaign while Bouchard struggled alone, his wife gone, his new amour, Audrey Best, unseen.

Before long, Gimaiel's attacks began to strike a chord. Above all, Bouchard demanded personal respect. Question his personal integrity and the surcharge of explosives in him risked detonating. Gimaiel went after him in a radio debate in such a way that it had this effect. Benoît Bouchard, who was now Mulroney's minister of transport, had been sent in to help out in the campaign. He recalled Lucien's eruption: "He was yelling and screaming—'I'm going to destroy this man! I'm going to just kill him! He will totally disappear from the political map!'" He continued pounding the table. Benoît Bouchard had never seen anything like it. "It scared me."

The media began attacking Bouchard for things he could not understand. The government was paying rent on a riding office. Bouchard was crucified for allegedly using the office for campaign purposes. Since, in the wake of Tory scandals, he was to be the party's new Mr. Clean, the charges carried some weight. He recovered, declaring that unlike other candidates, he would refuse all business and corporate donations for his campaign, accepting only individual contributions of $3,000 or less.

While a noteworthy initiative, the last thing this candidate had to worry about in this campaign was resources. The Tory organization in Ottawa, seeing this as a key test, a dry run for the autumn election, was prepared to break the bank for the new star. The spending included day-to-day tracking polls which provided Bouchard with critically important intelligence. Early in the campaign they showed him trailing badly, ten points behind the Liberal, with the NDP candidate, Jean Paradis, starting to show well.

Lisa Van Dusen, a journalist covering the election for *Maclean's*, was a close friend, and later the wife, of Ian MacDonald. One night she phoned and filled his ear with horror stories from the Bouchard camp. Bouchard, she reported, was having nightmares about the decision he had made to enter politics. He dreamed of being back in the salons of Paris. He was so ill at ease on the hustings that he didn't want to shake hands with constituents.

MacDonald walked down the hall to the hotel room where Mulroney sat in his bathrobe. "What would you say," asked MacDonald, "if I told you that our candidate in Alma walked into a bank yesterday and walked past a line-up of thirty people, did his business, then walked out without shaking hands with any of them?" He told him more. Before he left the room, Mulroney had grabbed the phone to call Bernard Roy to start an airlift to Alma.

A batch of Cabinet ministers were sent in. Mulroney himself made plans for a visit and Luc Lavoie became the manager of the campaign. He found a shaken and exhausted Bouchard, angered and hurt by the lack of support and by the disarray in his campaign. Taking his cue from polls revealing that the candidate was perceived as an outsider using the riding as a stepping stone to big things in Ottawa, Lavoie set about overhauling his image. He wanted Bouchard to become a local man, talking about local issues, making pork-barrel promises to respond to voters' needs. It was a tough assignment. Bouchard was never a glad-hander, never a small-talker, never one who could easily abide the obsequious byplay of voter ingratiation.

Lavoie wanted to film an advertisement at the Bouchard family farm—the shrine—just outside Alma. Though he had been moved away as a baby, his family roots were clearly there, in the riding, and Bouchard badly needed to rid himself of the parachute-candidate tag. The ad was to feature Bouchard, coat flung over the shoulder, emerging from the stereotypical barn in back of the family home. To the accompaniment of braying animals he would declare, "This is where I was born." Then he would walk down to the edge of the creek and look out onto the horizon with an expression of deep concern for the plight of his fellow citizens. "A real cliché," said Lavoie, "but it works in politics."

Bouchard was put off by the idea. On the first couple of takes, he couldn't keep a straight face. He tried again but cringed in dismay. "This is phoney, this is stupid," he complained. "I'm not going to do it." He went over, sat dejectedly on the balcony, and wouldn't budge. "This is not what I'm in politics for. This isn't what politics is about. Politics is about ideas."

Lavoie ultimately persuaded him to do the filming. In order to negate Bouchard's ambassadorial, man-in-a-limo impression, he had another idea. He wanted Bouchard to ride a bicycle through the streets of Alma—just an ordinary Joe on a two-wheeler. Bouchard demurred. He'd look like an idiot, he said. He hadn't ridden a bicycle in twenty years. Finally, he got on the bike and wobbled his way through the streets.

Overcoming his shyness took time. He toured a shopping mall, miked up, with television cameras in tow. For a politician on the stump this was normal fare, but Bouchard was devastated by the experience. "For hours," he would later recall, "I walked around under the constant fear of being ridiculed or insulted live."

Local issues also were difficult for him. They were small potatoes compared to La Francophonie. In the first televised campaign debate, Bouchard, who could have been expected to do well because of his command of the language and brilliant mind, was "badly prepared because he wouldn't listen to anybody," said Lavoie. "He got beaten up on the local issues." Lavoie waited outside the studio that night to drive Bouchard to Quebec City. Not one to sugar-coat anything, Lavoie told him he had done badly. Bouchard didn't have to be told. He knew it and sat in mournful silence for most of the trip.

He was thinking now of the likelihood of defeat. He told Lavoie he had to prepare himself to lose with dignity. "Why don't you just shut up about that?" Lavoie responded. "I don't like working with losers."

The polls were slow in starting to turn. But the prize card had yet to be played. In the crunch, Lucien Bouchard always had a friend he could count on. Brian Mulroney was about to come to the rescue. With the PM's visit to the riding, the assistance of some other unlikely political friends and with the help of the pork barrel, the campaign could still be a winning one.

"When in doubt, start paving the roads" was always a good principle to go by. In Alma, Tory promises, with ample government money to finance them, cascaded one upon the other. There was the restoration of the wharf at the picturesque village of Ste.-Rose-du-Nord, the repaving of an airport strip, a major grant for a job creation centre, a feasibility study for a highway all the way to James Bay, funding for the clean-up of a nearby river and the promise that with Lucien Bouchard in Ottawa, the big new Canadian Space Centre would be located in Quebec. For the latter, Bouchard told voters that he had already gained the commitment of the prime minister. His statement left no doubt as to the clout he felt he wielded. "Do you think Mr. Mulroney would risk not being on my side," he told voters. "We are too close."

With the pledges came the inevitable charges that the Tories were trying to buy the election. Opponents put the price tag of promises at a fabulous billion dollars—a mere $875 million more than the Bouchard team's estimate. The candidate noted how it was no coincidence that the most disparaging stories written about him appeared in the English media. Liberal leader John Turner, as well as national journalists, pointed out mockingly that Bouchard began the campaign as Mr. Clean but was ending it as Monsieur Duplessis.

The national media, while soiling Bouchard's broader image, didn't count for much in the riding of Lac Saint-Jean. The Tories' day-to-day polling showed that the promises were starting to pay big dividends. Was the campaign bought? A good question, said Roger Banford, the president of Bouchard's riding association, as he recalled the time. "There is certainly a part of the truth in that."

As well as federal government largesse, other backing, decidedly uncustomary, came Bouchard's way. The Liberal Gimaiel might normally have expected the support of fellow Liberal Bourassa. But Mulroney struck again. Owing to the special friendship he had carved out with Bourassa, the Liberal leader sent in his troops to work for the Tory. Bourassa wanted the Meech Lake Accord passed and he felt that Bouchard's election would be a plus in this regard. Gimaiel had been combating the rise of sovereignty in his region of the province for a decade. And now this. A leader of his own party was throwing his weight behind a nationalist. It was a funny business, thought Gimaiel. The Liberals in Ottawa, he felt, had been the spur to the growth of nationalism in the first place. "The force of the nationalist movement has its base in Radio-Canada. The network, with its millions from Ottawa, nourished the nationalist culture."

Along with the Liberals came another peculiar support group for the Tories—the Parti Québécois. Bouchard's past alliance brought many on board. Corinne Côté-Lévesque, the former premier's widow, and senior voices such as house leader Guy Chevrette, another former Cliche Commission member, came out openly in support of Bouchard. The one sour note was the cold blast from PQ leader Jacques Parizeau. Always suspicious of Bouchard, angered when he boarded the Tory bus, Parizeau wanted little to do with such an opportunist. He announced at the outset of the campaign that he preferred to remain silent. In the final days when the outcome was in doubt, Bouchard came pleading. He couldn't understand it, he told a press conference. "I am a fervent admirer of Mr. Parizeau's," he stated, already having given Lavoie, de Belleval and others the exact opposite assessment. "He is one of the most brilliant politicians of his generation, an extraordinary man." How could Parizeau not support him, he wondered. Did he really want to see one of those Liberals elected "who shoved the repatriation of the Constitution down Quebeckers' throats"?

His supplication brought only more silence. Gimaiel offered the media an explanation. Bouchard was an architect of the collapse of PQ support through his about-face in the public service contract negotiations, he asserted. Then "Lucien Bouchard was the first to leave the boat—as soon as the PQ began to experience problems—and jump into the patronage cradle of his friend Brian Mulroney."

The campaign added a lasting dram of poison to a Bouchard-Parizeau relationship, which was never a good one. It created strains as well in the important rapport between the two Bouchards. Benoît Bouchard had come in to help. Widely popular, an emerging star within the Quebec caucus, he was a top contender to become the Tory boss of Quebec. The arrival of Lucien Bouchard, he knew, would change all that. So, while he admired Lucien's talents and while he could see that the party could benefit from his recruitment, Benoît was of two minds about his ascendancy. When Mulroney had telephoned to recruit him for the campaign, Benoît was not overly enthusiastic. In a sense it was a request for him to get up there and start digging his own grave. He told Mulroney, "Brian, I have a big department to look after and I don't have the time." Mulroney responded: "Benoît, I'm not asking you if you would like to go. I'm asking you to go. Our man is losing."

Benoît Bouchard spent the last three weeks of the campaign in Alma. He called together seventy-five key campaigners from the 1984 election and tried to spur them to action. "I worked sixteen hours a day," he said. "I never believed I could be a good soldier." His degree of self-esteem being as lofty as that of most politicians, if not higher, he faced some trying experiences. When Mulroney visited the region to mark the 150th anniversary of the arrival of the first settlers, a televised church service was the central event. As the prime minister entered, Benoît Bouchard moved to his side to take the seat next to him. As regional minister for Saguenay-Lac Saint-Jean, this was the appropriate protocol. But he was barely there when a Tory official told him to move out of the way so that Lucien Bouchard could occupy the place and be seen on television with the prime minister. It seemed a likely request given the campaign in progress, but sensitivities being what they are in the business, Benoît Bouchard was terribly offended. Not only at this but at other moments when Lucien was put front and centre. "I will never forget it," Benoît would recall years afterwards. "I will never forget and I can give you other examples. There were many others where I was screwed or short-circuited by Lucien."

He was not entirely aware of the fact that Luc Lavoie and Lucien Bouchard didn't even want him around. They found him more of a hindrance than a help. "He was a fucking disaster in this by-election," said Lavoie, not mincing his words. "Just a major fuck-up. We didn't know what to invent to keep him away from us... He had a very serious problem because next door a new star was being born and his name was the same." Gimaiel didn't see it this way. Benoît Bouchard was "a key factor," he said.

Mulroney's visit came with the election nine days away. The prime minister spent two days in the riding imploring voters to send his friend Lucien to Ottawa. The media exposure was heavier than at any other event in the campaign. The PM visited the Bouchard family farm, showing none of the reluctance to ham it up for the cameras that Bouchard had demonstrated in trying to film the campaign ad. Bouchard wondered what his father would have thought had he witnessed the stampede of cameras across the shine. But this time he enthusiastically got in on the act, posing for a photo with a cow. "Congratulations!" came a message from Ian MacDonald, citing the bovine pic. "You've just won the by-election!"

In a rating of the leaders, Mulroney was the preferred choice as prime minister by a wide margin over John Turner. The prime minister repeated the message that a vote for Bouchard was a vote against Turner. Lavoie filmed an effective commercial on the visit which ran the rest of the campaign. By consensus, the Mulroney visit was the vital injection of momentum which pushed Bouchard over the top.

On election night, the tabulations showed Bouchard winning by a surprisingly substantial margin. He took in 16,986 votes against 10,726 for the Liberals. Weighing heavily in the outcome was the late collapse of the support of the NDP candidate, Jean Paradis. This was the prime source of the heavy switch-over to Bouchard in the final week.

While it was a high-stakes test for the PM and by no means simply a case of just doing a favour for a friend, the fact remained that Bouchard could not have won without all the help the PM sent in—Lavoie, the Cabinet ministers, the money, the pork barrel, the provincial Liberal machine, not to mention Mulroney himself. It was a campaign won from the outside, not by the candidate. Again, Mulroney had come to the aid of his pal in time of need. He had given him Cliche, he had given him Paris, he had given him a Cabinet post and he had given him a by-election victory.

Bouchard was appreciative. But as time would demonstrate, he had a funny way of showing it.

11. THE FIRST BLACKMAIL

He was emotionally relieved as he took the podium to declare his pride in winning the election. He spoke of Quebec uniting behind a Tory vision and how this campaign would be a forerunner for the coming autumnal test across the land.

France was on his mind. Shortly before the close of the polls, Bouchard told the media that it was time for the people of Quebec to rally behind grand objectives like they did in the old country. In France, they spoke with one voice on culture, on defence and on the role of their country in the world. "In Quebec we have very little in the way of consensus like this. On the contrary we are frequently divided, the latest example being the 1980 referendum period."

Ottawa was the conduit through which the grand dreams could be realized, Bouchard asserted. Though French power had come to Ottawa in force beginning in the late 1960s, he was pleased to note that the interests of Quebec were now being deeply embedded in the federal consciousness. "*On est en train de Québéciser la politique féderale*," he said.

He laid things out clearly. "Now we live in the Canadian Confederation. It's what we have decided. We are there. It's there that it is happening for us, at least in the medium term, and we can believe, as I do, in the long term."

On June 28, 1988, the prime minister and his deputy Don Mazankowski escorted Bouchard into the House of Commons for the first time. As the Tory benches exploded in celebration, the face of Brian Mulroney glowed with a measure of satisfaction that some of his ministers would never forget. Absent was the look of smarm, the forced political face the PM often wore because he thought the game demanded it. This was as genuine as he could get. "Lucien represented so much for Brian," said the other Bouchard, Benoît. "All that Brian was not, Lucien was. And all that Lucien was not, Brian was." Luc Lavoie got to know them both from close range.

What Mulroney admired about Bouchard, he said, was his insatiable work capacity, his thirst for excellence, a quality Mulroney shared, and his passion. "Lucien is a man with a heart, which Mulroney admires," noted Lavoie. "Lucien instinctively cannot connect, for instance, with a Trudeau who is basically a rational mind, whose entire life has been about how to keep emotions under control."

The championship season was upon them. Two momentous issues, free trade and the Constitution, were soon to be resolved, one way or the other. Mulroney had come a long way. Before becoming prime minister, he had sat in Conrad Black's study in Palm Beach, Florida, seeking support from members of the establishment. Black saw vaulting ambition in Mulroney but few ideas. He wondered whether he was all hat, no cattle. Mulroney frankly acknowledged that it was power more than ideas that lured him but that nonetheless he had goals.

Once in office, he swept aside any and all doubts about lack of vision by attempting a simultaneous overhaul of the two hallmark features of the Canadian definition—relations with Quebec and relations with the Americans. Free trade and Meech Lake now hung in the balance. For each great measure, electoral support from Quebec was vital. For that support, for the final thrust to the goal line, what the prime minister needed was the infusion of one dominating star player. Now he thought he had him.

They weren't long in the chamber, Lucien Bouchard looking shy and tense, when Mulroney singled him out. Opposition leader Turner raised the matter of free trade, wondering why Trade Minister John Crosbie had not yet read the agreement. Crosbie hadn't thought it was necessary. He used to sell vacuum cleaners, he noted, but he'd never vacuumed a room in his life. Mulroney jumped in to chide Turner for having had the gall to raise the free trade issue. The voters had just pronounced themselves on it, the prime minister said. Then, pointing at Bouchard, he thundered, "And here's the evidence!"

Bouchard told reporters he was not in Ottawa as a miracle worker, only to serve proudly "to conclude the Meech Lake Agreement and the Free Trade Agreement." In addition to this and his secretary of state duties, Mulroney had handed him an immediate task—the preparation of conflict of interest legislation to prevent Tories from getting caught with their hands in the till.

Bouchard had fared reasonably well in his first few seat-less months. Though rocked by the indifference of his Anglophone colleagues on the Saskatchewan and Alberta language fights, he waded his way through the muddy waters. He faced the nettlesome matter of indemnification of Japanese Canadians for Canada's deportation and internment of them in World War II. Previous ministers, Liberal and Conservative, had tried but been unable to settle the matter. But Bouchard was determined and was quickly able to arrange suitable reparations. On another issue, the fight against illiteracy, he pushed through funding for new programs. Critical to his success on each matter was full access to the prime minister and full support from him.

His deputy minister was Jean Fournier, who had worked as a personal assistant to Chrétien at Indian and Northern Affairs. Fournier maintained close ties to Chrétien, whom Bouchard loathed, but Bouchard and Fournier worked smoothly together. Upon introduction, Bouchard impressed Fournier, saying with a subservient smile, "And what can I do for you?" Usually with new ministers, it was the other way around. Working nine months with Bouchard, Fournier found him exceptionally gifted. "He was really an extraordinary person to work with. The intellect. He always asked the right questions, worked hard. He was demanding, but in the right sense of the word." His most important possessions, noted Fournier, were his books. "They were like his clothes."

The one matter that made Fournier wonder about Bouchard was his fragility on sensitive Quebec issues. At press conferences on departmental business, the media began putting questions about the Constitution and Quebec and Bouchard's PQ ties. Rather than refrain from comment, Bouchard rose quickly to the bait and made unguarded, sometimes incendiary remarks. When controversial stories appeared the next day, Fournier received irate calls from the PMO. "Don't you guys know how to close a press conference. How did you allow this to happen? Can't you control him?"

Fournier found Bouchard to be "another man" on these occasions. From calm and reasonable and sometimes brilliant, he turned deeply fragile and suspicious. "He was a totally different personality. He would lose the kind of lucidity and balance he had shown on other matters."

The media, particularly the Anglophone scribes, bothered

Bouchard because he felt they didn't know Quebec. He had always feared the media's capacity to randomly destroy reputations of fine people. Just a few months into office he was already looking for a way to restrain them. In a speech to the Canadian Bar Association, he proposed that the media introduce self-policing measures so that there would be somebody to watch the watchdog. Just as the legal profession had a disciplinary body, so should journalists. His recommendation was predictably batted down by journalistic executives who did not want their powers diminished.

His most delicate moment arose over Mulroney's legislation, Bill C-72, to increase minority language rights. In the spring, Bouchard had angrily lashed out at any suggestion Ottawa would actively promote the English language in Quebec. Only with permission from the Quebec government could it do so, he claimed. In the summer he backpedaled, now toeing the party line and saying the legislation had to be applied as written. Parizeau and sovereignist associates were infuriated, claiming Quebec had primacy over language matters and alleging a federal power grab. The matter heightened tensions between Bouchard and Parizeau. Bouchard vigorously denied he was seeking to bilingualize Quebec. At the time, Ottawa was spending about $18 million to promote French outside Quebec and about $2 million to promote English in Quebec. Meetings between Fournier and Quebec officials eased concerns over how the law would be implemented. But the controversy, which was to rise again, was symptomatic of the dilemma Bouchard found himself in. When he sided with the federalist position, he was berated by his former PQ colleagues. When he sided with Quebec nationalists, he was berated in his own party.

He delivered his maiden speech in the House of Commons— "Madam Speaker, this occasion fills me with awe and respect"—on August 29th. It was a tame effort, focusing not on the unity issue but, with the election looming, free trade. In the same month he tabled his hastily prepared study on ethics and morality in government. It called for new ways of awarding government contracts, financing political parties and dealing with conflicts of interest for politicians and their spouses. In the face of charges that his by-election victory was bought, it was a difficult sell. While defending the measures in the House, he faced the inevitable hoots and catcalls from opposition members, but rather than let them roll off his back like the more seasoned politicians, Bouchard was provoked. "Listen! I know that the person who has the floor should remain indifferent to all these shouts, but since I am not as thick-skinned as my honourable colleagues, I should like to be able to say quietly what I have to say, without being interrupted by all these untimely remarks."

He went on with his holier-than-thou posturing, occasioning only more ridicule from his opponents. "Oh, scold us, Lucien," they shouted. "Scold us!"

As if wanting to demonstrate he was a cut above, Bouchard peppered his treatise on ethics and morality with references to the luminaries of Ancient Greece, throwing in Pericles, Dionysius and, for good measure, Phidias. House members looked as if they didn't know what he was talking about.

He even introduced some Latin into Hansard, telling honourable members to beware the proverb of Dionysius—"Oderint dum metuant." (Let them hate me, as long as they fear me.) This was a rule all tyrants lived by, Bouchard explained. But nowadays politicians had to play by different rules. He then told the story about Pericles' erection of a golden statue of Athena and, for those who were still awake, moved on to Roman times with a yarn about Cicero. Cicero who championed Pompey had also distinguished himself, Bouchard explained, in a struggle with the evil wretch Verres, a proconsul of a Roman province who had been on the take.

While there may have been some relevance in the stories to modern conflict of interest guidelines, incredulous opposition members shelled him. He could well talk of Athena's cloak of gold, hollered Sheila Copps. He had just spent "a billion dollars here and a billion dollars there" on his by-election triumph! And where in his ethics measures, cried John Rodriguez, was a clause requiring disclosure of gifts to a prime minister from his political party? The NDPer was targeting Mulroney's alleged storehouse of tassled loafers. "Why no Gucci clause?"

Bouchard's cauldron was starting to boil over. This debasing of his monologue with cheap personal accusations explained, he indignantly offered, why good people refused to go into politics. "I personally know the prime minister. He is one of the most honest men I know in the world." What a disgrace, he asserted, that at such great historical moments members of Parliament go on about "the shoes of the prime minister."

The ethics episode—his report was referred to a committee for further study—was a tough outing. A columnist termed his "oderint dum metuant" speech "one big yawn." More significantly, opposition members were beginning to see that Lucien Bouchard suffered from a flaw which was often deadly for politicians. He could easily be provoked. He bled like a haemophiliac.

In the fall he had to return to Lac Saint-Jean for the general election, in order to reclaim the seat he had won just a few months earlier. It was a quiet campaign of the foregone-conclusion variety, but Bouchard was never one to avoid stirring the pot. The first tempest flowed from a broadside he levelled at John Turner over the language-rights issue. The feverish Liberal leader was making noises suggesting his Grits would abolish the notwithstanding clause of the 1982 Constitution. The clause allowed the provinces to exempt themselves from laws propagated under the Charter of Rights and Freedoms. It was therefore seen as a way for Quebec to protect its controversial Bill 101, which had made French the official language of Quebec. Though it had come with the repatriation package Bouchard claimed to detest, the same Bouchard certainly liked the notwithstanding clause—and so, he said, did Quebec. If Turner wanted to remove it, he asserted, he was writing off Quebec in this election campaign.

His words might have passed quietly but for the fact that in attacking John Turner, Bouchard was also attacking Brian Mulroney. As recently as June, Mulroney had called the existence of the notwithstanding clause "a mess" and suggested strongly that he was in favour of its removal. In an interview with *The Globe and Mail*, he said it was a surrender of "inalienable" Charter rights.

Following Bouchard's defence of the clause, a Mulroney spokesman came forward to affirm the prime minister's opposition. Since Bouchard and Mulroney had long been at loggerheads over so much of the Trudeau record as it applied to Quebec, it was hardly surprising the matter was starting to come home to roost. A time bomb was set ticking.

Bouchard's next target was the Liberal premier of Ontario, David Peterson. With rhetoric many deemed far-fetched, he said opposition to free trade in Ontario was a plot by the province's establishment to maintain its wealth and power. He went so far as to suggest that there was a parallel between the free trade debate and the 1980 referendum campaign because in both "Liberals, Ontarians, intervened heavily to scare a fraction of the Quebec population into preserving the status quo." There would be a resurgence of the separatist revolt in Quebec if the Free Trade Agreement was not passed, Bouchard warned.

"Have you ever heard such a crock in your whole life?" Peterson responded. Mr. Bouchard "has to really rethink whether he is capable of being a national politician." He was pitting region against region with "extravagant rhetoric."

As the Tory standard-bearer for Quebec in the election, Bouchard had trouble finding the right issue on which to focus. The morality issue didn't develop into much, nor did the Tory record on the environment, which he was prepared to defend. In mid-campaign, when it had become clear that free trade was the only game in town, he spent a couple of days boning up and then campaigned on it.

The Conservatives received a scare midway through the campaign when Turner did well in the debates and his party moved out in front. But the Tories surged in the late going to nail down another majority. In Quebec the result was never in question. Since Trudeau's departure, support for the Liberals had withered. Moreover, Quebec favoured free trade more than any other province. Bouchard crushed his opposition in his home riding, gaining 23,045 votes in almost quadrupling the tally of second-place finisher Jean Paradis of the NDP. The Liberals had had trouble finding a candidate to go against Bouchard and finally sent in a real estate consultant who was living in Montreal. He finished third. During the campaign, 71 percent of those identifying themselves as Péquiste said they intended to vote for Lucien Bouchard. Despite his animosity towards some press reports, Bouchard took comfort in the results. He had formed an abiding distrust of *The Montreal Gazette*, refusing to submit to interviews from its journalists. "I read in *The Gazette* that I'm a fascist," he said, finally sitting down with a reporter from the paper. "It's incredible. I don't have a high opinion of *The Gazette*, OK? I put my cards on the table." The reporter went through files to find the "fascist" reference but couldn't locate one.

Within a fortnight of the Tory triumph, a second straight

majority for Mulroney, the Supreme Court issued a ruling invalidating Quebec's Bill 101 as it pertained to unilingual public signs. When he heard of the decision, Bouchard had a premonition that a decisive moment was at hand.

The ruling prompted a wave of protests by Quebec nationalists demanding that Bourassa keep the bill in force. As Bouchard was to note, "All these people belonged to my political family, and even my real family." Lucien's mother, Alice, got on the phone to him. She didn't normally weigh into political debates with her boys, but this time she spoke about Lucien's niece, Catherine, and how proud she was that she had marched with the protestors in the ice-box temperatures in Jonquière in support of Bill 101.

Bourassa had options. He could comply with the court decision and allow the English to post their signs. Or he could invoke the notwithstanding clause and exempt Quebec from the ruling. His choice was of great importance since it could have an impact on the Meech Lake process. What would be the reaction in English Canada, which was debating Meech Lake, if the premier of Quebec turned his back on a court ruling favouring his English minority?

Bourassa was a notorious fence-sitter, a shaky federalist who tended to cower whenever nationalists showed their teeth. In 1974, he had brought in Bill 22, restrictive language legislation which embittered the Anglophone community. In 1971, owing to nationalist pressures, he had backed off on the constitutional accord agreed to at Victoria.

Now, he was spooked again. In view of the growing nationalist opposition, he decided to invoke the notwithstanding clause to disavow the court decision. He didn't go all the way, however. He tried to throw each side a bone. Bill 101 would remain, insofar as it applied to signs on the exteriors of buildings. Only French signs were allowed there. Indoors, the Anglos would be permitted to post their messages.

His hurried compromise appeased no one, certainly not the Anglophones. It sped Mulroney and Bouchard on a collision course which would have profound consequences—for themselves and for Meech Lake.

The positions of the two men on the notwithstanding clause had already been publicly staked out: Mulroney in opposition, Bouchard in favour. A game of political chicken now began to see who would back down first.

Shortly after the Quebec premier's announcement, Mulroney met with Bouchard and senior government officials at 24 Sussex Drive. The decision was taken to send a letter of rebuke to Bourassa. This was consistent with Mulroney's approach to Grant Devine when the government of Saskatchewan took steps inhibiting minority language rights. Bouchard didn't protest the Sussex decision strenuously. Norman Spector, who was now in charge of federal-provincial relations in the Privy Council Office, detected a mood of resignation from him. Spector, who had been brought into the PMO after serving in the provincial government in British Columbia, was sensitive to Bouchard's concerns. The two men got along well. Since Bouchard tended to judge people by the number of books they read, and Spector read a lot of books, they could talk of matters beyond politics. Like others, Spector thought that in terms of raw talent Bouchard was head and shoulders above the others in Cabinet. But he saw him as terribly unseasoned. Instead of building alliances, which is the real art of politics, he had only one man to go to. He was relying almost wholly on his close ties with Mulroney. The other aspect of Bouchard that worried him was his inflexibility. On some matters, his views were held in the soul, and it was hard to compromise with the soul.

Bouchard returned to his home after the Sussex meeting and called Luc Lavoie, asking him to come over. Lavoie was busy and wondered if it could be put off until the next day. "No, I'll send a car over."

Lavoie found him calm but somewhat shaken. "I just don't understand this place, Ottawa," Bouchard told him. In the Saskatchewan case, no one in Ottawa cared about sending any letter of criticism until he, Bouchard, raised the matter. But now, in a similar case, the federal politicians and bureaucrats wanted to climb all over Quebec. He wondered why they could not see that Quebec's situation was so different. The English language was obviously safe on the continent. French obviously needed extra protection. The crux, recalled Lavoie, was that "Lucien didn't think anyone in English Canada should come into Quebec and tell Quebeckers how to handle the language issue." Lavoie told him that he was going to win some and lose some in Ottawa and that he had to be prepared to take the bad with the good.

Bouchard, however, was not one to shrug something off and move on. He now determined to go to war with his friend, the prime minister. No matter what the consequences, he resolved he was not about to stand idly by and allow Mulroney's letter of reprimand to be sent to Bourassa. The letter was to be written in diplomatic, highly muffled language. It would have likely resulted in a day or two of controversial press reports, not much more. Most politicians, considering the prime minister was entitled to the final word, would have swallowed their pride for a day and let the matter pass. That would be all the more probable in a case where the prime minister was a personal friend who had done umpteen favours for the colleague in question. Moreover, it would eventually become clear that Bouchard wasn't terribly offended by the notion of English signs in Montreal. He would reveal one day that he thought the Bourassa decision was an inadvisable one.

In terms of logic then, it appeared he didn't have much of a case for drawing a line in the sand over the planned letter. But in times like these, as so many who worked with him would attest, Lucien Bouchard did not operate on the basis of logic. What spurred him was emotion—the baggage of the bloodlines.

The day following the Sussex meeting, top-level officials met again with Bouchard in the Langevin Block. Bouchard had asked Lavoie to stand by. Mulroney, who also enjoyed good relations with the go-between from Rimouski, asked him to do the same. He wanted reports.

Every so often Bouchard emerged from the meeting to tell Lavoie what was going on. "These guys think they are going to have me at their disposal," he said at one point. "They won't." The meeting ratified the decision to criticize the Quebec premier. As it adjourned, Bouchard told Lavoie in heavy French, "Fuck them. If this letter goes, I go."

A short time later, Lavoie walked into Bouchard's office and found him drafting a letter of resignation. He'd been in government less than nine months. He had just been elected with Mulroney to a majority. Free trade was passed and now they were moving on to the big one, Meech Lake. Mulroney had guided him every step of the way to prominence and now, as a result of a fuss over a letter, Lucien Bouchard was prepared to walk away from it all.

Lavoie urged him to reconsider. Just then a call came from

Mulroney's office, two floors above. The prime minister wanted to see Bouchard. Their conversation was low-key and grave. Mulroney at one point held up a picture from his by-election visit to Bouchard's riding. Mulroney pointed to a man in the photo whose identity he did not know but who, he told Bouchard, bore a striking resemblance to his father, Ben Mulroney. Bouchard was moved by this, a seeming suggestion that this anonymous supporter was of Mulroney vintage. When he emerged from the meeting, Lavoie could detect how charged it had been. Bouchard wasn't in tears, but not far from it.

Though touched, he was not deterred. Mulroney's attachment to the convictions of his father, as Bouchard would put it, "did not excuse me from my duties toward mine." He began again to write the resignation draft.

Lavoie informed the prime minister, then tried reasoning with Bouchard. "You're making a fool of yourself. You're making an issue where there is no big issue." He sought out others to talk to Bouchard. Derek Burney, Mulroney's former chief of staff, was in Thunder Bay preparing to go to Washington as Canada's ambassador. Bouchard held deep respect for Burney. So did Mulroney. Few had ever run the PMO with such crackerjack efficiency as Derek Burney. Lavoie called him to brief him on the problem and suggested he talk to the prime minister.

Ten minutes later, Mulroney called Lavoie. "Tell Bouchard there will be no letter to Bourassa."

Bouchard had won the showdown. He had forced his friend and superior into total capitulation—with senior ministers and staff all witness to the surrender. One could easily guess Mulroney's feelings about this. His pride was the size of Mount Royal, where he had owned a house—right at the very top. He didn't like backing down to anyone in such a way. He was the prime minister.

But Lucien Bouchard still wasn't finished. He would rub his nose in it some more.

Mulroney had retreated in order to avoid the full-scale crisis that the departure of his prized Quebec lieutenant would trigger. That done, the PM wanted to avert a public disclosure of the rift between them. The Opposition would have a field day. But Bouchard denied him this. After scoring his victory, he told Lavoie that he wanted to meet the press. Lavoie implored him not to do it, but Bouchard insisted, saying the journalists had been after him and he had to respond. He picked up the phone and called Pierre April of the Canadian Press and asked him to come over. He told the reporter that Robert Bourassa was fully justified in using the notwithstanding clause to undercut the Supreme Court decision. The survival of fundamental values in Quebec, such as the French language, had to be assured.

When Lavoie informed Mulroney of this interview, the PM was incensed. This was a public breach of Cabinet solidarity. There would be headlines across the country. Mulroney had only just learned that the Manitoba government of Gary Filmon, responding to Bourassa's ruling, had decided to withdraw the motion from its Legislature to adopt the Meech Lake Accord. Citing this, Mulroney then sent a message to Bouchard. Recalled Lavoie: "I remember Mulroney saying to go talk to this fucking guy and tell him that there are big things going on in this country, bigger than his own fucking ego."

Bouchard had violated Mulroney's first rule of politics—loyalty. Nothing in politics meant more to the Irishman from Baie-Comeau than this. He was a guy who had gone to the wall for his friends all his life. When they were in trouble, Mulroney was the first one there. It was one of his strong points as a politician. He took care of his own. In his first term in office, he had to manage a caucus of 211 MPs and had done so, as almost all agreed, magnificently. Because he had been so loyal to Bouchard, he expected loyalty in return.

When Pierre April's story hit the streets, the House of Commons was sitting and the Opposition was primed. For Question Period, they knew Mulroney and Bouchard, at opposite ends of a key issue, would be sitting ducks. The Tories wanted to get Bouchard out of town on official business of some kind, but he didn't want to leave. He was prepared to go into the House and fight it out. On the one side was the argument that since his job was to safeguard minority languages across the country, and since he was now supporting a decision that did the opposite, he was in flagrant dereliction of duty. On the other hand, he could argue that the provinces had been awarded the right to exercise the notwithstanding clause and Bourassa had acted within that right. As secretary of state he could say he was safeguarding the minority language—French.

Finally he was prevailed upon to leave Ottawa. After scrambling around, his staff was able to arrange a "crucial" meeting in Toronto with Ontario environment minister James Bradley. (Bouchard was also acting environment minister at this time, sitting in for Jean Charest, who had been suspended for phoning a judge.) Bouchard left for the Ontario capital grumbling that he was being forced to behave like a coward, running away from it all.

He now told friends that coming to Ottawa was a mistake, that Mulroney should have left him in Paris. "I had not turned down Lévesque in order to be guardian of the crown jewels in Ottawa." Lucien's brother Roch, teaching at the University of Ottawa, was seeing him from time to time. He found his brother "profoundly shaken by the lack of understanding of Quebec in Ottawa." This "really struck him." Moreover, he was already beginning to lose faith in Mulroney, Roch said. Mulroney was politically astute on Quebec and surrounded himself with good advisers, Roch observed. But he didn't understand the province in an in-depth way and Lucien was coming to realize this. "On the notwithstanding crisis, Lucien found Mulroney lacked force in Ottawa," Roch said.

While Bouchard fidgeted in Toronto, the Turner Liberals demanded his resignation. "*La tête de Lucien Bouchard est réclamée*," ran the headlines. Mulroney was pinned down in the House with questions like the one from Grit MP Robert Gauthier: Who speaks in the name of the government—you or Bouchard? Mulroney did an agile job of nuancing his way through it, putting different spins on his answers, depending on whether he was speaking in French or English. At this time none of the members in the House knew (it wouldn't become public until years later) of Bouchard's threat to resign. This made it easier for the prime minister to play down the split. They didn't realize he had been subjected to an ultimatum. As for Bouchard's absence, which extended over three days, Deputy Prime Minister Don Mazankowski told the Opposition that he was "attending to some very urgent matters."

The crisis came to a close with passions inflamed in Quebec, with Manitoba backing off Meech Lake, with relations between Mulroney and Bouchard indelibly scarred.

What could have prompted his friend to go so far as to blackmail him, Mulroney wondered. Those who bore witness or were close to the action had explanations. Peter White, in a revolving door between the Black empire and Mulroney administration, was back as principal secretary to the prime minister. In Bouchard, whom he liked, White sensed unstable elements, as did Spector. "His initial reaction to many things was an emotional one, not a rational one," said White. "But he's also highly intelligent, so there was the constant battle in composing both sides of his character as he thought things through." Jean Fournier and Benoît Bouchard noticed that on issues that were one step removed from the ones that touched the Quebec soul, he was brilliant. Touch the hot buttons, however, hit on the mythologies of his old-stock Quebec youth, the landmines of his Quebec conscience, and a different man, a volatile, brooding figure, appeared. It was as if he was jolted into a different psychological sphere. In its worst incarnation, as in his explosion in front of Benoît Bouchard at campaign headquarters during the by-election, the man of logic, seized by emotion, turned into an embittered, seething demagogue. "In these instances, what he may have said to you yesterday, no matter how important, means nothing anymore," said Benoît Bouchard.

Speaking from the perspective of someone who greatly admired Bouchard, Luc Lavoie acknowledged his deep emotionalism. "When something affects his integrity, or when something affects his private life or his family, he goes fucking nuts. Really nuts."

Following the crisis, Peter White soon detected a change in Bouchard's attitude. He was more independent of the government. "He was probably saying to himself, 'I'm going to stay on as minister but I'll sort of do what I want and if they don't like it they can fire me.'"

Bouchard knew his relations with Mulroney were forever damaged. "As proud as he was," Bouchard would later reflect, "the prime minister wouldn't readily forget the retreat I had forced him into with the knowledge of his ministers and principal associates. I drew no satisfaction from the situation." In his relations with his long-time ally, he began to feel he had made a big mistake in believing, as he put it, that friendship and power could coexist.

No thought was given to dumping Bouchard. In the midst of the impasse, Mulroney had called upon Bernard Roy, who had returned to practise law in Montreal, to come to Ottawa to try and

calm him down. Keeping Lucien calm would become a preoccupation with the Mulroney camp. Roy and Bouchard were good
friends. They met in the Château Laurier and Roy gave him the
loyalty pitch and he felt—wrongly—that by the end of the session
Bouchard was ready to try again to be a team player.

One of the problems with Lucien, Roy felt, was that "if he
wasn't getting things his way, the world was against him." But as a
fellow Francophone, Roy could understand some of his friend's
frustrations. "You're thrown into this unreal artificial environment
of Ottawa, with the media frenzy, working with [Anglo] bureaucrats
whose jobs have been transmitted from father to son, and you read
in *Le Devoir* and *La Presse* that Quebec is not getting its fair share of
this and that and you start to believe those goddam statistics." The
atmosphere, Roy said, was one in which, despite his tightness with
the PM, Bouchard could easily feel left out.

Bouchard had to cope with these frustrations, noted Roy, and
"he had to cope with something that was very painful for him to
accept—the ostracism from his own family." Though Bouchard
had privately faced down Mulroney, it wasn't enough. Family
members felt he was still too tied to Mulroney's federalism. Gérard
thought he had made a mistake, after Paris, in joining the Mulroney team. Roch had come to believe that Mulroney was too federalist to meet the needs of Quebec. So did the poet Claude
Bouchard, who was a strong *indépendantiste*. Their mother, Alice,
sided with these three sons more than with her eldest boy.

For Christmas 1988, Lucien Bouchard didn't make his custom-
ary trip home to the Saguenay to be with family and friends. He felt
too uncomfortable. He didn't want to face the looks. Bernard Roy
noticed his degree of distress. "I had him for Christmas to our place
in the country with my wife and our folks. He had no other place
to go."

12. The Environmental Centralist

Gérard Bouchard, tall, erect, slimmer and greyer than Lucien, was a man with fierce determination in his eyes. His commitment to Quebec nationalism shone through them, right into the heart of his brother.

Gérard's offices at the University of Quebec in Chicoutimi were in a one-storey, flat-roofed, pearl-painted structure that had all the appeal of an abandoned strip mall. They were located on Chicoutimi's upper plateau of fast-food and crass commercial out-lets, this in contrast to the quaint, postage-stamp town below which stretched the stark majesty of the Saguenay.

The Spartan surroundings wouldn't bother him. Like Lucien, his tastes were straightforward enough. Work, discipline, duty came first in life. Like Lucien, he had inherited a strong sense of responsibility from his parents. Like Lucien, such instincts could not be easily shucked off. They were bred in the bone.

Gérard's fine work as a demographic historian was known well beyond his parochial setting and Lucien would often boast of Gérard's progress. The two of them had been close since child-hood, and now they had another bond, that of achievers. "Lucien holds Gérard in admiration," recalled Bernard Roy. "He venerates Gérard, and Gérard has never hidden his nationalism."

But politics was threatening to break the bond. Lucien's joining hands with Mulroney had deeply troubled him. His ambassador's stint in Paris was tolerable. Gérard had visited him there and Lucien had guided him into his library and offered him a stack of books he had no time to read himself. But his brother becoming a federalist Cabinet minister was going too far. He didn't share Lucien's fondness for Mulroney. The Meech Lake Accord could serve as a starting point, Gérard felt, but he could see that Mul-roney was surely caving in to pressures from English provinces to water it down. "I was afraid Mulroney was going to go too far and that my brother would be caught in the middle of something very difficult to stand."

He was prompted to write a harshly worded letter to Lucien stating why he was in error. The politics of secession being such serious business in the Bouchard home, the letter caused a rupture. Lucien was bitter at being attacked by the most junior brother. Communication was cut off. They didn't talk to one another for days, weeks, months.

Lucien moped about this state of affairs to many in the Mulroney circle. "My being in Ottawa, you see what it is doing. It is breaking my family. My brother won't even talk to me anymore." His listeners got the impression that he wanted them to know what a sacrifice he was making and how much it was hurting him. He wasn't even welcome home for Christmas.

Years later, Gérard would not like recalling the breach. In an initial interview, he spoke defensively of the dispute, saying too much was made of it. In later correspondence, with an astonishing change of mind reminiscent of his brother, Gérard denied the existence of the letter. "I have no personal memory nor any trace of the supposed letter in question. I would be lying to you in saying anything different." When he was presented with evidence that Lucien, Roch and many others had talked about it, Gérard sent a note saying that yes, in fact, the letter did exist. He said he had checked with Lucien, at this time premier of Quebec. The premier had searched through his files and found the letter, Gérard said.

His attempt to erase it from memory was suggestive of his protectiveness towards his brother and of the upset the episode had created. It had been so serious that for Lucien's second wedding in February of 1989, Gérard was not in attendance.

The sense of rejection Lucien felt from other sovereignists preyed on him as well. Bouchard's two close friends, de Belleval and Gaston Ouellet, felt he was being deceived. "I found Meech a trap to say the least," recalled de Belleval. "I couldn't see where it would lead us. And my friend Ouellet agreed with me. We felt it would be taken by English Canada as not a first step, but a last step."

In Quebec, Bouchard was accused of being a sell-out to the federalists while in Ottawa the charge was that he was a sell-out to the separatists. Opponents, including newspaper editorialists, continued to press for his resignation in the wake of his stated differences with Mulroney on the use of the notwithstanding clause.

"Bouchard is certainly free to express his opinion, but if he wants to contradict the prime minister, he can't remain in Cabinet," argued the Liberal Herb Gray. He cited the examples of Anglo-phones—Clifford Lincoln, Herbert Marx, Richard French—who had just quit Bourassa's provincial Cabinet after denouncing the premier's actions on the language bill.

Mulroney didn't have much choice but to keep Bouchard on. Even if he had only wanted to demote him from the Cabinet ranks, he knew it was too risky. It could occasion a revolt in the Quebec caucus, which was largely behind Bouchard. Moreover, Bouchard's ego was not one that could tolerate diminution. He would likely be gone the next day. The dilemma was one of the burdens Mulroney had brought upon himself in inviting so many nationalists into the party. They could hold him to ransom.

Rather than punish him, the prime minister went the opposite route. For his blackmail of December, Lucien Bouchard was pro-moted a few weeks later. Mulroney moved him up from secretary of state to a Cabinet post of major and timely rank, environment. As well, he granted Bouchard's wish for membership on the all-powerful Cabinet body, the Operations Committee.

Instead of being thanked, the prime minister was immediately blind-sided. At his first press conference in the new portfolio, Bouchard made a power grab which astonished the Tory hierarchy and fed the printing presses with "Loose Cannon on Deck" headlines. Bouchard called together twenty journalists. He talked first about the $28 billion deficit. "This deficit question. It's absolutely dramatic. We are killing this government, slowly but surely, if we don't do some-thing very radical." That said, he exempted his own new department from all cuts. He asserted that previously announced lay-offs of 360 environment bureaucrats had been cancelled. "We will not dismiss the people we were supposed to dismiss."

This measure had not been officially endorsed, but it was small fare in comparison to Bouchard's next edict. From now on, Bouchard announced, his environment portfolio would monitor all new government spending projects. "It will not be possible for the government to make a decision without environmental assessment." And, "when environmental considerations conflict with economic considerations, environmental considerations will prevail."

If anyone wasn't sure what this meant, Bouchard cleared it up for them. His department, he stated, will "on a practical basis be invested with a kind of veto power."

The power grab—"*l'état c'est moi*"—stunned Mulroney, not to mention Finance Minister Michael Wilson, who had experienced running battles with Bouchard and was now witness to this usurpation of his powers. Peter White recalled Bouchard's announcement as one of the most ridiculous claims he had ever heard.

Mulroney, undermined by his friend a few weeks earlier, had turned the other cheek, and now the other cheek had been swatted as well. Rather than dress him down personally, the PM had Paul Tellier, the privy council clerk, and deputy PM Mazankowski, call Bouchard up on the carpet and try to drive some sense into his head. A Bouchard spokesman was soon trotted out to make a statement suggesting that no, not all spending projects would be submitted to Mr. Bouchard for his approval.

Bouchard had yet other things on his mind in this dramatic winter. He decided to marry Audrey Best. He had been courting the slender, blond Californian, more than two decades his junior, for almost two years. He boasted frequently to office staff about her. "*Elle est forte!*" ("She is strong!"), he would say, placing particular emphasis on the "t." Though there were gaping differences in age and cultural background, Bouchard's companions thought her a fine choice. She had intellect, strong fundamental values, spoke French, and was perhaps easygoing enough to cope with Bouchard's explosive nature.

The news came as a disappointment to many women. In his making up for lost time, the post-forty Bouchard, dark, virile, simmering with hot Latin vitality and with political power, had become an energetic suitor. He had a long list of women to call on. When he had made his choice of Audrey, he had to get the word out to his many other female friends that he was no longer available. A member of his office was startled one day when he gave her the assignment of calling them up to let them know he was now off-limits.

While most of his Tory colleagues were happy for him and Audrey, there were exceptions. Mila Mulroney still harboured a strong animosity towards Lucien for having left his first wife, Jocelyne. This had created an awkward social situation, but attempts to resolve it, such as orchestrating meetings between Mila and

Audrey, proved unsuccessful. "After the split," recalled Mila, "Audrey would go to my hairdresser, and it was funny how we kept being scheduled at the same times."

At one such session, Audrey opened up on the subject to Mila, tearfully telling her that she was sorry for what had happened. "Look, Audrey," the prime minister's wife responded, "I have no problem with you, but as far as I'm concerned Lucien does not exist." True to her word, when Mulroney held a reception at 24 Sussex Drive for Lucien after the February 1989 wedding, Mila was elsewhere.

Trying hard to keep his friend happy, the prime minister helped out before and after the nuptials. He had Ian MacDonald arrange a bachelor supper for Bouchard at a chic Hull restaurant. Many old friends, dating back to college days in Jonquière and Laval, were invited and the prime minister himself attended, though he didn't stay long. Bouchard gave a moving speech about how the reconciliation effort between French and English was still worth pursuing. He saluted the fine team Mulroney had assembled in Ottawa and said nice words about him.

On a day of freezing temperatures, the wedding, held in the Hull Court House, was a small affair limited to about ten members from immediate families. The prime minister's photographer was on duty there and at the reception. Mulroney presented Audrey and Lucien with a beautiful photo album.

In two big ways Bouchard was beginning a new life. He had a new wife who thrilled him and who could bring him children. He had a new job which freed him of his Mr. Canada garb and engaged him in an issue of global significance. The new environment title played to Bouchard's grand-scale instincts. He could dream big in this portfolio. He could lead nations in a campaign to cleanse the planet. On being appointed he spoke to cabinet colleague Tom McMillan. Bouchard told him he had never done anything of grand significance in his life, but now he had his chance. He gave McMillan the impression that the job meant more to him than anything.

Mr. Clean was becoming Mr. Green. Mulroney was putting some distance between Bouchard and the delicate unity issues, between the bull and the china shop. At the same time, he was bringing gravitas to a department that could use some.

To the new responsibilities, Bouchard brought new staff. Some who might normally have transferred over with him from the old department thought better of it. One who departed said she could no longer tolerate his tantrums. His temper would surely ruin him, she thought. On some days Bouchard was the perfect minister, but on others, she said, it was like demons within had taken over. She considered him brilliant, honest, but too torn and tormented between loyalty to Canada and loyalty to Quebec to maintain a stable equilibrium.

Camille Guilbault, who in her role as overseer of the Quebec caucus saw him frequently, considered Bouchard emotionally immature. She recalled him threatening to resign on a repeated basis. "Why am I staying here! I've got my whole family against me!" Around the staff, he didn't try to hide his anger. On his bad days, he berated people with foul-mouthed binges. Different staffers would try their luck at calming him down.

Another who left, chief of staff Claude Boucher, had many run-ins with Bouchard, but they may have been as much his own doing as the minister's. Boucher had helped him in his success with La Francophonie, and Bouchard thought he had done great work and asked him to take on the new assignment. But Boucher, according to Luc Lavoie, couldn't stand the heat. Lavoie told Bouchard that he therefore should get rid of him. Another employee, however, regarded Boucher as a high-quality professional. She said Bouchard treated Boucher in an inconsiderate, hellish manner, once pulling rank and shouting, "You're just a civil servant. Do what I say."

One of the newcomers was Martin Green, a bright, energetic young man from a good Tory family who had occasioned Mulroney's sarcasm for having supported Joe Clark in the bitter leadership battle. After winning his landslide majority in 1984, Mulroney had spotted Green at a Christmas cocktail party. With a vindictive look, the new PM, in his deep honeyed tones, asked: "Now tell me this, Martin, don't you find Christmas in power to be a little more satisfying than in opposition?" Green responded that it depended on how the power was exercised, and the conversation ended.

Green was highly enthusiastic about joining Bouchard. Little of the behind-the-scenes turmoil of recent weeks was known. Environment was the hot portfolio and Bouchard was the star, the coming force. Many close to Mulroney felt that the PM had brought Bouchard to Ottawa with the intention of grooming him as his successor. Despite all the problems in his first year, it was a view still held by many Conservatives, most notably leadership aspirants.

Bouchard and Green established warm relations on the first day and didn't look back. During the initial briefings by departmental seniors, one official showed a particular enthusiasm for coating his thoughts in bureaucratese. In responding to a Bouchard query, he opined, "Well sir, I don't want to tell you more about that issue now because we are preparing a menu of evolving targets on it." Leaving the meeting, a puzzled Bouchard asked Green, "Martin, this menu of evolving targets, what on earth might this be?"

"I think it's bullshit, sir," Green replied.

"Yes, absolutely," said Bouchard. "Bullshit. That's what I thought too. Thank you, Martin."

No sooner had Bouchard moved into his new offices in Les Terrasses de la Chaudière in Hull than he was hit with a mini-scandal over furniture purchases. Press reports alleged he had spent $40,000 in taxpayers' money on office renovations, including a tidy $2,700 for a glass door. For Bouchard, the tempest brought back intolerable memories of his supposed squandering of public money on taxi trips and on a pair of fancy courtroom trousers while working for the Quebec government. He responded quickly this time, firing off letters to newspaper editors explaining that increased staff required desks and chairs. The costly glass door was to separate the minister's secretarial pool from the other workers.

Another potential brouhaha was occasioned by the arrival of an exorbitantly priced set of mahogany bookcases to house Bouchard's leather-bound classics. Before it arrived, Bouchard had received a press alert—a freedom-of-information inquiry on the cost of his new accoutrements. When the bookcases were deposited in his office, Bouchard asked the price. "$12,000," came the reply.

Martin Green was there to see his new minister go through the roof. "$12,000! How could you do this to me! I want those book-cases out! Out!" Green promptly followed the order, had them shipped elsewhere, and reckoned that within a couple of days the matter would pass. But he didn't yet understand Bouchard's degree of sensitivity to questions affecting his personal honour. "Bouchard," recalled Green, "got so emotional about these god-dam bookcases that he wouldn't work in the departmental offices anymore." The offices were forever stigmatized. "He'd only work in his office on Parliament Hill. He wouldn't go back to the department. Just the memory of the bookcases."

Bouchard went to Ikea, bought cheaper ones and insisted on installing them himself. His foray to the store made news and Ikea took advantage. It ran big ads in the local newspapers saying "Lucien. Your Order Is Ready." The ad thanked him for showing both fiscal responsibility and good taste.

Green found Bouchard delectably naive, especially when in English Canada. One time the two of them journeyed to Athabasca, Alberta, where the issue was the impending demise of a pulp and paper mill partly because of costly environmental regulations. Appearing before the local chamber of commerce, Bouchard announced that he really didn't wish to talk about the mill, but rather about Meech Lake.

With all due sincerity and innocence, he entered into a long and boring treatise on the Constitution, this in a province where the C word was arsenic. Seated in the audience, Green began to sense the discomfort. Muffled groans were audible. "Oh, Jeezus Christ," muttered one despairing listener. Then, as Bouchard droned on, a man sitting next to Green tapped him on the shoulder and pointed at the minister. "Does this guy know where the fuck he is?"

Before long, many among the listeners got up and walked out. "I thought," recalled Green, "we were going to be lynched."

On the road they would sit down to dinners with provincial ministers or other officials and Bouchard would inevitably pull out his own credit card to pay. Green would remind him that this was government business and there was no need. "Really!" Bouchard would reply. He'd often pay himself anyway, not even thinking about it.

Bouchard impressed Green with his knowledge of political philosophy. He waxed on about the American Revolution and Thomas Jefferson, a figure whom he placed right near the top of his list of heroes. Green knew enough about the career of the Virginian to sense why Bouchard might be so interested. Jefferson was a lawyer, an ambassador to Paris, the founder of a new political party, the governor of a state, an author of the Declaration of Independence and the president of the new independent nation. "This was a great man," Bouchard repeatedly told his aide.

Another new staffer was Patricia Dumas. She had worked as a newspaper reporter for *Le Devoir* and *La Presse* and had recently served as an adviser in Ottawa to another suspiciously sovereignistic Tory from Quebec, Marcel Masse. Her job was to streamline Bouchard's office operations and help him wade through the bureaucratic maze of government. Bouchard, she noticed, had come to Ottawa thinking he could just step in and change the world. "He hated the process of big government machinery. He didn't know how the system really functioned. His power was political. His power was being close to Mulroney, and his power was his mind and his charisma." For Bouchard, Dumas noted, the principle was what counted. Once he got the principle right, that was it. All other considerations could be swept aside. This was a very Gallic mind at work in this regard, thought Dumas.

She was only a few weeks into the job when she wanted out. The intellectual, charismatic side of Bouchard certainly had its appeal. But Dumas found him erratic, foul-mouthed and bitchy, sometimes "a monster" in his dealings with people. Her plan to overhaul the office organization led to a bitter confrontation with him, but relations modestly improved.

For Quebec issues, Bouchard brought in Robert Charest, Jean's brother. Bouchard's relationship with the young Jean Charest, one of Mulroney's favourite ministers, was close at this time, making things all the better for Robert. Like Martin Green, he was enthusiastic about coming on board because he thought Bouchard had a great future. "What Lucien wanted, Lucien would get. He just had to place a phone call to Brian." Bouchard's refreshing candour initially appealed to him. He wasn't straitjacketed by bureaucratic and political tradition. He vigorously opposed, for example, the tradition of party discipline mandating that MPs vote the party line in knee-jerk fashion even if their consciences told them differently. How did this make sense, Bouchard chafingly wondered. One such piece of legislation was Michael Wilson's GST. Bouchard hated it but had to support and promote it, travelling to Quebec to tell lies about its benefits. This drove him into a rage, recalled Dumas, an absolute rage. He was being asked to defy his own principles.

Though he admired Mulroney, it was clear to his advisers that Bouchard didn't relish the idea of being number two. They began to sense a rivalry between them. They didn't find Bouchard to be cravenly ambitious in the sense that he was always shrewdly planning his next career move. But when he was involved in something, he wanted to control it. He was "a control man," said Dumas. "He was absolutely at ease with total control." Robert Charest, who grew disenchanted with Bouchard, felt he had a spoiled child's mentality in that he always demanded to get his own way. With his very selective memory, he said, he could always convince himself he was right. "He reminded me of my five-year-old son."

Bouchard knew the PM so well, analysed Green, that he could always tell how he would come down on issues. "But one of the things I noticed about the relationship was that there was obviously a hugely competitive streak between the two of them. I think when you have friends like that it's not sort of uncommon. I think the prime minister let it be known once in a while that he was prime minister, that I'm the guy who is making the decisions here." In his own mind Bouchard appeared to feel that he was entitled to the favoured place in such a competition. He confided to one of his advisers, this after spending a year in Ottawa, that he was losing faith in Mulroney, that Mulroney was not as bright as he had originally thought.

Their bond, loosened by the events of winter, was not helped by other players' movements in the PMO. Bouchard's friend Bernard Roy had returned to Montreal to practise law. His Anglophone ally Derek Burney had left to become ambassador in Washington. Burney's replacement, Stanley Hartt, was no fan of Lucien Bouchard, nor did he have much sympathy for the interests of the Quebec caucus. The other figure of enormous importance in the Langevin Block was Paul Tellier, the clerk of the Privy Council. The environment minister's relations with him were up and down. He respected Tellier's ability but complained often of the vast power he and other unelected officials wielded. They had not submitted themselves to the democratic will of the people. How did they rate such power? It was a lament which struck some as rather curious, given that Bouchard had wielded so much power as an adviser to Mulroney and as ambassador in Paris.

In the environment portfolio, Bouchard mastered the issues quickly, impressing the deputy minister and other senior bureaucrats. In the initial months, he brought together ideas for a grand scheme, a master plan to ensure the protection of the environment for decades to come. While preparing it, he announced programs to reduce the incidence of ozone-damaging chlorofluorocarbons, to check water pollution from pulp mills and create more national parks. For Bouchard, forests were treasures, the parks of Canada "a mystical thing." On parks policy, he agreed with Jean Chrétien who, two decades earlier, had created two new spectacular parks in Quebec, one in his own riding of La Mauricie. In so doing, Chrétien had met strong resistance from the Quebec government for allegedly interfering in its affairs. Bouchard thought in instances like this that Quebec nationalists were going too far.

He was quickly embroiled in a controversy over the illegal transport of toxic wastes into Canada from the United States. *The Globe and Mail* revealed that Bouchard's department had been warned about the wastes—including cancer-causing PCBs—but had not acted. Opposition MPs hounded him, but Bouchard handled the situation with aplomb, coming clean, admitting it could have been handled better while pointing to mitigating circumstances for why it hadn't.

In the fall of 1989, he began talking up his grand Green Plan, a five-year commitment that "will change radically the way of life" for Canadians. While not revealing the details, with each month in office he ratcheted up the rhetoric. Canada was facing a "terrible, insidious danger," he said. On the greenhouse effect, which led to global warming, he grew highly eloquent, as if he'd been reading his Churchill biographies. "We must find a policy for this country to fight this terrible enemy, this subversive enemy, this silent enemy which is destroying the planet now."

He was the new eco-statesman. What better way to appeal to his heroic ideal than leading a campaign to save the planet? The fight for the environment, he asserted, was "the fight for life itself."

To his distress, he had difficulty persuading Cabinet colleagues to think the same. In Cabinet, outside of some Quebec members, he had few allies. His style, which at times bordered on the intellectually arrogant, tended to alienate the others. He had the problem of being seen by larger players as a possible threat to their own ambitions. Because of his precipitate actions, as in his initial environmental edict, he was viewed as a prima donna. Green watched him in Cabinet committee meetings. "A number of the more experienced ministers treated him with a lot of scepticism and a lot of it was Bouchard's force of personality. Sometimes you saw it didn't have a lot to do with the issues. It had more to do with—who is this upstart coming in here and telling us what will happen? They didn't like his style. Bouchard would say 'yes, of course, I'll be making a decision on that,' not realizing that two or three other ministers had an interest."

Egos were wounded. Green noticed jealousy over his relationship with the prime minister, a jealousy that led some to try and block him. "I think this had a lot to do with the attitude Lucien came to have towards English Canada and Ottawa. He felt that he wasn't getting the support from his colleagues that he should have." One exception was Joe Clark, who he had gotten along well with in Paris after some initial tension and who often backed him at the Cabinet table. Clark, by now, was savvy enough to realize not to mess with the PM's kingpin. The kingpin was touchy. When Charles Caccia, the environment critic for the Liberals, suggested Cabinet would not support his grandiose Green Plan and Bouchard would suffer political defeat, Bouchard made headlines with a suggestion he was prepared to stake his career on it. "I'm not that concerned about my political career; I care more about the environment."

For many who worked for him, the words had too familiar a ring. Here was Lucien casting himself as martyr again. He had threatened to resign over the dispute on the notwithstanding clause. He was intimating with his statements on Meech Lake that he would resign if the accord was not passed. Now he was suggesting he would be prepared to sacrifice his career for the sake of his Green Plan.

His performance in the portfolio was striking for other reasons as well. As environment minister, Bouchard was a centralist. His lifelong political credo, of course, had been of the opposite strain, supporting a broad devolution of powers from Ottawa to Quebec. Now, viewing the country from the federal government's perspective, his tack altered. In a remarkable speech in Montreal, Bouchard urged governments to forget sterile arguments about which level has jurisdiction over what. If anything, the speech, at least in terms of environmental policies, appeared to suggest less power to the provinces. In the British North America Act the word environment or its equivalent wasn't mentioned, meaning the only certainty in regard to jurisdictional powers was ambiguity. To premiers like Alberta's Don Getty and Quebec's Robert Bourassa, Bouchard was going overboard in pressing for federal regulatory powers.

Under Bouchard, a new tool, the Canadian Environmental Protection Act, was passed which gave the federal side added clout in overriding provincial regulations. Bouchard's first use of it was against Quebec, a province which had jealously guarded its powers of environmental oversight. At St.-Basile-le-Grand in 1988, a PCB fire spewed dangerous toxins into the atmosphere, prompting Bouchard to step in, label the affair "a national embarrassment" and sign an order under his new act, regulating PCBs. The new protection legislation, observed Amir Attaran, a specialist in environmental law, gave Bouchard "a lovely stick with which to beat polluters and do-nothing provincial governments." With the action at St.-Basile, "Mr. Bouchard had introduced Canada to federal environmental primacy." As minister, he "styled himself at the sharp edge of environmental federalism."

In a dispute over Hydro-Québec's Great Whale River dam project, Bouchard went to war on Ottawa's behalf against Quebec's environment minister, Pierre Paradis. Paradis argued that only 5 percent of federal lands would be affected by the project and that therefore federal input should be limited accordingly. Bouchard wanted no such limitation. He pushed for a federal review process with independent commissions holding public hearings. Legal precedent required such a role for Ottawa, he stated. Court interpretation of federal authority meant that if such a process wasn't carried out, anyone would be legally free to bring forward an injunction and stop construction on major projects such as the one in Quebec.

André Tremblay worked as an adviser to Bourassa during this period. Tremblay had changed since his Laval days and had become a federalist. He was shocked that his friend Bouchard, who had moved in the other direction, could take such a strong stance against Quebec. Of his legislation on environmental impact studies on new projects, Tremblay said Bouchard was "responsible for the enactment of one of the most centralizing acts ever adopted by the federal government. This legislation meant that in the final analysis Hydro-Québec was under the supervision of the federal

government. You cannot sweep under the rug this reality."
Bouchard and Bourassa generally got along well, Tremblay noted,
but relations turned sour over what the premier saw as Bouchard's
power grab.

Many of Bouchard's policies in Environment created an impression that he wasn't so concerned about which level of government
had the power so long as he, the control guy, had the power.

Just as intriguing as his environmental centralism was his new
take on bilingualism. One aspect of Trudeau's governance that
Bouchard always appeared to support was his bilingualization of
the public service and of the education system across Canada.
Beginning in the 1950s and in his editorials in the Jonquière student paper, Le Cran, Bouchard had called for a great broadening of
linguistic capacities.

As late as 1987, in speaking of La Francophonie and the reach
of the French language in an interview with a Quebec magazine,
Bouchard said that in Canada, "the bilingualism instituted by
Pierre Elliott Trudeau and Gérard Pelletier has even been a means
of healing differences. It has allowed high-level Francophone civil
servants, for so long confined to the Quebec government, to come
into the federal government in Ottawa. Today, to have a successful
political career in Canada, you have to be bilingual."

In Toronto in November 1989 in a speech to the French-
Canadian Association of Ontario, he appeared to switch gears.
Bilingualism in Ontario too often amounted to Francophones
speaking English, he charged. Twenty years of bilingualism hadn't
stopped the assimilation of Francophones. Trudeau and Chrétien
dreamed of a "homogenized Canada" in which the provinces were
a necessary evil. "This country, which is Trudeau's, is not a country.
It's the concept of a bureaucrat in which division dominates and
confrontation replaces the willingness to work together."

Quebec was too inward-looking, and it was time for it to
create a solidarity with Francophones in the rest of Canada,
Bouchard said in his speech. By giving more powers to the
provinces through the Meech Lake Accord, minorities like the
Francophones outside Quebec would have their rights much better
protected than under the federal government, he added. Such
words also appeared to constitute a remarkable about-face. In his
role as secretary of state, Bouchard had recently seen what could

happen to minority language rights when the provinces had more say. He had been stunned when, left to their own devices, Saskatchewan and Alberta had brought in laws striking down minority Francophone rights. He had led the federal government intervention. Then he had watched as Quebec turned its back on a Supreme Court decision protecting the English language in that province.

His Toronto speech did not go unnoticed. "You can accuse Pierre Trudeau of all kinds of things," wrote Lysiane Gagnon in *La Presse*. "But the last thing you can reproach him for is not coming to the aid of French minorities or the cause of the French in Canada." For years Trudeau had been denigrated throughout Western Canada for trying to force the French language down people's throats. It was clear, wrote Gagnon, that anyone who could make Bouchard's type of accusation had rarely set foot in English Canada. "Never will one hear a Francophone living in English Canada criticize the Trudeau vision of minorities. Under Trudeau the French language emerged from the darkness and profoundly transformed the face of English Canada." Urban elites across the country were sending their children to French-immersion classes. The language had become an important part of the Canadian culture and a symbol of prestige for professionals. All this, wrote Gagnon, "comes directly from that vision of bilingual Canada that Mr. Bouchard, with extraordinary thoughtlessness, tries to demolish."

Bouchard's seemingly contradictory stances raised the question, as they had before: What could lead such an extraordinarily bright man to such strange leaps of logic? The response of Patricia Dumas was the same as that of many others. "When you're driven by passion," she said, "you're not rational."

13. "HE JUST EXPLODED"

There was still that chance as the decade closed that they could bring it all together; that Lucien Bouchard would find in himself a spirit of compromise and become a team player, that Meech Lake would be passed, that his Green Plan would make it beyond draft form. There was even a chance that Canadian politics could one day see Bouchard succeed Mulroney, thus blending the solitudes and forging a new national harmony.

All was possible, but improbable. The fire in one man's insides burned too deeply for this kind of peace. Clashes of ego and pride now took centre stage in the drama and darker instincts ruled the day.

In the final month of 1989, Bouchard lost about twenty pounds. Some strange gum infection drained away his strength, leaving him pale and weak. Rather than the brimming combatant with the rapier thrusts of a Cyrano, Bouchard now wore a haggard look of discontent. The mouth drooped. He moved about like the grim reaper, seeing enemies at every stop.

At the best of times he didn't have the typical politician's adren- aline, the stuff that drove them to press flesh and work rooms and gorge on the small talk and sound pathetically pre-scripted. Bouchard hated that, couldn't feed off it, could not—at this stage anyway—wade into a crowd of well-wishers and come out renewed. The adrenaline wasn't the same as, say, Mulroney's. Bouchard's nat- ural habitat was to be alone.

Rather than burn and renew, it seemed to aides that Bouchard was working on one—seemingly inexhaustible—tank. The family still worried about his degree of resilience. He had always overex- tended himself. But he was never under the kind of stress he was now. His mountain-climbing friends, de Belleval and Ouellet, did regular physical workouts to prepare for their excursions up the cliffs, but Bouchard never prepared. Nonetheless he assaulted the mountains with the same vigour and boasted of how he could keep up. So they didn't worry about their friend's health—though they knew the stress was accumulating.

This pressure was augmented when the prime minister appointed him Quebec lieutenant, leader of the big Quebec caucus, early in the new year. He was heading the taxing portfolio of the environment, he was trying to sell Meech Lake across the country, he was on the top Cabinet committees and now he had all of the Quebec Tories to keep happy, not to mention his other families.

In the early 1960s, Lester Pearson heaped a comparable burden of responsibility on his shining star from Quebec, Guy Favreau. He was justice minister, House leader and Quebec lieutenant, and he couldn't cope with it all. In the corridors they said the workload might kill him. He mismanaged a couple of controversies, became enmeshed in fabricated scandals and slowly receded from the action, a broken man. A few years later he died prematurely, acute stress among the reasons.

Arthur Campeau, a reputed Montreal lawyer, was appointed by Mulroney as a special envoy on the environment, in part to ease some of Bouchard's burden. Having worked at Mulroney's former law firm, Campeau was a very close friend of the PM's and the appointment did not sit well with Bouchard. He was suspicious, even jealous, thought Campeau. Bouchard didn't want anyone presuming to share the special access he had. He soon grew to detest Campeau. "Keep that man away from me," he told his staff.

His degree of suspicion was due, in part, to exhaustion, the special envoy thought. "You almost needed a superhuman to carry the load he was carrying," Campeau said. At one point he suggested to both Bouchard and the PM that Bouchard should take a few days for some rest and recreation. But Bouchard would have none of it.

On long overseas flights, Campeau expected the environment minister to put his seat back and rest his mind. But no sooner would Bouchard be done with official business than out would come the heavy reading. "He took out these great big thick goddam books and I wondered where the hell does he get the time to read something like that," recalled Campeau. "The books were always, you know, Alexander the Great, Julius Caesar. Invariably they related to some monumental figure in history."

Early in 1990, Bouchard was facing crises or near-crises on several fronts. On the environment, forces of retrenchment led by

Michael Wilson were ganging up on his prized Green Plan. Bouchard appeared to recognize the gravity of the budget problem but not as it pertained to his own department. On the Meech Lake Accord, a push that was on to make changes to satisfy dissenting provinces incensed him. A rebellion was brewing within his Quebec caucus on this account. It was his job to keep the lid on—though many suspected what he really wanted to do was rip it right off.

To work his way through the thicket it was apparent that now, more than ever, a very close collaboration with Brian Mulroney was necessary. It was a year since the split over the notwithstanding clause and Bouchard's wild announcement on taking over the environment portfolio. When he had been told of Mulroney's angry reaction to the latter, Bouchard, with an exclamation point, had told a colleague to relay a message: "You have to take me as I am!" Rarely had a Canadian prime minister been saddled with such an unruly lieutenant. Henri Bourassa's fractious relations with Wilfrid Laurier led to a profound split, though they later re-established good personal relations. Lester Pearson's close ally Walter Gordon eventually left him after the disaster that was Gordon's 1963 budget. But Gordon was a much more calm and stable force than Bouchard. Trudeau had some bruising clashes with his dear friend Jean Marchand, who left the government over a dispute on bilingualism in air-traffic control. But Marchand wasn't one to berate the PM publicly and they remained friends. Trudeau humiliated his close colleague Jean Chrétien when he tabled what was tantamount to a mini-budget in 1978 without telling Chrétien, then the finance minister, of his plans.

But Mulroney could only dream of having a lieutenant as loyal as Chrétien was through the Trudeau years. In 1978, Chrétien swallowed his pride and stayed on. As he excitedly told voters with his cement-mixer voice, he was always prepared to carry the load for the boss. He liked the football analogy. "Trudeau give me da ball. Everybody pile on me. But when dey get up, who still got da ball?? Da little guy from Sha-win-igan!!!"

Mulroney and Bouchard had always viewed each other as equals, as part of a team. In Ottawa this worked for a time, but after a year or so the hierarchy was imposing itself. "Their souls connected until they knew they were put in a situation that one was boss of the other," said Luc Lavoie. "Lucien could not accept that."

With all the changes in the front office a third force had entered the mix, and it proved to be a lethal one. Stanley Hartt, Burney's replacement as chief of staff, was a distinguished Montreal labour lawyer and a friend of Mulroney's. When Mulroney became PM, he coaxed Hartt into coming to Ottawa as deputy minister of finance under Michael Wilson. Hartt had a brilliantly logical mind and was never one to doubt its immodest capacities. Initially he got along passably with Bouchard, but as the new decade opened, the relationship turned bitter.

As chief of staff, Hartt wanted to control the Mulroney agenda as Derek Burney had. But Hartt was no Derek Burney. Hartt was bilingual, had studied in Paris, lived most of his life in Quebec. Burney was unilingual without a Quebec background. But paradoxically it was Burney who showed a diplomatic sensitivity towards Quebec and Lucien Bouchard. As for Hartt, PMO staffers were almost unanimous in their estimation of him. He was antagonistic, often brazenly so, to the Quebec caucus, to anything smacking of Quebec nationalism and to Lucien Bouchard.

Bouchard soon found himself without the same easy access to Mulroney he had before. A pit bull was guarding the door, one who didn't want to hear any whining about the maltreatment of Quebec. Hartt treated the Quebec caucus "like a bunch of hoodlums," said Camille Guilbault. She had a hard time believing her ears when he continually downgraded Quebec priorities. Luc Lavoie was astonished. At the beginning of the year he saw a memo in which Hartt had listed the top five priorities for the government in 1990. Not one Quebec issue was on the list, recalled Lavoie, not even Meech Lake! "I've been twenty years in Ottawa and I've got a pretty thick skin about this stuff. But I never heard anyone speak so openly against French Canadians as Stanley Hartt did, so openly it was driving me nuts, it was driving Bouchard nuts, it was driving a lot of other people nuts."

Hartt felt he could match wits with anyone, and it seemed, as Norman Spector looked on, that he wanted to knock Bouchard down a peg. He had "just a very quick mind and an even quicker mouth and he would engage Lucien in some pretty fundamental discussions and not always with the greatest of diplomacy," said Spector. "He thought he could win such arguments. As opposed to trying to reason through them, he was trying to win them."

Some of the disputes, or "pissing matches" as one observer termed them, became rather heated. Bouchard's attitude, recalled Lavoie, was, "I'm the minister. I sit at the Cabinet table. You don't. So shut up." Hartt wasn't always prepared to shut up. He held an important advantage. As chief of staff he had the prime minister's ear on a daily basis while Bouchard was away working with his departmental bureaucrats.

Another change in the PMO dynamic frustrated Bouchard. With Hartt in place, noted Norman Spector, Paul Tellier had much greater access to Mulroney than he did under Burney. Bouchard's relations with Tellier had been cooling considerably and now he had another interlocutor on the PM's doorstep whom he couldn't rely on for support.

The bad blood with Hartt reached the point where communication was severed. Bouchard stopped returning his calls. He began to put the word out that Hartt was sinking the ship. "I heard frequently from Bouchard how he felt that Hartt was impossible to deal with," said Peter White. Hartt, noted White, was like many lawyers in that he was "disorganized and didn't know how to run things." As for managing the delicate Quebec situation, "Stanley didn't have the patience or political inclination to do the job."

The Hartt problem, inspired, some believed, by Hartt's experiences as a member of Montreal's Jewish minority, did not escape Mulroney's attention. His political antennae were too sharp for that. But rather than move to mend the breach, Mulroney made a decision which deeply exacerbated the antagonisms and drove Bouchard to the breaking point.

Ever since coming to Ottawa, Lucien Bouchard had been making it bone-crushingly clear that he would tolerate no alterations to the Meech Lake Accord. But faced with mounting opposition to it, Mulroney had little choice but to try and reach some kind of compromise—modifications or supplements to the accord—which would appease the naysayers.

The opponents of the pact were primarily Liberals: the Liberal governments of Newfoundland and New Brunswick, Liberal opposition leader Sharon Carstairs in Manitoba, whose support was vital to the future of the accord in that province, and the presumed leader-in-waiting of the federal Liberal Party, Jean Chrétien. In a speech in January 1990 which was vetted by Pierre Trudeau,

Chrétien stated his reservations to the priority given the distinct society clause in the accord. He said there had to be changes in order for him to support it. Bouchard was furious. "Chrétien is constitutional disaster," he said.

Mulroney decided that Chrétien was the key in the mix. If he could get him on board, the dissenting Liberals in the provinces would follow. But Mulroney knew he could not be seen to be making a pact with a man Bouchard considered the devil incarnate. It would have to be done with the utmost secrecy.

Norman Spector headed up the federal-provincial relations secretariat. He seemed a likely choice to carry out the secret mission. But Spector was seen as a little too close to Bouchard in his sympathies. Mulroney wanted someone of the opposite stripe, someone with whom the Liberals would feel comfortable. He chose Stanley Hartt.

Hartt began meeting on the sly with Eric Maldoff, a close Chrétien associate. Not even the man in charge of the file, Spector, was informed of what was going on.

As Pierre Blais and other Tory Cabinet ministers were discovering, Bouchard was far less effective without a tight lifeline to the boss. Blais, a lawyer who represented a riding in Bouchard's region, had spent two weeks campaigning for him in his by-election. They had become reasonably good friends, going out together occasionally with their wives. Unlike Bouchard, Blais had worked his way up the political ladder the hard way. He didn't know Mulroney, or the top Tory brass. He fought to get a nomination, to get his name known, to win a seat, to establish credibility once in Ottawa.

He was somewhat taken aback to see how easy it was for others, to see Bouchard roar in from Paris and act like he owned the place. "Him, you know, if there was a problem, if he was discussing it around the Cabinet table with other ministers, and there was a roadblock, what did he do? He turned to the little table beside him, he picked up the telephone and telephoned Mulroney and said, 'I want it.'"

Lucien "never knew what it was to pull his own weight in politics." He'd been spoiled, and when he found out he could no longer get his own way, said Blais, it didn't take a genius to figure out how he would react. He'd go away and pout and shout and curse the gods. Mulroney knew of his mercurial nature. But in the crunch, no matter how many warnings he was receiving, he believed Lucien would stick with him.

While Mulroney opened the secret channel through Hartt to the Grits, a second clandestine operation was set in motion, this time from the other side of the trenches. The Parti Québécois, still in Opposition, saw an opportunity to enhance its position by exploiting the growing divisions among the Tories over Meech Lake. The PQ had lost some supporters as a result of the nationalist net Mulroney had cast across Quebec. Now the party saw a way of bringing them back to the fold. By encouraging the split, by destabilizing the federal Quebec caucus, it could help provoke defections. The idea had been long floated in the party of creating a federal wing. There was talk now of using Tory defectors to form a base for such a party—an Ottawa bloc.

Two prominent PQ members began making secret contacts with Tory caucus members. One was Marc-André Bedard, Bouchard's long-time friend from Chicoutimi who was practising law back home. The other was Bernard Landry, a leading lieutenant in the Lévesque years, one of the strongest and most capable members of the party. They made calls and held meetings with potential dissidents. Pierre Blais estimated that about fifteen within the Quebec caucus were pressured during the initial months of 1990. Bedard and Landry's pointman inside Mulroney's Tories was François Gérin. An MP from Sherbrooke with a strong nationalist bent, Gérin was ready to defect and to try and take a pack with him.

Bouchard's staff had a sense of what he was up to. "I kept warning Bouchard about Gérin," recalled Robert Charest. The PQ plotters would claim that they didn't contact Bouchard about their plans. Bouchard himself would leave the impression of being unaware of the draft-back movement in the early months of its existence. Several who worked for him, however, had different recollections. They said he knew very well what was going on and was in no hurry to stop it. "Bouchard would talk about the possible formation of a bloc," said Martin Green. "But he pretended he didn't want to hear much about it."

Always a man of alternating political allegiances, he was playing the cunning double game again—just as he had done in Paris, just as he had done with federalists and sovereignists throughout his career. Despite his mountain of problems, he was still a prize commodity both for the Tories and the PQ. On the federal side, he was clearly the dominant force in the Quebec caucus. Mulroney could not afford to see him go. At the same time, his popularity among nationalists in his home province had grown. Though he was a centralist on the environment, his vocal fervour on Meech Lake, his defence of Bill 101, his piercingly pro-Quebec rhetoric more than compensated. Anyone contemplating the idea of a PQ wing in Ottawa would first have to think of Lucien Bouchard.

Martin Green accompanied him to Quebec on several visits and was struck by the reaction. "It was unbelievable. It was like people there were seeing some sort of movie star. He was revered. He was the most popular politician in Quebec." His friend Mulroney meanwhile was falling terribly, along with his party, in public favour. One of the few things he had going for him was Bouchard, and Bouchard was leaning in an opposite direction.

Bouchard had two paths wide open before him—Mulroney's unity train and the PQ's sovereignty track. The more obstacles thrown up in front of him in Ottawa, the more he tended to look the other way. Mulroney's declining popularity had an effect on him as well. Mulroney, he told advisers, had become too caught up in his own importance and had lost touch with average Canadians. His boardroom style and his hyperbole, Bouchard told Green, cut him off from the ordinary people. "I think Bouchard thought there was a bit of the boy-in-the-bubble thing happening to Mulroney. Mulroney would often talk to Bouchard about all the heads of state he'd been speaking to and the big international meetings and so on. Bouchard was very cognizant about this." Bouchard would point to the polls and say to Green, "By the way, here's where we get elected—by the people."

The Prime Minister's Office was hearing of possible defections from its Quebec membership. It had indications Bouchard himself could not be counted upon. This became ringingly clear one day in February when Ian MacDonald went to see Bouchard at his Parliament Hill office.

The speech-writer had been made to wonder about the environment minister's loyalty in a previous conversation. Bouchard had been doing some campaigning for the Tory candidate, Serge Bégin, in a Quebec by-election. Bouchard told MacDonald a story about meeting up with a constituent who was shovelling snow. "Meech Lake is worth nothing," the snow-shoveller said. He made reference to the Quiet Revolution—*la révolution tranquille*. "Next time," he told Bouchard, "we'll do *la souveraineté tranquille*." Bouchard drew great significance from this observation. He told MacDonald there was a moral to the snow-shoveller's story: "Brian is screwed."

The meeting in Bouchard's office concerned a big speech on Meech Lake to be given to Toronto's Empire Club on Flag Day, February 15th. MacDonald had looked at a rough draft and found some of the stuff Bouchard wanted in the speech to be a little harsh for Anglophone sensibilities. He visited Bouchard to talk about it over breakfast. It was January and it was white outside and pristine—a perfect Canadian winter's day. The cold sun fired through the environment minister's office, highlighting the furnishings in golden splendour. MacDonald surveyed his surroundings, and noticed the Quebec flag, the fleur-de-lis. It stood out sharply, but there was no Canadian flag next to it. MacDonald looked around the room. No Canadian flag anywhere!

MacDonald left shaking his head, wondering what kind of statement this minister of the Crown was trying to make. He had the information relayed to a disbelieving prime minister. The next day a Canadian flag was put up in Lucien Bouchard's office.

His speech to the Empire Club was a source of deep aggravation. Given his eloquence, Bouchard was accustomed to writing his own speeches. He didn't like team productions, but this speech was being vetted to death. The missing flag hadn't exactly inspired confidence in his allegiance. When the day of delivery came, he was handed a final, approved copy just before he scaled the podium. As he read it, he discovered the emasculators at the PMO had taken all the juice out of it, robbing him of a big moment. The next day when he picked up the newspapers, he could hardly find any coverage. He was smoking mad and made a vow. "I decided I would never again let anyone reduce my speeches to platitudes."

During these times, he was full of strange acts and strange declarations. Having condemned English-Canadian provinces for backsliding on the Meech Lake Accord, Bouchard came to a press conference to tell a different tale. More likely, he asserted, his own Quebec brethren had prompted the mounting opposition to

Meech Lake. In bringing in Bill 178 forbidding the use of the English language on outdoor commercial signs, the Bourassa government had triggered opposition to the accord in the rest of Canada.
After all, noted Bouchard, how could English Canadians be expected
to be sympathetic towards French minorities when Francophones
were introducing such scornful legislation? Of the anti-Meech
movement, Bouchard said, "the determining factor, the event that
triggered it, was Bill 178." He added, "I can't hide it. The reaction
of the rest of the country, English Canada, is definitely negative."

At the press conference, he made reference to his own position
on the legislation. As an original defender of Bourassa's bill at the
time, Bouchard, by extension, was including himself in those to be
faulted for Meech Lake's problems. Contradictions sometimes
come back to haunt politicians, but in this case the media didn't
dwell on his rather startling pronouncement. His words were soon
forgotten, never to be raised again, even when he poured all the
blame on the other side and none on his own.

Very much complicating matters while the Meech drama
played out was the beating Bouchard began to take on his master
plan for the environment. He wanted to spend $5 billion on envi-
ronmental protection. The plan, featuring a whole set of new
national standards, would include vast new amounts of funding for
university research and pollution monitoring, mandatory environmental assessment of federal projects, a carbon tax based on levels
of carbon dioxide emitted from fossil fuels and a raft of other new
regulations on resource use and conservation. Bouchard had
received Cabinet approval in mid-1989 to develop the plan. The
vision was to make Canada the most environmentally friendly
country in the world by the year 2000. Because of his stature, his
clout, his big-thinking, he had elevated environmental questions to
a plateau never before seen—and was duly applauded by environmentalists and many in the media for his efforts.

But he soon ran headlong into Michael Wilson. To Bouchard,
Wilson was the Cabinet's dinosaur, a social regressive who "ruled
with an iron fist." He was also closely allied with Stanley Hartt.
Economics was their agenda, not Quebec or fantastic new sums for
spending on green space and clean air. Wilson, who could be forgiven for a little outrage over Bouchard's earlier bid to usurp his
powers, had a strong case. The debt and deficit were staggering.

The timing for a Green Plan could hardly be more inappropriate. On the other hand, Bouchard could well look at the overall financial management of Wilson in partnership with Bank of Canada governor John Crow and wonder who was spiking their drinks. As the country tumbled towards recession, Crow continued on the fiercest anti-inflation campaign the country had ever seen. As a result of his zealotry, backed by Wilson, interest rates jumped. Higher interest rates meant a much higher deficit. They contributed to a much higher Canadian dollar, which diminished trans-border trade just as the prime minister was trying to sell the country on the merits of his Free Trade Agreement. They meant a faster, deeper and longer recession than the country would normally have endured.

It was difficult, given this disastrous policy initiative, for Bouchard to sympathize with the Wilsons of the Cabinet. A dispute between the two arose over whether the Green Plan measures should be presented as part of Wilson's February 1990 budget. Wilson demanded this, saying the program involved major spending initiatives. Bouchard wanted to go his own separate route and drum up public support for big expenditures as opposed to having to operate under the veil of pre-budget secrecy. In the hands of the finance minister, he knew, the meat cleaver would be taken to his dream scheme.

Wilson won the fight. Major funding was not forthcoming at budget time, and the Green Plan was sidelined for further study and development. Bouchard told reporters the defeat was "no big deal" and that he would commence public hearings to fine-tune it and gather support. But he was privately fuming and publicly taking it on the chin. As Jim Fulton, the highly regarded NDP environment critic, suggested, it was a significant setback. Fulton wasn't one to mince his words. "I think Lucien Bouchard is finished, axed, wiped out, hatcheted. Michael Wilson has sunk a large broadaxe between Lucien Bouchard's eyes."

Part of the problem was Bouchard's inexperience in Cabinet. Sometimes he got the lip-service treatment and didn't realize he was being taken for a ride. He would present his proposals, as Martin Green recalled, and be told, "that's great work you've done here Lucien, you're doing something really important. Now just a few things have to be flushed out. So why don't you have another look, then we can go ahead." Bouchard would leave thinking he had done well. "He didn't realize," said Green, "that he'd been given code words for the big shove-off."

When he found he'd been taken, the frustration mounted. When his Green Plan was stymied, he had a hard time viewing the process objectively. He interpreted it as an Anglophone gang-up on him. The fury in his eyes upon losing in Cabinet, noted Benoît Bouchard, was something to behold; the sheer intensity of the anger, a face which screamed, "You can't do this to me!"

Camille Guilbault observed Bouchard at the Quebec caucus breakfast meetings. "The prime minister is being manipulated by the Anglophone ministers," he bitterly complained. "We're not being strong enough. We should tell him what we want. Michael Wilson decides everything in Cabinet. We should decide."

He knew his currency with the prime minister was declining and told his staff as much, saying that he would have to go it alone. But for all his force and brilliance of argument, he couldn't carry the day without Mulroney. He hadn't played the political game, he hadn't built the network of alliances and worked the trade-offs necessary to garner support. In other words, said a staffer, "he broke the first rule of politics. He didn't kiss enough ass."

His staff found him increasingly overworked, fed up and distracted. Patricia Dumas noticed he wasn't even taking the time to read and study the Green Plan documents. Usually he was so conscientious and thorough in preparation. But the Quebec issues preyed on him more and more. His old friend Fred Bild, number two to him in Paris, visited him a couple of times during this period. He had thought Bouchard would be really challenged by the environment portfolio. "What could be more important than an international mandate for the environment?" But by the time Bild saw him, the enthusiasm had waned. He was disengaged. "It was just a job. It didn't fire his passions. Maybe he had already become disillusioned." Ottawa, concluded Bild, wasn't where his heart lived.

In March, Martin Green accompanied Bouchard to Vancouver on environmental business. There, as he had done before, Bouchard stood in awe again, talking of the magnificent geography of the place, waxing poetic about the wonders of Canada. On his agenda was an appearance on the popular Rafe Mair radio show.

He was supposed to talk about environmental subjects, but callers weren't so interested in those. Instead they held forth, some of them very angrily, some of them using one of the more popular "f" words in the province ("frog"), to denounce Quebec on the unity issue. This time, Bouchard didn't rise to the bait. Green sat listening in his hotel, quite impressed. His minister was at his diplomatic best, saying he could understand how things looked differently in British Columbia.

The calmness didn't last. When Bouchard got back to the hotel he nearly blew the roof off. He went "absolutely nuts," recalled Green. "Just off the walls." It was no momentary outburst. This tantrum lasted twenty minutes. New combinations of curse words exploded through the chamber. His body shook with rage. He paced the floor in full holler. "The Anglos!" he cried, as Green roughly remembered it. "They're not even listening! They don't understand anything! What is the matter with these people! This country can't work like this!"

Green tried to interrupt a couple of times, but couldn't get a word in. "You don't understand anything!" Bouchard shouted. It took him the longest time to calm down. The emotional fever he had brought upon himself would not subside. What he had heard had struck the most sensitive chords.

He had other reasons to be disturbed in Vancouver. It was there he heard about New Brunswick premier Frank McKenna's resolution for amendments to the Meech Lake Accord. Mulroney announced he intended to have the resolution studied by a parliamentary committee. Bouchard interpreted the resolution as altering the essence of the accord. He was particularly incensed by a suggested change of the wording on the language issue. The accord said it was Ottawa's responsibility to "protect" linguistic duality. McKenna wanted to change that to "promote" linguistic duality. This, in Bouchard's view, would leave the federal side too much room to interfere in Quebec. He said he felt "manipulated," and could not possibly support McKenna's wishes.

During this time, Norman Spector tried to reason with him. He could engage Bouchard on an intellectual level and sought to explain how the essentials of the Meech Lake Accord would remain in place with some tinkering at the edges. So much controversy had erupted over the accord that Spector was sceptical. Even if passed, its efficacy would be limited, he felt. But it was better than nothing at all, and so he tried hard to persuade Bouchard not to fret about the possibility of side clauses. He was able to make headway, but only on one level. "On a rational level we connected, but so much of this was symbolic and emotional." Bouchard's opposition wasn't substantive, Spector found. It was all about the symbolism, "the symbolism of Quebec being humiliated and defeated by having to reopen this after passing it. Bouchard had already said that it was Bourassa's action that had led to the reopening of the accord. But this no longer seemed to factor into his thinking. This was his view at another time, at another press conference.

What counted were the emotions of the moment. Past facts could be shut out, guiltlessly cast aside. It was the type of behaviour which gave rise to the psychiatrist's speculation of something unusual at work in this man—the esthetic character disorder.

Spector witnessed some of the Bouchard behaviour that Green and others had seen. At a Cabinet committee meeting, the subject of Senate reform, allowing provinces equal representation in the Red Chamber, was raised. Quebec opposed this because it would diminish its weight in the body. At the meeting, seeing detailed proposals for the first time, Bouchard was overtaken by anger. "Lucien just exploded, I mean just exploded," recalled Spector. "'Where is this from? Who endorsed this? What are you people doing!'" The meeting was in the Centre Block, a dozen startled participants looking on. "It was not typical behaviour of a Cabinet minister," recalled Spector. Nor, he said, was it tactical. Some felt Bouchard's temper tantrums were sometimes deliberately staged for dramatic effect. But "this was from the guts." Not being in "the business of psychoanalysis," Spector said he was at a loss to explain it.

Bounding from one crisis to another, Bouchard now found himself at war with Newfoundland. The legislature in St. John's adopted a motion withdrawing support for Meech Lake, support which had been given before Clyde Wells came to power. Bouchard and Quebec's intergovernmental affairs minister Gil Rémillard were in Quebec City when they received the news. Bouchard said, "One can imagine a situation in which English Canada will have to choose between Newfoundland and Quebec." Canada without Quebec, he added, wouldn't amount to much. Rémillard put in, "And Canada can live very well without Newfoundland."

Referring to the new 1982 Constitution, Bouchard asserted that just as Quebec found itself isolated, Newfoundland may well find itself the same. Wells, he claimed, "has posed an act that is politically retroactive and that creates a serious precedent in a parliamentary democracy. There are not too many precedents where a state reverses a constitutional decision taken by a previous Parliament." Wells, however, had won an election on an anti-Meech platform and thus had a democratic mandate from the people to withdraw approval for the pact.

The statement asking Canadians to choose between Quebec and Newfoundland brought forward a hailstorm of protest. *The Gazette*'s Don MacPherson termed Bouchard an unreconstructed Péquiste. He was behaving, he wrote, as if he was an ambassador to Ottawa of an already independent Quebec. Brian Tobin, the vituperative Liberal MP from Newfoundland, the rock of the Rock, tore into Bouchard in the House of Commons, demanding an explanation. When none was forthcoming, Tobin launched a personal attack. "He hasn't got the backbone to get up on his hind legs and clarify. He hides behind the prime minister's skirts." He "has no backbone and is a coward."

Now Bouchard was up on the floor. "Nobody can say this of me!" They berated one another some more, whereupon Bouchard cried, "Okay then, let's settle this outside. Come outside and we'll settle it. Nobody calls me a coward."

Tobin withdrew his allegation of cowardice, only to replace it with the suggestion that Bouchard was "unfit for national office." Conservative House leader Harvie André jumped to Bouchard's defence, shouting at Tobin, "Sit down, you little jerk." As he continued yelling, Speaker John Fraser told him to control his temper. In response, André bellowed, "I have my temper under control."

Mulroney, Mazankowski and André tried to argue that Bouchard's original remarks on Newfoundland had been taken out of context. But Bouchard undermined that line of defence, saying he had in fact been reported accurately. "If I'm asked to repeat them here or elsewhere, I will gladly do so." Asked outside the chamber if what he said on Newfoundland was dangerous, he replied that the truth was never dangerous. "We are not Jean Chrétiens in Ottawa."

Having observed the dust-up with Tobin, fellow Tory Jean

Charest came over to Bouchard. He had a suggestion. When guys like Tobin try to get under your skin, he advised, don't even bother responding. Just ignore them. Bouchard looked aghast. *"Mais, l'honneur!"* he cried. But what about my honour! My self-esteem!

The tempest constituted another example, though a minor one, of Bouchard breaking ranks with Mulroney. The first had come shortly after returning from Paris when he contradicted the prime minister on his official languages legislation, declaring that despite any intent of the bill, he would seek approval from Quebec before introducing measures to promote English in the province. He had then split brutally with the PM over Bourassa's protection of Bill 101. Then, with no approval from Mulroney, he tried to turn his environment portfolio into Chancellor of the Exchequer.

The Newfoundland controversy was barely behind him when another free-for-all was sparked by Liberal MP John Nunziata's statement that separatists in government were "traitors" to Canada, "no better than racists or bigots." Defending his position, Nunziata declared that he had as much right to his point of view as MPs who "ask Canada to choose between Newfoundland and Quebec." Bouchard fumed as to how it was outrageous that he and other Quebeckers were always having to justify their loyalty to Canada. "Don't ask us to forget we are Quebeckers. Don't ask us to forget that we are from a society whose survival is a constant struggle."

On the environment he had begun his public consultation to fine-tune and build support for his Green Plan. The effort, after his earlier setback, had the look of an afterthought. One of his proposals, an environmental tax, was badly timed since the country was already in an uproar over the GST.

On most fronts he was faring badly. He was losing on the Green Plan, he was losing on Meech Lake, he was losing his influence with Mulroney and he was being battered by Wilson in Cabinet and by Hartt in the PMO. When he examined the two paths available to him—federalism or sovereignty—the latter was beginning to look more appealing.

Benoît Bouchard, who was becoming bitter over proposed changes to Meech himself, thought he had made a deal with Lucien. "I had so many conversations with him over a period of three or four months. He said to me, 'If you leave, don't leave me alone. Tell me before you are leaving, and we'll do it together.'"

Benoît Bouchard replied that he had decided he would wait until the June 23rd Meech ratification deadline and make his decision then. He explained that he and Lucien at least owed Mulroney this.

He thought he had Lucien's agreement. But in retrospect he said he should have known better. Lucien, he said, was now in one of his high-octane emotional phases. "Lucien Bouchard was already gone mentally" from Ottawa. "He was still there physically but he was not there anymore."

14. THE HUBRIS COMPLEX

Most days at around three o'clock, Bouchard and some on his staff took a break. In a quite formal and polite manner, Bouchard would announce, "I think I'll have my tea and biscuits."

One afternoon, when he settled back to enjoy his Earl Grey and Arrowroots, he discovered his favourite cookies weren't there.

"Where are my biscuits?" he thundered.

Staff explained that there were none left, but that there were other treats he would surely enjoy.

"What!" clamoured Bouchard. "There are no biscuits! There are no biscuits! None of my favourite biscuits."

He was told it was okay, there were others. "You can have another kind of cookie today, Minister." Bouchard didn't want another kind. He wanted his biscuits. Soon, his temper at a fever pitch, he was berating the staff as incompetents. How could they not know this? How could they not have his cookies ready?

Martin Green suggested that, well, if he was that alarmed about the situation, not to worry: He would run out and buy a package of Arrowroots. He got to the store, located the cookies and, to his relief, the minister was put at ease. The latest "conniption fit" was over.

The drama of the missing biscuits made the rounds at the office, and it was the general opinion that Bouchard needed a good rest. Many began to wonder—along with Arthur Campeau, who Bouchard seemed to think was some kind of spy—if he was emotionally unstable.

It wasn't a good time to be in a highly fragile frame of mind. Too much was in play. Robert Charest got the feeling that what was making the minister particularly hot these days was his sense of isolation. The phone from the PM's office wasn't ringing. He was being left out of the loop on the Meech business. Stanley Hartt had won, walling Bouchard off from his lifeblood in federal politics, Brian Mulroney. So now he had to sit and stew, wondering what plotting was going on behind his back. He didn't know about Hartt's secret channel to the Liberals, but he sensed something was in the works. Hartt, Bouchard would later tell journalist Graham Fraser, was the thorn in his rapport with Mulroney, "He played a considerable role in the deterioration of our relationship."

Robert Charest informed the PMO that Bouchard's frustration was mounting. His message—"you have got to cut him in." In fact there was an opportunity for this. Mulroney was forming a parliamentary committee to study possible modifications to the Meech Lake Accord. Bouchard was given the opportunity to hand-pick the chairman. He wanted Jean Charest, who had campaigned for Bouchard, as had seemingly half of the Cabinet, in his by-election. Charest was not an ardent nationalist, which made Bouchard's choice of him for this job rather peculiar. But the MP from Sherbrooke had voted Péquiste in the past and Tories remembered seeing a picture of René Lévesque on his wall. More important was the family connection—Bouchard having brother Robert on his staff. Bouchard could use a special line of communication on the Meech deal. He was fearful that at the end of the day some Anglo bastard was going to pull another rabbit out of the hat. Another night of the long knives.

Initially Charest didn't want the committee assignment. He had been recently suspended from Cabinet for telephoning a judge, and he wasn't sure he wanted to jump into the spotlight again so soon. Camille Guilbault, Mulroney's Quebec liaison chief, hosted a dinner to try and sell him on the idea. Bouchard and Audrey Best attended with Charest and some others, including Pierre Blais. Bouchard poured on the charm and the pressure, telling Charest how important it was that he take the job, that he was the right man for it, that the prime minister was strongly in favour. Everyone noted how satisfied Bouchard seemed with the idea of the committee. They drew two possible conclusions. One was that he had softened and would entertain minor changes to the accord. The other was that he thought he'd be able to handle Charest like a puppetmaster and beat down every suggested modification.

Charest listened to the dinner-table flattery, gave no immediate commitment, but later signed on.

As the committee began deliberations, Bouchard, who would later claim to be blind-sided by some of the group's recommendations, was kept intimately briefed on its dealings. "I talked to him on a daily basis on where the committee was going," recalled Robert Charest. "I asked him to phone Jean and I made sure that Jean phoned him regularly to brief him on procedures. They spoke on several occasions and talked of all the permutations. When I had access to preliminary reports I handed them over to him."

In the meantime, as Robert Charest knew, Bouchard was intensifying contacts with hardliners in the caucus, including François Gérin. Officially this was being done under the guise of Bouchard trying to keep these radicals from resigning and sitting as independents. But Robert Charest and others grew suspicious that Bouchard was actually cozying up to them, warming to the idea of a pro-sovereignty bloc of MPs in Ottawa. Many were left to wonder whether he was working the federalist side or the sovereignist one. Some wondered whether he knew himself.

As the Charest committee continued its work, Bouchard prepared for a major thirty-four-nation conference on sustainable development in Bergen, Norway. Though second to Meech Lake on his list of priorities, he was still anxious to make a mark in the environment portfolio. It was obvious now he wasn't going to be the saviour of the planet Earth. But Bergen had some important work before it. At issue was global warming and the push by European countries for specific carbon dioxide reduction targets to combat it. Three options were available: One was to set reduction targets. Another was the stabilization of emissions at existing levels. A third, favoured by the US, was to take no action until more research was done.

In the days before Bergen, a telex leaked in Washington suggested Bouchard would support the American position. Canadian environmentalists expressed outrage. Only a month earlier Bouchard had publicly derided America's go-slow position on the environment, saying that "the price of inaction is too high." Now he looked like he was saying one thing and doing another. The story made headlines and Bouchard was understandably furious. He had been misrepresented.

He told associates someone was out to get him. The culprit, he was persuaded, was Mulroney's special envoy on the environment, Arthur Campeau, whose conservative positions were more in line with Washington's. In Bergen, Bouchard told his aide, Martin

Green, that Campeau was spying on him and reporting back to Mulroney. At the first briefing session of the Canadian delegation, Bouchard tore into Campeau, alleging he was doing America's bidding and that his policy positions were unfounded. The intensity of the attack shocked those at the meeting. Pierre-Marc Johnson, the former Péquiste leader, now devoting a lot of his time to environmental causes, could hardly believe his ears. This kind of flogging normally took place in private, if at all. Campeau hadn't expected it. He knew Bouchard felt uneasy with him around, but why this?

Going into the conference, Canada had not finalized its position on carbon dioxide emission targets, though it was closer to the American than the European one. But Bouchard, as if determined to prove that he was entirely independent of Washington and win back his honour, began sounding as if he would commit Canada to targets even more radical than Europe's plans. To Campeau, this smacked of policy-making based on personal pique. He had it out with Bouchard, telling him to hold on, that there was no mandate from Ottawa for this cockeyed strategy.

The conference failed to win agreement on any reduction scheme. But Bouchard, taking matters into his own hands, came forward with a shotgun announcement. Canada would go it alone and stabilize carbon dioxide emissions at their present levels until the year 2000. That it was a loose-cannon commitment was evident in his own assessment. "It will be done, but I cannot announce how it will be done." Since the announcement did not conform with planned Ottawa policy, deputy minister Len Good, who got along well with Bouchard, got on the phone to Ottawa to try to explain the announcement to startled officials.

Meanwhile, Bouchard continued to stalk Campeau. At one point, Campeau innocently mentioned how he was looking forward to the end of the conference so he could go to his cottage in Maine for a rest. Maine happened to be the location of President George Bush's summer home. Bouchard, immediately picking up on the connection, weighed in with a zinger. "Oh," he said, "so you're going to Kennebunkport to report to George, eh?"

Campeau demanded to know what he was talking about. He was now really beginning to think Bouchard had lost his equilibrium. "It was bizarre...It was as if he thought I was some goddam CIA agent."

Earlier Campeau had attributed Bouchard's yo-yo swings of temperament to either exhaustion or deliberate calculation. As a lawyer himself, Campeau knew some of the tricks Bouchard had learned in the courtroom. Faked fits of temper were often a good tactic, but the more he saw Bouchard, the more he doubted that this was the case. Now he was beginning to think that Bouchard wasn't fully in control of his own levers; that he randomly rotated from rational zones to twilight zones.

"I came to think," he said, "that there are about eight Lucien Bouchards living within the same body and that he shifted from one plane of awareness to another plane of awareness without even realizing that he had." It was the Dr. Jekyll and Mr. Hyde syndrome. "I'd start off a meeting with this guy, with one Lucien Bouchard, and end up the meeting talking to another Lucien Bouchard. It was really bloody weird."

Campeau asked Pierre-Marc Johnson to have a talk with Bouchard to find out what the hell was eating him. Johnson found him nervous, edgy, complaining about Hartt and Charest and what they were doing to Meech Lake. At this time, Mulroney was using Benoît Bouchard to keep Lucien informed of what was going on back home. Hartt was also trying to call him. This rattled Bouchard. He was getting the surrogate treatment. Why, he asked Johnson, wasn't Mulroney phoning himself? As Robert Charest had noticed, Bouchard felt excluded, and Johnson got the impression he couldn't tolerate it.

Bouchard and Johnson had gotten along well since meeting a decade earlier. They went down to Bergen's old harbour, where they sat on a terrace and ordered beer. Johnson mentioned how Bouchard's treatment of Campeau would be unlikely to win him a place in the annals of diplomatic charm and etiquette. Bouchard explained in general terms that he was unhappy. He despaired over the lack of family time. He felt paralysed in the federal power structure in regard to the environment and Meech Lake. He underlined how the PMO was trying to isolate him. Mulroney, he granted, was under tremendous pressure from the Maritimes and the West to modify the accord. But he was highly critical of his friend for not showing more force in batting them down.

Johnson began talking about Bouchard's career. He spoke quietly because members of the Canadian delegation were seated at surrounding tables. He then put a simple question to Bouchard. "What do you want to do with your life, Lucien?" There was a pause, before Johnson answered the question for him. "You want to be premier of Quebec, don't you?"

Bouchard nodded his agreement. Back at the conference, he was soon in another spat with Campeau. Bouchard stated that he wanted to leave early, before the final press conference of all the participant nations. Realizing that Mulroney would be irked by this undiplomatic gesture, Campeau urged him to stay. Bouchard said he had a plane to catch to Paris to see his wife and child. Campeau offered to charter him a plane so that he could meet his commitments. Bouchard demurred. "He wanted to get the hell out of Bergen," recalled Campeau. The special envoy hadn't noticed that Bouchard was gobbling up the telex traffic from back home relating to the negotiations on Meech Lake. He didn't realize that Bouchard had other urgent business to attend to besides Audrey and son Alexandre.

During the Bergen conference, Martin Green found a bit odd the frequency with which Bouchard brought up the subject of the coming tenth anniversary of the 1980 Quebec referendum. The Parti Québécois would be marking the event at a party meeting to be held, coincidentally, in Alma, in Bouchard's riding.

Bouchard was planning to send a message welcoming the PQ to his constituency. This sounded innocent enough, but Green wondered why Bouchard kept asking questions about it. Why would he care what Green thought about it? Was he preparing him for something?

Green didn't know, nor did anyone in the PMO, that Bouchard was already in communication with the Péquistes on how he should word the message. He was considering sending a telegram intimating support for the PQ. Coming from a federal Cabinet minister, coming as the clock on Meech was winding down, it would send shock waves. Specifically he had spoken to Marc-André Bedard, the ringleader of the movement to set up an independent bloc of MPs in Ottawa. Years later, Bedard, though refusing to elaborate on the type of wording they talked about, would confirm having discussed the proposed contents with the environment minister. It was clear that before he left for Bergen, before the Charest report came out, Bouchard was contemplating dropping a bombshell.

On the flight over from Canada, he told Green, "It's really on my mind. What should I say in it?" His adviser responded bluntly. "I think you should put 'Welcome to my federal riding. I hope you all spend lots of money and do the economy very well and enjoy the local scenery and have a happy and safe time.'" When Bouchard complained he wanted to do more than that, Green replied that he was walking a fine line. The timing was so sensitive. Meech hung in the balance. For Bouchard to embrace the PQ in any way at this time could have fantastic repercussions. If he sounded too supportive of the secessionists, Green warned, he was finished in federal politics. "You'll be resigning."

In Bergen, Bouchard also discussed the telex with Pierre-Marc Johnson, who warned against any strongly worded message. It was important, Johnson told Bouchard, that he talk over all his problems with Mulroney.

Though the business of Bergen was the environment, Bouchard was preoccupied with the constitutional drama. Much had transpired. *Le Devoir* had published an article shortly before Bouchard left for Bergen, citing Bernard Landry as saying twenty to twenty-five federal Tories were preparing to bolt the party. Bouchard told Mulroney not to worry. He'd hold the fort together.

Marcel Danis was Mulroney's quiet sports and fitness minister. He was told that a member of Bouchard's staff, Jacques Bouchard (no relation), had attended secret gatherings with the new-party plotters. Danis had been invited to attend. Alarmed, he stayed away and instead went to Lucien Bouchard to raise the matter. Didn't Bouchard consider it inappropriate to have one of his aides actively involved in such plotting? Bouchard said he knew about the meetings, but he didn't take them too seriously. A staff member plotting with separatists to undermine the governing party? This, wondered Danis, was not serious?

His temptation was to alert Mulroney, but he backed off. "I was there as a junior minister from Quebec, dealing with the leader of the Quebec caucus," he told Peter Newman. "It's widely known that the PM helped him all through his life, made him ambassador, Cabinet minister, Quebec leader. Christ, I couldn't pick up the phone to tell him what I'd heard. He would have thought I was crazy."

The Charest committee prepared its final recommendations on the Meech Lake Accord. Bouchard had a good idea of what the main proposals would be. He'd been shown a draft report at a Quebec caucus meeting in Mont-Tremblant. He'd met with Jean Charest and expressed his general satisfaction. He'd been to a dinner in Montreal with Mulroney to celebrate the fifteenth anniversary of the Cliche Commission and expressed no reservations there. But he was sending different signals to the other side, the sovereignty camp, which was hoping he would bolt. Conrad Black saw Bouchard at this time. He found him irritated over Meech Lake but had the feeling he was searching for a pretext that would allow him to show his true separatist colours. He was "cranking up to be able to say 'there, I tried it, but it didn't work.'"

If he was planning to flee one army to join another he would indeed require a strong pretext. Bouchard had two of them. Even though he had pushed Charest to head the committee, the pending publication of the report would provide grounds, whether in fact it was offensive or not, for a *coup de théâtre*, a feast for the persecution complex—Quebec wronged again! Secondly, the PQ meeting in Alma on the anniversary of the referendum would provide the occasion for an incendiary message of welcome.

Before Bouchard left for Bergen he had met with Paul Tellier. As the clerk of the Privy Council, he was now playing a big role in Meech, a fact which deeply bothered Bouchard. He knew Tellier's background. In the late 1970s, Trudeau had appointed him to head up the federalist office for the coming referendum campaign. Tellier, in Bouchard's mind, was a killer of the dream.

It wasn't a pleasant meeting. The clerk informed Bouchard that it was still necessary to do something to bring on board the three dissenting provinces (Newfoundland, New Brunswick and Manitoba) on the Meech package. His message was that statesmanship required compromise. The Charest report would likely have to recommend federal responsibility for the promotion of minority languages across the country, including Quebec. This change alone was enough to make Bouchard burn. He could see that Mulroney was going to cave in to the compromises demanded by the Liberals and Jean Chrétien, the Uncle Tom "who represented everything I abhorred in politics." He had been led to believe, by Charest, that the promotion of linguistic duality would not be part of the report.

Bouchard's sensitivity on the issue struck some as a bit extreme. They didn't realize that shortly after coming to Ottawa in 1988 he had experienced one of those defining moments that politicians do not forget. It occurred in Montreal, at the funeral of Félix Leclerc, the chansonnier of the Quiet Revolution. In his see-sawing positions over Mulroney's bill on the protection of minority language rights, Bouchard had most recently come out in support of it, even though it gave Ottawa linguistic authority in his province. On the way out of the church, a man stopped Bouchard and looked him in the eye. "You are from Lac Saint-Jean?" the man asked. "Yes," replied Bouchard.

"So am I," said the man. "The difference is that I am not a traitor to Francophones."

Bouchard didn't say anything but the man's words hit hard.

After the Tellier meeting, he had dinner with Bernard Roy at Mirabel Airport before boarding his flight. The two were still close. Bouchard expressed reservations about not having been directly involved in proposed Meech Lake changes and stated his opposition to the linguistic duality clause. But Roy did not go away from the meeting overly concerned. Bouchard had mentioned that Mulroney was the master political strategist and that a lot of gamesmanship was going on. Roy was persuaded that he would give the PM time to work his magic.

In Bergen, his mind whirled—the Charest report, the question of the telex, Campeau's spying? In the midst of it all, he took a long reflective break.

Sunday at the conference would not be a busy day. On Saturday afternoon, he told Green, "I have a ministerial request. No, a ministerial command. Tomorrow we'll have breakfast and then we'll go for a long walk." Green was excited. He was one of the favoured few on Bouchard's staff, the minister inspiring occasional jealousy among others by taking him on trips. But even for Green there hadn't been many times like this, when he could be alone with this exceptional man and his thoughts. Usually it was business, business, business.

The walk turned into a marathon. It lasted six hours. They strolled over the hills of the delightfully pristine Scandinavian town. They walked through galleries and churches and paused, with Bouchard deep in thought, among the lily-faced Norwegians to observe a christening. They took a funicular up and down the steepest slope and stopped at a café. The minister wanted his tea and biscuits.

For much of it, Bouchard told Green the story of his growing up in small-town Quebec, emphasizing the importance of religion, the pull of the church. His face lit up as he talked of the day Monsignor Morin, with Bouchard's parents looking on, put his biretta over Lucien's brow and intoned, "Lucien will be our cardinal."

It was in these moments, when invoking the idea that he had a special role in life, that Bouchard became most passionate. He spoke of René Lévesque, of how he had told him (Bouchard) that he was one of the chosen few who must carry on the fight. "He remembered this," said Green, "in a very emotional way."

He talked of his father and of the sense of injustice Quebeckers carried with them and of their strong will. He talked bitterly about the rich Anglophones in Montreal who had owned everything and controlled everything and who never saw fit to help the rest of the province develop. Green got a sense of the wounds Bouchard felt, wounds that had never healed. Despite the great progress made through the Quiet Revolution, despite the arrival of all the French power in Ottawa, despite this and the program to bilingualize the country, the wounds were still there. His mind was stuck in the past, in a bygone era.

There were lighter moments during the six-hour walk, but even they bore a message. Bouchard told the story, one he often recounted, of the young Quebecker who left his Saguenay home to go to work in the textile mills in the north-eastern United States. He returned home several years later to his family farm where his father was hurt to find him speaking only English. How could he have forgotten his native tongue? The son explained that English was the language that counted. It was the way of the future. As they strolled through the farm, the son stepped on a pitch fork and it shot up and smashed him on the head. "*Colliste! Ciboire! Tabernack!*" the son cried out, using every French curse word in the book. A big grin crossed the father's face. He new his boy was home and that the true blood was still in him.

For Martin Green, the experience of the long walk was beginning to feel like a valedictory address, as if Bouchard was preparing to leave and that he wanted his friend to understand the deep motivations for it. When Bouchard ended the walk on an ominous note, raising again the subject of the telex, there remained few doubts in Martin Green's mind what was to come. It was as if it had been planned.

Bouchard left Norway and arrived in Paris as the Charest report was released. It was a coincidence heavy with portent. Paris was rife with symbols all pointing in one direction. This was his second home, the spiritual and cultural anchor of his family line. This was where, as ambassador, he had moved Quebec closer to its patrimony via his central role in the creation of La Francophonie. This was where Bouchard's Frenchness shone, and it was the worst place Mulroney could have dreamed of having him when the report came out and the referendum anniversary took place. Had Bouchard flown home to Ottawa from Bergen and been coddled by the prime minister, instead of having all these other chords clanging in his ears, the following few days might well have taken a different turn.

The report was faxed to him in Paris. He saw that it contained the clause on the promotion of languages and other suggested changes to the Meech Lake agreement that he deemed offensive. He was predictably furious and there was no one to cool him off, to emphasize that there was nothing final about this report, that it was only a working document.

Jean Charest phoned three times to embassy officer Marc Lortie's apartment where Bouchard was staying. Bouchard wouldn't take the calls. Benoît Bouchard tried to reach him to say not to worry, this report wouldn't count for much. Lucien wouldn't take his calls. Again he raised the question, telling Green, "Why isn't Brian calling me? I don't understand this. Why does he think I'll deal with these people?" It was as if the others were minions and the seigneur did not wish to hear them. Where was the prime minister?

It was hubris that came calling, not the PM. Bouchard's pride was assaulted. He was not being shown respect, so now he would show them. By now, he had his cruise missile—the telex—ready; and now, in a mood of defiance, he was prepared to send it.

The telex, in its most controversial section, read that the commemoration of the referendum "offers another opportunity to recall the sincerity, the pride, and the generosity of the 'Yes' we defended at the time, around René Lévesque and his team.

"René Lévesque's memory will unite us all this weekend. He was the one who led the Québécois to realize they had the inalienable right to decide their own destiny."

Bouchard instructed his press secretary, Micheline Fortin, to dispatch it, adding that she must keep it hidden from Green. He didn't want to hear Green's counter-arguments and perhaps was trying to protect him from possible career damage owing to any implication in the act. Green saw Fortin as a sovereignist, one who was always pushing Bouchard in that direction. Lay off, he had told her many times in the past; this guy could be prime minister some day. Now, outside the apartment, she refused to show him the telex. Green became adamant. "Give me the fucking thing!" At a restaurant, as he threatened to rip it out of her purse, she finally relented. Upon reading it, his suspicions were confirmed. "This isn't a telex of welcome," he told her. "This is a resignation letter. You have to tell him this." He coaxed her to make the call, but the response from Bouchard was just as he anticipated: The four-letter-word send-off.

This was to be one little speech, Bouchard vowed, that was not going to be censored by the PMO. Green went with Fortin to the Canadian embassy, the place Bouchard knew so well, to send the missile. Green had a sense it was all over now. Instead of returning to see Bouchard, he booked an early flight home.

The telex was addressed to David Cliche, the son of Bouchard's beloved Robert Cliche. All this had been previously arranged among Bouchard, Bedard and others. Cliche would deliver it straight to the PQ executive in Alma. Bouchard wanted no communication foul-ups. He didn't have to be too brilliant a schemer to realize that if he was intent on resigning, it was better to lay some groundwork first. The telex would prompt headlines across the province enhancing his sovereignist status. The people would be waiting for him with open arms. When Jean Marchand quit the Trudeau government in 1976, he had sided with the nationalists. But in leaving he didn't denounce federalism. Had he done so, he remarked to a reporter later, he would have been greeted as a hero in Quebec.

The thought of dumping the Tories and jumping aboard the sovereignty train had a lot of appeal to Bouchard at this time. The sovereignty option was climbing swiftly in the Quebec polls. He was astute enough to realize that in leading the charge against a diluted Meech, his stock in Quebec, already high, would soar further. He could lead a new party of sovereignists in Ottawa if he wished. He would be his own boss. Or he could practise law and combine it with politics.

When the PMO got wind of the telex, Paul Tellier was instructed to call Bouchard. But if there was anyone Bouchard didn't want to hear from, it was Tellier. He caught Bouchard coming out of the shower dripping wet and dripping mad. Tellier inquired about the telex. As expected, the headlines were making their way onto the front pages. Tellier spoke on and on, telling him of the damage he was inflicting. Finally Bouchard interrupted. "I don't give a damn about the telex. The Charest report, that's the problem. You knew I could not accept these changes. Wait till Monday. Things will be happening."

Arthur Campeau had just made it from Bergen to his cottage retreat in Maine. It had been a tough time in Norway and he relished the prospect of the break. He was about to put his feet up when Brian Mulroney called. "What the fuck is going on?" the prime minister inquired. Campeau wondered what he was talking about. First, Mulroney addressed the matter of Bouchard's early exit from Bergen. "Why the fuck did he take off? What was so urgent?" Before Campeau could explain, Mulroney said, "What the hell is this bloody telex?" Campeau explained how Lucien had been acting strange through much of the conference. "We've been calling him," Mulroney said. "The fucker won't answer the phone. Where the fuck is he?"

Mulroney was placing calls everywhere, trying to get an explanation. He found Ian MacDonald on vacation. "Well, what do you think of our friend this morning?" he said over the phone. He read the telegram, but MacDonald didn't find it so traitorous. "It doesn't really say anything more than what you said about Lévesque on the night he died," he told Mulroney. Bouchard himself would later profess to be rather surprised that his message, though provocative, was viewed as a full-fledged leap into the arms of the PQ.

Luc Lavoie arrived at 24 Sussex Drive on the Saturday afternoon, not knowing about the telex. He had come to consult with Mulroney on arrangements for Soviet leader Mikhail Gorbachev's state visit. Lavoie found the prime minister pale and shaken, like he had been hit over the head. "You're aware of the news?" Mulroney said.

"No."

Mulroney pulled out his small Sony radio he carried around in his pocket. He turned it on and just then Jacques Parizeau could be heard reading out the Bouchard telegram to a crowd in Alma. The roar of approval was tumultuous, stirring. It was like a victory on election night. Mulroney looked nightmarishly at Lavoie, and didn't say anything.

Lavoie started to ask him about arrangements for the Soviet leader. Mulroney would normally have been very caught up at the prospect of hosting a giant of history such as Gorbachev. He would want to know and approve every detail. Now he didn't want to hear anything. "You decide," he told his aide. "I agree with everything."

Bouchard arrived back in Canada the next day, the Sunday of the Victoria Day weekend. He had a huge list of messages from people demanding to see him that night, but it was Luc Lavoie who was again to get an exclusive ringside seat on history in the making. He was the only one Bouchard chose to see. Lavoie arrived at his apartment on Laurier Avenue at 6 p.m. and stayed beyond midnight. Audrey, who didn't care much for politics, and the baby, Alexandre, who was crying, were there with Lucien. Over a spaghetti dinner, they talked into the night, Bouchard calm, but resigned. Lavoie put the case forward for his staying on the team. He explained how Bouchard was confusing the substance of debate with tactics. Only a first ministers' conference could change the Meech Accord, not a committee headed by Charest. "So why the hell do you make this report into something that it is not?" Lavoie asked. He was not dealing with a naive man when it came to this kind of thing. "You were a negotiator, for god's sake. You know the difference between tactics and substance."

He could tell, however, that Bouchard was no longer impressionable. It was the calm after the storm, and his course had been decided in the eye of it. Bouchard did not come out and say flatly that he was resigning, but his mind was made up.

Lavoie tried playing the loyalty card. How could he treat his friend Brian this way after all he had done? This didn't work either. As far as Bouchard was concerned, Mulroney was now listening to the likes of Chrétien, Charest and Hartt more than him.

Lavoie knew that this was where the core of the problem lay, that the Charest business was not the crux, that the real story was all about pride, hubris, wounded ego. Lavoie's testimony and that of others pointed in the same direction. Anglophone-Francophone relations were being thrown into crisis and sped perhaps on a disastrous trajectory because Lucien Bouchard's childlike sensitivities were not being coddled enough. The reason Bouchard decided to quit, said Lavoie, "had very little to do with Canada and Quebec and everything to do with somebody who could not deal with the fact that Mulroney was his boss. He will hate me for having said this. But I don't care. I've told him that."

Pierre Blais, Bernard Roy and Paul Tellier all had follow-up meetings with Bouchard. Give Mulroney a chance, they pleaded. At least wait until the June 23rd Meech deadline. He can still get Meech through without the Charest changes. Give him a bit of time. You at least owe him that. Their arguments also fell short. Bouchard was no longer listening. Mulroney, he would later say, "gambled on thirty years of friendship, on my weakness in accepting to play the game on the McKenna resolution, on my attachment to Environment Canada, on the five billion dollars he had promised me for the Green Plan, and on the difficulty of breaking with a party and a whole group of friends. He was wrong, that's all."

Bouchard met with Mulroney for the last time on the night of May 21, 1990, in the prime minister's study at 24 Sussex Drive. Mulroney began on a conciliatory note. "Whatever happens, we won't erase thirty years of friendship." But despite the tragedy of the circumstance, a sense of competition prevailed. Mulroney knew Bouchard's mind was made up. He didn't want to leave the initiative with him and let him resign. Better to fire him first. The telegram was unacceptable, he told him; he clearly didn't wish to modify his behaviour and there was no logical reason for this behaviour. He would have to ask for his resignation.

Bouchard said the telegram had nothing to do with the fundamental issue—the Charest report. Mulroney and his colleagues believed, however, that the missive was the signal he was moving to the PQ camp. A disagreement with the prime minister over Meech alone would have caused less damage. It wouldn't have been seen as the act of party disloyalty the telegram constituted.

After debating the Charest report, Bouchard handed Mulroney

his prepared resignation letter. The prime minister read it closely. He asked that Bouchard not table it for a day and that he delete the portion in which he said that when Trudeau had recast the Constitution in 1981 even he had not gone so far as to include a clause on the promotion of bilingualism. Mulroney did not want to see a reference to that. Bouchard agreed to remove it.

On the porch on the way out, Mulroney asked that while resigning from Cabinet Bouchard remain in the caucus. The intent was clear. By keeping him in caucus, Mulroney could keep his Quebec MPs on the team. Thinking about it on the way back to his office, Bouchard concluded that this would be ceding too much ground. He telephoned Lavoie from his car to ask to see him at 7:30 a.m. the next day to coordinate the logistics of his resignation announcement. Back at his office, he phoned Mulroney and said that he would no longer be staying in the caucus.

The PM reasoned he had done a lot for Bouchard. On Meech he felt he was only trying the art of the possible. He was showing some bargaining flexibility to get it done. Even if there was some dilution, Quebec with the accord would still be further ahead than Quebec with no accord at all. He asked only that his friend give an inch or two. He felt that loyalty was worth at least that much.

After the Sussex meeting, Bouchard and Mulroney never spoke again. Nor did a great many of Bouchard's other Tory colleagues ever want to see him. Bernard Roy heard him out before resignation day, but concluded that his supposed reasons for leaving didn't make sense, that he had clearly made up his mind to leave well before the Charest report. This whole thing, Roy believed, was a "*coup montée*"—a planned strike. Pierre Blais couldn't countenance his behaviour. He had sat there at the dinner table only a few weeks earlier. "He pushed Charest to accept the committee assignment, then used the committee as an excuse to leave the party. I can never forgive him for that." For Benoît Bouchard it was a manifestation of the tragic flaw in Bouchard, the vulnerability to be "totally blinded by his emotions." For others it was a matter of ego, of not being able to tolerate being number two. Patricia Dumas recalled him in the weeks before his resignation. He was reading the great revolutionary speeches of history.

On May 22nd, Bouchard rose in the Commons. Brian Mulroney sat about five metres from him. They exchanged not a glance. Then Bouchard spoke of the "ghetto of frustration" to which the people had been condemned. "I felt that in reading the accord for the first time that Quebec had managed to overcome its humiliation and its just indignation... I felt we had to leave the ghetto of frustration to which we were confined by the arrogant structure of Mr. Trudeau. And I felt that this was an occasion to turn the page from the bitterness of the past..."

He had regarded Mulroney's signature, he said, as a sacred thing. And, "I had no reason to believe that the Meech Lake Accord with the signatures of the premiers of New Brunswick, Manitoba and Newfoundland would be dishonoured." This was "deeply shocking."

He recognized that the Charest report was only a negotiating document to be used as the basis for convening a first ministers' conference. But, he said, this was still too much humiliation for him to bear. "In giving this type of weight to the report the government is making an alliance with those who want Quebec to continue to be humiliated." These were people who wanted "to deal Quebec a final blow."

"This report should not have existed. I am against it. And I find that I will have to leave the government with pain and with sadness and I will have to sit as an independent member of Parliament."

A commentator would write of the speech that "Lucien Bouchard needed hundreds of words to say what Charles de Gaulle had said in four: *Vive le Québec libre.*" The irony was that Bouchard, only a few years earlier, had brought on the great thaw in Canada-France relations that de Gaulle had put on ice. Now, the old general must be chortling in his grave, the commentator wrote. Bouchard had topped him—with an inside job.

After the speech, there was dead silence. Mulroney got up, took his briefing books in hand, turned his back on Bouchard and left the House.

The stated reasons for the abandonment of his party by the man from the Kingdom of the Saguenay were greeted with incredulity, even by his friends. Had he really resigned over a "negotiating document" issued by a fellow-Quebecker whom he himself had hand-picked? Even his ally Lavoie, who saw him from such close range through these times, couldn't swallow this one. The Charest report, he said, was "a pretext."

15. DE GAULLE WAITING FOR THE CALL

As he was leaving Bouchard's Laurier Street apartment the day before the resignation, Luc Lavoie issued a warning to Bouchard. "You go through with this," Lavoie told him, "and you will quickly become a footnote in history."

Bouchard froze. He looked at Lavoie coldly, not saying anything. Lavoie knew his words had struck deep.

The following day, Monday, the Victoria Day holiday, Lavoie had work to do with the Soviet advance team in preparing for Gorbachev's visit. He was at the external affairs department when a phone rang. Preparing for his resignation act, Bouchard had many things on his mind, but there was something he had to tell his visitor from the night before.

Lavoie picked up the phone to hear the deep and emphatic voice. "I just want to tell you," said Bouchard. "This business about me being a footnote in history. You may well come to eat your words."

End of conversation.

Bouchard's dreams and ambitions certainly weren't diminishing with his decision to abandon Mulroney. More likely, they had hardened. The political chessboard was an unfathomable maze at this point. Bouchard could not determine how the match would play out. Nor could anyone. But having worked both sides of the board, he had a hunch about which side held the most promise for him. The arrival of his first child in the previous autumn had quickened in Bouchard—as he told his friends from school days—the desire to implant the flag of sovereignty. He wanted to build a secure Francophone homeland for his children. When Bouchard began having a family, recalled Paul-André Gauthier, "he said to me it was the main reason he would seek independence, because it was opening the future for his children. And I think he was deadly serious. He said that to me and he repeated it to a class reunion."

Bouchard was a believer in fate, not in a superstitious way, like

Mackenzie King, but in the romantic sense. He believed that among the masses dwelled some men of destiny. When he sat on the top of the Charlevoix mountains with Denis de Belleval they would talk of fate and the power if it. They would talk philosophy. They loved being on the mountaintops because, said de Belleval, from there "you could look at the stars and believe for a moment you were superman."

Many believed, following his desertion of Mulroney, that only the act of a superman, only all the fates pulling in his direction, could restore Bouchard's credibility.

That credibility could be questioned on several fronts:

• Before the Charest report was published, Bouchard was already planning to send his telegram of support to the PQ meeting. He had talks with Marc-André Bedard, who was trying to form a sovereignist bloc in Ottawa, about how to word it.

• If Bouchard was so traumatized by the Charest report, why did he refuse to accept phone calls from Charest, his hand-picked committee chairman, to hear him out? Did he have a fine tale of humiliation in hand that he did not want undermined by counter-evidence? Was the report just a pretext?

• He had stated in clear language at a press conference that it was Bourassa's questionable use of the notwithstanding clause that had driven a hole in the support for Meech Lake across the country. How could he turn around and blame English-Canadian premiers for its problems without including the Quebec government as at least equally culpable?

• His confidant Luc Lavoie, who had sat with him for hours before the resignation, was saying his stated reason for leaving was hogwash.

• At the beginning of the Meech process in 1987, Bouchard had told his federal partners in Ottawa that it was a good deal. In response to demands from Quebeckers for more concessions, he had sat at the meeting in the PMO in 1987 and responded, "Screw them!"

His comportment in the Meech crisis reminded Alain Dubuc, the editorialist for *La Presse*, of everything except statesmanship. In order for political men to cope with the intense heat of action,

Dubuc wrote, they must sometimes be able to clear away emotional baggage. "They must transform themselves into statesmen and demonstrate qualities of calm, of patience, of self-control, of endurance, of coherence. Mr. Bouchard has not manifested them." Dubuc was joining many in saying this episode was about vanity, a desire to write history. "A classic case of hubris," said Peter White. It was all about the "hero-syndrome," wrote Jeffrey Simpson. "Self-aggrandizers do these sorts of things. Mere mortals prefer remaining part of a team at least until the final whistle blows." Pierre Blais, who had sat in many Cabinet meetings with Bouchard, preferred a sports analogy. What Bouchard had done would be like Wayne Gretzky quitting the game after two periods when the going got tough; then going home to weep on his mommy's shoulder because he didn't get his own way.

While federalist elites saw the story in this light, the nationalists of Quebec had a very different take. They had a new hero in their midst. His name was Lucien Bouchard.

Following his resignation, Bouchard was scheduled to deliver a speech to the Montreal Chamber of Commerce on the topic of the environment. It couldn't be cancelled because tickets had been sold. Bouchard agreed to appear only if he could change the subject to the political crisis at hand. He had no prepared text and would have to shoot from the hip. The chamber did not normally attract a nationalist audience, and this worried him. But he need not have been concerned. The moment he stepped into the hall the applause began. The din grew thunderous as the businessmen of the city rose to their feet. The headlines created by the Bouchard telegram and by his resignation over Meech Lake had registered the impact he hoped. At this instant, Bouchard knew Quebec was with him. Public opinion, as indicated in surveys, had been moving towards the sovereignty option in recent months His gambit in fleeing the federalists had dramatically accelerated the process.

Enormously relieved, Bouchard told his listeners of the great sacrifices they had been making for the rest of Canada. "Quebec has compromised," he said. "It has stripped itself naked. It has nothing more to give but still it is being asked to give. What more could we give up if not our honour and what's left of our pride. What I'm saying is 'enough is enough!'"

While many in Ottawa wondered how he could have repudiated

his own signature with the Cabinet and the prime minister, Bouchard was turning the tables—accusing others of repudiating him. In the speech, he invoked the image of his grandfather building the country and wondered how this man could possibly have imagined so many premiers reneging on their signatures in order to beat down Quebec.

He called for a non-partisan union of Parizeau and Bourassa and all Quebeckers to come together to forge a new consensus that would end the humiliation. "We have children to bring up," cried Bouchard. "We want them to be musicians, astronauts, scientists. We want them to do meaningful things in life. We don't want their lives torn apart. We don't want their lives twisted and tormented by politics. We want them to be integrated fully into the modern world." On the Mulroney team he had boasted not so long ago of how the Free Trade Agreement served the purpose of helping integrate Quebec into the modern world. And before that he had gone on about the glories of the Quiet Revolution in giving Quebeckers what he now demanded—the chance at great careers in all the varied fields.

He reached back in his speech to an old phrase he had first employed at Laval, the need for Quebec to engage in a "*rapport de forces*" with Ottawa—the strategy of wringing new concessions from Ottawa by threatening to leave if it didn't get them. "Quebec is dying of ambiguity," he stated. The province had to strike hard, choose a strong course, go its own way. Great upheavals of applause, the likes of which the chamber had rarely witnessed, interspersed his oratory. At its conclusion, the 650 businessmen were falling all over themselves with wondrous assessments. Bouchard "touched the mind and soul of the people in the room," said Guy de Grandpré of the Desjardins Caisse Populaire. "I think it's time to go beyond political parties."

Bouchard left the room feeling that he made the right decision in fleeing Mulroney. Having mused about a return to the practice of law, he was now convinced that politics was the way. In the following few days he received similar grand receptions while speaking to the Quebec Bar Association in Pointe-au-Pic and at a political meeting in Alma.

He was one who always found it difficult not to personalize the debate. In Alma he launched his toughest assault yet on Jean

Chrétien. Chrétien was leading the race for the Liberal Party leadership at the time, so Bouchard had special cause to have at him. "Jean Chrétien has come back to haunt us like an old ghost dragging its chains." He had made a career "riding on the back of anti-Quebec prejudice." He would never form a government in Ottawa, he said, because Quebeckers wouldn't forget that he worked against them. Nor, he said, would he win another referendum campaign.

Backing for sovereignty surged to close to the 60 percent level. Bouchard's sense of vindication heightened and those thinking he would become a footnote in history could only take note. He appeared to be casting himself as the spiritual heir to René Lévesque. He told reporters, "I believe that the solution is sovereignty-association." The term has "never been properly defined. English Canadians refer to separatists. This is a cold term. We have to remake the country."

Bouchard lacked Lévesque's street-corner, nicotine-stained sociability, but as a leader of a new crusade, his dynamic persona had wide appeal. He was fiery and dark, brooding and brilliant, a man with the mien of a martyr and the cast of a seigneur. Unlike Parizeau, who could break bread only with the hardline secessionist element of the population, Bouchard had positioned himself magnificently in the political middle so that he cut across all lines. He was a quasi-federalist, a quasi-separatist sharing much in a Lévesque-styled ambiguity that incorporated the fluctuating allegiances of the Quebec populace. He was a coalitionist who could passionately bend and blend with the shifts and swings of the tormented political seasons. Fierce in his willpower, he could carve up anyone who got in his way, no matter how close his earlier alliance with them. "Mulroney's Brutus," one columnist called him. And if he cut down Mulroney, what about Parizeau, for whom he had no affection, and what about Bourassa, whom he found too irresolute, and what about any others he considered obstacles? From his position in the middle, all could be targets and all could be friends.

One figure he was not anxious to berate was Brian Mulroney. Down deep he felt badly about what he had done to the friendship, and he wasn't about to lump the prime minister with the likes of Trudeau and Chrétien. After his resignation, he wouldn't talk about Mulroney, not even to his family members. "It was too painful for him," said his brother Gérard. "It was a real friendship."

Gérard wondered why the focus was always on the one side of the story. "No one has ever gone into the business of the possibility of some betrayal on the other side... Which one has betrayed whom? This is a very good question." Lucien was a close friend of Brian's, but "does that mean you have to go against your basic principles because of that friendship?" While the conventional wisdom suggested Bouchard had used Mulroney to advance his career, the opposite, Gérard noted, could also be said. Mulroney had used Lucien to obtain his overwhelming Quebec support. "Mulroney knew what political capital he could get from Lucien."

Indeed, there had been political advantage to be had from a figure so attractive to voters, and Mulroney certainly reaped some. On balance, however, it appeared, taking into account what happened earlier in their careers as well, that Mulroney had given far more than he had received. Bouchard had declined to enter the 1984 election as part of the Tory team. His part in the preparation of the reconciliation speech in that campaign was significant. But that speech came after John Turner's many blunders had already turned the Quebec tide in the Tory favour. The victory would have been won without the speech. In Paris, Bouchard's work as ambassador was outstanding, but it went largely unnoticed by the media back home. When he finally did decide to enter politics, it was Mulroney's sending in of the money and the troops as well as his own prime ministerial appearance that turned a failing Bouchard campaign into a winning one. In the 1988 federal election that followed, free trade was a far bigger factor in carrying Quebec than anything Bouchard had done. Then, once in the Cabinet, while a strong and vital force, Bouchard had also been a divisive one, publicly contesting the prime minister, then abandoning him at a critical moment.

On June 9th, twenty days after Bouchard's resignation, Mulroney won agreement from all the premiers on the Meech Lake Accord. By borrowing from some of the Charest recommendations, he was able to swing over the recalcitrant provinces.

The development appeared to be disastrous news for Bouchard. His future political hopes rested on the division a failed Meech Lake Accord would foster. Celebrating Tories talked about how he was finished as a political force. He would return to the Saguenay as an anonymous practitioner of law. Their glee, however, was premature. The new agreement, to Bouchard's immense relief, collapsed within two weeks as Newfoundland and Manitoba refused to ratify it. But even if the new pact had held firm and the accord was stamped into the constitution of the land, it likely would not have been enough to sink Bouchard or the secessionist ship. His response, in the few days during which the agreement held, was instructive. He took the line that the accord was not acceptable. In so doing, he aligned himself with Péquiste friends who had opposed the pact in the first place. Meech was only, as they had said, to be a first step anyway. Other, more pronounced devolutions of authority were supposed to follow. Bouchard and his new company were prepared to seize on the weaknesses of the Meech pact, charge that no new second deal was on the horizon, and conclude that they therefore had to take matters into their own hands.

When Mulroney reached his tentative deal with the premiers, Bouchard had begun writing a column for *Le Devoir*, the small, literate nationalist organ for which his views were suited. In one of his efforts, he scorned the eleventh-hour Meech pact. "There were two great voids" in the new arrangement, he wrote: "Honour and enthusiasm." They were the very words he had used back in 1984 in writing the reconciliation speech for Mulroney—Quebec had to be brought into the constitutional fold with honour and enthusiasm. Bouchard now charged that the closed negotiations with the premiers were a "masquerade." No honour there. And though the meat of the original accord was in place, solid enough for Bourassa's approval, Bouchard found it vague on a number of points. No enthusiasm there. He said it was unclear, for example, whether the distinct character of Quebec society was being confirmed. It looked too that perhaps Bourassa was conceding ground on the idea of an elected Senate, a prospect Bouchard opposed. Furthermore, he wrote, Mulroney's having to wait for further confirmation from Newfoundland on the deal constituted another humiliation for Quebec.

He was planning to move ahead on a sovereignty crusade, even with the new constitutional agreement in place. Its sudden collapse provided a dramatic kick-start to his new sovereignty campaign. Luck had struck. Instead of undoing him, the Meech Lake drama had put his career on the fast track. He could now say that he had been right all along. English Canada wasn't prepared to give Quebec its due. Public opinion in favour of independence and in support of Bouchard now scaled even higher. In his own riding, he launched a fund-raising drive for the new nationalist crusade. Control of the purse strings would assure him a lead role. Fifty thousand dollars was to be raised for his personal travel expenses. In the words of one pundit, Bouchard now saw himself as "de Gaulle waiting for the call."

Five Conservative MPs had followed Bouchard to sit as independents in the days after he resigned. Considering the lobbying effort from the PQ side that had gone out throughout the year, it was a small number from a Quebec caucus that numbered twelve times that many. Bouchard announced that the dissidents would sit as an independent group of MPs. No political party, he asserted, would be formed. "My feeling and that of my colleagues is that Quebeckers don't want any more parties."

As the most popular Quebecker in Ottawa, Bouchard became the de facto leader of the independent MPs. This gave him some clout, but he soon received more. Robert Bourassa, in close alliance with Mulroney, had just witnessed Bouchard's desertion. Bourassa had also received a pillorying by Bouchard for having stayed on negotiating with Mulroney after the tabling of the Charest report. But the same Bourassa now came running to Bouchard. And Bouchard quickly removed him from the snake pit to which he had been recently relegated and welcomed him with open arms.

In the light of the clamour over the Meech collapse, Bourassa decided to appoint a commission to chart Quebec's political future. Looking at opinion polls, noting who was on top of the sovereignist heap, he had little hesitancy in deciding who would be his first choice for membership. Bouchard was climbing the Charlevoix mountains when the premier called him to Quebec City. The two men met for an hour on the sunning deck atop Bourassa's office. Bouchard agreed to be named to the commission. Their talks, warm and friendly, set the basis for a temporary alliance which would prove important, perhaps central, to Bouchard's emergence. Having discarded Mulroney, Bouchard now needed a new political patron. The Quebec premier would do nicely.

The new deputation, soon to be called the Bélanger-Campeau Commission, effectively took over the work Bouchard had proposed for his great nationalist consultation. Bouchard and his group of associates had been operating under the name Forum-Québec. Many of them became members of the commission. It provided Bouchard with a new platform, an infrastructure and guaranteed media attention. "Perhaps Bourassa didn't realize this," Bouchard would say, "but it was almost a miracle. The Bélanger-Campeau Commission was a bigger, better Forum-Québec, financed by the state."

But the commission was only one gift from the wily Bourassa. Another would help assure him Bouchard was kept at a safe distance from provincial politics. The way to do that was to help this fledging new group of sovereignist MPs develop into a full-scale political party with Bouchard as its leader. Bourassa raised the subject of the pending federal by-election in Montreal and asked if Bouchard was planning to run a sovereignist candidate. Bouchard replied that he was thinking about it. Bourassa soon turned that thinking into action by supplying him with polls showing that a Bouchard-sponsored candidate would carry the riding easily. The polling numbers were an important spur for his decision to proceed.

Bouchard had strange political bedfellows all his career. Author Jean-François Lisée, who would become a top assistant to Bouchard, would go so far as to say that Robert Bourassa was the godfather of the Bloc Québécois.

For Bouchard, another significant ally was Jean Lapierre, the fire-breathing shout-champ who had the look of just having jumped out of a box. All his life he'd been an in-your-face Grit—and a highly effective one. Most recently he had co-chaired Paul Martin's long-shot bid to deny Jean Chrétien the Liberal leadership. Martin paid the price for supporting Meech Lake while Chrétien skirted it. With the simultaneous election of Chrétien and fall of Meech, Lapierre had had enough. He, along with another member of the party, Gilles Rocheleau, bolted the Liberals to sit as independents aligned with Bouchard's sovereignists. An important part of Lapierre's decision was the encouragement from his friend Bourassa.

The federal by-election was in the Montreal riding of Laurier-Sainte-Marie. After some indecisiveness, Bouchard settled on Gilles Duceppe, the son of the actor Jean Duceppe, as his candidate. Duceppe, once a Marxist of the Maoist persuasion, initially brought a Luciferian intensity to politics as well as an ardent social-democratic commitment. The mere fact that he was Bouchard's hand-picked man shot him to the forefront of the race. Although other candidates were pushing the sovereignty buttons, they got nowhere. Duceppe's low-budget campaign was run out of a run-down east-end beer hall. Since Bouchard's group did not have a party organization, the Péquistes ran the show with considerable input from Lapierre.

Bouchard's independents needed a name. The reference that popped up in media reports was "Bloc Québécois." It stuck. On August 13th, Duceppe became the first member elected under the Bloc banner, coat-tailing Bouchard's popularity to register an impressive 67 percent of the vote. Mulroney's Conservative candidate was crushed. The prime minister knew now that his dream of emulating the Liberals in building an enduring fortress in Quebec had ended. His ally since law school had walked off with the key to the maintenance of it—the nationalist base of support in Quebec that had been central to almost every Tory federal election victory.

In mid-September, when the Commons reassembled and the Bloc gang took their seats, a *Montreal Gazette* headline greeted Bouchard with a vicious swipe: "PM Faces His Judas Across the Commons Floor." The atmosphere bristled. In the spring Bouchard had been a member of the Tory team. Now the Tories cried traitor. As "Judas" put forward his first question, one on agriculture, Mulroney paid no attention, looking down at his notes.

Bouchard was the type to be deeply pained by such treatment. Like virtually all public men, he craved popularity. More than others, he went out of his way to make up with people he had offended in the past.

His political course had a consistent pattern. He was always hitching himself to the popular political movement of the day. He had marched under Trudeau's banner when Trudeaumania swept the nation in 1968. When Trudeau's star began to fade, the ascendant René Lévesque became Bouchard's new man. When Lévesque's fall was imminent, it was Brian Mulroney to whom Bouchard turned. And when Mulroney's numbers plunged terribly, in Quebec as well as the rest of Canada, it was bye-bye Brian. The low popularity ratings were only one of a number of factors in his decision to leave, but an important one. Had the prime minister been in grand favour, Bouchard would have been more likely to ride with him. Now, finally he, Lucien Bouchard, was the most popular, so it was his own star that he followed.

The remarkable numbers kept coming in. By the fall, just a few months after its birth, the Bloc already surpassed all other federal parties in Quebec in the polls. In personal popularity, Bouchard scored higher than PQ leader Jacques Parizeau. Among Francophones in La Belle Province, he registered higher than the premier. Bourassa could feel vindicated with his decision to help the Bloc get off the ground and keep Bouchard on the federal side of the fence. As media speculation suggested, he was a threat to the job security of both Parizeau and Bourassa. Although more identified with the PQ, his soft sovereignty made him also comfortable to provincial Liberals who, bending to the political winds, were moving fast to catch up to the new sovereignist trend.

In Ottawa, being leader of the Bloc was no joy. The little party was a target of scorn. It was limited to one question a week. Its seats in the Commons were barely in the building. It was a muddy mélange of a party featuring true-blue conservatives, leftists like Duceppe, Liberals like Jean Lapierre, who became its house leader, and Lucien Bouchard, who could fit any and all categories depending on the day of the week.

Some in the ragtag grouping found Bouchard exceedingly difficult. It wasn't only the federalists who worked for him as a Cabinet minister who despaired of his violent mood swings and authoritarian manner. Nic Leblanc, the right-winger in the sovereignist band, found him, particularly in the early months, "too emotional for politics." Bouchard was dictatorial, loved to exercise power, and didn't like compromises. In rows with Leblanc over policy matters he quickly turned to rage. Leblanc's assessment was hardly comforting. "He didn't have the patience democracy demands," he said. Luc Plamondon, the group's best organizer, found Bouchard overly impatient, insistent that everything be done right away.

At times, however, he counterbalanced his intensity with charm and warmth. Once he took the Bloc members to dinner in Montreal where he regaled them with tales of his sumptuous lifestyle as ambassador in Paris. The waste of taxpayers' money in these embassies was scandalous, Bouchard revealed. He told his troops of six or seven officials there who had limousines—Mercedes. There were so many servants, he reported, even one to take his coat. When he was about to take his first bath at the embassy residence, a lackey asked him what temperature he would like the water. "Well, let's try 72 degrees," Bouchard responded. Upon stepping out of his 72-degree tub, another valet was there to hand him a robe—a room-temperature robe. "It was completely crazy," Bouchard told his laughing cohorts.

Compensating for the limited exposure Bouchard received in the capital was the spotlight he garnered at the Bélanger-Campeau Commission. The commission, which began hearings in November 1990, was to report by the following spring. Most expected it to recommend the calling of a sovereignty referendum for the late spring or fall of 1991. The mood of Quebec made the secessionist scenario sound highly promising. Even the esteemed personage of Léon Dion, the political and constitutional sage of Laval University, had given up on the chances of a calm compromise being reached with the rest of Canada. Given the rejection of the Meech Accord, he told the commission, it was obvious "English Canada will only yield—and even this is not assured—if there is a knife at its throat." Hearing words like this from such a source, Bouchard knew he had the wind in his sails. Dion, after all, was a federalist.

Bouchard's position was hardening. If people had wondered about his inconsistency in the past, they hadn't seen anything yet. In the course of this one year, he appeared to take on three incarnations. From the federalist who had been backing Meech Lake in the spring, he had moved to the sovereignty-association solution of Lévesque in the summer. Now, in the fall, he was talking of complete sovereignty, a Quebec that was a real country. "Quebec must become sovereign just as a child is born, a flower blossoms, a tree grows, conscience awakens and maturity develops. For one must be whole to be able to live up to one's potential and make one's contribution to the universe."

In the early hearings of the Bélanger-Campeau Commission, Richard Holden, the member of the Legislature for Montreal's Westmount and a long-time Mulroney friend, charged that Bouchard was little more than an opportunist who would be a nobody were it not for his riding Brian Mulroney's coat-tails. Bouchard fumed. This was a "lowly, mean provocation" to which he would not stoop to reply, he said. Then he issued his reply.

"I did not enter politics because of friendship...I wanted to give Canada one last chance and see the Meech Lake Accord approved. After two years [in Ottawa] I found out that the country that English Canadians had in mind was not the same one I had in mind. They want a homogenized, centralized country..." Few could agree with his assessment. Because of soaring deficit and debt levels, the trend in Canada was less towards centralization than towards conservative-minded governments, federal and provincial, bent on decentralizing and privatizing to reduce expenditures.

On the issue of the environment, Bouchard favoured centralization himself and got in a brouhaha with Quebec's energy minister, Lise Bacon, for his stance. When Bacon rebuked the federal government for insisting on environmental reviews on Hydro-Québec's power projects, Bouchard jumped to Ottawa's defence. "For the time being Ottawa has powers and jurisdictions in the environment. And it might be that even some nationalists in Quebec must thank God for that because Quebec is not taking care of the environment now." Bacon responded harshly. "I think Mr. Bouchard has always given us a demonstration of opportunism and incoherence in what he has been doing and this is a demonstration that he is still doing it."

More worrisome for him than these criticisms was one of the first pieces of bad news to hit his new sovereignist bandwagon. The financing campaign which was to bolster his nationalist mission had come up empty. Launched in the summer with the target set at $50,000, the Bouchard boosters had collected only $776 five months later. Backers were now on the point of dropping it. "We are very disappointed," said Gérard Deschenes, one of the fundraisers. "We don't understand why Lucien Bouchard, who has an important network of friends in the region, doesn't get more support from his people." The people weren't prepared to move yet, he said. They wanted to wait to see what developed.

Bouchard was working, with some success, to gather a consensus at the Bélanger-Campeau Commission for the calling of a quick referendum. The commission's membership had been divided quite evenly between federalists and sovereignists, but it was the latter, led by the trenchant persuasiveness of key figures like Bouchard, who dominated the proceedings. As commissioners like Senator

Jean-Claude Rivest noticed, Bouchard demonstrated the brilliant litigious and conciliatory skills honed in the courtroom and in countless hours of labour negotiation. Rivest was amazed at how confidently he viewed the prospect of getting commissioners as divergent in opinion as labour leader Gérald Larose and the Liberal André Ouellet to sign a report advocating a referendum. Rivest raised the thorny matter with him. "No problem," Bouchard responded smilingly. Then he went to work with charming, soothing words and a soft smile to do it.

To end the year it was the turn of the ghost dragging his chains, Jean Chrétien, to appear before the commission. Led by Bouchard, commissioners dissolved into laughter and ridicule at the prospect of his coming. Chrétien had just won a by-election in the Beauséjour riding in New Brunswick to secure a seat in the House of Commons. He had not run in Quebec because his former seat in Shawinigan was now occupied by a Conservative. Bouchard noted how Chrétien had won the by-election by only 4,000 votes—even though the riding hadn't even been contested by the Conservatives. Wait till Chrétien tried to run back in Shawinigan against a Bloc Québécois candidate, said Bouchard, in a sarcastic, mocking voice. Then, with a great burst of laughter, he left the room.

Bouchard was on holiday in Europe when Chrétien appeared before the commission, thus robbing a province-wide TV audience of a potentially searing spectacle. Others, like Larose, took up the hammer for Bouchard. "In 1981, during that famous night of the long knives," said Larose, using the line of attack Bouchard would have favoured, "you buried yours in the back of Quebec." Chrétien was on the defensive, choosing not to use a raft of rebuttal arguments the federal side had at its disposal. Instead of pointing out that Quebeckers said in polls they wanted the new constitution, instead of vigorously repudiating the hyperbole of the long knives analogy, instead of using the argument that Bourassa had long-knifed Trudeau and the rest of Canada in 1971, instead of pointing out how the Charter of Rights had realized for Quebeckers an objective sought for a century—the right to a French education in the nine provinces outside Quebec—Chrétien argued, without great success, about how the independence route would hurt the majority in the province.

His performance was reflective of a malaise on the federalist side from which Bouchard and his supporters would benefit enormously. Bouchard was able to gain ground because nobody was prepared to lash back at him and undermine his core arguments. If, with his graphic and poignant oratorical skills, he was spouting fiction, no one on the other side was sufficiently skilled as a debater and thinker to expose it as fiction. Trudeau was off the centre stage. Mulroney was not in a position to challenge Bouchard's analysis of the Trudeau years because he had flipped from being a Trudeau supporter to a denigrator. Joe Clark didn't have the gravitas to beat down Bouchard's arguments. On the Liberal benches, John Turner was no great admirer of Trudeau either and there would be few reverberating corrections to the record from him. Robert Bourassa had support from soft-nationalist quarters in Quebec that he did not wish to alienate. Chrétien was no longer the aggressive street fighter. Once as a young MP, when a nationalist denounced his federalism, he had wheeled around and flattened the man, Marcel Chartier, with a vicious right uppercut—this in full view of chief justices and their wives at a meeting of the regional Trois-Rivières Bar Association. Now he treated sovereignists with kid gloves.

In English Canada there was no great tribune. It had rarely produced the politicians of trenchant force they had in Quebec— the Lauriers or Lévesques or Lesages or Bouchards. The Tory tornado John Diefenbaker may well have had a field day exploding the contradictions and backflips and holes in the reasoning of a Bouchard. But the Chief was gone and no one was there to replace him.

The result saw a fine irony. English Canada was effectively pilloried by a Quebec leader who was as ill-informed on English Canada as almost any the province had produced. Under the barrage of his thunderous rhetoric, the greater part of the country was often defenceless. Federalists flinched. Bouchard had open field. If he had myths to sell, he could sell them.

16. THE POLITICS OF RESENTMENT

Among nationalists in Quebec, the cool, professional Pierre-Marc Johnson saw two strains. One was the city-based rationalist school which preferred the more detached and clinical analysis of the situation. This was the group he felt comfortable in. The other was the more rural-based emotional school which tended towards the politics of resentment and ethnicity. Members of the emotional school were often minorities who tended to see—sometimes before it was even expressed—a bias in the other side's eyes. If it wasn't real, it could be easily imagined. They felt pushed around. Their feelings were easily hurt. A paramount mission was the winning of respect. In the case of Bouchard, winning respect for himself, his family, his Quebec was the lifelong quest. Respect could never come from minority status—only equal partnership or independence.

In his 1995 analysis for the federal Liberals, the psychiatrist Vivian Rakoff explained that the politics of resentment arises from such deep, symbolic hurt that it can never really be compensated for—no matter what the majority population tries to do. Hence, efforts by Mulroney were never sufficient for Bouchard, nor was French power or bilingualism under Trudeau.

The dynamic of the politics of resentment as practised by Bouchard, wrote Rakoff, sees the goalposts always being moved further away. There is "an addictive need for something almost transcendental which cannot be fed by ordinary positivist stuff." When the Tories were nearing the goal line with the Meech Lake Accord, Bouchard backed away. Feelings of exasperation—the Liberals, Chrétien, Mulroney's dealings with them, possible amendments—inundated him. The prospect of a constitutional pact with the key elements in place, though partially diluted, was not good enough. From then on only sovereignty would do.

How could something like Meech make up for the shame of it, for the shame of being held back, of being robbed of the patrimony by Anglo overlords? "Part of Bouchard's life," said Rakoff, "is the rehabilitation of his father and therefore of rural Quebec, and a redemption of those years of priest-dominated, semi-literate, hard-scrabble farming that wasn't part of the experience in France. No enlightenment, no French Revolution, no glorious nineteenth-century explosion of arts and letters. They didn't really share any of that." Quebec governance, he noted, with its imposition of the Catholic Index prohibiting much of the great modern tradition of French letters, was a foremost part of the problem. But people like Bouchard, raised in the years of the Index, focused the resentment on others, not his own.

With the goalposts forever moving, Bouchard could never be satisfied with what the political parties offered him. He had tried so many. He had tried the NDP, the Trudeau Liberals, the Lévesque Péquistes and the Mulroney Tories. Now he had boarded another train in the hopes of reaching the faraway destination. The Bloc Québécois was much smaller, but it had one big advantage. It was his own. He was the overlord. He could shape it to his wishes. "I feel so good about politics since I left the government because now I make all my decisions myself," said Bouchard in a telling remark. "I just consult my instincts."

Bouchard still had to choose among three options: keeping the Bloc in its present form; making it a full-fledged political party; or returning home to practise law with an eye to succeeding Jacques Parizeau as PQ leader. He left little doubt among his Bloc colleagues that his eventual goal, as he told Johnson, was to become premier of Quebec. Though he liked being boss of the Bloc, there were drawbacks. It was small. He didn't like being in Ottawa, where he was estranged from his home and surrounded by hostile faces. He was in his fifties, he had a family to support, a wife who wasn't working and a mere $60,000 salary as an MP. No perks, no lackey to set the water temperature for his baths, and buses instead of limousines.

Most within the Bloc wanted to see it formalized as a political party running a full slate of candidates across Quebec in the next federal election. Another thought Bouchard pondered seriously was turning the Bloc into a new sovereignty party in Quebec. It would be a party of moderate sovereignists of the Lévesque breed. Parizeau's hardline approach, defenders of this idea maintained, would never garner enough support to carry a majority of Quebec in a referendum.

The idea appealed to Bouchard's regal instincts. He wanted Quebeckers to unite under grand projects and grand leaders as they had done in France, but eventually he dropped the idea for the obvious reason that an attempted coup against the PQ would split the sovereignty movement, touching off a bloody internecine battle. The Bloc's progress was already creating unease among PQ pooh-bahs. They weren't sure they could trust Bouchard. "We had legitimate doubts," said party vice-president Bernard Landry, "about the solidity of Bouchard's conversion and his constancy, which was understandable because he had changed his mind several times…" They worried about Bouchard's close ties to Bourassa and Quebec Liberals. They worried that he was not, nor would he ever be, a bare-knuckled separatist.

It was never Bouchard's style to define himself narrowly. The divisions within his own mind wouldn't allow it, nor would his ambition to be a *rassembleur*, a leader who could bring together the disparate elements under the vision of a bold dream. His goals required a more chameleon-like posture.

To Péquistes, he didn't have enough of the old-time religion. To Liberals, like Bourassa adviser Jean-Claude Rivest, he had too much religion, too much ethnocentricity. "What I don't like is the religion of sovereignty," said Rivest. "I look at people I like a lot, like Lucien Bouchard. I call him the modern Abbé Groulx. It's terrible, he has all the same bad reflexes. I don't like people who are full of themselves, and I don't like navel-gazing."

The comparison to Lionel Groulx, Rivest noted, was not to imply Bouchard shared the worst of Groulx's instincts—anti-Semitic and fascist ones. But it was still quite an indictment coming from a friend. For decades Groulx had preached a romantic, almost messianic nationalism involving a sacred mission for French Canadians. His pontifications had sometimes a xenophobic ring. Although Bouchard was no longer a devout Catholic, he was a man of religious faith who, as Rivest noted, spoke like a curé sometimes. His political mission had a religious old-stock fervour about it. It was about more than politics. It was political religion of an exclusionary kind, which bothered Rivest. "We are not only Quebeckers. We are human beings first of all."

Lucien Bouchard didn't just want to be a political leader, noted

Benoît Bouchard. He wanted to be a prophet. He wanted to lead Quebeckers to the promised land. He was the new Moses. "Moses was the symbol. Lucien is the symbol of Quebec. Lucien represents Quebec with its frustrations, with its hopes, with its beautiful characteristics. He believes he has a mission to fulfil."

The conjuncture of time was favourable for such a mission. Since the 1960s, the immense pull of the Catholic Church in Quebec had evaporated, giving way to secular enthusiasms. The population was in need of a new religion, a messiah of sorts, and political nationalism, given a charismatic tribune, could well be it. Bouchard was dated enough in his tastes and outlook and reading to appreciate the power that could be generated by a union of the secular and the religious. In a Western democracy, no such hegemony—as realized, for example, by the Ayatollah Khomeini in Iran—was possible. But Bouchard was not a man lacking in messianic blood.

Occasionally Luc Lavoie, whose unshakeable federalism was surprising for a native of nationalist Rimouski, would try to knock him off his pedestal. He needled Bouchard about his parochialism and victim complex. Bouchard would bite back with a maze of arguments pointing to secession as the only way. These debates sometimes took a most unpleasant turn. Over dinner once, while they were vacationing together, they got so worked up, so brutal with their accusations, that the vacation ended before dessert arrived. Lavoie got up from the table and stormed out. "I told him to fuck off and left the day after."

Bouchard was embattled the first year with the Bloc. Internal rivalries shattered the peace. François Gérin, who had been in on the party's creation even before the Meech Lake crisis broke, felt he was entitled to special status. Bouchard bristled because Gérin wouldn't submit to his dictate. Gérin made public statements out of turn, and exerted constant heavy pressure on Bouchard to turn the Bloc into a formal party. What particularly irked the leader, however, was Gérin's close ties with Bernard Landry and the Péquistes. Bouchard was determined that the Bloc be seen as independent of Parizeau and Quebec City. He wanted to be seen as running his own show. He hadn't forgotten how Parizeau snubbed him when he asked for support in the by-election or Parizeau's arrogance on other occasions. The Bouchard-Gérin feud ended in a bitter exchange in which Bouchard excoriated him for indiscipline. They didn't talk after that and Gérin declined to run for the party in the 1993 election.

Despite the splits in the group, despite low to no visibility in the House of Commons, despite the uncertainty over its future, the Bloc had a monthly injection of good news to sustain it: opinion polls. Support kept growing.

The development that could kill it, ironically enough, was success. Hanging over the Bloc's head like the proverbial sword of Damocles was the possibility of another referendum on sovereignty. A successful one would render the Bloc obsolete in infancy. A referendum appeared inevitable as a result of the work of the Bélanger-Campeau Commission. Here, Bouchard was helping forge a consensus among the thirty-six members representing all the political colours of the province. The hot nationalist mood of Quebeckers made such a consensus possible. The commission recommended the holding of a secession vote by the fall of 1992, at the latest.

The province was now governed by the Bourassa Liberals, but the premier agreed to the deadline. Bouchard appeared convinced sovereignty could be won under the slippery federalist. Quebeckers were chomping at the bit. "I do not see how the Bourassa government can get out of it," Bouchard said of the calling of a referendum. "It would be political suicide. The government that would try to evade this obligation does not exist."

As fine a negotiator as he was, however, Bouchard, along with the other commissioners, left Bourassa an escape clause. They agreed that in the event of further constitutional offers from Ottawa, they would first have to be considered. In so doing, "Bouchard had provided Bourassa," wrote Jean-François Lisée in his brilliant dissection of the period in his book *The Trickster*, "with his mandate, his legitimacy, his breathing space, a licence to try the *beau risque* yet another time."

It was a remarkable turn of events. On Meech Lake, with the publication of the Charest report, Bouchard had seen the Quebec premier stick like glue to Mulroney. It was a seemingly clear sign where Bourassa's sympathies lay. It appeared likely now that Bourassa would go to Mulroney in search of a new offer. The prime minister, having felt the sharp end of Bouchard's knife sink between his shoulder blades, would welcome Bourassa with open arms.

Reverting to the 1970s phase of his life when he signed on with the PQ, Bouchard had now become openly contemptuous of the federal system. His condemnations of its leaders grew more and more harsh and outrageous.

When Mexican president Salinas visited Ottawa, he made some seemingly routine remarks on the importance of Canadian unity. Bouchard got all in a lather. Mulroney, he charged, was "perverting" the laws of international diplomacy by "forcing" foreign visitors to promote Canadian unity, he charged. This, in his view, was a further humiliation for Quebec.

As the Bélanger-Campeau hearings proceeded, the Quebec Liberal Party brought forward the Allaire Report. It was to provide the basis for a constitutional platform for a Liberal Party devoid of one since Meech Lake. Ex-judo champion Jean Allaire and his colleagues tabled a radical document, recommending that Ottawa hand over control of twenty-two powers to the province. Bouchard rubbed his hands in glee. "This practically leaves the federal government with little more to do than lick their stamps," he said.

He didn't want to hear of new unity offers from his friend Mulroney. He began likening the PM's speeches to Jean Chrétien's. Mulroney was becoming "as orthodox as Trudeau... He shouldn't take us for imbeciles and naive people." Taking advantage of the Bélanger-Campeau outlet, Mulroney was preparing another offer of the Meech Lake variety. The plan was to hold a national referendum on a new set of proposals, but if they were defeated in Quebec, the result was not about to be forced on the province. It was, as most saw it, an honest effort by the federal government to find a compromise. But Bouchard pictured it as Mulroney in league with Chrétien concocting a dire plot. The Bloc leader alleged in May of 1991 that they were conspiring to force constitutional changes down the throat of an unwilling Quebec. It was going to be a "*coup de force*" without precedent. "We are faced with mortal perils," Bouchard stated. "The danger is devious and very real." His former Tory colleagues wondered what he had been smoking.

Bouchard and Mulroney squared off brutally in the House of Commons over another set of federal proposals on the Constitution contained in the Beaudoin-Dobbie Report. Bouchard termed the offering inadequate, not even up to par with Meech Lake.

Mulroney glared across the floor. The report was not a final position, he replied. And "for someone to claim—especially someone
who had supported the five conditions of Meech—for him to
denounce as insufficient a document that is Meech plus, plus—that
is hypocrisy without precedence in the House of Commons."

Bouchard responded that even Robert Bourassa didn't consider
this a better deal. Mulroney, he said, was being dishonest to suggest
otherwise. Now Mulroney, stung by the allegation, was on his feet
again. "I don't think there is anyone in Canada or Quebec who
thinks we have lessons to learn from this member of Parliament on
honesty or loyalty!"

As his benches erupted into rousing cheers, Liberal MP Beth
Phinney held up both hands, giving the Mulroney rejoinder a perfect score of ten.

With searing sarcasm, the prime minister continued his assault.
Mr. Bouchard "has become legendary and we will talk about him
for decades. I'm sure that for generations to come, they will be talking about him as a model of truth and loyalty."

The thirty-year bond between the two men had been reduced
to bitterness and sniping. Bouchard's support in 1988 for Bourassa's language bill banning English on outdoor signs had provoked
the split that sent the relationship on a downward spiral. Later
Bouchard had acknowledged this and conceded that the episode
also had badly damaged chances for the success of the Meech Lake
Accord. Now Bouchard went further. He called the Bourassa measure discriminatory and awful. "I recognize that the Law 178 is a
terrible thing," he said. "The Anglophones were let down by the
premier…I recognize that it was traumatising for them." He went
on. "For me, to prohibit the use of a language, to prevent English
from being used, I can't abide it."

From a man of spectacular about-faces, there could be few
more spectacular than this. By a simple progression of logic,
Bouchard appeared to be including himself as one of the architects
of the demise of the Meech Lake Accord. He had resigned from the
government because of what he imagined were the foul deeds of
others. Now, he was making a brutally honest admission, but there
was no suggestion he was accepting blame or responsibility for getting it wrong in the first place. He wasn't apologizing to Brian Mulroney. It was simply a matter of him seeing things this way at this

particular point in time. As Michel Vastel, a journalist who knew him well, wrote, Bouchard was never seemingly bothered by contradictions. In fact, they hardly seemed to register with him. It was an aspect of his character that lent credence to what Arthur Campeau said of him: Lucien Bouchard seemed to operate on different planes of awareness. It was consistent as well with Vivian Rakoff's suggestion that he lived in the scene and the emotion of the moment.

The most cynical interpretation of his U-turns came from author Peter C. Newman: "This is a man capable of anything. He inhabits a world where only what fuels his ambition carries the stamp of reality." But how would his declaration on the language bill fit the theme of ambition? The answer perhaps lay in a statement he made to *Le Devoir*. "We have to keep the Anglophones on our side," he told its editorial board. "I'm convinced that we need them to gain sovereignty."

In June 1991, he officially turned the Bloc Québécois, with its eight MPs, into a political party at a convention in Sorel-Tracy. The founding document, which he and Jean Lapierre drew up privately, made the point that with the advent of the Bloc, federal MPs from Quebec would no longer be used to keep Quebec in its tidy federal place. Mulroney's Tories from the province had reacted to the failure of Meech Lake, the document said, in a way that did not represent the people of Quebec. They had been co-opted by a federalist party. Only an independent political force in Ottawa could combat federal stratagems.

The Bloc leader now made it his goal to win more seats in the province than any of the federal parties. Bouchard was out to show that it was he who incarnated the thinking of Quebec, not Bourassa, not Mulroney, recalled the Bloc MP Luc Plamondon. His potential base of support among Péquistes and Liberals was far-reaching. There was constant speculation that he would be Parizeau's successor. When the PQ leader said that in the event of a loss in a coming referendum, he would resign, the talk intensified. Bouchard did not deny interest, but told the media, "I think you should stop musing about these things."

For the second half of 1991 and the beginning of '92, while Bourassa struggled with the question of how to fulfil the referendum mandate of the Bélanger-Campeau Commission, Bouchard spent much of his time writing a memoir of his career to date. He did it the old-fashioned way—in longhand, with a fountain pen. Having been active in political life only six years, three as a faraway ambassador, the decision to write a book was a curious one, particularly since he was so guarded about his private life. More predictable would have been a treatise on the political culture of the province.

But, as he noted, he wanted to explain all the twists and turns in his life in the context of machinations in his province. The book would also set the historical record straight before other biographers had a crack at him. It would serve to heighten his political profile at a time—before a referendum and before a federal election—most favourable. He was likely quite mindful of the success of Jean Chrétien's memoir, *Straight from the Heart*, which sold over 100,000 copies and served Chrétien's image as the little guy from Shawinigan rather nicely. Lastly, there was the matter of profit— and given Bouchard's modest political income, he could certainly use some of that. The advance, $25,000, was hardly lavish, but good sales could well boost the dividend.

The book, *À Visage Découvert*, insipidly translated as *On the Record*, was a notch above most political memoirs and was reasonably well received by the Quebec critics. Bouchard quipped at the launch party that "if all my political enemies rush out to buy it, I'll be in business." It sold moderately well in the French edition but was a dud when it appeared later in English.

With his political career at full throttle, Bouchard was out to make friends, not enemies. The volume therefore did not stir controversy. People Bouchard spoke of in dastardly terms privately escaped the guillotine of the printed page. Though, for example, he had told journalists that Stanley Hartt's antagonistic attitude towards him contributed to the split with Mulroney, Hartt received gentle treatment in the book.

For an intellectual, it was a surprisingly straightforward rendering of his life. This was not a work in which he in any way tried to emulate the autobiographies of Rousseau and St. Augustine he had taken with him on the retreat in 1980. His text shone in the early pages, his considerable writing talents evident. But the remainder was a largely factual rendering of his career which studiously avoided personal life, private thoughts and other driving imperatives. As well as ignoring his mother and his first wife throughout the text, Denise Bombardier was not mentioned, nor were some of his closest associates. As is to be expected in political autobiography, the writer was selective and heavily one-sided in his interpretation of events. Few attempts were made to explain the dozens of serious contradictions in his public statements and actions. Many unpleasant episodes were ignored. As a great reader and lover of biographies, Bouchard must have realized he was leaving yawning gaps in his story.

The psychiatrist Rakoff wrote in his appraisal of the work that "it signals a 'Bildungsroman,' a modernist journey towards the discovery of an authentic presence—a true identity." What was revealed in the memoir and Bouchard's other writings was enough for Rakoff to issue a discomforting caution to Ottawa. Bouchard was a force who could fuse with the Quebec people in a way stronger that Trudeau or Lévesque. "The dichotomy articulated in the brilliant but now clichéd joke that René Lévesque is what Québécois felt they were and that Trudeau is what they want to be, is healed in Bouchard," wrote Rakoff. Bouchard, he said in so many words, was both. "His origins are humble but his maturity is polished—seigneurial." But "the polish he has acquired isn't tainted by the internationalism, the caricature Britishness of Parizeau who while asserting the Frenchness of Quebec, radiates clubland whiskey/soda, Colonel Blimp. Bouchard's superior attainments don't seem to produce a feeling of superiority like Trudeau, nor the uneasiness among square rural folk generated by the slightly farouche smoking, drinking, womanizing, bohemianism of Lévesque…"

In Bouchard's personal history, Rakoff saw a course running parallel with the larger society of Quebec in the past many decades. "He moved from a rural, ecclesiastically-dominated society to a highly sophisticated secularism, struggling to define itself in its own terms." Quebec was dissociated from the history of France, which achieved its enlightenment and anticlericalism much earlier. Quebec then compressed all these changes into the last four decades—and so did Lucien Bouchard. "Like all magic political leaders, he seems, on the surface, to be seamlessly connected to his constituency," Rakoff analysed. "He is them, he speaks for them.

When he addresses them, starting slowly and moving into a more rhythmical declamatory style, he doesn't so much tell them what he thinks, as articulate more nobly and passionately what they already think and feel."

If this "gifted national poet," wrote Rakoff, "is at one with Quebec, in history, sentiments and loyalties, then acting in self-interest is acting in the interests of Quebec."

To the former head of the Clarke Institute, Bouchard bore the stamp of an anachronistic larger-than-life figure. "He could have been one of those young non-aristocratic men who at the beginning of the new enlightenment came to Paris to stoke the fires of a new age." He was like Diderot or David Hume. Or, wrote Rakoff, he was perhaps better seen in the light of a Bolívar, the last American liberator, "the last great anti-colonialist."

These were grand references but Bouchard's threat to the unity of Canada was hardly a trifling matter. In spearheading the fight for the independence of the Spanish colonies of Venezuela, Peru and Bolivia, Bolívar was heavily influenced by one of Bouchard's favourite thinkers, Rousseau. In 1819 at the Angostura Congress, Bolívar spoke of his Spanish-Americans as a separate breed. "We are not Europeans, we are not Indians, but an intermediate species between the Aborigines and the Spaniards; American by birth, European by right." Bouchard and a great many sovereignists hewed to this "we are a people" thinking in pursuing their dream. It could be said perhaps that they saw themselves in terms of an intermediate identity between the French of France and North Americans.

Bolívar exhibited several character traits consistent with the independence leader of Quebec. As analysed by the historian Paul Johnson in *The Birth of the Modern*, Bolívar was not so interested in the truth of what he said, but the effect. He too was given over to alarmist interpretations and manic episodes. He could radiate ferocious disapproval and frenzy in his intent. His ultimate difficulty, said Johnson, was that he could not persuade himself that the popular will was sound and solidly behind him. He was burdened with "a fundamental pessimism which Bonaparte never knew."

Only by going back far into history like this, Rakoff reasoned, could Bouchard be understood. His ethnic-based nationalism had its roots in old Europe, and "the call of powerful mythologies which go far beyond mere language as an instrument of daily communication." A part of Bouchard wants a nineteenth-century ethnic state, analysed Rakoff, and he needs a contemporary disguise for the longing. Thus, Bouchard and other sovereignist leaders camouflage the more unsavoury aspects of their nationalism by "packaging it into a late twentieth-century notion of a pluralist society, bound only be the use of French as the lingua franca." In fact, said Rakoff, many in the movement are not so intent on pluralism. They are "xenophobes knitted from the yarn of ancient dreams."

His profile heightened by his book, his message more defined, Bouchard ventured back into the political fray, knives as sharp as ever. Bourassa, he kept saying, was pinned down on his commitment to calling a Quebec referendum. Bourassa was perhaps the great Houdini of Canadian politics, but now, he said, he was padlocked and chained in such a way that he could never get out.

But the great Houdini escaped again. In October 1992, Bourassa agreed to hold a referendum on Mulroney's new federal offer, this one put together after some hard slogging by Constitutional Affairs Minister Joe Clark. Bouchard savagely condemned Bourassa's new turn, calling it "a desecration of democracy" and other choice phrases. He could drop allies just as fast as he could take them on. Bourassa had helped him through his first by-election victory, in the formation of the Bloc Québécois and in appointing him to the Bélanger-Campeau Commission. But now, because the same Bourassa wished to take a more compromising attitude towards a national unity solution, he was discarded.

The premier's decision triggered the resignation from the Bloc Québécois of Jean Lapierre, who had assured Bouchard that the Liberal leader could be counted upon to hold a referendum on the secession question. A job offer from radio station CKAC in Montreal at $100,000 a year helped Lapierre in the decision-making process. It was a tough blow to Bouchard because Lapierre was a pillar of his little party, and with him and Bourassa went the Bloc's tentative ties with the provincial Liberals. The Bloc was now woven more tightly to the PQ, diminishing Bouchard's hopes of forging the great rainbow coalition.

Key organizers also left at this time. "Morale was at its lowest,"

Bouchard told the journalist Manon Cornellier. "We didn't have any money. I was always taking the bus. Things were really tough." Operating without support staff perhaps helped explain why Bouchard made so many statements without seeming regard for the established record. He visited Mulroney's home town of Baie-Comeau far up the north shore of the St. Lawrence to rebut the PM's claim that Quebeckers working for the federal government would lose their jobs if Quebec chose the sovereignty route. The vote would have the effect of putting up a wall around Quebec, the prime minister alleged. In Baie-Comeau, Bouchard shot back that it was Ottawa that was keeping Quebec locked behind walls. Only sovereignty, he claimed, would open the way to the world. Sovereignty was the way out through the bolted door of federally imposed parochialism. But it was the same Bouchard who not so long before had been so laudatory about the creation of La Francophonie and the winning of the Free Trade Agreement. They were paramount examples of openings to the world Quebec had achieved under federalism.

On the Charlottetown Accord, as the new constitutional agreement eventually came to be called, Bouchard's argumentation had more weight. He was able to mount a good case suggesting the accord was not Meech-plus, but Meech-less. The federal side maintained the new pact contained no less than thirty-one gains for Quebec. Among them: recognition of Quebec as a distinct society, limits on federal spending powers, compensation for opting out of federal programs, a promise from Ottawa to withdraw from six exclusively provincial jurisdictions including labour market development and training, a guarantee of three Supreme Court judges and 25 percent of the seats in the House of Commons. Bouchard countered that the distinct society clause was so diluted it applied only to language, culture and civil law; that changes to the Senate creating equal representation for each province would leave Quebec on equal footing with the likes of Prince Edward Island; that the seven sectors from which Ottawa talked of withdrawing were already under exclusive provincial jurisdiction in the 1867 Constitution. The Bloc leader bolstered his case by stressing through most of the campaign—until a text eventually did appear—that there was no legal text of the new accord and that many of the proposed changes were so ambiguous they would lead to only more constitutional wrangling for years to come.

The campaign was a high-stakes affair for Bouchard. If the federal side won approval for the agreement in Quebec and the other provinces, his electoral prospects would have substantially diminished. Bouchard may well have folded the party.

No such dénouement was to take place. Events turned in his favour, as if the gods of fate were smiling on him. When his career needed a lift, they were usually there. The ambassadorship in Paris had come at a time when he was at a low ebb. Meech Lake had died when it had to. The unlikely figure of Bourassa had helped him get the Bloc off the ground.

Now came another slice of manna from heaven. His former Laval friend André Tremblay, now constitutional adviser to Robert Bourassa, made a cellular phone call in which he denounced the same Bourassa for selling out Quebec in the Charlottetown negotiations. The phone call was recorded by an outside party and leaked to the media and replayed in the newspapers. For Bourassa and Mulroney, it was like the sky had fallen.

Tremblay hadn't seen too much of Lucien since the old law-school days when they met every night in their apartment in the heart of the old town and opened the cheap wine and set about analysing every problem and every issue they could think of. By now they had switched identities, Tremblay going federalist, Bouchard the other way. In Tremblay's eyes, his friend hadn't changed that much. He was still the angry man, "born angry, born unsatisfied," that Tremblay knew at school. He was still equipped with a fierce willpower to get what he wanted. Tremblay felt Lucien would stop short of nothing to get his way. He will "address you right in your back."

He marvelled at the many different disguises Bouchard could take on. He was like Bourassa in this way, thought Tremblay. But he found a vital difference between the two. Bouchard was also a man of the people. You could call him immature because of his wild emotional outbursts, but these tantrums worked in his favour, said Tremblay. They showed the real man of burning Quebec heart and soul. His friend Lucien was authentic, intellectually brilliant, possessing "an art of dialectic that very few people in Quebec possess." This, while Bourassa, for whom Tremblay now worked, was "a lazy person" lacking in Bouchard's intellectual rigour. During the

Charlottetown campaign, the bloodless Bourassa would say that "in politics, you can't let yourself be led by emotions." He didn't know Lucien Bouchard.

The negotiations leading to the Charlottetown Accord had disappointed and angered Tremblay. He could see Bouchard's point. Quebec was getting undercut this time. Bourassa wanted so badly to get an agreement, thought Tremblay, that he was going the appeasement route. His frustrations with the premier reached the point where he returned to his hotel one night and made the ill-fated phone call. It was to his colleague, Diane Wilhelmy, deputy minister responsible for constitutional affairs. For twenty-seven minutes he vented his dissatisfaction and she responded in kind. When it became apparent the media had a tape, Wilhelmy unsuccessfully tried to get a court injunction to stop publication of the transcript. This only served to heighten media and public interest. When Mulroney got wind of the leak of the tape, he knew Charlottetown was dead. "We're fucked," he told colleagues.

Parizeau and Bouchard established a big lead for the No forces in the campaign. Bouchard worked out of the media spotlight with focus and determination. Those who travelled with him talked of his strength, his demands on his staffers and his demands on himself. "In briefings," said Evelyn Abitbol, newly hired for help with the media, "he kept going over points repeatedly. If he didn't understand something he would go back and forth, back and forth until he was dead certain."

He sometimes insisted on going on long campaign trips by car instead of airplane to save funds. Once on the highway to Rivière-du-Loup he played tapes of speeches by Winston Churchill for inspiration. He had been moved at a rally the night before when he noticed ordinary Quebeckers, people who obviously didn't have much money, making contributions to the campaign and the party. If they could make this sacrifice, he told his staffers, how could he possibly spend their money on the comforts of airplane travel?

As he often did, he talked of his father. He wished that his father, who had died seventeen years earlier, was there to see how well he was doing. If there was something that bothered him deeply, Abitbol found, it was this. How proud his dad would have been.

Abitbol, a woman of Middle Eastern and European background, talked to him at length on matters beyond politics, but there was a sense of formality about Bouchard that was hard to break through. Once they tried to use the more familiar "tu" in speaking instead of the formal "vous." They tried it for five minutes, but both felt uncomfortable and went back to "vous." Even with his good friend Luc Lavoie, Bouchard still used the "vous."

Bouchard's temper rose at an alarming rate, but Abitbol found that he came down from it just as fast as he went up, and she wasn't bothered. How much virtue was there in being in such control of yourself that you're like a machine, she wondered. And while his speeches were often full of vitriol and name-calling, she could see a tender and considerate side to him which was wholly contradictory. No one, for instance, had heaped as much public abuse on Jean Chrétien through the years as had Lucien Bouchard. But there was no predicting this man. On the campaign bus when his aides began making jokes about Chrétien and tearing him down, Bouchard scolded them, saying they should show more respect. Leave personalities out, he said. It was the issues that counted. People had to make a lot of sacrifices to be in politics. Don't make it worse.

He and Chrétien met in a televised debate from studios in different locations. They were each so anxious to knock the other down that their voices frequently drowned one another out. Bouchard unsurprisingly went after Chrétien for his role in the patriation of the Constitution and in opposing Meech Lake. Chrétien, he charged, wanted Quebeckers to be docile and submissive. Chrétien, who had started life burdened with physical handicaps and made it to the top, hardly saw himself in this light. He asked how Bouchard could have been such a stalwart proponent of Meech Lake federalism one day and the PQ the next. Bouchard, he told listeners, would never be satisfied no matter what Ottawa offered. Neither was victorious in this debate.

In the campaign, Bouchard also tried to lure Mulroney into such a debate forum. He wished he hadn't. In the Commons, Mulroney paid brief tribute to the late Quebec premier René Lévesque. Bouchard noted how the prime minister had spoken of a "dead sovereignist" and asked him how he'd like to meet up with a live one in a televised debate. Mulroney rose and straightened his cuffs. "Well, I'm a living Canadian," he asserted and, pointing to

Bouchard, added, "and that's one I brought to life." It was the first time Mulroney invoked the highly sensitive business about his friend having ridden his coat-tails to prominence. Bouchard again challenged him to a debate. "The last time I took up the challenge," said Mulroney, levelling Bouchard once more, "my wife and I travelled twice to Lac Saint-Jean to elect my friend as a member."

The Bloc leader was stung. "This stuff is for English Canada," he told reporters outside the Commons. "This is small stuff... In Quebec it would never fly. He wouldn't dare say that in Quebec. I tell you, I tell you, he's dead if he says that in Quebec."

He survived the bitter personal slights to win the bigger game. The Charlottetown Accord went down in flames on October 26, 1992. The lasting image was of a desperate-looking Mulroney in Sherbrooke explaining how Quebec would be throwing away historic gains if it voted against the accord. For dramatic effect, he tore up the list of them and threw it on the floor in front of a startled audience.

Quebec voted almost 60 percent against the accord, with every region except the island of Montreal and western Quebec turning it down. The strongest vote of rejection came in Bouchard's home area of the Saguenay. The victory constituted "a massive repudiation of the Canadian political establishment," said Bouchard, with justification. Virtually all the Canadian elites were behind the agreement, but not the ordinary people. In English Canada, it was rejected as well.

He now looked forward to the federal election, which would come within a year. Having spent a lot of time on the ground in Quebec, he had a feel for what might happen. He predicted Mulroney's Tories would collapse and that his Bloc Québécois would win an astonishing 50 to 60 of Quebec's 75 seats. Most thought he was crazy. Bouchard knew better. He'd hold the balance of power in the next Parliament, he forecast. And he'd make the government "dance."

17. THE CAMPAIGNER

The old country was never far from his mind. With the federal election less than a year away, with criticism mounting over his absences from the Commons, Bouchard returned to his literary homeland, France, to close 1992. He met in Paris with members of the Academy of International Diplomacy to explain the results of the Charlottetown referendum. But primarily he was there to sink into the cobblestones and indulge the romance of his historical passions. He lamented that there were no more giants, no more de Gaulles and Churchills. It was next to impossible for the modern leader, he thought, to recapture their grandeur. The electronic media and technologies had reduced the world to a sound bite and every attention span was too short. The gravitas of old leadership had given way to flyweight and ephemeral images. "We are all victims of our pursuit of images and clips," Bouchard observed. "We are asked to reduce to ten seconds our thinking on anything and everything." Intellect didn't mean much in politics anymore, as Ronald Reagan had surely proved. What did depth and erudition, qualities Bouchard had in abundance, have to do with it? More important than the *Discourses* of Livy, Bouchard had sadly concluded, was the colour of your shirt. He knew, he said, that blue came across better on TV than white. He was now wearing blue.

While yielding somewhat to the vulgarity of the new age, his heart still yearned for the world of nationalisms, enlightened kings and great ennobling movements. He sensed perhaps that his day was coming and he could turn back the clock a bit.

Twelve members of the European Community had signed the Maastricht Treaty in December 1991. It laid the groundwork for closer political and economic union, for common foreign and defence policies and for a single currency. The target date for the reformations was 1999. Its evolution marked a sterling example of a trend away from nationalism, of a move towards continental cohesion. The North American Free Trade Agreement (NAFTA) marked a similar orientation, though of lesser degree.

Bouchard, however, saw possibilities in the Maastricht model for Quebec and Canada. An overarching structure could be created with an independent Quebec and English-Canadian nations within it. Robert Bourassa, who had studied the European Community while away from politics, had raised the possibility in 1992, offering the model of Maastricht in a positive context. Bouchard took him up on it. "We would do well to look closely at the Maastricht Treaty. There's a case where nations come together to broaden areas of cooperation and deepen what they have in common all the while conserving the base of their sovereignty." If Germany and France could proceed to such a logic of cooperation, why not, he wondered, Canada and Quebec?

The idea was a non-starter in the rest of the country. The rest of Canada, stuck in its ways, could barely come to terms with the notion that Quebec was a distinct society, never mind entertain the thought of reconfiguring Confederation to recognize it. PQ leader Jacques Parizeau was demonstrably unenthralled with the Maastricht proposal for this very reason. He felt negotiations would go nowhere. They would only put off the big dance—another sovereignty referendum.

His position and Bouchard's underlined their differences in approach. The flexibility of Bouchard vs. the more focused persuit of Parizeau. The contrasting styles would be critical as a struggle between the two for the control of the sovereignty movement evolved. Despite his break with the provincial Liberals, Bouchard still liked to be the man of all the people, the *rassembleur*. Only by casting the wider net, he realized, could the referendum be won.

The process of undermining Parizeau—or did Parizeau undermine himself?—began with modest steps which would grow larger with time. As the federal election year of 1993 began, Parizeau, chortling with triumphalism, cast an eye across the voter landscape and saw no chance for consensus. It looked to him like five federal parties would divvy up the seats rather equally. The resulting tumult would resemble nothing less than "an Italian parliament." His suggestion was that Bouchard's Bloc could then obstruct Parliament, thus creating chaos in Ottawa, thus boosting Parizeau's sovereignist drive at home, especially with a provincial election on the horizon. Bouchard didn't like Parizeau nosing into his affairs.

He responded that the Bloc had no intention of playing such an obstructive role. "I don't believe Quebeckers want a government in chaos in Ottawa."

In the highly sensitive relationship between the two men, such small disagreements could take on disproportionate meaning. On the surface they had gotten along well in the campaign against the Charlottetown Accord, though Bouchard had not been pleased by being relegated to such an obvious secondary role. The accord was a federal initiative and Bouchard, after all, was the leading sovereignist at the federal level.

The two men got a chance to agree on something when *The Lafferty Canadian Report*, a Montreal investment monthly, published a confidential offering to its subscribers. Its analysis said that Bouchard and Parizeau based their appeal entirely on nationalism. By way of comparison, the report invoked the demagoguery of Nazi Germany, saying, "Hitler's success was based entirely on fear and these are the tactics of the Parti Québécois."

Bouchard described the comparison as "absolutely unacceptable, almost surreal." He and Parizeau launched a lawsuit against the authors for defamation of character. The baseless comparison brought them sympathetic press coverage from usually antagonistic quarters.

More serious for Bouchard was a similar association made later in the year by the respected former Ontario premier David Peterson. In an interview on TV Ontario, Peterson said: "Bouchard is building his whole campaign on the basis of Quebec's humiliation. Hitler built the whole Nazi movement on the humiliation ... of Germany after the First World War." Peterson said that while he didn't wish to compare Bouchard to the dictator, it was very dangerous for politicians to build movements exploiting feelings of rejection.

The Bloc leader had come to expect harsh criticism from the more redneck segment of the Canadian population. In August, Tory MP Bob Horner, who was chairman of the Commons Justice Committee, suggested Bouchard should be tried for treason. This he could shrug off, but when it was someone he had respected, someone like Peterson, it was another matter.

In the context of such comparisons, it was Bouchard's misfortune to have a demeanour that was confrontational. His persona sometimes resembled that of an old-stock autocrat. With his disarming grin, René Lévesque could come across as charming and benign in the rest of Canada. But for Bouchard, any efforts at creating the image of a nice-guy nationalist were more difficult, particularly given the way he had bolted the Mulroney government. He appeared often as an edgy and bitter man, bearing chips on his shoulder the size of manhole covers. His fiercely intense look, his thuddingly authoritarian verbal thrusts and his penchant for psychodrama were sinister enough to bring to mind unpleasant comparisons. In casual conversations among ordinary Canadians, the frequency with which the comparison to the German dictator was made was alarming.

In rebutting Peterson, Bouchard claimed his movement did not feed off the humiliation, as the former premier alleged. "I never use the word [humiliation]. It is a word I have banned from my vocabulary because Quebeckers aren't humiliated." Bouchard had just used the word in his book, referring to "the humiliation of 1981-82." He had used it so much that columnists like Jeffrey Simpson made a point of saying how tired and predictable he had become in doing it. His newfound view that Quebeckers weren't humiliated was an unfortunate choice of words given his track record. After this episode, however, he did refrain from using the term.

More credible than the references to old Germany were questions raised in the Quebec media by Francophone commentators such as Marcel Adam of *La Presse*. In Adam's view, Bouchard was advocating a *"unanisme,"* or unanimity, which was more consistent with the hegemony preached by Abbé Groulx than it was with democratic healthiness. Bouchard was calling for Quebeckers to vote en bloc for the Bloc while sweeping away the traditional federalist parties in Quebec. The thrust of Bouchard's argument, noted Adam, was that it was impossible to be both a federalist MP and at the same time a passionate defender of Quebec.

Had the province grown out of religious unanimity only to topple over into monolithic nationalism, Adam wondered. Others engaged in similar speculations. How open-minded was this form of nationalism Bouchard was preaching?

Part of the problem stemmed from the one-note nature of the Bloc Québécois. Bouchard's party had been coming under criticism for preaching sovereignty and nothing else. With the 1993 federal election approaching, it decided to put some meat on its bones by issuing a policy platform.

On the political spectrum, Bouchard was a shifting figure, never easy to pin down. He had learned the good lesson of politics—that it was always harder to hit a moving target. He weighed many issues not from a tight philosophical framework but on the basis of merit alone. He thus ricocheted between right and left with regularity.

On economics he was not well-schooled, either academically or from his casual reading, or his career experience. He was right wing on trade policy, wishing to give vent to the market through strongly enhanced continental and global trade liberalization. But on social spending, he told voters the Bloc was the party that would take care of the little guy. In the Bloc's proposed debt-reduction program, no social programs were targeted. He wanted a humanist approach, "*un pacte d'humanisme*." He told reporters of how right-wing ideologues, "some in power in Quebec," were threatening an entire class of poor people. "It's time to close ranks," he said. "There are values of a civilized society and social justice to defend." In taking a position considerably to the left of what he would do as premier of the province, he pilloried as underhanded and hypocritical any axe-wielding in the social program area. Better to go after the tax shelters of the rich. "These are anti-social tax shelters."

His party proposed a $10 billion deficit reduction scheme, $3 billion of it to come from reductions in military spending with most of the rest to be derived from elimination of government waste and the closing of tax loopholes. He'd pour half of the $10 billion that was saved into job creation and schemes such as a high-speed train from Quebec to Windsor.

For Bouchard, the massive deficit and debt was all the fault of the English. "Quebeckers were always told that English people knew all about business and that it had to be left to them," he asserted at his nominating convention in his riding for the autumn campaign. "But we let them run Canada and now we have a country on the verge of bankruptcy." With such statements he left himself an easy target for those even modestly acquainted with Canada's debt history. It had been under a French-Canadian prime minister, Pierre Trudeau, that the debt took wing. In the Diefenbaker and Pearson stewardships of the previous decade, there was no debt to speak of. Trudeau's profligate path was abetted by the work of many of his Francophone ministers. In Quebec, premiers Lévesque and Bourassa ran up debts as great as in any province. In Ottawa, under another Quebecker, Brian Mulroney, the debt raged out of control. One of Mulroney's big spenders was Lucien Bouchard himself. With the deficit already at record levels, he had demanded billions for his environmental Green Plan and had taken great offence at attempts to downscale it.

Bouchard and his party rigidly opposed the death penalty. They were pro-union, they were nationalist on culture vis-à-vis the United States and, as could be imagined, strong devolutionists in pushing Ottawa to cede vast powers to the provinces. On immigration, Bouchard professed an open-door policy for Quebec. In other areas such as the environment, native affairs and justice, the Bloc was vague, and since it wasn't running with any intention of forming a government, it could get away with generalities. More specific policies in these areas would be developed after the election.

More central in the build-up to the campaign than his own platform was Bouchard's villainizing of his federalist opponents. After blaming Anglophones for the deficit and the debt, he unleashed an assault on Ottawa, saying that federalism had cheated Quebec out of billions of dollars. The Maritimes and the West received far more in regional development money, he alleged. In research and development, Ontario received much more than his province. In agriculture for the years 1980 to 1987 federal subsidies to the rest of Canada had tripled, while in Quebec, Bouchard claimed, they had only gone up 37 percent.

An internal study in his own Quebec government by Aurèle Beaulne of the department of industry and commerce painted a different picture. For investments in science and technology, Quebec received a substantially greater share than its proportion of the population entitled it. For industrial research and development outside of the Ottawa-based federal institutions, the same was true, as it was for federal contributions to university research in the sciences. In agriculture, it was generally agreed that no one got a better deal from Ottawa than the Quebec dairy industry. In his study Beaulne issued what was tantamount to an apology for the biases and distortions coming from the mouths of Quebec politicians. "In the first place, we must, to our regret, recognize as an important factor prejudice and partisanship..."

The prejudice and partisanship were, of course, reflected in the way the media in English and French Canada interpreted events. From one media perspective, Bouchard was trying to break up the country. From another, he was on the noble road towards creating one. From such divergent starting points, it was small wonder journalists saw the news differently. Bouchard received a tough run from the English media, and softer coverage in Quebec, with the notable exception of *The Montreal Gazette*, which did not have much clout among Francophones.

Bouchard was not an easy man to challenge. Reporters who crossed him could be searingly rebuked. One such journalist was *The Gazette*'s Sarah Scott. Scott was a bright, sassy writer who had risen through the ranks to become one of the leading political reporters at this, a newspaper Bouchard equated with prejudicial scribble.

She had followed Bouchard across the province for many weeks before the campaign began. In mid-October, shortly before the election, she wrote a lengthy profile of him. The article made passing reference to the fact that Lucien's father Philippe drank too much. "His father was a truck driver with a drinking problem who could barely write." Bouchard had written himself about his father's near illiteracy in his biography. But the reference to the drinking problem was another matter. Many, including Lucien's mother, believed Philippe drank too much. But the reference drove Lucien Bouchard to near apoplexy. He met in an emergency session with family members. He demanded a formal retraction. He distributed copies of a letter to the editor of *The Gazette* to individual members of the press. He re-routed his campaign. He took days to recover. Before the outburst, Scott had developed what she considered to be a reasonably good rapport with Bouchard. Listening to him on the hustings, she was moved by his great flights of poetry, his romantic vision of the world. He could be so impressive. But at the same time she wondered about his emotional stability. Her reservations mirrored exactly those of so many others who had a close-up view. The man was strange. She found that his mind was so easily and ephemerally carried off into different zones of excitability. He rushed into contradictions, into new areas of commitment with no seeming regard for antecedents. Yet there was no evidence of dishonesty or deceit. "I think he is completely convinced of whatever it is he believes in at that particular time."

Prior to her controversial article, she had an experience with him which made her shudder. She was interviewing Bouchard in the Outremont district of Montreal in the presence of his press secretary and the Bloc candidate for the area. She had been given a delicate question by her editor to put to Bouchard. William Johnson, the virulently federalist columnist, had written an analysis mentioning how some of the words in the Bloc program were strangely coincidental with the phraseology of Nazi Germany. Realizing that this would be a sensitive question, Scott waited till the end of the interview before popping it. Before she could finish, Bouchard jumped from the table, his face lit in burning rage, his voice at full bellow, raining down denunciations on her. "How dare you! How dare you! How can you ask this! Who do you think I am! What kind of journalist are you! Your paper is mad!"

As the big, dark cormorant hovered over her, spewing bile, Scott tried to withstand the assault. She offered that she had a right to ask tough questions. Bouchard raged at her some more, and then stormed out of the room, leaving her, the candidate and the press attaché behind, mouths agape.

Scott was incredulous. She had never witnessed a greater fit of emotional immaturity from a public figure in her life.

Sometime later, Bouchard patched things up. He took Scott aside and said he was sorry for what had happened, that things had gotten out of hand. Relations were normal until mid-October when she wrote, in the fifteenth paragraph of her story, the offending words about his father's drinking. Bouchard reacted as though the sacred honour of his family reputation had been despoiled. It was character assassination. "I find it revolting," said a livid Bouchard. "A lying attack," he termed it. "It's a scandal."

Earlier in the campaign, a reporter for an English-language newspaper had described Bouchard's wife as a "Valley Girl," a phrase suggesting a California party animal with a head full of air. The Bouchards were understandably riled by this. Audrey Best was a well-travelled and cultured young woman. As she had informed reporters, she hadn't even been to a rock concert.

In her story, Scott hadn't thought twice about inserting the drinking reference. Fathers with drinking problems were hardly out of the norm in the culture of the time. She wasn't saying he was an alcoholic. Two sources, one a relative, had told her that Philippe Bouchard often liked to have a couple too many. Lucien's brothers later revealed that their mother made such scenes over it that the rest of the family was embarrassed. Moreover, André Tremblay, while an admirer of Bouchard's father and not considering it a big deal, reported how he sometimes made his lumber deliveries smelling of beer.

After writing a strong letter of rebuke to *The Gazette*, Bouchard, with Sarah Scott aboard, re-routed the campaign bus to make an unscheduled side trip to his ancestral family farm. He stopped in the living room, Gérard at his side, and they began singing good wholesome songs from their childhood. Peter Stockland, a columnist at the scene, reported: "He wanted to demonstrate, graphically, that the Bouchard family was not of a kind to be headed by a drunk. His emotions displayed the ferociously sentimental side of his personality: a sense that family, roots, heritage must never be violated."

Bouchard didn't talk to Scott for months. She was snubbed by her former friends in the Francophone media as well and was surprised they would turn on her as they did. "There was a tribal reflex... It's then you realize how you can be an outsider in your own country."

The episode didn't affect Bouchard's opinion poll ratings. They continued their upward climb. One of the imperatives for the viability of his party was to appear as he had just appeared—excessively hurt and offended by English Canada. Anglos were destroying the integrity of his great Quebec family. Anglos had caused the debt. Anglos had said no to Quebec for thirty years on the Constitution. Support for sovereignty required a constant downgrading of the status quo as it existed under the federalist system. Exaggeration was the requirement of the day.

To run an election campaign based on emotion and hurt was an easier sell for Bouchard than an appeal based on logic. Logic would pit Bouchard against some hard facts. In trying to make a case against Canada, he had to make a case against what the United Nations rated as the number one country in the world in terms of quality of living. If he wished to make a case against the way the country was run, he was up against some equally contrary evidence.

At the top level, Canada was run by his own people, French Canadians. A Quebecker had been prime minister for almost all of the last quarter of a century. Moreover, the great majority of the most prominent and powerful positions in Ottawa were occupied by Francophones. The PM was French. The leader of the Opposition was French. The official Opposition party was French. So was the clerk of the Privy Council, the chief justice of the Supreme Court, the Speaker of the House of Commons, the leader of the Senate, the Governor General, the chief of staff to the prime minister and a slew of the top Cabinet ministers and civil servants.

One of Bouchard's favourite themes was that the country was over-centralized. But here too he faced a brick wall. Canada was generally considered, outside of Switzerland, the most decentralized federation in the world.

If the Bloc leader wished to highlight another charge—how Quebec had been beaten down by English Canada in constitutional negotiations—he had to confront a statistic that flew in the face of it. For more than two decades the negotiations had been headed up by Quebeckers themselves: Trudeau and Bourassa, Trudeau and Lévesque, Mulroney and Lévesque, Mulroney and Bourassa, later to be followed by Chrétien and his Quebec counterparts.

In so many instances he was arguing not against the politics of English Canadians, but the politics of his own brethren. To find another federation like this one was not so easy. In the unity debate, in the battle for Canada, the argument could well be made that the great majority non-Francophone population was the off-Broadway act. It was the Bloc member Nic Leblanc who, speaking of federalist and sovereignist Quebeckers, said of the dynamic, "*C'est une lutte entre nous*" (It's a fight between ourselves).

In the face of the evidence, to turn the tables and portray Quebec as a deprived minority seemed to be asking too much of anyone. But to say such was to underestimate the appeal that the emotional fervour of Lucien Bouchard could muster. And it was to forget the potential of the federalist side to blow its case. Though equipped with a barrage of devastating ammunition, it would not use it.

Bouchard was able to tap not the facts but the folk-soul. He could wear wounds. Esoteric clauses on a piece of constitutional parchment had negligible effects on the daily lives of average Quebeckers. But with the traumatic spin Bouchard brought to bear on the subject, it could be made to feel of paramount importance. In an exceptional triumph, Bouchard was able to revive the repatriation of 1982 as a landmark event in the humiliation of Quebec. In the federal election campaign and again later, his charges went largely unanswered. No less remarkable, given his role in it, was the portrayal of the failure of Meech Lake as a rejection of the Quebec people by English Canada. Not only were most of the key players in the drama Quebeckers—Mulroney, Chrétien, Bourassa, Charest and others—there was also a welter of evidence suggesting that Bouchard himself had played a culpable role. But, yet again, his version of events would go unchallenged.

As the prosecutor of Canada, he was able, with his courtroom experience, to take the defence team to the cleaners. Roland Fradette, his old legal master, would have been most proud of the performance, if not the content. On the battlefield of Quebec, Chrétien was badly wounded, painted too boldly by Bouchard's poetry of the blood as a turncoat, an Uncle Tom. He had been put forever on the defensive, unable to take the fight to Bouchard as Trudeau had taken it to Lévesque in 1979 and 1980. In that war of logic versus emotion, it was Trudeau, the master logician, who had conquered. But Chrétien was no Trudeau and Lévesque, for all his charm, was no Bouchard. His indignation was never as acute.

At the time of the 1993 campaign, the country was coming out of a long recession. The pain was real, not imagined. Quebeckers had suffered. The greatness of the country didn't mean much in times like this. Recessions bring a thirst for change. As head of a single-issue party representing a single province, Bouchard could devote all his time to campaigning in Quebec while Chrétien and the Tories' Kim Campbell could only spend a fraction of their time there. In the campaign debates, Bouchard honed his message for this market. He had built an opinion poll lead going into them and played it safe, not allowing himself to fall into the trap his advisers worried about—overreacting to an insult and detonating in front of the cameras. One of the few times he started to smoulder was during the French-language debate when Kim Campbell related that PQ leader René Lévesque was opposed to sending separatists to Ottawa. Bouchard instructed the Tory leader to "leave René Lévesque's ashes alone." A hush fell over the proceedings. Bouchard had scored a poignant and palpable hit.

He ran what commentators termed an almost perfect campaign. A moment symbolizing how everything was going right for him came when, with the cameras rolling at a golf course, he took a putter in his hand and with a flick of the wrists calmly drained a twenty-five footer.

His platform combined a call for a strong attack on the nation's deficit with repeated promises to come to the aid of the poor and disadvantaged. "I am not a Conservative," he said in appealing to the latter group, "and I never was a Conservative."

He attempted the impossible in portraying himself as an honourable dismantler of the country. With many soft words for Anglophones about how he would behave responsibly, he almost pulled it off. Sovereignty wasn't about resentment towards English Canada, he told an audience in Toronto—even though he spent many other speeches detailing the wrongs inflicted on Quebec.

There were moments, such as over the Sarah Scott affair and the charges by David Peterson, when his temper overcame him. On another such occasion, Kim Campbell drove him bananas with a misinterpreted suggestion that she might have to call new elections if the Bloc scored really well. Bouchard admitted to leaving a lot of rubber on asphalt when he heard her, but told a journalist that his reaction was ill-advised and that he was working hard to keep himself under control. "I've decided that the road that must be taken is the road of rationality."

Bouchard had the support of the PQ's strong provincial electoral machine—for which he had Parizeau to thank. With a provincial election coming soon, Parizeau was taking a risk. A poor showing by the Bloc would demoralize his forces and sap momentum. On the other hand, a good showing would further elevate the stature of Lucien Bouchard and thus lend him more of the look of a PQ leader-in-waiting.

The use of the PQ infrastructure proved important to Bouchard. He had this, he had the sympathetic home press, and he had the benefit not only of Jean Chrétien's impotence but also that of Campbell's, whose party had presided through the long economic downturn. Bouchard wisely sized up Campbell early in the campaign. He said she had skills, but was terribly unseasoned, not ready for such prominence. He was right again when, in witnessing Campbell profit from photo opportunities in the dog days of summer, he observed, "People who try to build credibility in politics by image will perish by image."

Campbell's brief bubble began to burst as soon as her shoddy campaign began. Beyond her feisty image, Quebeckers couldn't find any reasons to vote for the Tories. The party's big nationalist base that Mulroney had created in 1984 was no longer there. It had begun crumbling the moment Bouchard fled Mulroney in 1990. The transfer of allegiance from Tory nationalists to Bloc nationalists was almost total. It was the story of the election in Quebec. The Tories won sixty-three Quebec seats in 1988. In 1993, it won only one. The Bloc didn't exist in 1988. In 1993, it won fifty-four seats.

Bouchard had a majority of seats from his province and had just missed a majority of the popular vote there, winning 49 percent. With the collapse of the Tories, the Bloc Québécois had become the official Opposition party in Ottawa. It was a remarkable triumph. Quebeckers were being asked to vote not only for an entirely new party, but one which had no chance of forming a government in Ottawa. The latter fact had persuaded many analysts to project a diminishing level of popularity for the Bloc as voting day approached. Quebeckers, they said, would follow the traditional route of voting for the federal party which was most likely to form the next government. They were wrong. Bouchard had a hold on the people. As a measure of his astute political instincts, he had been forecasting for two years the magnitude of this voter shift.

He spent election night in Alma, not far from the Bouchard family shrine. It was in Alma where, in his shining black wing-tips and ambassadorial suits, he had looked so out of place as a campaigner in his first by-election only five years earlier. He had returned now as a well-seasoned political pro. "I say to our friends in English Canada that our victory tonight represents a unique occasion to forge a new relationship grounded in truth and respect," Bouchard said on victory night. The Bloc would "fight for jobs, for the unemployed, and for the poor." Quebec independence is the only option left, he added, since Canadians had failed to accommodate the province through constitutional change.

His personal appeal was analysed by Alain Giguere, president of the polling firm CROP. Bouchard, he observed, came across as the prototype of the old-stock Francophone Quebecker. He incarnated the image these Quebeckers would like to have of themselves. He was "the ideal mirror." Bouchard "has a sense of drama, of tragedy. The way he recounts Quebec's history seems to be inspired by the libretto of an opera." While grace under pressure may have been the model for a successful leader in other Anglo-Saxon jurisdictions, it wasn't the case in Quebec. Bouchard combined the class of Trudeau, the common touch of René Lévesque and the fire of Réal Caouette, the passionate populist who led the Créditiste party in the 1960s and '70s. There had rarely been a mix more potent.

He had acknowledged during the campaign that he came with faults. In an interview he was asked to name his three worst ones. He responded immediately, as if they had been on his mind for some time. Impatience, an excess of pride, pessimism, he said. But he was working on them. "I decided rather late in life to be patient, to insist on pride in Quebec and to be optimistic." His successes were indeed bringing forth a newfound optimism. The surfeit of pride in himself and in Quebeckers was always with him. But few could attest to seeing much evidence of more patience. Those around Bouchard still often found him brusque and impetuous.

After the election, as leader of the Opposition, it was time for him to swear allegiance to the Queen. He managed to do it with a straight face. He seemed determined to show, initially at least, respect for the country and its institutions. Parliament would function without obstruction, he promised, issues would be debated in good conscience, and sovereignty would not be the only entrée on the menu. Showing a sensitivity to the feelings of many, he chose not to move into Stornoway, the official residence of the Opposition leader. Symbolically it would not have looked right, neither from his side of the fence nor the other. He kept expenses for office space and equipment for new Bloc members to a minimum.

In December he demonstrated more good will by fullheartedly supporting the appointment of Raymond Chrétien, the prime minister's nephew, as ambassador to Washington. While others cried foul, citing nepotism, Bouchard lauded this Chrétien as one of the best diplomats of his generation. Though Chrétien was a federalist, Bouchard said this ambassador would present a better image of Quebec to Washington than his Anglophone predecessors. There were reasons for his generosity. He had known Raymond as a fellow law student at Laval, and when Bouchard went to Paris as ambassador, Raymond Chrétien, a senior official in External Affairs, went out of his way to support him and make his passage easy. Bouchard was soon planning a trip to Washington. He could use a friendly ambassador in the US capital.

He confessed to feeling nervous over the Christmas holidays in preparation for Parliament's grand opening. Only five from his band of fifty-four Bloc MPs had previous Commons experience. He worried that some would make fools of themselves and that he might not be able to handle all the new responsibilities. But preparations were thorough. Even before election day members of the party executive had begun planning for this eventuality. Bouchard himself was a firm believer in the old adage—failing to prepare is preparing to fail.

The Commons was electric when the new Parliament sat on January 19, 1994. Chrétien's benches rose to their feet when the prime minister—who had put in thirty years in anticipation of this moment—invited Bouchard to move forward with him towards the next century at the forefront of a multicultural, tolerant country. "This is a Parliament of different colours, religions and languages, all members of the same family in my party, all members of the same country, Canada," said Chrétien, as his deputy, Sheila Copps, fought back tears.

Bouchard had emerged from his oak-panelled Opposition leader's office, which was once the office of the prime minister. Mackenzie King had plotted the nation's course in World War II from this very space and it was here that Lester Pearson had chosen a flag for Canada. That so much was different now was evident when he stood in the Commons and rebutted Chrétien with scorn. The prime minister was offering nothing but "escapist platitudes." He was ignoring the message of Quebec voters who had sent a majority of Bloc members to this chamber. "He should know the future of Quebec as a sovereign country is just ahead of us, a sovereign country which is a neighbour and a friend of Canada."

It had been obvious all along that this day in Parliament, with Quebec MPs representing the sovereignty option, would come about, he continued. It was inevitable "that these old walls would one day hear the speech of members who would never compromise Quebec's interests in Ottawa." Bouchard spoke rapid-fire for an hour, leaving no doubt that he was deadly serious about his separatist mission. His air of truculence and his impassioned flights engendered some feelings of uneasiness. Chrétien refused to engage him in a debate on the unity question, saying that now was not the time. Foreign Affairs minister André Ouellet scored some points, cautioning Bouchard that he did not speak for all of Quebec, that the Bloc, after all, represented less than half the voters in the province. But most of the pundits awarded the day to Bouchard. The power of his oratory had shaken the Commons.

"Take a look at the Western world," Bouchard asserted. "Ninety-five percent of its population lives in nation states. And the fact is, Quebec is the only nation of more than seven million people in the Western world not to have attained political sovereignty. I invite the members of this House to reflect upon this."

18. DEFYING THE ODDS

While he now had the status of Opposition leader and a bigger salary, he still chose to live in the Holiday Inn at $65 to $80 a night. For lunch he ate smoked meat sandwiches and for dinner it was often take-out chicken from the St. Hubert chain. He was concerned about his physical condition. All the flaring emotion he carried inside him equated with stress. His one body carried the stress of twenty, colleagues related. Sometimes they could practically hear the tension ticking within. In his by-election campaign of 1988, when the subject of his flying off the handle came up, he was candid, telling reporters, "I concentrate three-quarters of my energy on holding back my aggressiveness."

Some mornings he was able to put in a forty-five-minute workout before heading to the office. In the evenings, he took a long time to unwind. He had an inactive social life, rejecting cocktail party invitations unless his presence was absolutely required. His chief form of entertainment, as always, was reading.

When the House was sitting, he returned on weekends to upscale Outremont in Montreal, where he had established a permanent residence to be with Audrey and their two sons, Simon and Alexandre. The choice of the name Alexandre for the first baby was hardly surprising, friends suggested, the great conqueror of ancient times being a central part of Lucien's historic imagination. Alexandre was four and Simon was two. Bouchard read Walt Disney books to them and took considerable care, along with Audrey, that they learned English as well as French.

Best had accompanied her husband on many campaign trips. She told reporters that the twenty-two-year difference in their ages was not the obstacle that might be imagined. "Without being of the same generation, we see many things in the same way: I'm rather conservative myself, traditional." She was also beginning to feel comfortable with her husband's sovereignty mission. It had a look of inevitability, she thought. "If it's not in this generation, it will be in our children's."

She got along well with the media, though there were occasional rhubarbs. Best liked to wear a lot of make-up, and her luxuriant blonde hair sometimes gave her a Barbie Doll look. One day, an Anglo reporter spotted her in the Commons' public gallery, looked up and remarked disparagingly to a colleague that she looked like the type of broad you'd find in a bar in Val d'Or, a faraway Quebec mining town with a reputation for low life and low ladies. A French reporter overheard the remark, relayed it to someone in Bouchard's office who told the leader himself. Bouchard turned so hot smoke practically billowed from his ears. The Anglo reporter was blacklisted.

Bouchard's time away from home grated on him and Audrey. If there was a difficulty in the marriage it was his long absences. When they lived in Ottawa, Audrey had demanded that he stop work and return home for dinner. He was able to follow the regime for some time but now they were separated by the two hours between Ottawa and Montreal. It was hard on the sons. "You know, Mommy," Alexandre said one day, "I love my daddy so much, but he doesn't have time to love me." Bouchard was told about the remark, and, recounting the story later to a journalist, had tears in his eyes. "It broke my heart."

To some degree, as Bloc colleagues reported, the arrival of the children and family responsibilities had softened the rancour within him. Heard less frequently was a favoured description of Bouchard—"A temper in search of a tantrum." But he was frequently bothered by the nature of the political game. Sometimes he would speak of how it energized him, other times of how it made him want to run and hide. Shortly before the 1993 election, he said, "I'm a politician who would like to get out of politics...I hate the word. I hate the job."

As head of the Opposition, he devoted a good part of his first year to spreading the gospel beyond Ottawa and his home province. His itinerary featured excursions to the US, to France and to the Canadian west. A Quebec referendum was perhaps not far off and he had to lay the groundwork for the coming schism. He had to defang himself and his message.

For his first major trip, he chose the power capital of the world. Parti Québécois leaders usually reserved the right of explaining sovereignty to the Washington establishment for themselves. But now the movement had two heads and if Parizeau didn't like Bouchard being diplomatic tribune for the movement, Bouchard wasn't about to worry about it.

In preparing for the visit he steeped himself in books of American history. His reading focused on the Civil War period—a biography of Confederate General Robert E. Lee and one on Abraham Lincoln. On meeting leaders, Bouchard liked to appear knowledgeable about their country and their history. But why was he backgrounding himself in the Civil War period when at this very time he was encouraging divisions within his own country?

As for his own background, he could be sure his hosts were well briefed. A separatist as Opposition leader in Canada was something the CIA would want to know about. As Jean-François Lisée had reported in his 1990 book, *In the Eye of the Eagle*, the American spies had kept René Lévesque closely under watch. The probability was high that phone lines were tapped to Bouchard and his Bloc and that the intelligence men had a file on him several inches thick.

He prefaced his visit to Washington with a stopover in New York for an audience with the unreceptive UN Secretary-General, Boutros Boutros-Ghali. Given the civil war in Bosnia, the division of Czechoslovakia into Slovakia and the Czech Republic, the break-up of the Soviet Union into multifarious units, news of a redoubled effort to splinter Canada did not go over swimmingly.

Bouchard had looked up to the United States since his boyhood. "The truth is," wrote Quebec writer Jacques Godbout, "our ideas come from France, but our myths, fictions, credit cards and comfort come from the United States." Bouchard tended to reflect that reality. He was dismayed by the lack of social equity in the superpower's polity, but looked to its Jeffersonian spirit. He was bent on fostering warm relations, warmer perhaps than with the rest of Canada. His economic message seemed well-tailored for a US audience as he complained of Canada's vast over-governance with extensive overlapping of provincial and federal jurisdictions. He had supported free trade wholeheartedly and, though favouring deep cutbacks in the Canadian military, had recently endorsed the continuation of American cruise-missile testing on Canadian soil.

Conceding that he could hardly expect Washington's support, Bouchard expressed hope that the world's only remaining superpower would at least remain neutral while Quebec made up its mind. As if Americans considered him a dark force, he felt compelled to disassociate his movement from the extreme forms of ethnic nationalism in the former Yugoslavia. "I myself have participated in the House of Commons in the general condemnation of Serbian expansionism and urged the Canadian government to stay the course in Bosnia."

But he was in no way trying to camouflage his intent. For the first time, Lucien Bouchard contentedly declared himself a "separatist." He had eschewed such a description in the past. With his blessing, Bloc members had frequently risen in Parliament to object to being called separatists as opposed to sovereignists. But now, said Bouchard, in giving the blunt term his imprimatur, "Things have to be clear. We can't allow ourselves to come to the United States and explain what's happening at home in terms they won't understand ... We want the separation of Quebec from the Canadian federation."

Neither President Clinton nor Secretary of State Warren Christopher saw him, which was a far cry from the days when Brian Mulroney went to Washington as Opposition leader and was ushered in for a warm audience with the Gipper himself. Mulroney and Reagan set the basis that June day in 1984 for an enduring camaraderie. Mulroney subsequently introduced Bouchard, in glowing terms, to Reagan, and Bouchard also had occasion to meet President George Bush.

Having graduated to Opposition leader himself, he was able to see only a clutch of Congressmen and an official from the State Department. But he won modest praise from the legislators, convincing them he was not about to establish a Cuba of the north. His charm-offensive was hardly in the league of a Gorbachev, who had the capital at his feet in his heyday, but generally Bouchard accomplished his defanging mission.

He had one advantage over predecessors. Since the end of the cold war, Washington viewed the prospect of Quebec secession with less urgency. With the Soviet menace gone, a unified and friendly country to the north was not as important. Americans had several countries to the south of them. A couple to the north would hardly be traumatic. Bouchard, overstating the case, went so far as to say there was no nervousness on the part of his hosts about separation. "The question in Americans' minds now is more related to how than why."

The leader of Canada's Official Opposition likely felt less a stranger on the Potomac than he did in Western Canada, the next stop. His visit was, in part, to promote the English translation of his memoir, *On the Record*, which was appearing two years after the French edition. *The Edmonton Journal*'s take on his tome might have provided him a foretaste of the attitudes he was up against. The critic Satya Das likened Bouchard to a Canadian version of Vladimir Wolfovich Zhirinovsky, the vodka-soaked hypernationalist of the Russian right. Bouchard was a leader, wrote Das, who sought out humiliation like most people look for love affairs. Bouchard's book revealed "an ardent tribalist, convinced of his moral superiority, an intense collector of real and perceived insult and humiliations, who has a full measure of contempt for Quebeckers who do not share his views."

The Bloc leader tried to be frank and at the same time unprovocative in the West. He was received respectfully by some citizens and commentators, but excesses piled up as he went along. In Alberta, callers identifying themselves as rednecks urged Bouchard to get Quebec out of the country as soon as possible. Bouchard responded that he'd be only too glad to oblige. In Calgary, following his address to the chamber of commerce, the deliverer of the intended thank you speech turned it into a lecture. Bouchard sat stone-faced, looking as lonely as his volume on the shelves of the bookstores. It sold like mudcakes.

A *Maclean's* magazine column suggested that it might be a good idea if Teddy Kennedy invited Bouchard for a drive home one night. The reference was to the 1969 tragedy at Chappaquidick wherein Kennedy's car plunged off a narrow bridge into the dark waters below, killing a female occupant. Alberta premier Ralph Klein joined the bash-Bouchard bandwagon, expressing wonderment that the leader of the Opposition wasn't expelled from the House of Commons. "I mean, Louis Riel was." Should Bouchard be considered a traitor? a reporter asked. "I'm not going to say it," Klein responded. "I was hoping you would."

Bouchard might have anticipated kinder words from his 250,000 Francophone brethren in New Brunswick. But there he was bluntly told that they didn't want any part of his separatist plotting; that an independent Quebec would be disastrous.

He had it tougher than other secessionists because he had only just changed masks. He had so enjoyed his rapport with François Mitterrand the first time round, but now, returning to France under his new guise, he was greeted coldly by the French president. No more long discussions of literature and history. Only basic questions: "What's happened? What have you done? What is the Bloc Québécois?" On his way out, Bouchard, taken aback by the chilliness, saw the Élysée Palace's Republican Guard emerge. They stood at regal attention, sabres and plumes, ruffles and flourishes, all the pomp and circumstance. "It's for Lucien!" one of Bouchard's aides excitedly told the media. Alas, it wasn't for Lucien. Just as he was leaving, the prime minister of Slovakia was making his way in.

Bouchard dropped by the Canadian embassy, where he had enjoyed many successes as ambassador. In his former chair now sat the other Bouchard from the Kingdom of the Saguenay—Benoît Bouchard. He had remained loyal to Mulroney and was rewarded with the prestigious post. The two Bouchards had hardly spoken since the split in 1990. Benoît had come to regard Lucien as a craven opportunist lacking in emotional stability. Lucien Bouchard's people had come to regard Benoît as a traitor to Quebec who had traded in his honour for a limousine. They managed in their meeting to evince a measure of politesse and the new ambassador declined any opportunity to impugn his rival in the media. Foreign Affairs minister André Ouellet had already spoken for the government. "I'll be very frank with you. I don't like Mr. Bouchard using his title as leader of the Opposition to travel through the world to promote the independence of Quebec. I frankly resent it."

The Bloc leader failed to get meetings with Prime Minister Edouard Balladur and the estimable Jacques Chirac, but Socialist party leader Michel Rocard endorsed his secessionist vision, as did Philippe Séguin, the chairman of the National Assembly. The success or failure of the *tour de France* depended on which media the Canadian reader chose. *Le Devoir* said that Paris had fitted Bouchard like a glove, that Senate and National Assembly members were stopping to shake his hand, that he was overloaded with invitations, that there were no snubs of any kind. It was the opposite of the impression left by newspapers outside Quebec.

At home, Bouchard was faring better. As Opposition leader he was garnering positive reviews from both English and French media. The consensus of the critics suggested that he had built a disciplined and professional team, that he easily outperformed the leader of the Reform Party, Preston Manning, and that if one were to subtract his secessionist purport, Bouchard would rate as one of the best Opposition leaders the country had produced.

The Bloc's effectiveness flowed from his domination and discipline. Because it was basically a single-issue party, it was far easier for its leader to maintain cohesion than it was for the leaders of the traditional Grit or Tory ensembles of disparate elements. But Bouchard gave the party force, presiding over it like an old-fashioned master of a *collège classique*. Nothing was slipshod, nothing left to chance. His MPs' schedules and duties were clocked by the hour. Decorum and dignity were enforced. Members were summoned to answer for even minor mistakes. Pierrette Venne, a Tory defector to the Bloc, was told one day to find out from the Speaker of the House if Bouchard would be given time to ask a question. Venne had trouble getting a specific response. Bouchard sent her back and she got some information from the Speaker, but not enough to please Bouchard. He was furious. He shouted that if she couldn't do it, he would bloody well do it himself. By the next day, he had calmed down and the incident was forgotten. Bouchard was extremely demanding, Bloc members said, demanding and sometimes severe, but since he was that way with himself as well, it was easier to take.

Daniel Turp was one who found that the party must speak with one voice. Turp, an international legal specialist and president of the BQ's policy commission, wrote an article endorsing the right of aboriginal people in Quebec to secede from the province. It was an admission heavy with portent. Turp was saying, in so many words, that if Canada was divisible, so was Quebec. It was the line that was to become the birth song of the partitionist movement in the province.

"The native nations," said Turp, "are in a position similar to that of the Québécois when it comes to invoking international law in support of the claim that they have the right to self-determination." Bouchard had already flatly declared in the Commons that aboriginal people did not have any such right in Quebec. The dispute, after making headlines, was soon resolved. Turp issued an aye-aye sir statement of clarification. His press release—*L'état c'est Lucien*—revealed that he would not be making any further declarations on the matter.

Nobody bucked the boss. His utter control was noticeable to all. Paddy Torsney, a young new Liberal MP, watched from across the aisle in awe and angst at how the troops fell in behind him. One afternoon, Bouchard was standing in the front row, firing on all cylinders, his disciples thumping their approval. Now Bouchard decided he wanted silence. His back to them all, his arms at his sides, he spread open his hands and lowered them. The slight downward gesture was all it took. His flock turned as mute as doves.

Paul Martin, the finance minister, had come to savour sparring matches with Bouchard in the House. Martin had become a powerful performer after a few years of on-the-job training. One night over dinner as the gentle waters of the Rideau Canal flowed by, he expressed wonderment at the Bloc leader. Some days in the House he was formidable. On other occasions, noted the finance minister, it looked like there was something wrong with him, maybe a health problem. Whatever it was, said Martin, there were days when Lucien "wasn't all there."

On average the Bloc spent two hours a day preparing for Question Period. Bouchard took the members through dress rehearsals, advising them on what to say and how to say it. The government's probable responses were speculated upon and follow-up questions set accordingly. Research was thorough not only on matters pertaining to Quebec. Bouchard, for example, put himself and the Bloc through exhaustive preparation on the issue of the defence of English-Canadian culture as it applied to book publishing. Ginn Publishing Canada had been sold to America's Paramount Communications. The deal was in apparent contradiction of the Mulroney government's Baie-Comeau policy, which decreed that if there were potential Canadian buyers, as was the case with Ginn, a sale to the Americans could not take place. Bouchard made hay of it in the House with an analysis deep in statistics and background. "Culture is the very essence of national identity," he asserted. "When it comes to the soul of the country, we have a duty to protect it." His voice grew harsh. "We must protect what we are!"

Beyond his secessionist message, the area in which Bouchard was becoming most vulnerable was on the matter of contradictions. His U-turns were starting to be noticed. For years he had portrayed the failure of Meech Lake as a rejection of Quebec by English Canada. Now, he was amending his thoughts on this—the issue that served as the very springboard for the formation of his party. The failure of Meech, he told Peter Gzowski on "Morningside," wasn't so much a rejection of Quebec. "My thinking about that has evolved. I might accept now that it was more the fact that English Canadians had a vision of their country and this vision called for equal provinces, no special status. And that they wouldn't recognize their own country if Meech was adopted."

He had spoken so often about how the English had held his province down through their domination of the Quebec economy. Now he was singing a different tune on this score as well. "They are full-fledged Quebeckers and personally I would do anything to keep them in Quebec because we need them to build a strong Quebec to succeed. They have been part of Quebec for hundreds of years and have been quite instrumental in the success of Quebec."

Journalists were tuning in. "Lucien Bouchard is in a curious position indeed," wrote Lysiane Gagnon in *La Presse*. "The man is playing so many different and contradictory roles that one wonders how he manages to remember who he is when he gets up in the morning."

For the Quebec provincial election campaign in the fall of 1994, his incautious pronouncements could sew divisions with Parizeau. The media would be on the lookout for clefts between one sovereignty-seeker and the other. Bouchard therefore stayed in the background. He kept his Bloc members on federal business and discouraged the press from following him as he attended a series of low-profile events to shake hands and plug the PQ slate. It was a comfortable few weeks. He stayed clear of controversy and bathed in the support of ordinary Quebeckers who simply wanted to shake his hand.

But the campaign might well have benefited from a higher profile of him. Parizeau had a sizeable lead over Liberal leader Daniel Johnson at the outset and was expected to win handily. He ran a non-aggressive campaign, beating the drum softly on the sovereignty theme so as not to scare voters. Meanwhile, Johnson worked vigorously, buying up three times as much air time and slashing away at the sovereignists' real intent. The results of the September 12th election were almost a dead head: The PQ squeaked by with only 13,744 more votes. It won a majority of seats, but only 44.7 percent of the popular compared to 44.4 percent for the Liberals.

At the victory rally, Bouchard looked like he was attending a funeral. In certain respects he was. But it wasn't his. It was a dirge for the man he wanted out. Bouchard had expected at least a 48 percent vote for Parizeau's PQ. It would be a good base to take into the next referendum campaign. But at the lesser number, he felt the prospects were sadly diminished.

Parizeau's loss, however, was Bouchard's gain. In the end, Bouchard's low-key strategy paid off because he didn't share in the blame for the disappointing results. Given Parizeau's performance, more and more sovereignists in Quebec now looked to Lucien Bouchard to lead them to the promised land.

Looking at the months and years to come, he was in a favoured position. If Parizeau went ahead and led the way to a referendum triumph, the goal of sovereignty would be realized. If Parizeau fumbled the ball—and the Bloc leader was only too willing to grease it for him—Bouchard's other dream would be well within reach. He would be premier of Quebec.

In late November 1994 he attended a party meeting and dinner at Mont Ste.-Anne near Quebec City. It was a festive occasion. He gave a speech, was in high spirits and joined in the dancing. The following day, a Sunday, he felt weak with what he thought was the flu. He took Monday off but felt worse. A pain had developed in the back of his left leg. He cancelled a scheduled dinner with the US ambassador and was admitted to hospital in Montreal on Tuesday. The initial diagnosis, which he later came to regret, suggested he was suffering only from an inflammation of the veins in the leg. The name of the malady, phlebitis, had become known to the public when Richard Nixon came down with it in the 1970s.

By Wednesday doctors discovered that Bouchard had contracted something many times more grave. It was an infection of an alarming, one-in-a-million kind called necrotizing fasciitis. The more lurid name for it was flesh-eating disease. As barbaric as it sounded, the term did not overstate the reality. The devouring and deadly process saw bacteria root under the skin. Then, in a cannibalistic frenzy, the toxins tore through the flesh, gorging on the body's nutrients.

No one was sure how Bouchard had contracted it. He had complained only of being very tired in the days before entering the hospital. Some, including family members, were led to believe that his draining work pace had taken its toll on his nervous system—he had lost all those pounds with the gum infection not so long ago—leaving him vulnerable to such bacteria. But no one knew. Some specialists speculated he could even have got it at the hospital. So many of these places were unsanitary.

Audrey Best had flown home from New York, where she had been visiting a friend for a few days. She was at her husband's side later Wednesday when doctors on the fourth floor at St. Luke's Hospital revealed to Bouchard the gravity of the situation. They wanted permission to amputate his leg at mid-thigh. Otherwise, at the rate the surging bacteria were progressing, they would reach his abdomen and chest. The news jolted the patient. He conferred with his wife and they informed the doctor, Patrick D'Amico, that, of course, his life was more important than his leg. They must go ahead with the amputation. He was wheeled to the amphitheatre where the operation was carried out. The surgeons hoped it would be enough, but soon they discovered otherwise. They were too late. The contaminants were progressing to the upper regions of his body.

On Thursday the physicians opened him up again to get into the abdomen and the chest to expunge infected muscle and fat. Meanwhile heavy doses of antibiotics were injected to try and stem the toxins' advances. Bouchard's wife looked on, never succumbing to high emotion or hysteria. She transmitted a message of strength and unswerving confidence that he would get through it.

But if the antibiotics didn't work—and it seemed they weren't working—Lucien Bouchard had no chance to survive. He was conscious enough to know the gravity of the moment. He had hours, perhaps minutes to live. They say that in such circumstances the images of the victim's life pass before him—a desperately timed highlight reel. Bouchard now had that experience. He was reliving "all my life, every second with my father, my childhood."

The hospital had informed the outside world that Bouchard was in serious but stable condition after the leg amputation. Inside,

Lucien's brother, Gérard, was being told the real story. The infection was progressing to the heart. The antibiotics were not kicking in. Nothing could be done. "The doctor, at some point during the day of Thursday, December 1, called me into a room," recalled Gérard. "He explained to me that Lucien was going to die."

Usually if there is any hope, the doctors offer it to those closest. But not this time. Gérard, the only member of Lucien's parental family at the hospital, was convinced it was over. He decided he had best be with his mother—his mother who had worried much of her life about Lucien's health—to deliver the news personally.

He phoned home and asked his wife to take Mrs. Bouchard from her senior citizen's apartment in Jonquière to their home. Then he booked a flight to Chicoutimi for the early evening. Among other things, he had to start thinking about burial arrangements.

In the meantime, the desperate physicians, led by Doctor Patrick D'Amico, were taking advantage of computer technology to research all the documentation on the extremely rare disease around the world. They found two cases that had been successively treated by an injection of a special cocktail of immunoglobulins taken from the blood of various donors. In both cases the flesh-eating disease had been halted. The physicians of St. Luke's were able to make such a concoction and in a final expression of hope, they injected Bouchard with it.

A couple of more hours passed. Gérard prepared for his flight home. "It was four o'clock. My brother was unconscious but still breathing." At five the doctors reported the progress of the infection had stopped. That didn't mean it wouldn't start again, but now there was hope. At six, the bacteria were still in abeyance. By seven, when Gérard had gone to the airport, still the same.

It was at this time that the impression leaked from the hospital that Bouchard had died. It spread to Prime Minister Jean Chrétien, who was in Europe. He was of a mind for some time that his arch-foe had succumbed. The rumour reached dinner parties in Ottawa, one being that of the *Globe and Mail* reporter Susan Delacourt. Tory leader Jean Charest and his wife, Michelle, were present along with several other guests. Chantal Hébert of *La Presse* told the gathering that she had heard a report from her newsroom that Bouchard was dead. She ran upstairs as a hush fell over the table. Jean Charest got up and walked across the room. He turned and, with his back to the wall, slowly started knocking his head against it; back and forth, back and forth. Delacourt asked if he was okay. Charest spoke of the emotional upheavals this man had put him through; the deceptions during the Meech crisis. He was full of conflicting feelings now and he didn't know what to say or do. He had come to detest Bouchard before this evening—and the feeling was mutual. Now he had to reconcile those feelings with the horrendous tragedy.

Gérard Bouchard arrived in Chicoutimi. He had been calling the hospital every hour, making sure there was no news that the march of the bacteria had recommenced. There wasn't, and he was able to tell Alice Bouchard that Lucien was going to make it through. Early in the morning he awoke and turned on the radio to hear more bad news. As well as a leg, the ratio station was reporting that Lucien Bouchard had now lost an arm. Was it going to be limb by limb? Fortunately, Gérard was able to find out before too long that it was a false report. Then the doctors held a press conference to announce that, barring the unforeseen, Lucien Bouchard was in the clear.

The gamble with the special medical treatment had worked. A combination of the availability of the computer technology and doctors smart enough to take advantage of it had most likely saved his life.

There had been one-in-a-million chance, according to medical estimates, of him contracting the killer virus. Then, given its progression, the odds were almost as fantastic against him surviving it. Lucien Bouchard had defied the impossible numbers both times.

His brothers spoke of the power of the presence of his wife and the magnificent steely confidence she transmitted. He had always spoken of Audrey as being so strong. It was confirmed now. Even more powerful perhaps was the picture of his two sons. He had to survive for them.

His fellow mountain climbers, de Belleval and Gaston Ouellet, talked to him. Bouchard spoke of the fates. "I could have won the Lotto, I suppose," he said. "Or I could have got the microbe." They knew from their experiences of climbing with him that he was a man of exceptional raw physical strength and stamina and they were convinced that this was what pulled him through. He knew it too, de Belleval said. "He knew he survived because of his resistance. He could have been killed as much by the side effects of the antibiotics. But he had the strength to ward it off."

Bouchard was deeply grateful for the work of the doctors. There was, however, the nagging thought, as he told friends, that they had goofed with the initial diagnosis in saying that his problem was nothing more serious than phlebitis. Had the bacteria been spotted sooner, his leg might have been saved. There was the possibility too, though, that the infection had set in at the hospital— and that the first time he was examined, the flesh-eating bacteria were not present.

His friends saw him in his ravaged state, his face sunken, ghoulishly pale and bloodless. His eyes were very, very soft and full of kindness and vulnerability. "He had the eyes," said de Belleval, "of someone who had returned from the dead." Luc Lavoie had tried to get through to Audrey Best during the ordeal. On Sunday she called him back and said Lucien wanted to talk to him. Bouchard came on the phone. He was choked with so much emotion he could hardly talk. He was panting weakly for breath and he wept throughout the conversation. Lavoie recalled he had a simple message. He only wanted to say that he was alive.

The nation's outpouring of sympathy was genuine. For a time it stood united, a strange kind of unity because it was for the country's leading force for dissolution. "At moments like this," said the prime minister, "we put political differences aside to express our personal solidarity with the suffering of a fellow human being." Reform MP Jan Brown, with her flare for the dramatic, walked over to Bouchard's empty desk in the House and placed a yellow rose on it. Jacques Parizeau asked his "old friend," as he called him, to hang on. "Show the same courage that you've shown so often in the past... And I hope that soon it will just have been a very bad dream. Hang on, old friend. Hang on."

There were, as might be expected, a welter of crass developments. There were reports that he was dead, that he had had other parts amputated, that Parizeau's office had already started funeral arrangements. There were reports speculating on the political impact of his ordeal—how would it affect sovereignty polls?— before he was even in the clear. The strange drama resulted in a damaging rupture in relations between the wives of Parizeau and Bouchard. Parizeau's second spouse, Lisette Lapointe, made an appearance at the hospital, getting past security to offer moral support to Audrey and family. The next morning Ms. Lapointe spoke of her gesture on television.

It seemed like a natural thing to do, but Audrey Best saw the TV clip and took great exception to it, feeling Ms. Lapointe was crudely trying to exact political gain. She was so disgusted that she told her husband she never again would attend a political event with Parizeau's wife. The two women had never enjoyed harmonious relations. Now the rift was such that it added to the tensions in the relations between their husbands.

Through these days, Bouchard's popularity soared in Quebec. As Claude Charron, the former Lévesque Cabinet minister, put it, he had moved from simply being the most loved politician in the province to one of near mythic stature. To endure the torment, the amputation, the ravaging of an affliction so horrible—was this not confirmation of legendary valour? Symbolism could be drawn for those who wished to draw it. He embodied Quebec's dream, and the dream had refused to die.

He would perhaps be the first to say his survival didn't require exceptional courage. In such instances, the circumstances take over, the circumstances of medicines and doctors' skills and countless variables of the body while the sufferer awaits the verdict.

But there could be no doubting the impact of the trauma on the collective consciousness of Quebec. While his life hung in the balance, while he was semi-conscious, he had scribbled a note to doctors. "*Que l'on continue, merci!*" ("Carry on, thank you!") Many saw the message as teeming with political connotation. Come what may, the afflicted man was saying, the march towards sovereignty must proceed. It was the ultimate act of altruism—the dying man thinking not of himself, but of the movement!

Gérard Bouchard had noticed that "the thing that people seem to like in Lucien is that he looks sometimes to be fragile, like they are. They don't see him as an iron man." Outside the hospital, Gérard found that many of the people who came by, night and day, were poor people. "I discovered the nature of the relationship they have with him." It was the same at home, in the Saguenay, he said. "It is not a story of power. It is not that at all. It is the story of humble people who believe that one of them, one like them, will be able to defend their interests." Now that Lucien had lost a limb, the special bond was intensified. Now he could be seen to be carrying their pain with him. He was their stricken hero, a martyr. He had survived, miraculously, to carry the torch for them.

Bouchard let it be known that he would be resuming political duties as quickly as possible. Within days of his operations, he was passing on instructions to his talented chief of staff, Gilbert Charland, and others. Bouchard worked determinedly at rehabilitation for a couple of months. He learned to walk with the prosthesis. He built up his shoulders and one good leg to formidable strength. When he began doing interviews, he was asked what his signed message from the hospital bed had really meant. "I had in mind the idea that we should not stop there," he told Radio-Canada's Jean-François Lépine, "that we had to continue, that Quebec's future was more than a poll...that it had to be more than one individual's fate." So it was a political message? "Oh, yes, it was political, I modestly confess, it was political."

But had he really—in the intensity of the emergency chamber, heavily sedated, hanging by a thread, surgeons hovering awaiting instruction, his past life flashing before him—been thinking of the future of a political movement to which he had only been committed on an intermittent basis? His staff thought not. Before the interview with Lépine, the staff had put out the opposite interpretation. They had said the message was obviously just a simple instruction to his physicians to keep going.

Later, when Bouchard realized confusion was mounting over the matter, he stepped back from what he had told the interviewer. "I never knew that they [the words] would be published and have a political character," he said.

With all the publicity surrounding the note, it appeared as though Bouchard had found himself in a quandary. He didn't want to lose all the political capital that went with the political interpretation. The best strategy, then, was to fudge his way through it—to make it appear it was a message of both medical and political significance. One of his final comments on the matter was to this very effect.

He came under some criticism for the mixed signals. Then he received a more sustained rebuke for allegedly trying to stage-manage his return for maximum public relations advantage. When he returned to the public arena in February, Bouchard redefined the term "exclusive interview." He gave about a dozen of them. To get one of the soul-baring exclusives, news organizations had to pass certain criteria. The stories had to run on the front page and they would follow in appropriate sequence. Exclusives given to more favoured outlets had to come first.

Chantal Hébert of *La Presse* compared the media blitz to the marketing extravaganza for the wedding of the celebrated chanteuse Céline Dion. Hébert's newspaper chose not to take part in this "dance of the seven veils," as she called it, declining an interview with Bouchard because of the conditions imposed. The story soon became not the Bouchard comeback but the tawdry fashion in which he was apparently exploiting it. Bouchard's reaction to all the criticism suggested he was back in good health. He fumed, just like in the old days.

In fact, the stage-managing of media coverage was an old and commonly practised art in politics, and Bouchard, in his unusual circumstance, could hardly be faulted for trying to gain the maximum advantage. But it didn't look right that someone who had suffered so much and was seen as a martyr could suddenly appear so calculating.

Yet again, he was a wellspring of conflicting signals. He told *The Globe and Mail* he hadn't had time to stage-manage his return, but in a press conference that followed that interview, he said he had made all the decisions concerning the nature of his return. He gave out differing interpretations on his scribbled message from his bedside. He said he was touched by a phone call from Jean Chrétien during his convalescence, but then lashed out, saying the PM was preparing a frontal assault on Quebec. Quebeckers can't let it happen, he said. "We'd be saying to Jean Chrétien, Hit us again. Go on. We like it." He questioned whether a sovereignty vote should be held at all in the coming year. But then a few days later, he reversed directions. "I can't imagine a referendum not taking place in 1995," he said.

The Globe's Susan Delacourt sat down with him for an interview. She read a direct quote Bouchard had given to Michel Vastel: "Perhaps we have been too harsh when we say we've hit a wall with English Canada."

Was he softening up? she wondered.

"I didn't say that," Bouchard responded.

Delacourt had the quote in her hands. "You didn't?"

"I might think it," Bouchard replied. "But I have no recollection of those words."

Then, having denied it, he added, "But I wouldn't deny it."

These backflips were of trifling consequence for a man in the vicinity of the gods. No Canadian political leader of the century had experienced anything close to what he had been through. Given his survival, given the extent of the adulation, he could be forgiven for believing that fate had chosen a special mission for him. What an impossible few years it had been. When he had quit the Tories and when Meech was temporarily approved, he was deemed to be finished. Then the agreement had fallen through and the skies had opened up for him. But who would have imagined that from ground zero he would form a party that in the space of one election would become Canada's Official Opposition? And who would have imagined that the deities would choose him for a flesh-eating disease?

He had returned from the dead twice and he could well wonder now what other miracles awaited him. He could think back to his time as a boy when he acted out scenes from the biographies of the giants of history. He could see now that he was writing his own exceptional chapters.

Rather than turn him away, the health calamity had made him even more keen on politics. "I am proud, so proud to have beaten death," Lucien told an interviewer. "Proud to have won the battle. I feel stronger as I now face life." He was more acutely aware of the limitations of time. There was much to do, and politics, he said, provided the fastest route of doing it. In the past, he'd been impatient, Gérard Bouchard noted, but "he did not have this sense of urgency in his political life and in his family life." He now realized "we have a certain number of years to do a certain number of things."

He felt closer to his family, to his party members, who sensed a greater "*souplesse*" or softness, in him for a few months, and to the ordinary people who kept vigil outside the hospital. Some old friends came back as a result of the crisis, though the gulf between him and Mulroney wasn't bridged. Mila Mulroney had contacted Audrey at the hospital to express the Mulroney family's concern, but the two men did not speak and had no plans to do so.

He returned to the House of Commons on February 22, 1995, less than the three months after the trauma. He joked to reporters that for his comebacks from future brushes with death, he would be careful not to stage-manage the media. He was awkward in trying to support himself on his artificial limb and he looked older than his fifty-six years. The rich, black sweep of hair had lost its glimmer. He had greyed, his face had thinned and his eyes, once so strong, now had a hollowed-out and haunted look. But there was no sense that the force had gone, or that the commitment to whatever it was he really sought had diminished. The fires inside were still burning—fervently.

In the House of Commons, the torrent of applause, three standing ovations, cascaded upon him. Tears streamed from the eyes of Bloc members and from his wife in the gallery. Testimonies of admiration were heard from all sides. Bouchard was shaken and looked noble as the spotlight beamed on him. He put his fingers to his eyes as if to stem a river.

"Yes, I have been looking forward to this moment since a certain day in December when technology and destiny combined to give me another chance," he said as the country looked on. "If the rallying cry of democracy is 'stand up and be counted,' I respectfully ask to be counted."

The unilingual Reform leader Preston Manning spoke entirely from a prepared French text. Chrétien praised Bouchard's courage and determination. Conspicuously absent was Jean Charest, who still could not tolerate the past acts of this man.

"I was able to observe first-hand how compassionate and generous our fellow citizens from English Canada can be," said Bouchard. "Who would not have been moved by these expressions of sympathy?" This did not mean, he noted, there would be many converts to his sovereignty mission, nor would it mean he would be renouncing his political path. "However, I am confident that sovereignists and federalists can discuss their options with dignity and without impugning each other's motives." These were heart-warming words on a heart-warming day. But if there were many federalists who thought that Lucien Bouchard would keep to high-minded thoughts, they didn't know how deep the wells of bitterness reached in him. The *souplesse* would soon be gone.

19. UNDERMINING PARIZEAU

Back in the days when he was in the Boy Scouts, they pinned an unfortunate nickname on Jacques Parizeau. "*Belette Vibrante*," they called him, "The Vibrating Weasel."

Half a century later, Parizeau had yet to shake off the look. The rodent-like, triumphalist grin was still there, lending a rather pompous air. Much of the bluster was soon to be taken out of him, however. Lucien Bouchard had him in his sightlines.

For the next many months, the plump premier sat on the wall, a caricature of Humpty-Dumpty himself, while his ally-turned-tormentor slid the bricks out from under him.

The tormentor was approaching sainthood. It was time to expand his power base. Time had amply demonstrated that the name Lucien Bouchard could never be synonymous with second in command. He craved the exercise of power too much for that. His hubris had him believe that it was his due.

At every career point, the appetite was evident. He'd gone off in a huff to form his own law firm. He accepted only the jobs in Quebec which gave him control. He chafed when anyone touched his speeches. He accumulated ambassadorial power in Paris like no other. He tried to turn his environment portfolio into the pre-eminent one of the entire government. He deserted his friend Brian Mulroney, timing his exit so as to capture the type of attention reserved for a Shakespearean soliloquy. Rather than joining the Péquistes, he formed his own secessionist party.

Bouchard was never bashful about his lone star proclivity. He told the journalist Manon Cornellier, "I'm probably someone who has not the capacity to work under someone else." Parizeau had probably guessed this by now. He may well have ruminated on the inevitability of what was to transpire. But he could have been forgiven for thinking he had time to brush his teeth.

Bouchard's health trauma had vaulted him far atop the sovereignist heap in popularity. Parizeau had not scored well in the election and support for his sovereignty mission was down. More-over, his style was ill-suited for leading the rebellious enterprise that engaged him. While his rival carried the hurt of the masses, Parizeau bore the self-satisfied look of a European aristocrat.

Bouchard had been barely out of intensive care when he started second-guessing the plans of the premier. Now in April, only four months after having rolled back the stone, he launched a pre-emptive strike. Before 1,400 delegates in Montreal at a convention of the Bloc Québécois, he proclaimed the need for a *"virage,"* or major turn, in the referendum strategy. He had met at length with advisers to choose a word that would make headlines. *Virage* fit the purpose. He proposed the referendum be held with the goal of creating a European Union–type of partnership with the rest of Canada, and he advocated a slower timetable in moving towards it. Parizeau, as premier, was in charge of the referendum strategy. He had already rejected Maastricht-style solutions. He had already said the referendum had to be held before the year was out.

The Quebec premier sat in the audience as the bombs dropped around him. Knowing his plans would meet with disapproval, Bouchard hadn't forewarned Parizeau of the speech's contents. Just like the media, the premier received a copy of the address only shortly before its delivery. It was a fait accompli, a *coup de théâtre*, reminiscent of a certain telegram Bouchard had once fired off from Paris.

The press jumped on the story. Newspapers bannered his *virage* just as he hoped. When reporters subsequently examined the details of his proposals, they found he had exaggerated the weight of them. On the PQ policy books were similar recommendations for joint bodies to govern the relationship with Canada in the event of the schism. But Bouchard's wish for a time delay was a signifi-cant change—and so was another gambit. Just in case Parizeau wasn't listening, his tormentor issued a thinly veiled threat not to participate in a referendum campaign if his views weren't heeded. "I have to wait before giving any unconditional agreement" on par-ticipation, Bouchard told reporters. "I will not sign any blank cheque to anyone. That wouldn't be responsible."

Parizeau, vibrating now as much as he ever did in the Boy Scouts, was quick to fire back. Bouchard's post-referendum scenarios were not much of a *virage* at all, he asserted. While acknowledging there were many who could be considered leaders of the sovereignty movement, he drew the line on the question of ultimate boss. "There's just one premier at a time. I'm the premier of Quebec, premier of all Quebeckers, and I have a certain number of decisions to make." Though the Bloc could put forward ideas, Parizeau stated that he was the one who would negotiate with Ottawa after a Yes vote. Then came another slap at the dauphin. "I said there will be a referendum on sovereignty in 1995 and there will be a referendum on sovereignty in 1995."

Bouchard tried to raise a white flag, pointing out there was no nefarious intent in his speech, just suggestions for the good of the movement. But parliamentarians, as well as both the French and English media, were quick to pin the Machiavelli tag on the Bloc leader. "The Knife Wounds in Jacques Parizeau's Back Look Familiar," ran one headline. "Bouchard Can't Stand Anyone Else Being in Charge," said another. *Le Devoir*, which tended to be on Bouchard's side, featured a report entitled "Mr. Bouchard Follows His Own Rules." Many parallels were drawn with what he had done to Mulroney. Now, with another inside job, it was Parizeau's turn. "Let me put it this way," said Jean Charest with barely disguised contempt, "We recognize the style...It's obvious that he has his own agenda."

The two sovereignty leaders didn't bother even trying to preserve the pretence of unity. The premier's entourage was enraged. They had been suspicious since the night of Parizeau's provincial election victory when Bouchard appeared on the stage looking like he'd rather be in Borneo. They were now convinced he was out to hijack the leadership. If not, why didn't he discuss the planned *virage* with Parizeau first? Why did he call it a *virage* when it was only a modification? Why had he acted as if he was the supreme commander? Why had he risked splitting the sovereignty movement?

Bouchard's call to delay the referendum looked suspect. Did he want it put back to give himself time to unseat the premier, so he could then be the one, the modern-day Bolívar, to lead the province to statehood? On the other hand, putting aside the evident opportunism, many agreed with the wisdom of the Bloc leader's suggestions. It made no sense, as he pointed out, to call a referendum with polls showing the secessionists on the losing end by a margin close to the 60–40 loss of the 1980 campaign. What was the hurry? Why impose a potentially suicidal deadline when four years remained in the mandate?

Knowing the idea of a hard and fast separation scared off voters, Bouchard's wish to moderate the pitch to sovereignty-association was also reasonable. The sovereignists, as polls suggested, needed the support of soft nationalists. One segment of the population sorely needed were those marching under the banner of Quebec's smallish third party, L'Action Démocratique (ADQ). It was led by a charismatic young star, Mario Dumont, and it had the support of 9 percent of the Quebec electorate. These constituted potentially crucial numbers in a close referendum fight.

Having inflicted a wound on Parizeau, Bouchard now sought to beat him up some more. He set his sights on an alliance with Dumont. Only months earlier, Bouchard was warring with the dark-haired youth, whose words flew as if shot from a gun. Bouchard had agreed to campaign for the PQ against Dumont in the young man's riding of Rivière-du-Loup in the provincial election. As well he had argued against the ADQ platform, which drew heavily on a partnership with the rest of Canada. However, Bouchard's *virage* speech, signalling a softer sovereignty, impressed Dumont. Bouchard was able to open talks with him aimed at conscripting his party to the sovereignty campaign.

Since Bouchard had the crucial factor—the vox populi—on his side, he was winning the war with Parizeau. In the previous December the premier had created eighteen Quebec regional commissions to promote, deliberate and report on independence. Their work didn't generate the anticipated excitement he hoped it would. Moreover, their recommendations leaned more towards Bouchard's referendum strategy. It was further bad news for the PQ leader but at least it made his surrender easier. The report allowed Parizeau to be seen as bowing to the will of the people as opposed to the BQ leader. Parizeau endorsed the report, thus signalling his own *virage*. "The squabble is over," he announced. "The report of the national commission has reconciled us, and Mr. Bouchard and I will conduct the referendum campaign hand in hand."

Keeping the upper hand in the relationship, Bouchard soon hit Parizeau again, criticizing the premier's decision to close hospitals in Montreal. The closures were strictly provincial business, something that was none of the Bloc's affair.

The urgent matter of business was to bring Dumont into the fold. Talks between him and Bouchard soon expanded to include Parizeau, who found no delight in having his arm twisted again. Each side made concessions in the tripartite negotiations on the make-up and powers of the institutions and common parliament to govern post-referendum ties. The sovereignty question was to be put in conjunction with an offer of a political and economic partnership with Canada that would follow a Yes vote. Ottawa would have up to a year to decide. If no agreement could be reached, Quebec would move to full independence.

The leaders signed the agreement on June 12, 1995, at the Château Frontenac. Bouchard understood the significance of the moment better than anyone. The sovereignty campaign now had three political parties united under one banner. He described the signing as a vital step that could well go down in history as the sovereignist camp's "finest moment." In Ottawa few seemed to grasp its importance. Summer had begun. Mario Dumont had a low profile. The press slept. One of the few to sound the alarm was former prime minister Joe Clark. Wake up, he warned, the sovereignists have just moved a big step closer.

The three sovereignist leaders agreed that autumn should be the date for the referendum, though Bouchard was prepared to push it back. As the fall approached, tempers warmed. Jean Chrétien suggested in the Commons that since Bouchard had admitted his only concern was now winning a referendum to break up the country, he should give up the extra pay he made as Opposition leader. Preston Manning suggested he might forfeit his pension as well. Bouchard was irate, indignant and non-obliging.

He then launched a lawsuit against a Montreal radio reporter who suggested his six-year marriage to Audrey Best was in trouble and that he had been frequently seen with Corinne Côté-Lévesque. The rumours about the marriage appeared to be based on little more than the cold body language between the two at public appearances, as well as Best's habit of spending time in the United States with relatives. Friends reported that there had been difficulties owing to Bouchard's all-consuming work regime but that the birth of the children and his brush with death had brought them closer. The allegation about René Lévesque's widow "could not have been further from the truth," said Luc Lavoie. Ms. Côté-

Lévesque "couldn't stand Lucien for other reasons." The rumour about a relationship with Côté-Lévesque drove Bouchard "bananas, crazy," recalled Lavoie. It fell into the hypersensitive area of personal business and Bouchard's quite appropriate abhorrence of the price politicians had to pay owing to media exposure of it.

Lavoie didn't like the general suggestion that Bouchard was an emotional time bomb, but was learning more about the degree of his volatility as it concerned private family business. Bouchard called him one night, his voice trembling. His son Simon had been sick with what he thought was the flu. However, in the middle of the night, with only Audrey at home, Simon began choking and turned blue. She rushed him to a hospital where doctors diagnosed severe tonsillitis. They operated because he couldn't get air.

Bouchard got home from Quebec City in time to see that the surgery had gone well and was immensely relieved. He then heard a rumour that the Liberal Party of Quebec had checked to see whether or not Simon had received preferential treatment because he was the son of the Bloc leader. It was too much for Bouchard. He began ranting and raving over the phone to his former assistant. "This is where he really gets out of control," recalled Lavoie. "On the phone to me he was out of control."

There was little time for personal matters. Parliament was to reconvene September 18, right about the time the referendum campaign would likely be kicking into high gear. Bouchard predicted a second No vote on sovereignty would have "disastrous consequences" for Quebec.

He promised a civil campaign, one without personal attacks. The sentiment was forgotten as soon as the word Chrétien crossed his lips. In the very same speech, he levelled the prime minister with several rhetorical kicks to the groin. The little guy from Sha-winigan was out to "finish his strong-arm job of 1982." He was dreaming every night of the week of new federal invasions into the jurisdictions of Quebec. Over time, Bouchard had called Chrétien "The enemy of Quebec's aspirations"; the man "who represents everything I abhor about politics"; the "scarecrow"; the "ghost of 1980 dragging his chains, coming back to haunt us"; English Cana-da's "hatchet man"; the "assassin" of Meech Lake and "the raper of the political will of Quebec."

There was more to come. As much as anything, the Bouchard

campaign would feature personal attacks. While the object of his
mission was to secede from English Canada, the target of his wrath
would again be his own people—the French Canadians, the Chrétiens, the Trudeaus, the Charests who had thwarted Bouchard's
grand desires in the 1980 referendum, on repatriation and on
Meech Lake. Though the press never reported it in such terms, it
was clear, to judge from Bouchard's words, that he considered his
own people the more guilty party.

In this campaign, the four main players would be Parizeau,
Daniel Johnson, Chrétien and Bouchard himself. In large part the
fight would pit Francophone against Francophone for the future of
a country that was three-quarters Anglophone-Allophone. While
Canada was spoken of as a nation of two solitudes, the split often
appeared as rife between Francophones themselves as between
French and English.

No two people better encapsulated the internecine Quebec
battle than the seething intellectual that was Bouchard and the
nuts-and-bolts commoner that was Chrétien. Their enduring differences had been set at the beginning: Chrétien came out of a
"*rouge*" family, an anti-feudal, anti-clerical tradition championing
open-border commerce and democratic liberties. Bouchard, by
contrast, descended from "*bleu*" stock which was parochial, devot-
edly religious, Duplessiste.

Chrétien was raised to look west and to look outward.
Bouchard was raised to look east, to France, and to look inward—
to New France—which was to be a nation. It was these two visions
which would clash in the referendum campaign.

The word "*peuple*" (people) to describe Quebeckers never
appeared in a Jean Chrétien speech. But on the weekend that he
announced his celebrated *virage*, Bouchard offered Quebeckers the
word in abundance. He used it more than a dozen times. "In a
word, [sovereignty] is necessary because we are a people, we have
always felt and behaved as one, we live on a territory where our
ancestors settled almost 400 years ago... We have a culture that is
distinctly ours and we have, as an official language, French, sacred
heritage of the struggles..."

In Jean Chrétien, Quebeckers were offered a model of federalist consistency, a linear politician with a mind uncluttered by the
intellectual and emotional tumult that was Lucien's inferno. Chré-

tien's lifelong Liberalism had seen few zigzags. Economically, he was in the conservative wing of the party since teaming up with Mitchell Sharp in the 1960s. Constitutionally, he'd been in Trudeau's camp—no special status—since the same period.

Bouchard, by contrast, was a gypsy-nationalist, a man never content in one political home. But his meanderings had not hurt him. Quebeckers found a strong rationale for his trek through five political parties. It wasn't opportunism. Bouchard, they said, was simply following the tortuous route of the Quebec conscience on the unity issue. Outside La Belle Province, however, the explanation appeared facile. English Canada had traversed an identity crisis with a big neighbour also, the one to the south. Canadians had swung between nationalism and continentalism and various positions in between. The trajectory did not bring with it justification for Canadian leaders to see-saw willy-nilly from one camp to another and back. To imagine, for example, a Canadian nationalist like Mel Hurtig twice joining parties supporting continentalism and twice returning to the nationalist fold, then being applauded for following the troubled conscience of the people would be to imagine the outrageous.

What could be said of Bouchard's career path was that he had shown a greater degree of flexibility than Chrétien. He had appeared, at least until now, open to more possibilities for a rejigged federation than Jean Chrétien, whose views were cast in stone. When nationalists like Bouchard spoke of demands in an accord like Meech Lake as being minimal, it was a language Chrétien couldn't understand. A good case could be made that such demands were in fact minimal. There were many areas of jurisdiction untouched: regional economic development, environment, coastal fisheries, aboriginal peoples, social policy, science and culture.

Now it appeared that Bouchard was locked into the sovereignty option and bent on waging a vitriolic campaign to get there. He told friends the campaign would be fought with an appeal to the soul of the people. As well as ad hominem attacks on fellow citizens he considered disloyal to the cause, he wanted to create a sense that Quebeckers had been suffering under the yoke for too long. For such an appeal, he was exceptionally fitted. As unfortunate and distressing as his artificial limb was, it was a magnificent political prop. To be able to sell wounds, it helped to wear them. The pictures of

Bouchard, as the old adage had it, were now worth a thousand words—even a thousand of his own precious words.

Prime Minister Mackenzie King used to visit President Franklin Roosevelt often. The president wore leg braces because of the polio he had contracted on New Brunswick's Campobello Island. Of FDR's broad public appeal, King wrote, "I think the president is reaching the people through his infirmity more than anything else." The people knew he was suffering.

In the campaign, Bouchard could blend his afflicted visual persona with his trenchant sense of injustice. A good part of him was steeped in martyr-complex theology. He could capitalize, like no one else, on the grievance culture that had built up through Quebec history. A selective rendering of that history lent credibility to the thesis. It had begun with the torturing of the Jesuits by the Iroquois, the subtext here being that the Quebec people would go to heaven for labouring for their faith. The story continued with the deportation of the Acadians, the Battle of the Plains of Abraham and the crushing of the 1837 rebellions. Then there was the hanging of Louis Riel, the enforcement of conscription in the two world wars, and the night of long knives. Bouchard had the gift of making all these events sound like they took place last summer.

Daniel Poliquin, a Quebec novelist and translator who wrote a study of the victim complex, saw Bouchard as the perfect agent of it. A small but typical example, noticed Poliquin, was Chrétien's appointment of an Acadian, Roméo LeBlanc, as Canada's Governor General. Acadia was the name given to eastern regions of the country settled by the French in the 1600s. The populations were dispersed by the British in 1755 but eventually resettled. Of the LeBlanc appointment, Bouchard said, "I am very happy for all the Acadians, knowing how much they have suffered." The suffering, noted Poliquin, was 240 years earlier. It was imposed by the British. The Acadians had returned to become a happy people in the Canadian home. What was Bouchard thinking, wondered Poliquin? Should modern English Canada bear the burden for 1755? Was there no limit?

The martyr complex brought with it a narcissistic sense of isolation and moral superiority that was "intrinsically fraudulent and totalitarian," wrote Poliquin. "Professional victims feel that anything goes, any gimmick and any lie, against an all-too-powerful enemy. That includes asking tricky questions in referendums and lying about its consequences."

Not all Quebeckers were consumed by this self-pity. They lived in ambivalence, attached interchangeably, for example, to Lévesque provincially and Trudeau federally. But like any population, they could be swayed by the magic of leadership. Bouchard was capable, through what Poliquin called emotional blackmail, of lifting the culture of grievance to the fevered heights of Greek tragedy.

He could do it with a clean conscience because he was so passionately tied to the myths of the Kingdom of the Saguenay—the family shrine, the traumatizing mother, the heroic father, the early poverty and isolation, the one-sided teaching of history in the schools. It was a past he could not shed. He had a duty to history. "His conviction," said Bill Fox, who worked closely with Brian Mulroney, "is a reflection of an earlier time. As a young student at Laval he was probably right. But that's not today's reality."

In the aftermath of the Quiet Revolution, it seemed to many that Quebec had moved beyond the politics of resentment to a nationalism based more on pride and accomplishment. When the Canadian-born, British-based writer Michael Ignatieff researched his book on ethnic nationalism, *Blood and Belonging*, at the beginning of the 1990s, he was struck by the changes in Quebec. "The old scores have been settled. It is now a rhetoric of self-affirmation."

But his conclusions were reached before Lucien Bouchard had achieved his mythic stature. Bouchard was turning back the clock. His past campaigns had been, in part, aimed at old scores. His plan for the referendum campaign was no different. In preparing his strategy, he was a smart enough politician to realize that unity and solidarity can be most easily achieved with the invocation of the demons of old, demons which were still at the door. Nothing could unify the people like the big bad wolf. Bouchard had read de Gaulle's book. In his memoirs of war, *Le Fil de l'Épée*, the general had written, "You cannot move the population without resorting to elementary sentiments, violent images, harsh invocations." The man of action, he said, "needed a strong dose of egotism, pride, toughness and trickery."

Bouchard was the revved-up, well-prepared combatant, while Chrétien, resting on a lead in the polls as the referendum campaign began, was bent on turning the other cheek. His old friends in

Shawinigan spoke of his deep animosity towards the separatists, their arrogant intellectualism and pompous put-downs of him. "You wait," said his friends who had played hockey with him as a boy on the streets. "Wait till you see our Jean in the next referendum. Wait till you see what he does to those guys. There you'll see the Chrétien of old." They didn't realize how the years of battle had worn him down. They didn't realize he'd lost his precious gift for politics—his rancour.

Of course, as the campaign opened, it was not so much Bouchard the prime minister worried about. Jacques Parizeau still sat on the wall, however precariously, and Bouchard had to defer somewhat. He was relegated to Ottawa, where he was to lead the charge in the Commons debate.

Having said that a No vote would be a calamity for Quebec, he was quick to amend his words. Voting against sovereignty, Bouchard asserted, would simply mean postponing the inevitable. The issue was not going to go away. Referendums were to continue until Quebec won one. His remarks, which caused the dollar to tumble, had a heads-we-win, tails-you-lose flavour to them. This game was like, as the Liberal Marc Lalonde would later point out, a form of Russian roulette: keep shooting till the bullet discharges. Conceivably the sovereignists could lose six straight referendums, but win the seventh and expect it to be the only one of binding value. The argument gave Chrétien an opening for rebuttal—if several federalist wins were of no enduring significance, why should one separatist victory be binding? But it was an argument he chose not to use. Not now.

The prime minister had decided to follow the low-key strategy Pierre Trudeau used in the 1980 referendum campaign. Trudeau gave only three major speeches, getting enormous media penetration from each. The tactic was deemed to have worked.

In the initial weeks, Chrétien had few concerns. Bouchard and all his grand campaigning possibilities were held at bay. Stuck in Ottawa, he couldn't let loose. Chrétien cruised.

In the debate on the economic ramifications of secession, each side posted doomsday scenarios. Bouchard, as well as Parizeau, claimed the Grits had a hidden right-wing agenda. After a No vote they would slash social programs and old-age pensions just as heartlessly as the Tory Mike Harris was allegedly doing in Ontario.

But even *Le Devoir*, one of Bouchard's favourite newspapers, criticized sovereignist outrage over Ottawa's cutbacks on social spending. Debt-strapped governments, the paper said, had little choice.

Finance Minister Paul Martin got under Bouchard's skin, saying there would be no economic union with the rest of Canada and no easy access for Quebec into the North American Free Trade umbrella. "It's so predictable," Bouchard angrily responded. "It's the federal strategy to make Quebeckers believe that if they take control of their own responsibilities they will not be able to conduct themselves like a real people, that only other peoples can take care of their responsibilities and not Quebeckers because they are incapable of it." The federal government would have no choice but to negotiate a new economic deal, Bouchard added, because the whole business of Quebec's share of the colossal Canadian debt would have to be sorted out. Canada would want the new plan for a federal union. "Otherwise," he threatened, "Quebec might not be willing to pay its full share of the debt."

Sovereignists' attempts to make the economic case for secession weren't helped by Quebec government studies. The reports detailed the potentially harmful effects of secession and cast doubt on how an economic partnership with Canada could work. One report was by Laval University law professor Yvan Bernier, another by George Mathews, Bouchard's former economic adviser. Bernier said the Parizeau government asked him to delete the controversial part of his report; Mathews said it had withheld his study. Bouchard was not about to depart from the traditional cynical behaviour of politicians by coming clean on these reports. If it wasn't good news, he wanted it buried. He dodged questions on them, trying to throw the ball back into the federal court by charging that Chrétien was camouflaging public opinion studies made by the Canadian Unity Office. Chrétien rejected the comparison, saying that internal Cabinet documents were privileged. He appeared to have the upper hand on this one. His studies, after all, were not about embarrassing consequences of a referendum win. Bouchard did concede there had been hitches on the Quebec side and promised more *glasnost* in the future. "Now everything is going to be published."

In the House of Commons he wasn't able to spark the grand debate on the Canadian future that he had hoped. Chrétien handled his attacks with comparative ease. He had numbers to refute

Bouchard's claims of unfair treatment at the hands of federal marauders. With 24 percent of the population, said the prime minister, Quebec was getting 30 percent of federal research and development spending.

The Bloc leader again stepped into landmines he himself had set. When Laurent Beaudoin, president of Bombardier Inc., hinted he might move his company out of Quebec in the event of a Yes vote, Bouchard spoke of how ungrateful this man was to Quebec. Look at all Quebec had done for him, he said. Bombardier had won a servicing contract of $1.3 billion for the CF-18 jet-fighters. It was a federal government contract. Quebec had lobbied vigorously for it, embittering bidders from the West who charged that too much favouritism was being shown to Quebec. Bouchard agreed that it was Quebec's political strength that got Beaudoin the CF-18 contract. But in so doing he was trapped. His statement could hardly help but take the sting out of previous arguments about how Quebec was always being shortchanged by Ottawa.

If the landmine wasn't contradiction, it was conflagration. Harvey Oberfeld, a TV reporter from British Columbia, went after Bouchard at a press conference. His questions suggested that the Bloc leader was a traitor. Bouchard couldn't help but jump to the bait. "Well-thought question," he replied sarcastically. "Should I be hanged? What is your choice, sir?" Then the Bloc leader waded further into the fray, listing the lugubrious possibilities—gas, the electric chair, lethal injection. Turning to other reporters, he said, "I think that guy would rather have me in the electric chair." The skirmishing continued outside, right to the entrance to the elevators. Bouchard then ensured the matter got more attention by filing a complaint with the parliamentary press gallery alleging that this kind of behaviour would prevent a serene climate from prevailing during the campaign.

Of course a serene climate was the last thing he had in mind. He needed to wake up his masses. At the end of September, four weeks to the October 30th referendum, the federal side held a strong lead. Parizeau, who had not an ounce of populist blood in him, was demonstrating again, as he had in the last provincial election campaign, that he could not connect with the people. That the sovereignist campaign was in a sorry state was confirmed by Bouchard's remarkable public musings that the date could still be changed. He kept opening the door for Parizeau to come forward and cancel the whole campaign.

Bouchard wondered about Parizeau and about the Quebec people themselves. Where was the passion this time? Why were they so quiet? Why weren't they in the streets marching towards their historic moment? "There is a kind of worrisome silence running through Quebec at this time, a sort of apathy," he said in Chicoutimi as October opened. He had been shocked by the muted reaction which greeted Chrétien's suggestion that the federal side might not recognize a narrow sovereignist win. "Never have Quebeckers accepted such a provocation as this," said Bouchard.

Péquistes now concluded that a mistake had been made. It had been wrong to keep Bouchard, their ace card, campaigning in Ottawa. They needed his passion, his pain, his martyrdom on home ground where the battle was being waged.

It was time for the second *virage*.

20. DEMONS EVERYWHERE

Bouchard let friends know of his enormous frustration with Parizeau's handling of the campaign. Why was he not emphasizing the partnership with the rest of Canada? This, Bouchard knew, was the vote getter. Quebeckers needed a security blanket if they were to break the bonds. Why then was the premier giving more vent to the separation angle?

Bouchard knew the answer. Parizeau had the partnership forced on him on the occasion of the first *virage*. While it was now part of his menu, he didn't have to eat it—and he didn't like the idea of serving it to others. One thing about him—he had a lot of separatist backbone. He didn't bend and twist with the tides of time—like someone else he knew.

In the realm of politics, Bouchard, schooled on Mulroney, was more pragmatic than principled. From the start of the year, his approach, recalled de Belleval, was to go with what could win. "His attitude was, 'I've got a job to do and I must confront Parizeau because I don't agree with what he is doing.'"

This time he did not have to be as devious towards the premier. This time, the rebellion was fermenting on its own. Others were doing it for him, one being a stocky little pugilist from the cast of the Cliche Commission, Guy Chevrette. He and Jean Royer, chief of staff to the premier, asked Parizeau to agree to a partial abdication of responsibilities.

Parizeau buckled. He could see the obvious—that there was a man on the ticket much more popular than himself. Swallowing his pride, he agreed to name Lucien Bouchard chief negotiator for the sovereignists with Ottawa. On the face of it, it didn't seem like much of a prize. For this to mean anything it required that the sovereignists first win the referendum, and second that the federal side then agree to protracted negotiations. But once decoded, the announcement, as journalist Rhéal Séguin was the first to tell the country, meant that Bouchard was now in control of the referendum campaign.

The declaration of the changeover came on Saturday, October 7th, little more than three weeks from referendum day. Taking charge was a considerable gamble for Bouchard. If the sovereignists went down to heavy defeat, the blame would no longer be principally Parizeau's. It would be Bouchard's in equal portion. But since signing the tripartite pact in June, the Bloc leader was confident victory could be gained.

The day he took over, the crowds got bigger, the mood more upbeat. In Compton Station in the Eastern Townships, a supporter of about Bouchard's age came over and as he steadied himself on his cane she reached for his hand. She told Bouchard of the many novenas she and her friends had said for him during his passage through the flesh-eating torment. She told him of a great man of history, a legendary figure of the independence wars, whom he reminded her of. "For me, you are Quebec's Gandhi, Mr. Bouchard."

As the premier of the province gradually receded further back in the news pages, Bouchard made it clear who was now in control. The Parizeau government, at a cost of millions of dollars, had produced a long line of studies on the impact of sovereignty. The studies, some of which were still to be released, were coordinated by Quebec's minister of restructuring, Richard Le Hir. Provincial Liberals, suggesting the reports confirmed major job losses, were beating the drums. In Chambly, Bouchard came forward and cut an imperious, peremptory swath that ended all the controversy. He ditched the Le Hir reports. No more! he said, responding to some pointed questioning. "I don't want to hear anything about the Le Hir studies. These are not my studies." His arrogation of power and his attitude towards it was evident in the use of the personal pronoun. They were not "his" studies. They were "in the past." As he was approaching a podium that day, an onlooker had shouted "Viva El Presidente."

Bouchard's dictatorial gesture flew in the face of his promise earlier in the campaign to disclose everything from then on. As well, it contradicted the words he had spoken just a few hours before dumping the studies. He had used one of the Le Hir reports to back his argument for Quebec's continued use of military bases.

As the columnist Allan Fotheringham, commenting on his remarkable leaps of logic, put it: "Lucien Bouchard has the attention span of a hummingbird."

While the Le Hir episode constituted one of his more cynical acts, the criticism was rather light and the controversy was soon forgotten. Its quick passing was a reflection of a critical feature of this referendum campaign. The central actor for the sovereignty side enjoyed an immunity rarely seen in Canadian politics. His survival of the brutal health trauma had won him a long period of grace. The sense among the Quebec population—how dare you question a man who's been through what he has?—was palpable. Those who did challenge him, as would be the case when Bouchard issued a controversial remark on race, did not get far. They were seen as challenging the words of a deity. It was like taking on a bishop in early-century Quebec. In a way, the monsignor who put his biretta on Lucien's head as a teenager had been right after all. Lucien Bouchard had become the cardinal of Quebec.

From dismissing Le Hir, he moved on to bigger fish—Mulroney, Gorbachev, Bush. Meeting in Colorado at a reunion, the three leaders, given a prompt by Mulroney, expressed the hope Canada would remain united. Bouchard bristled. What credibility did Mulroney have? he asked. Mulroney, he said, had to retreat to the United States to make such pronouncements because it was the "place where he'd be the least booed." As for Gorbachev's plumping for federalism, the cardinal was equally dismissive. He found it disgraceful that someone from a country with a history of intolerance and repression like the Soviet Union should offer advice to a country like Canada.

The word "tolerance" got a good working over in the campaign. Bouchard based a lot of his rhetoric on the "we are a people" notion but at the same time denied his movement constituted ethnic nationalism. Now, he stepped into the quagmire of race talk with an injudicious observation while musing about the low birth rate in Quebec. "Do you think it makes sense that we have so few children in Quebec?" Bouchard asked at a rally. "We're one of the white races that has the fewest children. That's really something. That suggests we haven't resolved our family problems."

The words "white race" hit raw nerves. Were Quebec women of pure white stock supposed to be having more babies for the good of the race? Were those not of the white hue a lesser breed of Quebecker?

In the House of Commons, Jean Chrétien pounced. "There are

Quebeckers of all colours and all religions," he said. The Bouchard credo, he charged, was that "in order to be a good Quebecker you have to be white rather than coloured, you certainly have to speak French rather than English, and you definitely have to be a separatist. If you're a separatist, you're a good Quebecker; if you're a federalist, you're not."

Women's groups, visible minority groups, the media and many other prominent Quebeckers joined in the attack. Liberal leader Daniel Johnson's wife, Suzanne Marcil, called Bouchard's comments "insulting, degrading, humiliating." Ottawa's intergovernmental affairs minister, Marcel Masse, said his African-born wife was as Québécois as any separatist. Bouchard, he said, was stating the view that Quebec stock was only white and French-speaking. "To me, that is a racist remark."

Bouchard's nationalism was intense and vociferously argued and his movement had a strong ethnic-nationalist colouring. But he could hardly be said to be a racist. His record did not support that claim. Bouchard had demoted one of his Bloc members, Philippe Paré, for complaining that ethnic voters could deprive oldstock Quebeckers of their dream of independence. The Bloc leader had also corrected a radio show host not long before for using the term "Quebecker" to describe only old-stock types. Liberal Claude Ryan and many others had spoken of the need for Quebeckers to produce more children. Columnist Michel Vastel suggested that perhaps the shoe should be put on the other foot. What about the 96 percent of non-Francophones who were supporting the No side, he asked. "That's not an ethnic vote? That's not a tribal reaction?"

Bouchard accused opponents of distorting his words out of a sense of panic. "They are trying to make a big deal of something that does not exist. They are portraying me as a racist. Me, a racist? Me, sexist? That's ridiculous. It will not fly." As the storm grew, he admitted that he inappropriately used the words "white race" to qualify the comparison. He jumped on a reporter who asked if he was apologizing. "I do not apologize. It's not like that. I know exactly what I said. I said exactly what I reported."

The attempt of the federalist side to make hay of the controversy was hampered by the restrained reaction of the Quebec media. The story didn't get half the play in Quebec it received in the rest of Canada. Bouchard's deity status, as supportive polls

showed, held. At a rally of a thousand women of the province, backing was strong for Bouchard. The Liberal Senator Jacques Hébert,
an old Trudeauite, had ignited a controversy by labelling a Montreal woman scholar a separatist cow. This mistake helped take some
of the focus off the baby-production controversy. Almost everybody in the crowd wore cartoon cows. Singer Carolyne Desbiens
told the cheering women, "What we must do in two weeks is not
feel regret—and vote the right way." She sang a song called
"Regret." In it she warned of the "day of assimilation" which awaits
"a people that says no to itself." Eight decades later, it was *Maria
Chapdelaine* all over again.

A major feature of the Bouchard strategy was to ease fears of
breaking with Canada. To this end, he set about painting a won-
derfully rosy portrait of a sovereign Quebec. "A Yes has magical
meaning because with a wave of a wand it will change the whole situation," he told a rally in Montreal. The wave of the wand would
create a fantastic new solidarity. "The day after sovereignty there
will be no more federalists, no more sovereignists. There will only
be Quebeckers."

At a news conference he was more affirmative. "I am sure there
will be no economic hardship if we vote Yes." Sovereignty would
provide huge benefits, making the people masters of their own
money and tools of development. "There will be no warring
between governments, there will be solidarity in Quebec and the
rest of Canada will be better off because it will be able to design and
shape the kind of country they want." Critics countered that the
studies by Le Hir were supposed to tell Quebeckers what it would
really be like. If it was so rosy, bring them forth.

A second prong of his strategy, heating up the anger in the people, was hardly a daunting challenge for the Bloc leader. For the
role of demonizer, there were few more suitable than Lucien
Bouchard. The scorching put-down came readily to him. Within a
week of taking charge of the campaign, his accusations and demagoguery surged. Anyone who wasn't a sovereignist fell under his
sword. As a federalist, he had detested anyone in Quebec casting
doubt on his allegiance. Now he heaped scorn on all those who
laboured inside the federal system.

Jean Charest, whom he had once greatly admired, was no
longer dignified with recognition. Bouchard refused invitations to

appear at forums where Charest would be present. Asked about him, Bouchard responded, "Who?" Again the question came. "Jean Charest?" asked Bouchard. "Who is he?" The discourse ended with him saying, "He's irrelevant."

Brian Mulroney, whom he had once greatly admired, had retreated, Bouchard charged, to the place he was least booed. Pierre Trudeau, whom he had once greatly admired, had committed, Bouchard charged, "reprehensible" acts against Quebec.

The media of Radio-Canada, which were thought to have a bias for his cause, were now, Bouchard charged, directed by puppets of the federal government. Big businessmen of the province were now, Bouchard charged, "spitting on Quebec."

As the journalist Benoît Aubin pointed out, they were all enemies now. Through the cardinal's dark lens, Daniel Johnson, who came from an honourable family of politicians—one who had been premier of Quebec and another a PQ leader—wasn't worthy of becoming premier of Quebec. He was participating in a plot, Bouchard charged, "to extinguish the spirit of Quebec."

Those outside his home province were skewered like the rest. New Brunswick premier Frank McKenna was high on the villains' list for having insisted on changes to the Meech Lake Accord. The same McKenna, however, had helped forge equal status for the French in his province where the large majority was English. He had laboured to learn French himself, it being especially difficult for him because of his dreadful accent. Bouchard levelled him. "There is nothing he likes more than to say no to Quebec."

The former Ontario premier Bob Rae often found himself on the hot seat for being too soft on Quebec. He had put up bilingual signs on highways and government offices and brought forward a bill to make the Ontario public service bilingual. But what Bob Rae wanted most, Bouchard charged, was to see Quebec stripped of its negotiating power.

The new premier of Ontario, Mike Harris, whom Bouchard would later embrace with open arms, was contemptuously dismissed. Harris had said the province's welfare recipients could get by on a reduced diet. Well, yes, explained the Bloc leader: "They can buy every month two boxes of cornflakes, no sugar. Two kilos of hamburger steaks, ten bananas." This diet of the poor, he cried, was what awaited Quebec if it voted No. "That's what will be imposed on Quebec by Jean Chrétien."

He had helped knock off a prime minister, his friend Mulroney. He had pushed a Quebec premier, Parizeau, closer and closer to the edge. One big fish, another prime minister, remained. As if all the other epithets were not enough, he now resorted to calling Jean Chrétien a traitor. The little guy from Shawinigan, whose family had lived on Quebec soil for 300 years, was anti-Quebec.

It was a form of intolerance rarely witnessed in modern Canadian politics. Those who didn't share Lucien Bouchard's ever-changing view of the world were unworthy or disloyal. Politicians regularly harpooned one another over disagreements on issues, with the disputes sometimes descending into personal put-downs. But rarely did the vitriol reach this sustained level.

Bouchard's loving brother Gérard was among those who sometimes looked askance. Lucien, he thought, was going overboard. The heat of battle was the primary cause, Gérard reasoned. During political campaigns politicians were under pressure to inflate the rhetoric. "The crowd goes crazy and you feel yourself overwhelmed and I think that kind of thing certainly happened. And I'm not saying that Lucien avoided every bit of this. Certainly not."

Bouchard lit up the speaking halls with his charges. He was a spectacular orator. With the cane as a sort of a religious symbol, he limped to the microphone, so human compared to all the other stiff suits who played the game. He started his speeches slowly, and gradually, very gradually, intensified the pace. The style was authoritative, pounding, theatrical, rhythmical. Soon he reached a feverish lather from which the vitriol shot like spears. He was in the hot zone now, his passion scorching, his mind locked in a decades-old time warp where all the old grievances sat like the great blueberries of Lac Saint-Jean, ready for the plucking.

In the referendum campaign, the malice and falsehoods could all pass because with a few exceptions—among them Mordecai Richler, lawyer Guy Bertrand, and the odd Francophone journalist—no one in his home province was prepared to take him on.

Taking him on was a risky business, as Tobias Fisher, a producer for the CTV network, discovered. Fisher had noticed that some of the premiers whom Bouchard was skewering with his black belt in rhetoric were the ones who were supposed to suddenly turn around and be warm neighbours as soon as the sovereignty vote passed.

Fisher approached Bouchard after a speech, asking how, in view of
the insults, he would be able to negotiate on good terms with them.
Bouchard had been in good humour but, as Fisher remembered, he
was suddenly fired with rage. "Insults!" Bouchard shouted. "What
insults? I've insulted no one! I understand the meaning of words.
There have been no insults!" He turned away for a second, then
came at Fisher again, demanding, "What's your question?" He
repeated, "There's been no insults."

The sense of denial, as evidenced on several other occasions as
well, was vehement in Bouchard. Fisher could see his eyes burning,
like Maurice "Rocket" Richard going around the defence. "Something snapped," recalled Fisher. "He lost it. It was a sort of a Jekyll
and Hyde thing."

Knowing he could get away with it, Bouchard repeatedly used
the night of the long knives episode against the federalists with
impunity. If anyone was vulnerable to the knife-wielding charge, it
may well have been Bouchard himself. The federalists had flesh-
and-blood examples at their disposal. They didn't use them. They
were watching closely to gage the Bouchard effect. In his first week,
they didn't see the tide turning. In the initial polls, Eddie Goldenberg, Chrétien's adviser, detected a jump of only two percentage
points for the sovereignists. Not much, concluded Goldenberg,
considering all the hoopla. No need to change the strategy.

In fact, there was no new strategy to bring on. Goldenberg
would be asked what contingency plan the federal side had in the
event the sovereignist campaign took off. "We had no contingency
plan," he said. Such eventualities could not be planned for, he
added. If the polls were suddenly to turn sour, there were no special ads, no special offers, no special events in the hopper. Polling
with focus groups had convinced Goldenberg and others on the
PM's team that personal attacks on the cardinal wouldn't sell.

While cast in his godly persona, Bouchard was trying to sell
himself as an ordinary humble fellow. He portrayed René Lévesque
as a giant of history, but a man who sadly had to face Ottawa alone,
and was therefore ganged up on. This would not happen again,
Bouchard promised, if the Quebec people were behind their
leader—"a very ordinary person like me"—in great number.

He carried his theme as a modest, put-upon man to a session
with the editorial board of *La Presse*. With a bit of the martyr's air,

he solicited sympathy for all the terrible cheap shots he had taken in the campaign. What insults? the editorialists wondered. "Well, they are treating me like a racist," he responded indignantly. As for his own venom, there was no hint of any remorse.

Bouchard and Parizeau debated between themselves the timetable for a declaration of sovereignty. Parizeau argued that the declaration should come first, negotiations for a partnership with the rest of Canada to follow. On the referendum ballot, however, the question said the exact opposite. Given this, the fact that a reversal of the timetable was even discussed was remarkable enough. But Bouchard, apparently forgetting the words on the ballot, at first appeared to support the plan for reversal. On October 19, 1995, in a morning press conference in Rivière-du-Loup, he stated categorically that sovereignty would be proclaimed, followed by a negotiation with the rest of Canada. "The mandate being solicited by Mr. Parizeau's government and by the sovereignists is that Quebec realizes its sovereignty and that, empowered by its sovereignty, Quebec will then move on to negotiate a partnership agreement." But that evening in Rimouski he completely reversed himself. Bouchard said now there would be two distinct stages. First the negotiations, then the declaration.

Confusion in the public mind resulted from such statements, but this kind of confusion didn't hurt. Polls suggested that up to one-third of Quebeckers believed that after voting to go their own way they would continue to elect members to Parliament. In a sense, it was the way the Bloc leader wanted it. For Quebeckers there had to be nothing to fear but fear itself.

The federal camp's initial hopes that his taking the reins would have little effect proved ephemeral. During his second week at the helm, the sovereignists moved into the lead. With a week to go, they were sprinting ahead. The Bouchardistes were in front by five to seven points and riding a wave of momentum. The turn in fortunes was a remarkable example of the power of leadership. Lucien Bouchard had touched off the greatest wave of enthusiasm since Trudeaumania in 1968.

The federal side looked beaten. Johnson and Chrétien added to their woes by crossing signals as the terrible polls came in. Johnson asked for a statement from Chrétien promising a commitment to a constitutional amendment that would recognize Quebec as a distinct society. Chrétien, who was in New York at a gathering of world leaders, didn't see the full text of Johnson's remarks. He replied that the issue wasn't the Constitution but the separation of Quebec from Canada. Bouchard lapped it up. The headlines across Quebec cried out that the PM was saying no to the province once again.

The Chrétien team considered bringing all the former prime ministers together on the same stage for a show of solidarity. It dropped the idea, afraid it might backfire. The strategy, it appeared, would remain the same—let's take it on the chin right up to voting day.

For his big rally in Verdun, a Montreal suburb, six days before the vote, Chrétien did break open a small box of news. To scuttle the impression that a vote for his side was only a vote for the status quo, he made three promises: recognition of Quebec as a distinct society, the granting of a constitutional veto and control for Quebec over labour-market training. No promise was made on the important question of entrenching the first two changes in the Constitution. He left open the possibility they would be done only through a parliamentary resolution.

The promises were not really new—even though the media reported them as such. They were part of the federalist package that had been sent out to all Quebec households. The press hadn't focused on them, Goldenberg recalled. Now was a good time to re-emphasize them.

The Verdun rally went reasonably well, but it was too early to tell if it had much impact. Polls were still bad. Jean Chrétien appeared the morning after the event at a meeting of his Liberal caucus. He was as shaken as anyone had seen him. He was bitter, drained and hurt. For his audience of MPs, he provided what he would not give the Canadian public—his real thoughts on Lucien Bouchard. He called his campaign a big lie. How could he say secession was risk-free? How pathetic it was that he was getting away with it. In his entire career in politics Chrétien had never encountered such garbage. How could the Quebec press keep reporting this "big pile of shit" as if it were the gospel?

The prime minister became emotional, recalling his visit a few days earlier to the fiftieth anniversary celebrations of the United Nations. He talked of how so many leaders from around the world had come to him to express their astonishment at how a country as great as Canada could be doing this. How could this be? His voice became more strained as he told the story. Then he turned away and lowered his head. Jane Stewart, the chairwoman of the caucus, tried to comfort him, but the prime minister could no longer contain his emotions. Lucien Bouchard had reduced Jean Chrétien to tears.

It was the first time he had cried at a political gathering in three decades as a politician. He had been proud after the devastating loss to John Turner for the Liberal leadership in 1984 that he had held back the tears. But now all the poison from Bouchard had gotten to him.

He was going to leave the caucus room but Stewart convinced him to continue. He spoke of the greatness of Canada and of the other times he had come back from the brink, such as the last federal election campaign in his own riding. With a few days to go he was trailing, and the separatists were celebrating. He stormed back and defeated his Bloc opponent handily. The same thing would happen now, the prime minister promised. "The people of Quebec will not fall into the trap of the magician."

In the evening, the federalists handed Bouchard another seeming gift. Chrétien had booked a five-minute address to the nation in each language. He was under no obligation to provide rebuttal time—in order to get savaged by the Bloc leader. Bouchard and Parizeau had their biggest rally of the campaign planned for the same evening, also in Verdun. They would be all over the TV screens of Quebec. Bouchard would have a major speech in which to respond to the prime minister's address. But the Chrétien team, again fearing a backlash, gave Bouchard equal time. He would follow Chrétien on the airwaves. Given that he was getting the last word, he would have the advantage.

In his sombre address, which was better in French than in English, Chrétien wished to remind voters that this was a do-or-die vote. The question was "to remain Canadian or no longer be Canadian." Because Bouchard had succeeded in de-dramatizing the consequences with talk of partnership, the federal strategy was to re-dramatize them with talk of the end of the nation. The speech in Verdun had hit on that theme. Chrétien's television address drove it home once again.

Now facing the nation was Lucien Bouchard. He was seated for the address, his cane hidden. But he had come equipped with a prop of another kind. He wanted to take the population back in time, fourteen years, to the night of the long knives. Since no one had forcibly challenged him on his interpretation of the event, he prepared to bludgeon Trudeau and Chrétien with it again. During his address in French, Bouchard dramatically pulled out an oversize copy of the front page of *Le Journal de Québec* from November 6, 1981. The sovereignist team had saved this for the last. Bouchard held it before the cameras for all to see: "Lévesque Betrayed by His Allies," the headline read. In the accompanying photo, Trudeau and Chrétien were seated behind a table, laughing it up. The message to be taken from the grins on their faces was unmistakeable— "We're screwing these people again. Isn't it fun!"

The photo, however, was not from the so-called night of the long knives or even the days surrounding it. It was from a different time. It was a different context. Bouchard, who had a habit of rewriting history to suit his purposes, used it anyway.

As he held up the pernicious prop, he told viewers the memory of the event was too fresh to be forgotten. "Mr. Chrétien, you won't pull the same trick twice on us."

Nothing enraged Chrétien so much in the campaign as the use of this front page. He saw it as a preposterous distortion. Lévesque had bargained away the veto in joining the gang of eight; he had also rejected signing a bill of rights that Quebeckers, in numerous opinion polls, strongly favoured. There was no night of the long knives anything like the way Bouchard described it. And even Bouchard had admitted that as a sovereignist Lévesque had no credibility in seeking a unity pact in the first place.

Earlier, during the day of the television appearance, Bouchard had accused Chrétien of having "brutally stuffed an entire constitution down Quebec's throat." Chrétien was a predator who had once before "eaten all the chickens in the hen house and this time [he] is telling us 'I don't eat chickens anymore—I've just seen a nice young tender one but I won't eat it.'" At the sovereignty rally the same night, the front page of the newspaper was blown up on two huge video screens and Parizeau and Bouchard used it to what they imagined would be devastating effect again. Always remember, Parizeau told the cheering throngs, the laughter on the faces of the federal leaders.

Bouchard devoted almost all of his Verdun speech—his last major one of the campaign—to an attack on the federal government. Almost no time was spent outlining a vision of an independent Quebec, or its glories. Instead it was an exercise in whipping up animosity.

No thought had been given to a strategy that the rest of Canada might well have been able to understand, such as the proposition that Quebeckers had not been accorded bad treatment or ill-will, they simply wanted to have their own country. To such an argument there could be little rebuttal from the other side. But Bouchard knew, as dangerous as this game was, that nothing unites the people like an enemy at the door, even if Chrétien and many of the other top power players in Ottawa were fellow-Quebeckers. His mindset was steeped enough in old Quebec to convince himself of scores to settle. Conrad Black, a student of the Duplessis years and Quebec history, was of the opinion that Bouchard's greatest grievance over the last twenty years was that Canada really hadn't furnished him with a real grievance. This ate away at him. Bouchard's pal de Belleval was not entirely in disagreement. "Bouchard is not against Canada. He is against federalism. He is against the way Canada is organized. We must destroy the federalist system as such." No degree of argument on the wonders of Canada would remove what was bred in the nationalist bone, de Belleval said. "I grant you we live in the best country in the world with the best political regime." But that wasn't the point, he said, turning indignant. The point was that the current relationship had to end.

In Verdun, to the backdrop of the deafening din set off by the crowd of the committed, Bouchard told of bitterly cold winds coming from English Canada in the form of budget slashers who would take $2 billion from the pockets of Quebec's needy. "The Liberal Party's programs are in fact the Reform Party's programs." Quebeckers had to "build up ramparts, sovereignty ramparts to protect ourselves and our social programs...The people before us built for us and we will not be the first generation simply marking time." Quebeckers had to make of themselves a people. It was something federalism would never allow them to do.

He imagined the prime minister on the telephone with "members of the long knives club" trying to see if there was anything that could be offered Quebec. The answer was "No!" It was the same answer, Bouchard said, that came from all federal negotiations.

When he wore his federalist hat, Bouchard had said "screw them!" to more demands from Quebec. As premier, he would carve into social expenditures much like the Liberals in Ottawa and the Harris Tories in Ontario.

For now, he could enjoy his saintly immunity. It appeared that he had won the TV square-off and that his Verdun rally had matched the power of the federal one. It looked like nothing could stop the sovereignty train now. Only a few days of campaigning remained.

Then at last Chrétien got some good news. His tracking polls showed that in the previous two nights, a major opinion shift had occurred. The federalists were on the way back. They had registered a whopping jump of eight percentage points. From six down, they were suddenly two up!

Two explanations were provided. Chrétien's three promises as well as his decision to dramatize a Yes vote as meaning the end of Canada had worked. It had brought voters to their senses. There would be no easy aftermath. The second theory was that Bouchard had overplayed his hand this time. He had gone too far with his personal attacks, his smearing of not only Chrétien but also Trudeau, who still had a strong following in the province. The use of the front page was one big distortion too many. It was overkill.

Not just his adversaries questioned Bouchard's comportment in this campaign. Friends like Jean-Claude Rivest could scarcely believe the depth of bile and demagoguery in him. "I hated that," he said of Bouchard's brandishing of the newspaper and his speech at the Verdun rally. "There is a bitterness there that I never heard from anyone on the other, federal side. It was so heavy and so harsh and Lucien Bouchard made a demagogic speech at that time."

As part of their emergency planning for the final week, the federal side had begun organizing a huge rally for Friday in Montreal. It was designed to send a message of respect and friendship from English Canada to Quebec. Surprisingly, the sovereignists planned no great event, no topper for their campaign. Instead of beating the drums harder in the final days, Bouchard lowered the pitch. It was a curious, and perhaps pivotal, decision. Looking at the bad polls from the previous two days, some sovereignists had concluded that they were getting too negative and had better cool off.

For conspiracy theorists, there was a more spectacular explanation. Bouchard, some were cynical enough to suggest, was having second thoughts. He was slowing the train because it was in his personal interest to do so. Politics was a me-first sport. Parizeau was thinking of stepping down in the event of a loss. But if Parizeau won the referendum he would be around a long time. He, Parizeau, would be the one to take Quebec to statehood. He, Parizeau, would be the first president. Why, Bouchard may have thought, take the ball the final few yards across the goal line, only to hand the crown of gold to Parizeau? This would mean playing second fiddle to a man with whom he had had bad relations for years. Vice-President to Jacques Parizeau! Bouchard couldn't stand being number two. His wife couldn't stand being in the presence of Madame Parizeau. From Bouchard's career point of view, a narrow defeat in the referendum would be the better outcome. Parizeau would be under great pressure to leave. Bouchard would surely be the one to take over for the final push to nationhood.

The thesis seemed far-fetched. Nonetheless, the way in which the sovereignty campaign flagged in the final days was curious. The federalists set the agenda, stole the headlines and, with them, the momentum. Two Quebec journalists researching a book on the referendum found the sovereignists' slowdown to be the most costly decision of the campaign. They had no final promises, no final push, no rally on the final weekend. A major demonstration in downtown Montreal on the Saturday or Sunday, a magnificent show of force to wash away the federal rally, would have given them the last wave of momentum and, quite possibly, victory.

Three reasons led the Bouchardistes to play it safe in the final days. Their polls were not showing as much slippage as the overnight federal polls and they therefore weren't terribly concerned. They thought, correctly perhaps, that people coming in from outside for the Montreal rally would have little effect. Lastly, they had concluded that they were too negative at the Verdun rally, and it was turning off voters.

The federalist demonstration, organized with the enthusiasm of Brian Tobin and Sheila Copps, saw close to 100,000 people from all over Canada converge on downtown Montreal to try and save the country. Airlines and bus companies offered reduced fares. The federal government gave employees the day off so they could attend, as did many corporations. On the way in, cars honked, Canadian flags flew from windows, Canadians stood on bridges cheering the motorcades passing under them and "O Canada!" rang through the streets. Jean Charest, Jean Chrétien, Daniel Johnson and others spoke at the rally. They could hardly be heard above the strong winds and the poor outdoor sound system and the cheering. But the point was made.

Sovereignists countered that corporate Canada was trying to buy a victory. The whole thing was a "disgraceful act," said a bitter Bouchard. The federal side was "ready to use any subterfuge. No matter what, they'll do it." The reduced fares broke the referendum's spending laws, he charged. "Friday, two days before the vote, they have to come to say they love us." But where were they in 1982 when they repatriated the Constitution, he asked, and where were they when Meech went down?

The rally's impact could not be easily gauged. Quebec television's all-news network estimated the crowd at a meagre 35,000. Other Quebec media were equally unenthusiastic. Tracking polls showed a slippage of one percentage point for the federalists, but this could be explained by the margin of error in the polling. Or it could have been that the unionists were sliding back and the rally stopped the slide from going too far.

By labelling the rally a disgraceful act, Bouchard was digging himself a much deeper hole in public opinion outside Quebec. Less than a year earlier Canadians from everywhere had reached out to him when he lay suffering. The prime minister and waves of political adversaries had offered their sympathy and support. Bouchard had seemingly been moved by it. It appeared that the motivations of most attending the Montreal demonstration were genuine and that good will towards Quebec was deeply felt. While commenting on his drenching vitriol that greeted the rally, *The Globe and Mail* peered into the Bloc leader's character: "We have come to know well the dark rages of Lucien Bouchard, and we despair of his mercurial manner. This is a man of chemical impulse and deep obsession, who thinks so little of loyalty that he changes parties the way he changes shirts."

On the day of the vote, cold tension could be felt throughout Montreal. It was like a city on the brink of war. Bouchard had whipped up passions and levels of animosity to dangerous heights, and later that night when the vote was in and large rival mobs gathered on the streets, it was a chilling indicator of what might have happened if the country had not held.

As the votes came in, as tens of thousands paced living-room floors, smiles widened on sovereignist faces. They took a good early lead. But when the results from the western side of the province started arriving, the No side began inching up, getting closer to the 50 percent level. The drama seemed to take forever, but ultimately the federalist vote crossed the majority line and held there, ever so perilously. When the final tally was in, the margin of victory was less than one percentage point.

The unionists had been down five to seven points with a week to go; the prime minister was in tears. The momentum had been on the other side. But the pan-Canadians had climbed back to win it. Quebec had voted for Confederation once again, and the secessionists saw a remarkable opportunity slip through their hands.

They had so many circumstances in their favour this time, circumstances they would likely never see again. They had the emotional wallop of a mythic champion returning from within an inch of death. They had a Canadian prime minister who was unpopular in his home province. They had a federal side too timid to respond to attack. They had the sovereignists as the Official Opposition in Ottawa. They had the support of another party in Quebec, Dumont's L'Action Démocratique with its youth appeal. It was a three-party push, two parties more than they had in the first referendum in 1980. They had thousands upon thousands of rejected No ballots and they had the obfuscatory question implying all the comforting business of partnership. Still, they could not win.

Bouchard spoke for only seven minutes. He was disconsolate. He had said earlier, in a categorical manner, that he did not want a moral victory. Now, coming so close, it was exactly what he had. "I am like you all, disappointed by tonight's decision. Never has the victory of the Yes appeared so close than these last days. To see it escape at the very moment we thought it was within our grasp, it hurts us." The population, he emphasized, in an important note, must accept the democratic verdict.

If he was hurt, the hurt was very short-lived. Fate was immeasurably on his side once again. Five years earlier, after he resigned from the government, two events had taken place which put him back up on the pedestal. The Meech Lake Accord collapsed and Robert Bourassa came to his side. Now, in the wake of the referendum defeat, two other developments would occur which would do the same.

One, ironically enough, was taking place in the major media outlets across the country. Millions outside Quebec were glued to their TVs this night. Naturally they were immensely relieved when the final verdict was registered. Strangely, however, the media were decidedly gloomy in their assessment of what had transpired. There were two possible story lines or spins. One was how the federalists, after enjoying a substantial lead at the outset, had come terribly close to blowing the whole thing. The other was the federalists' remarkable comeback in the last week to deny Bouchard and Parizeau a victory.

But despite the federalist victory the media in English Canada chose the losing angle, sending the nation to bed in a sullen state of mind.

The interpretation played beautifully into Bouchard's hands. He couldn't have asked for a better response. Instead of post-mortems about what went wrong in his final week; instead of long analyses of his distortions and name-calling and multitude of contradictions, Bouchard was saluted. His stature grew.

The second gift—a much bigger prize—came from Jacques Parizeau. While pacing the floor, waiting for the final numbers, Parizeau had a few drinks. He was stung by the result and now his tongue was loosened enough to let drop some searing words. In a hostile tone, he said "money and the ethnic vote" had cost Quebec its dream. He was categorical in this announcement, leaving his listeners incredulous.

It may have been the drink, it may have been the subconscious, it may have been the heart. Perhaps it was a concoction of them all. Whatever the cause, Parizeau was not alone in his race-related faux pas. It was a trap into which all his top brethren, in varying degrees, were falling. Less than three weeks before, Bouchard had found himself in a bind over his remark about the "white race." Earlier, Parizeau had been compelled to dismiss Pierre Bourgault, one of the founding fathers of Quebec separatism, from his team when he too had raised the race issue. Bourgault had said there could be trouble if the Francophones voted in majority for sovereignty and were denied victory because of non-Francophones.

On the night of the defeat, Deputy Premier Bernard Landry came across a Mexican-Canadian at the check-in counter of his hotel. Landry lashed out in bitterness, using words to the effect that it was wrong for immigrants to vote according to their grandmothers' chromosomes. His anger was palpable and threatening and the hotel employee called security. Later, when Landry discovered that the scene had been videotaped, he issued an apology.

Four sovereignist leaders. Four fractious declarations on race. It was as if they were all reading from a script by Mordecai Richler, as if they were all trying to prove his point that, notwithstanding the many secessionists of good will, the movement was a xenophobic, ethnic nationalism. In his report prepared for the Liberals, Vivian Rakoff noted that incidents like these tore away the cloak of respectability and revealed the inner souls of the authors. "When the pressure is great the rational shell of pluralist territoriality cracks and the true impulse leaks out like involuntarily exposed lava. The French-speaking Haitians, and Algerian Jews, the Allophones, the Anglophones are told, 'We know who you are. And you are not us.'" Rakoff further explained that the rationalization of the movement as an attempt to create a modern pluralist state simply cannot square with that of the "myth-driven national enthusiasm... the yearnings grounded in blood, history, ancient wrongs."

Parizeau's rash pronouncement, however accurate, brought on a storm of protest—though little from those in attendance at his speech. He had left conflicting signals about whether he would stay on in the event of a loss. In a TV interview he taped before the vote—but not to be played until the result was in—he said he would leave. Coming so close, however, could well have prompted him to change his mind. Now, in the wake of his incendiary blast, his mind was made up for him. His assertion stirred such controversy, within his own party as well as without, that he had little choice.

In the spring his tormentor had left him wounded with his preemptive *virage* announcement. Now it was as if Parizeau was saying, "Here, let me finish the job for you," while plunging the knife in himself. Within twenty-four hours he resigned the premiership. Before the ink was dry, the inevitable was already transpiring. The people of the province were falling to their knees beseeching Saint Lucien to become their pope.

And so again fate had struck and the tides had turned for him. For Bouchard defeat had been turned into stunning triumph. His fall on referendum day had turned into the realization of his dream: Lucien Bouchard was the leader of Quebec, a Quebec which he believed was but a step away from statehood.

21. DR. JEKYLL AND MR. HYDE

After the resignation of Parizeau and the stampedes towards him to succeed, Bouchard played the media like a symphony conductor. None of his closest friends doubted that he wanted the prize of the premiership. This was what he had been targeting for years. This was the penultimate step. But instead of appearing to be grasping at the chalice, Bouchard allowed himself to be wooed. As do many politicians with an eye for the headlines, he left the longing throngs in doubt. He let linger the suggestion that he might retire from politics to be with wife and children.

The media lapped it up. The number of "will he or won't he" stories reached the uncountable. It was a public relations agent's dream. The underlying message was one of altruism, martyrdom. If Bouchard decided to accept the premiership, it would be out of pure sacrifice for his people. Just as it was when he left Mulroney over Meech Lake. Just as it was with his interpretation of the note from the hospital when he was at death's door.

The decision taken, he resigned from the House of Commons to make way for his coronation as leader of the Parti Québécois, his fifth political affiliation. On his last day in the House, Jean Chrétien made a statement of friendship, saying—while managing to keep a straight face—that he regretted Bouchard's departure. Bouchard was touched by the kind words and decided to pay the prime minister a courtesy visit.

The tête-à-tête opened tensely. Chrétien gave a frank assessment of the campaign Bouchard had run. He did not use the words "pile of shit," as he had before his caucus, but he came close. His chief of staff, Jean Pelletier, had addressed, item by item, Bouchard's distortions in a letter to the editor of *La Presse*. Directly to Bouchard, Chrétien expressed his bitterness over his brandishing of the newspaper page with the out-of-context photo. He explained to him how it amounted to a monumental misrepresentation of the facts.

Instead of rebutting, Bouchard heard him out—sympatheti-
cally. He appeared, remarkably, to be contrite about it. "I told Mr.
Chrétien: 'Give your own version of the facts, say what happened.
Me, I was only reporting what was said at the time.'" After blud-
geoning Chrétien and Trudeau for a decade on the repatriation
matter and widening the unity division in the country in so doing,
Bouchard now appeared to be thinking that there was perhaps
another side to the story. Maybe he had gotten it all wrong.

Early in the New Year the prime minister finally went on the
attack. He gave tacit approval to a movement known as partition.
In three areas of the province—the north, the Outaouais and the
West Island of Montreal—breakaway groups were organizing. If
Quebec voted to secede from Canada, they would then vote to
secede from Quebec. Chrétien came forward to say that if Canada
is divisible, Quebec is divisible too. The declaration sent alarm
bells ringing in the offices of the Bouchardistes. The federal side
had rarely moved this boldly. The years of playing strictly defence,
while letting Bouchard set the agenda, were over. In Canada's cold
war, the federal side was deploying its deterrence strategy.
Bouchard was being given some of his own medicine, Chrétien was
saying that if you do it to us, we'll do it to you. The threat left
Bouchard with the prospect of a Pyrrhic victory, with the prospect
not of a sovereign Quebec but of a sovereign mishmash—three big
slices of his pie carved away.

To Chrétien's tit-for-tat strategy, he had great difficulty finding
a rational response. Indeed, two very close associates of Bouchard's
granted that partition was the best weapon the federal side had. If
he knew his territory was going to be split up, they said, he might
not even wish to call another referendum. In a Southam
News/Compass poll, 21 percent of independence voters said that if
they knew they would end up with less territory, they would change
their minds.

Unopposed, Lucien Bouchard became leader of the PQ in January 1996 and premier of Quebec the following month. Support
for sovereignty had climbed above 50 percent and Bouchard's
personal following was huge. Since he was a newly acclaimed
leader, since the PQ had been defeated on its sovereignty plank,
speculation suggested he would seek a new mandate from the people with a snap election. In Ottawa they feared the worst. What if

Bouchard called an election on the basis of seeking a mandate to proceed with secession? In an election-cum-referendum, given his stature, given his momentum, Bouchard would likely carry the day. The country would be plunged into crisis yet again.

But Bouchard pulled back. In so doing he may well have missed an historic opportunity. It was improbable that his popularity would ever again be so high. Soon, his tragedy and the immunity it gave him would be well behind him. Soon, as with any leader, time in office would acquaint the population with lesser qualities.

His reason for hesitating was that Quebec had to get its financial house in order before going its own way. It was an understandable explanation, though it hadn't stopped him and Parizeau the last time—and there was no indication that the province's deficit was a major factor in the referendum outcome.

Assessments of Bouchard's first term as premier would have to await its conclusion, but for the initial period, he was a strong and effective leader. Inheriting a deficit of almost $4 billion, he faced an emergency financial situation. Governments in all other parts of the country were tackling their debts, but Quebec had yet to begin. Leading a party of social democrats, leading a population inured to generous social programs, leading a party in the grip of strong unions, Bouchard faced a decidedly unwelcome challenge. This wasn't Alberta, where the politics of the right were the only winning politics, and it wasn't Ontario, which had been dominated by Conservative governments for four of the five previous decades.

As well, Bouchard confronted cleavages of opinion on the language issue, the sovereignty timetable and relations with the Anglophone, Allophone and business communities. As the referendum result had shown, it was a province split in half. Under the circumstances the chances of consensus-building were prohibitive. But Bouchard's popularity, his enormous skills as a persuader, his command of material allowed him to begin assembling the factions under one roof. At socio-economic summits, where tensions threatened to undermine him, his force of character controlled the proceedings, allowing him to wrench out compromises in the final moments. Pursuing a conservative agenda in which he curried favour with the business class, he was able to set his ship of state on a course towards financial health. Business wanted the secession talk struck from the ledger to encourage stability and investment.

Hardliners in Bouchard's party insisted he keep the momentum going from the high showing in the last vote. Bouchard answered both calls. One day he vowed not to talk of sovereignty for a long time to come. Then, shortly thereafter, he appeared before students to weigh in on the subject, proclaiming that sovereignty was the number one priority of the government.

It was largely a one-man show. All power flowed from Lucien. He holed up in his office, living there most of the week, returning to his family in Outremont on weekends. A small, Spartan bedroom was attached to his office in the Legislature. He would finish his twelve-hour days, often eating at his desk, then he would make his way, cane in hand, to his room, where he would sit and read before retiring. His bunkered life prompted a feature article in the magazine *L'Actualité* entitled "Prisoner of Power." On seeing it, Bouchard, as could be expected, blew a few more fuses.

As premier, he was the monk who was master of all. He ran the government around the clock, just as he had done in Ottawa, overseeing even minor press releases as environment minister or with the Bloc. Virtually everything came under his purview. He centralized power, placing much influence among the unelected officials in his office—a practice he had abhorred a few years earlier in Mulroney's PMO.

In the middle of 1996, he attended a first ministers' conference in Ottawa. Recalling the Mulroney days, Chrétien welcomed him to 24 Sussex Drive with a sardonic slap. "Well, Lucien," he said. "I guess you've been here a few times." Not much could be done at the constitutional tables. Bouchard's scorching anti-country rhetoric had left a climate of opinion outside Quebec which was hardly conducive to conciliation. For their part, instead of even deigning to consider a reconstrued Confederation, Chrétien and the majority of the premiers held to their inflexible ways. When Thomas Courchene, the economist from Queen's University, came up with a model for a highly decentralized Canada, it was quickly dismissed by all but Mike Harris and Ralph Klein. Bouchard saw a lot of good things in the report, but could only throw up his hands at the reaction. It was a signal to him that nothing would change, that the rest of the country was stuck in the status quo.

Achieving the summit of power in Quebec had not calmed him. In the fall he went to the convention of the Parti Québécois where he faced the standard confidence vote. The premier's staff had suggested he would receive as much as 95 percent support. But many party members were disappointed over his language policy supporting bilingual commercial signs, his austere economic policies and his softness on the sovereignty question. They showed it by voting a 76 percent approval rating. Bouchard was traumatized by the announcement. He hurriedly retreated from the convention hall. Word passed, accurately enough, that he was even thinking of resigning or calling a snap election. His attitude had the look of wounded hubris—how dare you do this to me? As had been the case in the Mulroney years, a calm squad was now sent in to try and cool him down. In this case, Bernard Landry and Guy Chevrette spent the entire Saturday evening with him and convinced him not to take drastic measures.

In the meantime, party stalwarts were rallying support behind Bouchard, enough to defeat a motion by the hardliners for unilingual signs. The leader received a raucous reception when he returned to the hall. He was overcome by emotion and could be seen wiping tears from his eyes. Now, feeling vindicated, he gave a speech laced with authoritarian threats. The party must close ranks behind him, he asserted. More discipline, more unity were needed. Otherwise, they might not have him to lead them. He would not be, he announced, an outcast in his own party.

The event, as some described it, was pure psychodrama—another chapter in a life that was full of it. A respite came from an unlikely source—the prime minister and the provincial premiers. Bouchard went on a trade mission to Asia with them. It was the type of thing Parizeau couldn't countenance, but that Bouchard was flexible enough to undertake. On the tour, the premiers found him a reasonable, calm and charming man. Friendships with federalists were built. The Quebec premier and Ontario's Harris, whom he had ridiculed not so long before, got along splendidly. They planned a friendly weekend together with their wives.

Without the power of his leadership, his old party, the Bloc, wasn't the same. After Michel Gauthier served briefly as successor, Bouchard helped engineer the election of his friend Gilles Duceppe, surviving a scare when Parizeau hinted that he might seek the position. In Duceppe, he had a surrogate in Ottawa, a man who marched to his drumbeat. But Duceppe couldn't bring the heft to the position that Bouchard did. In the 1997 election the Bloc couldn't hope to match the 49 percent of the popular vote it received in the 1993 campaign—which in turn was the same number the sovereignists received in the referendum. That it still won 44 seats and almost 40 percent of the Quebec vote in an error-plagued campaign spoke to its strong base of support.

In any new referendum campaign, Bouchard felt he could bank on the potential of a strong campaign boosting numbers to the brink of 50 percent or over. He would be without many of the advantages of the 1995 campaign. The federalists would be much better prepared. He wouldn't have as strong a Bloc Québécois. He wouldn't be as mythical as he was the first time around. But given the rate at which he was tackling the deficit, he would have the province on a firmer financial footing. More of the fear would be gone. Without the fear he felt he could win.

As premier, his popularity slipped somewhat but he still placed far ahead of any rival. Given the rash of problems he inherited, he was holding up well. He had talked while Bloc leader of the need to build a rainbow coalition to achieve sovereignty. Now at a measured pace he was trying to fashion a concord, a unanimity which would be the foundation for the launch of a new state by the turn of the century. Being a moderate sovereignist of the Lévesque mould, he was nicely placed at the centre, the best location from which to try and pull together the various strands.

If anyone was capable of it, it was Lucien Bouchard. No other politician in the land combined in such abundance the qualities he possessed—the voracious work capacity, the depth of intellect, the power of prose and the burning charisma. Brian Mulroney's early read on him as a man with exceptional gifts was well vindicated. When he brought him to Ottawa, Mulroney had such big dreams for him. What a union of the solitudes they might have fashioned, had he been able to hold on to him.

The former prime minister, in his new function as globe-trotting dealmaker for his old Montreal law firm, didn't dwell much on those times. He didn't like to speak of Bouchard anymore. But he told his long-time buddy Sam Wakim why he lost him. By the time Bouchard landed in the nation's capital to take up the challenge of being a Cabinet minister, he was about to turn fifty. By then he had too much of the drug of the Kingdom of Saguenay in him. Mulroney had underestimated the pull of these old-stock bloodlines in Bouchard. He could stand on the balconies of Vancouver and rhapsodize on the magnificence of the larger Canada. But these were only moments. The siren songs of *la patrie* were too loud. "He came to Canada too late," Mulroney told Wakim. "Too late to understand."

The mind that was hostage to old history defied conventional analysis. Since childhood when Gérard noticed the high-voltage flights of temper which came and went without seeming reason, it had been evident Lucien Bouchard was someone who worked in strange ways. On reaching his goal of becoming premier of Quebec, not much had changed.

He met with a New England governor, William Weld of Massachusetts. Among other subjects, they discussed the unity issue. Following the session, reporters asked Bouchard if the subject was raised. Bouchard said no. He repeated the denial seven times. Later, the governor's people corrected him and Bouchard had to awkwardly come forward and admit the falsehood. He had been tired, he explained. This was probably why he made the seven denials.

What could be said of this? What could be said of a man who after all the vicious swipes at Jean Chrétien could turn around a few months into his stewardship as premier and assert, "I respect the man and I respect his ideas…I have no personal problems with Mr. Chrétien. Honestly. You know him. He's a straightforward guy. We have a lot in common. We are all Quebeckers…" What could be said of a man who, three months after holding up the newspaper with the betrayal headline, would then say to reporters that he had never used the word? "Betray! Betrayed? Those [words] don't pass through my lips," Bouchard indignantly insisted. "I respect people too much to do that."

In the premier's chair such fantastic contradictions and denials continued to pour out of Bouchard as if from a conveyor belt. He vociferously rejected the suggestion that he would give up his federal pension. Then he gave up his federal pension. Having devoted his key speech of the referendum to a denunciation of Ottawa's planned cuts to social spending in Quebec, he then went ahead and ushered in the cold winds himself, bringing in deep cuts similar to those of Ottawa and the provinces. As premier, he made several strong statements about not increasing taxes, then increased taxes. In a dispute with Newfoundland over power rights in Labrador he insisted on how the rule of law must prevail, but in reacting to Guy Bertrand's court challenge on Quebec's right to secede, he said the rule of law wouldn't count.

Contradictions were part of the territory in politics. Everybody made them. Trudeau was notorious for reversing himself on his promise not to impose wage and price controls, Mulroney did an about-face on free trade, Chrétien was all over the map on the question of withdrawing the GST. It could be argued that some reversals of opinion showed integrity on the part of politicians. Having learned more about an issue, it was right that they changed their minds. But Bouchard was a special case entirely. His spectacular volume of reversals (see list of fifty in Appendix) dwarfed those of other leaders. Jean Chrétien had been much longer in the political game, but his contradictions didn't reach a fraction of Bouchard's. Very few of Bouchard's could be regarded as examples of a maturing politician. Some fantastic backflips were made on the very same day and on questions as fundamental as the declaration of sovereignty. Some, such as the episode with the newspaper page, brought on heated denials from him when the truth of the matter was glaringly apparent for all to see. Some touched on issues of extreme importance, striking at the very heart of his beliefs.

Of Bouchard it could be said—as preposterous as it sounded— that at one time or another he had pulled the rug out from under himself on almost every fundamental position he stood for.

Even on as primal a question as Canada's stature as a country he had done a complete about-face. "I am proud to belong to this country," he offered after joining the Mulroney team. "Quebec will achieve more prosperity within Confederation." Some time later, he angrily declared, "Canada is divisible because Canada is not a real country. There are two people, two nations and two territories and this one is ours."

He had stood for a federated Quebec several times and he had stood for a sovereign Quebec several times. He had blazed his way through five different political parties. He had blamed English Canada for rejecting Quebec on Meech Lake and then said he didn't think this was the case. He had turned from a social democrat into a fiscal conservative. He had blamed the federal side for failed constitutional agreements when history showed that his own people, Lesage and Bourassa, had reneged on two of them. He had blackmailed Mulroney on the notwithstanding clause controversy, only to turn around and put the responsibility on the shoulders of Bourassa. After helping establish La Francophonie and free trade as a federalist, he decried federalism for keeping Quebec locked behind closed doors. There were these, and there was the ultimate contradiction: that of blaming the rest of Canada when most of the time it was his own people, Quebeckers, who were making the key decisions in Ottawa.

As stunning as the contradictions themselves was his utter lack of a sense of having made them. No one seemed to think Bouchard was deliberately deceitful. Rather, it seemed to be a case where his mind was capable of jumping from one self-contained island of commitment to another. At times he could completely shut out past history and live only in the moment. This could help explain the incident with the governor of Massachusetts, or his saying he never used the word betrayal after holding it up on a banner in front of millions of TV viewers.

Vivian Rakoff had come across examples of this phenomenon in the early 1970s before he took charge of the Clarke Institute, and they prompted him to coin the term for the behaviour—the esthetic character disorder. "It's a capacity for compartmentalizing the discontinuity," he said, the tendency "to embed yourself totally in a reality and then once that particular scene is over you move on." Bouchard was "an inspired actor-orator" who could deliver himself "a visage" at any moment that "seems absolutely convincing." The changed uniforms brought with them "no guilt of conscience," said the doctor, "because that was then. Now is now." Rakoff said he didn't like "psychiatrizing the world." He was only talking about symptoms, not hard evidence of such a problem. But the wealth of symptoms Bouchard had demonstrated were hard to discount. So many of those who dealt with him raised questions concerning his emotional stability.

From her experience in Paris seeing him, Adrienne Clarkson considered Bouchard on a wavelength that was not rational. She was one of many who, observing his swings of mood and commitment, wondered about his emotional stability. Few had met a more emotional man than Bouchard. He bled all over the place. In his by-election to gain a seat for the PQ, he came across a scrutineer in a polling booth who refused to shake his hand. Bouchard was seized with wrath, repeatedly demanding of aides in a how-dare-he kind of way the identity of the individual. The small incident was caught by the TV cameras and flashed throughout the province, receiving widespread comment.

Combined with the emotional intensity of Bouchard was a heavily rational component. Those who dealt with him on non-sensitive matters found him cool, logical, brilliant. Some said that the more time he spent in the premier's chair, the more he was learning to control himself.

What got in his way was his pride, a mushrooming hubris that had been evident since childhood. This aspect of him helped explain his thirst for power. Given his humble beginnings and those of his family, Bouchard craved respect. What brought respect, Bouchard knew, was power. Power unto him would help make up for past grievances. Throughout his career, he had always hitched his wagon to the rising star, be it Trudeau, Lévesque, Mulroney. He left each of them when they were in decline. Admitting he couldn't tolerate being number two, he sometimes plotted to undermine the number ones who got in his way. With the blessings of fate he moved to the top of the heap.

In the end, while he had yet to dispense with Chrétien, there was only one star left to follow—his own. Friends described his multicoloured trajectory as simply following the will of the Quebec people. Adversaries saw a fierce opportunist at work, every impulse in his body channelled towards realizing the fantastic dreams of the conquerors he read about as a boy.

He was at once the most formidable and the most flawed political leader in the land. The description many gave to him was Dr. Jekyll and Mr. Hyde. Indeed, there were two Lucien Bouchards. One was the rational, brilliant leader of Athenian ideals. The other was a thin-skinned, demagogic tribalist.

To a large extent, the future of Canada would depend on which one showed up. The country could not know the answer for the simple and potentially tragic reason that Lucien Bouchard himself did not know. As his fantastic convolutions of the mind had demonstrated, it was as if there was something in him he could not control. It was there. He responded to it.

His career tended to lend credence to what many had said of him at the outset—that he was too emotional a man for politics. History—and at what cost?—was full of leaders swept away by emotion, by the pull of the bloodlines, rather than by reason and logic. Lucien Bouchard was one of them. His mind, in all its traumas, was too often trapped in a bygone era—that of pre-1960s Quebec. He couldn't shed ancient hurts, prejudices, venom. He therefore stood as a man who sought to divide people rather than unite them.

In that his mission was endgame, in that he was often driven by emotion more than reason, in that he possessed almost hypnotic powers over portions of his population, it could be said of Lucien Bouchard that he posed a greater threat to the unity of the country than any political leader of the century. In his emotional hot zones there was no telling what he would do. He had brought the country considered the best in the world to the brink once; and now, as Canada turned to the new millennium, he was planning another assault on its stability, one that could spawn worse discord.

"When one enters the arena of the dream," Vivian Rakoff wrote in his report to the Liberals, "the rules of reason are suspended." Lucien Bouchard, as the psychiatrist and so many others knew, was in the arena of the dream too often.

AN APPENDIX:

A Man of Many Minds

As is explained in the text of the book, all politicians make contradictions and flip flops. It is part of the territory. Changing one's mind is often laudable, more laudable than a steadfast stubborness based on unwillingness to recognize previous error.

This said, Lucien Bouchard's record of reversing himself or brazenly contradicting the existing record is such that it bears special note. Bouchard has seemingly reversed himself at one time or another on almost every fundamental belief. By comparison in a political career many times longer I could count only a handful of occasions when Jean Chrétien made the political u-turn. Some of Bouchard's contradictions, as listed below, are part of a regular education cycle and understandable. Others seem to defy explanation. They are part of the mystery that is the man.

1. In January 1989, stating his support for the Canadian nation, Bouchard said, "Quebec will prosper better within Confederation." He added, "I am proud to belong to this country." In January 1996, he angrily asserted that Canada is divisible because "Canada is not a real country."

2. In December 1995, Bouchard said of Jean Chrétien, "I respect the man and his ideas... I must say that I have nothing against him." Prior to this declaration, Bouchard had called Chrétien the man "who represents everything I abhor about politics," the "enemy of Quebec's aspirations" and "the scarecrow." He described Chrétien as "the ghost of 1980 dragging its chains, coming back to haunt us," English Canada's "hatchet man," the "assassin" of Meech Lake and "the raper of the political will of Quebec."

3. In the 1995 referendum campaign, Bouchard held up a newspaper headline in front of millions of TV viewers. It said that Trudeau and Chrétien had "betrayed" Quebec. Three months

later Bouchard vigorously denied having used the term. "Betray! Betrayed?" he responded. "Those [words] don't pass through my lips. I respect people too much to do that."

4. Bouchard wrote in editorials for the college newspaper in Jonquière that Quebeckers must contribute actively "to the building of a big and great Canada." Isolationism for Quebec, he argued, must be avoided. He then moved on to law school at Laval. In editorials for his college newspaper there, he wrote that Confederation was "a cupboard of junk," that Canada couldn't work, that Quebec must use the threat of separation to exact concessions from the federal government.

5. Bouchard left Laval to begin work as a lawyer in Chicoutimi. He dropped his sovereignist-styled pitch and went federalist again, becoming a supporter of Pierre Trudeau. He campaigned for the Grits at both the federal and provincial levels. He then dropped the Liberals and took up again—this time in a formal way—the sovereignty cry. He joined René Lévesque's Parti Québécois.

6. As a middle-aged professional, he chose to discard sovereignty and return again to federalism. This time, it was with Brian Mulroney's Progressive Conservatives. He then dropped federalism again and became a secessionist, this time forming a new party, the Bloc Québécois.

7. In 1976 Bouchard worked in the Tory leadership campaign as a writer and policy maker for Brian Mulroney. Mulroney followed a strong Trudeauist line on policy towards Quebec at the time. In the same year, Bouchard actively supported René Lévesque's Parti Québécois in the election that brought the sovereignist party to power.

8. In sizing up Quebec's history between 1960 and 1980, Bouchard wrote in his book *On the Record* that "it had been a beautiful trip." Listing all the advances, he said that Quebec had made "enormous progress." The Liberal Party had been in power for most of those years in Quebec and in Ottawa. Bouchard abandoned both parties during this period. While on

the one hand he said tremendous progress had been made, on the other, he said Trudeau had been a disaster for the province, keeping it "a simple module."

9. Bouchard vigorously opposed Chrétien's and Trudeau's positions in the 1980 referendum and during the repatriation of the Constitution in 1981–82. Brian Mulroney strongly supported the federalists on both occasions. He gave a ringing endorsement of Jean Chrétien for his outstanding performance in each case. Bouchard then decided to ally himself with Mulroney and the Tories—before Mulroney changed his position in regard to repatriation.

10. Bouchard often talked of being a man of principle. Principle was what counted for him. In the Tory leadership race in 1983, Joe Clark was considerably more amenable to the politics of Quebec nationalists. Clark, like Bouchard, had opposed Trudeau's repatriation; however, Bouchard supported Mulroney over Clark in the leadership contest. Before going to Paris as Canada's ambassador to France, he heaped praise on Mulroney. In an interview in *Le Devoir*, he said Mulroney had an understanding of Quebec superior to almost all other politicians.

11. Bouchard claimed repeatedly that the repatriation of 1981–82 was shoved down Quebeckers' throats. After resigning from the Mulroney government, he would use it, along with the defeat of the Meech Lake Accord, to spearhead his drive for sovereignty. In a remarkable statement in his book, however, Bouchard said that René Lévesque really had no business trying to reach a unity pact with Trudeau and Chrétien in the first place. In doing so, Lévesque lacked credibility, he wrote, because he was a sovereignist. This was the point made by Chrétien and other federalists in the wake of Lévesque's rejection of the constitutional accord. He didn't really want an accord, they said. A unity pact would have undermined his party's raison d'être.

12. In 1979 Bouchard had headed up negotiations with the Quebec public service on a new contract, and a generous settlement was reached. Two years later, Bouchard and a cash-starved govern-

ment reneged on the deal, scaling back the original gains. Though he was acting on behalf of the government, critics pummelled Bouchard for the about-face, saying he could have taken the honourable route and chosen not to be party to the rescinding of the contract.

13. Bouchard alleged that the repatriation of the Constitution was done against Quebeckers' will. Opinion polls taken at the time showed a majority of Quebeckers in favour of repatriation, and particularly of Trudeau's Charter of Rights and Freedoms. Despite his charges, Bouchard conceded two years later, in September of 1985, that support for the Charter was high in Quebec. Polls indicated that there wasn't too much apprehension over the constitutional package among Quebeckers even after repatriation. They showed a continuing low level of support for sovereignty.

14. The Meech Lake Accord became the second great weapon in Bouchard's arsenal to try and bludgeon federalism. When the original Meech Accord was being negotiated in the early months of 1987, an irate Bouchard told Jean-Louis Roy, Quebec's envoy to Paris, as well as others, that the deal was no good. Concessions to Quebec did not go nearly far enough, he said.

   The same Bouchard told Mulroney and members of the Tory hierarchy that it was a good package. He told the House of Commons that Quebec was on the way to realizing its dream. In a meeting at the PMO, the issue of more demands coming from Quebeckers was raised. "Screw them!" Bouchard responded.

15. After serving as ambassador in Paris, Bouchard alleged in his book that his Quebec brethren who were ambassadors to France had their policies forced on them by their Anglo masters back home. Fred Bild, the second in command at the embassy, who had served two decades in Paris, had briefed Bouchard at length on the subject. He found it curious that Bouchard was so interested. When he read Bouchard's interpretation of the history he had given him, Bild was astounded. He found it to be in total contradiction to what he had said.

16. In 1988 Mulroney brought forward language legislation allow-ing Ottawa to promote bilingualism in Quebec and other provinces. Bouchard, as secretary of state, said categorically that the legislation would not be applied in Quebec without permission from provincial government. The statement under-cut the intent of the legislation—and Mulroney. A few weeks later, Bouchard backtracked, saying the law would be applied in Quebec as elsewhere. Then, a few weeks later, he changed course again. A modus operandi was worked out wherein there would be some consultation with Quebec.

17. Quebec premier Robert Bourassa invoked the notwithstanding clause at the end of 1988 to override a Supreme Court decision. The Court, in effect, had invalidated Quebec's Bill 101, which banned the use of English on outdoor signs. Contradicting Mulroney's policy opposing the use of the clause, Bouchard supported Bourassa. Mulroney planned to send a letter of admonition to Bourassa. By threatening to resign over the mat-ter, Bouchard forced Mulroney to withdraw the letter.

   Following his resignation from the government in 1990, Bouchard, in one of his most stunning about-faces, reversed his position. He then said Bourassa was wrong to use the clause. He acknowledged also that its invocation dealt a serious blow to the changes of Meech Lake being approved.

18. One of Bouchard's most basic positions over the years was that Ottawa's powers needed to be decentralized to give Quebec more control over its future. But as federal minister of the envi-ronment, Bouchard implemented measures strengthening the power of Ottawa over environmental issues as they affected Quebec. More control was necessary from the centre, he argued. (Bouchard complained repeatedly that Canada was an overcentralized government, although it was generally acknowledged that it was one of the most decentralized feder-ations in the world.)

19. As a Cabinet minister, Bouchard bitterly complained of the power of unelected officials surrounding Mulroney. As Mul-roney's adviser and speech-writer and ambassador, Bouchard exercised major influence as an unelected official himself.

Then, as premier of Quebec, he centralized power in his office, giving unelected officials much clout.

20. Bouchard mounted his case for sovereignty on the woes allegedly inflicted on Quebec by English Canada. But the Canada he spoke of was governed by his Quebec brethren. Quebeckers occupied the prime minister's chair for most of the three decades from the late 1960s on.

    At the time of the 1995 referendum, French Canadians were dominant in the power structure. The prime minister was French Canadian. The Opposition leader was French Canadian, as was the entire Opposition party. The Clerk of the Privy Council was French Canadian. So was the Chief Justice of the Supreme Court, the Speaker of the House, the Governor General, the chief of staff to the prime minister, the leader of the Senate and a slew of the top Cabinet ministers. Canada was rated the best country in the world and Quebeckers, in large part, had the run of it.

21. After holding English Canada responsible for the defeat of Meech Lake, Bouchard later reversed his position. He told Peter Gzowski in an interview on "Morningside" that he didn't really think it was an act by English Canada against Quebec. In fact, the people Bouchard railed against far more than others over the failure of Meech Lake were his own people— Chrétien, Charest, Trudeau and Paul Tellier.

22. After resigning over Meech Lake, Bouchard vowed not to form a political party from his bloc of dissident MPs. He said Quebeckers did not want another political party. He then turned the Bloc Québécois into an official party.

23. Having left the Mulroney Tories, Bouchard derided the federal system for keeping Quebec locked in a closet, unable to open itself to the world. As a Cabinet minister, he had played a leading role in the development of La Francophonie, the commonwealth of French nations. At the same time he was a grand promoter of the Free Trade Agreement which allowed Quebec to open its economic borders. As premier of Quebec, he joined the Chrétien trade mission to Asia because it allowed for the

same type of expansion.

24. In November 1989, Bouchard attacked Trudeau's bilingualism policy, saying bilingualism didn't exist outside Quebec. The attack flew in the face of his decades-long support for bilingualism going back to his days as a student in Jonquière. Prior to the outburst, he had embraced Trudeau's policy.

25. Bouchard scorned Robert Bourassa for taking part in negotiations to alter the Meech Lake Accord in the spring of 1990. In the summer, as a newly conceived sovereignist, he leaped into Bourassa's arms. He became a supporter when Bourassa invited him to sit on the Bélanger-Campeau Commission and when Bourassa helped him in a by-election to get the first Bloc member, Gilles Duceppe, elected to Parliament.

26. In a strong outburst in April 1993, Bouchard blamed English Canada for saddling Quebec with an enormous debt. Under Anglo prime ministers Diefenbaker and Pearson there was no debt to speak of. Deficit levels took off under the stewardship of a French Canadian, Pierre Trudeau, and skyrocketed under another Quebec prime minister, Brian Mulroney. As a minister in the Mulroney government, Bouchard demanded $5 billion in new spending for his environmental Green Plan. In Quebec, the deficit rose sharply under its Francophone premiers Lévesque, Bourassa and Parizeau.

27. Bouchard pledged in December of 1993 that the question on the next referendum would be a straightforward Yes or No on sovereignty. He then led a successful campaign to have the question watered down to include a proposal for a partnership agreement with the rest of Canada.

28. In October 1993, Bouchard said he never used the word humiliation "because Quebeckers aren't humiliated." Reporters had lost count of how many times he had used the word in talking about himself or the treatment of Quebeckers. However, he did not use it after that.

29. On his visit to Washington in the spring of 1994, Bouchard

explained, while agreeing that Quebeckers were often the ones running the country, that Quebec still needed independence. The reason was that the province's economic growth was stunted within Canada, he said. Quebec lacked power over the economic levers.

In direct counterpoise, Bouchard then said it was Quebec which was responsible for bringing about what he called the biggest economic change of the Canadian century. Without Quebec's support, Bouchard stated, the Free Trade Agreement would not have passed.

30. Bouchard never liked the term "ethnic nationalism." On his visit to the United States he told reporters in New York that "ours is not an ethnic nationalism. Our is a territorial nationalism." In April 1994, he said "in a word [sovereignty] is necessary because we are a people..." In the speech he used the word *"peuple"* (a people) to describe Quebeckers more than twenty times.

31. As Bloc leader, Bouchard was initially opposed to the partnership proposals with the rest of Canada forwarded by Mario Dumont's fledgling party, L'Action Démocratique. In late 1994 Bouchard agreed to campaign against Dumont in the young leader's own riding in the provincial election. A few months later, Bouchard reversed himself, forming an alliance with Dumont and borrowing from his partnership message.

32. Bouchard often used the image of Machiavellian dealings and back-stabbing by federalists in condemning their behaviour towards Quebec. Without warning, the same Bouchard abandoned his close friend Mulroney, and plunged his government into crisis in May 1990 on the eve of the Meech Lake ratification. His telegram from Paris in apparent support of the PQ was described in back-stabbing terms. In 1995 he undercut Jacques Parizeau, announcing a *virage* or major turn in separatist strategy without forewarning the premier, who was seated in the audience for the speech. That Bouchard could accuse others of underhandedness occasioned reactions of utter incredulity from anyone who had been party to these episodes.

33. On his trips to Paris and Washington, Bouchard, as Opposition leader, promoted the break-up of Canada. But when Mexican president Salinas visited Ottawa and spoke in favour of a united Canada, Bouchard, still Opposition leader, raised a storm. He chastised Salinas for meddling in Canadian affairs.

34. "I am a politician who would like to get out of politics," Bouchard said while Bloc leader. "I hate the word. I hate the job." While in the same job, Bouchard asserted, "I feel so good about politics since I left the government because I make all my decisions myself. I just consult my instincts."

35. During his brutal health crisis, Bouchard scribbled an instruction to his doctors: "*Que l'on continue.*" ("Please carry on.") He later claimed in an interview with Jean-François Lépine that it was a political message to the sovereignty movement. He was asking people to believe that in the heat of the emergency room, hanging on to life by a thread, his body having been carved open, a leg having been amputated, his system under severe stress from massive doses of medication, he was preoccupied with the sovereignty movement—this after having been a federalist three times over!

     Later, when reports from associates suggested that obviously the note was just an instruction to doctors, Bouchard began to back away from his original statement.

36. After many years of service to René Lévesque's PQ, Bouchard declared in 1988, "I don't like the word separatist. It's not the reality." On his trip to Washington in 1994 he declared he was a separatist because that was the reality.

37. He was asked in early 1995 about his remark that perhaps it was "too harsh to say we've hit a wall with English Canada."

     Was he softening up? the reporter, Susan Delacourt, wondered.

     "I didn't say that," Bouchard responded.

     Delacourt had the quotation in front of her. "You didn't?"

     "I might think it," Bouchard replied. "But I have no recollection of these words." Then he added, "But I wouldn't deny it."

38. Following his torment with flesh-eating disease, Bouchard was accused of stage-managing his return to gain maximum publicity. In an interview he told *The Globe and Mail* he hadn't had time to stage-manage his return. However, in a press conference subsequent to the interview he said he had made all the decisions himself concerning the nature of his return.

39. In a dispute with Newfoundland over hydroelectric power rights in Labrador, Bouchard vowed that the rule of law must apply. In the case of lawyer Guy Bertrand's challenging Quebec's constitutional right to secede, Bouchard said, in effect, that the rule of law should not apply.

40. Bouchard complained bitterly in the referendum campaign of 1995 that the federal government's attacks on the deficit would take millions of dollars from the pockets of Quebec's poor. As premier of Quebec, Bouchard undertook a deficit-cutting plan which dug into social programs in a way comparable to federal efforts.

41. Bouchard ridiculed Ontario premier Mike Harris for forcing a basic diet on the underprivileged classes of Ontario. As premier of Quebec, while bringing in his heavy deficit-cutting measures, thus moving away from his promised "pact of humanism," Bouchard became good friends with the right-winger. Bouchard and his wife got together with the Harrises for a weekend of vacation and work.

42. Bouchard alleged that all constitutional negotiations between Ottawa and Quebec had resulted in failure. During the referendum campaign he worked his audiences into a lather, charging that Ottawa had reneged on its promises.

    In 1964 Quebec premier Jean Lesage reached an agreement with Ottawa to repatriate the Constitution under the Fulton-Favreau formula. Quebec then reneged on the agreement. In 1971 Quebec under Bourassa reached a constitutional accord at Victoria which gave Quebec a veto over constitutional changes. Bourassa went back on the deal.

43. Early in the referendum campaign, controversy emerged over

the Quebec government's failure to publish studies on the potential effects of a secession vote. Bouchard promised that from then on everything would be published. A short time later he ditched the Le Hir studies, a multimillion-dollar series of reports on the impact of sovereignty undertaken by Parizeau's team. Some had yet to be published. Bouchard said he didn't want to have anything to do with them. They were in the past.

Earlier, on the same day in which he jettisoned the studies, Bouchard used one of the Le Hir reports to back up his argument for Quebec's continued use of military bases.

44. In the midst of the referendum campaign, Bouchard attacked Laurent Beaudoin, the CEO of Bombardier, for suggesting he might move the company out of Quebec in the wake of a pro-sovereignty vote.

As a mainstay of their campaign, Bouchard and Parizeau had been making the case that Quebec did not get its fair share of federal largesse. In 1986 Bombardier had received a $1.3-billion jet-servicing contract from Ottawa. Bristol Aerospace of Winnipeg had been a strong bidder and the award to Quebec triggered protests in Western Canada of favouritism to La Belle Province.

Bouchard agreed with the critics. "If Mr. Beaudoin hadn't been a Quebecker and if it wasn't in Montreal, he wouldn't have gotten the contract. Bouchard said, stunning observers by tearing a hole in his previous line of argument. "It's Quebec's political strength that got him the CF-18 contract."

45. On October 19, 1995, Bouchard stated in a morning press conference in Rivière-du-Loup that sovereignty would be proclaimed after a Yes vote, to be followed by a negotiation with the rest of Canada. That same evening in Rimouski, Bouchard declared there would be two distinct stages. First the negotiations with the federal government on a partnership, then the declaration.

46. After meeting with Governor William Weld of Massachusetts in early 1996, Bouchard repeated—seven times—that they did not talk about the issue of Quebec secession. Bouchard was

soon corrected by the governor's aides. He then conceded, following his seven denials, that indeed they had talked about it.

47. As premier of Quebec, Bouchard suggested strongly that no tax
hike would be brought in to combat the deficit. A short time
later he brought forward a tax increase to combat the deficit.

48. As a result of Chrétien's support for Guy Bertrand's legal challenge to the right of Quebec to secede, Premier Bouchard
vowed he would not meet with Chrétien and the premiers.
Bouchard met with Chrétien and the premiers.

49. Bouchard attacked Tory leader Jean Charest in the 1997 federal election campaign, saying he had worked out a secret deal,
behind Quebec's back, to dilute the Meech Lake Accord.
    Bouchard had personally convinced Charest, a fellow
Quebecker, to head up the committee to study possible side
clauses to the accord. Charest's brother, Robert, worked on
Bouchard's staff. Bouchard was briefed on the committee's
actions every step of the way, and was shown drafts of the
report being prepared by the committee. In the days before he
resigned, ostensibly over the Charest committee report, he
refused to return phone calls from Charest.

50. Leapfrogging among political parties, Bouchard, by age fifty-
eight, was with his sixth. In college he moved from his Union
Nationale family background to become a supporter of the
NDP. He dropped the NDP in the 1960s to become an active
Liberal Party member. He dropped the Liberals in the early
1970s to joint the Parti Québécois. He dropped the PQ in the
1980s to become a federal Progressive Conservative. He
dropped the Tories in the 1990s to become a member of the
newly formed Bloc Québécois. He dropped the BQ in 1996 to
return to the PQ.

NOTES

Unless otherwise indicated, all interviews referred to herein were done by the author, specifically for this book. The interviews took place between October 1995 and April 1997. With a couple of minor exceptions, all interviews were on the record.

In many cases the sources of information are evident in the text. Dates of some newspaper articles quoted are not specified when the time frame is clear from the context. Unless otherwise noted, the newspapers are *La Presse*, *Le Devoir*, *The Globe and Mail*, *The Toronto Star* and *The Ottawa Citizen*.

CHAPTER 1: BURNING INSIDE

1   In his office in the philosophy department at the University of Ottawa, Roch Bouchard recalled at length the nature of their upbringing in the Bouchard home. He followed up the interview with a letter to me expanding on some of his views. Three phone conversations followed. All information from Roch in this chapter is from the interviews.

2   The reaction of Alice Bouchard to her husband's beer-drinking was recounted by Roch and confirmed by Gérard Bouchard, who was interviewed at his University of Quebec offices in Chicoutimi. Conversations by telephone followed. All references to Gérard in this chapter are based on the interviews.

5   Lucien Bouchard's reference to the cult of family is from Lucien Bouchard, *On the Record* (Toronto: Stoddart, 1994).

5   A close associate of Lucien Bouchard's suggested that owing to Roch Bouchard's problems with depression, he wasn't the best interview source. However, he was working at his office and appeared in good health when interviewed. Further-

more, certain information he gave was checked with others and verified.

CHAPTER 2: THE MYTHS OF THE KINGDOM

6   Roch told the author about the humiliating experience of working in the labour camps. The author wrote to Lucien Bouchard asking for more information about the incident, but he declined to respond.

6   Description of life in Arvida is from interview with Joan Bell in Ottawa and from her thesis on the subject.

8   Information beginning here on the history of the Saguenay-Lac-Saint-Jean region is from interviews with Gérard Bouchard, Roch Bouchard, Joan Bell, historian Camil Girard, Lucien Bouchard's biography, and from information provided by Lucien Bouchard's classmates at Le Collège de Jonquière. Also from Camil Girard and Norman Perron, *Histoire du Saguenay-Lac Saint-Jean* (Quebec: Institut Québécois de Recherche sur la Culture, 1995), and Christiane Laforge and Mona Gauthier Cano, *Notre Histoire à Petits Pas* (Saint-Fulgence, Que.: Les éditions du Gaymont, 1987).

11   Background on Jean Chrétien's youth compared to Lucien Bouchard's: Lawrence Martin, *Chrétien: The Will to Win* (Toronto: Lester Publishing, 1995).

12   The memories of the Bouchard brothers vary somewhat over the details of their father's background. The version here is largely that of the historian in the family, Gérard.

12   Denise Bombardier, the Radio-Canada broadcaster and author, maintained in a telephone conversation that during her relationship with Bouchard in Paris, the poverty of his youth was a theme he returned to again and again. It marked him forever, she said.

13   In an interview, Paul-André Gauthier recalled the charismatic demeanour of Lucien Bouchard's father.

14   André Tremblay spoke to the author for two hours on the balcony of his apartment in Montreal on his memories of

Philippe Bouchard and of Lucien and Roch. To this day, he is not sure of the source of the anger and bitterness he always saw at the core of Lucien Bouchard.

14   The anecdote of Philippe Bouchard admonishing Lucien at the dinner table is from Marci McDonald's profile of Bouchard, in *Maclean's*, June 13, 1994.

15   On the stash of one hundred books, see Bouchard's *On the Record*.

16   Episodes of Lucien on the football gridiron and of his fights with neighbourhood toughs were described by Roch Bouchard.

CHAPTER 3: THE CLASSICS STUDENT

19   Bouchard was expansive and candid in an interview with Jeffrey Simpson on the one-sided view of Canadian history he was taught. See Simpson's *Faultlines: Struggling for a Canadian Vision* (Toronto: HarperCollins, 1993).

20   On wrestling for years with the likes of Horace and Virgil, see René Lévesque's *Memoirs* (Toronto: McClelland & Stewart, 1986).

21   Of the thirty classmates Bouchard had at Jonquière College, twenty were interviewed for this book. A consensus of their views informs this chapter, as does Bouchard's own recall of the period in his autobiography.

22   Though forty years had passed since he taught Lucien Bouchard, Lionel Lamonde, who was interviewed in Jonquière, remembered well his outstanding qualities.

24   Yves Villeneuve, Bouchard's rival for top academic honours at college, noted in an interview that the Lucien Bouchard he sees today as premier of Quebec has changed little from the intense fellow he knew at college.

25   The story of the monsignor placing the red biretta on Lucien's head is from Bouchard's memoirs.

28   The editions of the college newspaper *Le Cran* containing all

of Lucien's early writings are available at Jonquière College.
Most of his articles were co-written with Yves Villeneuve.

CHAPTER 4: CULTURAL TRANSFORMATION

34   Normand Simard, who recounted the blind-date story in an
      interview, said the evening marked the first time Jocelyne
      Côté and Lucien Bouchard had met. Others suggested they
      may have become acquaintances prior to that evening.

35   The description of students from the Saguenay as from the
      boonies is from an interview with Nicole Arseneault.

36   Bouchard meeting de Gaulle: see Bouchard's autobiography.

38   Roch Bouchard revealed the story of the desecration of the
      Confederation monument in an interview.

40   In interviews, Bouchard's room-mates André Tremblay and
      Bernard Angers described the Laval years. While Tremblay
      was forthcoming, Angers said one area he would not talk
      about was Lucien and women. Other students interviewed
      for this chapter included Bernard Roy, Sonny Mass, Peter
      White, Yvon Marcoux, Denis de Belleval, George McLaren
      and Peter Kilburn. Also interviewed were several classmates
      from Jonquière College who then moved on to Laval, but
      were not in the law faculty.

43   Bouchard's wholesale change in political attitudes from one
      college to the next is evident in the editions of Le Carabin,
      from which his quotes are drawn.

45   For Chrétien's bitter exchange at lunch in Trois-Rivières, see
      The Will to Win.

45   The reference to the comparison of Bouchard and Trudeau
      is from Michel Vastel's biography Lucien Bouchard: En Atten-
      dant la Suite (Outremont, Que.: Lanctôt Editeur, 1996).

48   Bouchard's classic description of Mulroney is from On the
      Record.

49   Peter Newman's comparison of Daniel Johnson and Brian
      Mulroney is from his The Canadian Revolution: From

Deference to Defiance (Toronto: Penguin, 1995).

50   Bouchard's first big political speech: interview with Denis de
     Belleval.

CHAPTER 5: THE YOUNG LAWYER

52   In an interview, Michael Cain recalled what Bouchard was
     like as a law partner.

54   Gérard Bouchard offered generally a more protective and
     positive view of his brother than did Roch, whose relations
     with Lucien were more stressful.

55   Assessments of Jocelyne Côté as an unsuitable partner for
     Bouchard came not only from de Belleval, but also from
     André Tremblay and other friends from Jonquière who knew
     them well.

56   Kristeva on Proust: see Julia Kristeva, *Proust and the Sense of
     Time* (London: Faber and Faber, 1993).

57   Bloom on Proust: see Harold Bloom, *The Western Canon:
     The Books and School of the Ages* (New York: Harcourt Brace
     & Co., 1994).

57   Trudeau's influences: see Christina McCall and Stephen
     Clarkson, *Trudeau and Our Times, Volume 2: The Historic
     Delusion* (Toronto: McClelland & Stewart, 1994).

59   Marc-André Bedard reported in an interview how he intro-
     duced Bouchard to the sovereignist cause.

61   In an interview, legal colleague François Lamarre recalled
     Bouchard's visit to Greece and the problems his turning to
     the PQ caused at the law firm.

62   Trudeau in Ottawa "to screw us": see Vastel biography,
     Lucien Bouchard: En Attendant la Suite.

64   Bedard told the story of Bouchard's signing the PQ mem-
     bership card in an interview.

CHAPTER 6: FLEEING THE FIRM

66   On Bouchard's split with the firm, Michael Cain and Lamarre's versions differed from that of Pierre Bergeron who didn't report having such a personal conflict with Bouchard at the time.

70   For the account of Mulroney and Bouchard at the Cliche Commission, see L. Ian MacDonald, *Mulroney: The Making of the Prime Minister* (Toronto: McClelland & Stewart, 1984). See also John Sawatsky, *Mulroney: The Politics of Ambition* (Toronto: Macfarlane Walter & Ross, 1991), as well as Bouchard's *On the Record*.

74   The funeral day: Gérard Bouchard interview.

78   In becoming a close friend of Lévesque's wife, Jocelyne Ouellette had a good sense of the Bouchard-Lévesque relationship.

79   The description of the labour negotiations by Bouchard as a Greek tragedy is from his autobiography, *On the Record*.

CHAPTER 7: LONG KNIVES OR LONG LIES

81   Bouchard's estimation that the years 1960–80 represented wonderful progress for Quebec is taken from his book.

83   Bouchard's remarkable admission on the lack of credibility of the PQ in the federal negotiation is from his book.

84   In an interview, Peter Blaikie recalled the night Mulroney scorned Joe Clark and praised the Trudeau strategy.

86   For a rundown of Lévesque's behaviour during the constitutional negotiations, see Robert Sheppard and Michael Valpy, *The National Deal: The Fight for a Canadian Constitution* (Toronto: Fleet Books, 1982).

87   Hugh Segal's observations on the so-called Night of the Long Knives are taken from his memoir, *No Surrender: Tales of a Happy Warrior in the Tory Crusade* (Toronto: Harper-Collins, 1996).

88   Jean-Luc Pépin provided his thoughts in an interview for

Chrétien: The Will to Win.

88   Bouchard's observation that the repatriation negotiation was the key event triggering all that would follow is from his autobiography.

91   Marc-Yvan Côté's view that Bouchard had major responsibility for tearing up the agreement with the unions was given in an interview. Bouchard later would strike back at Côté, labelling him a right-winger out to bash the poor.

92   Bouchard's view on being "humiliated as never before" is from his book.

93   Pierre-Marc Johnson reflected in an interview on the impressive abilities of Bouchard as a negotiator.

CHAPTER 8: BRIAN AND LUCIEN

101   In an interview, Charles McMillan recalled the fight he had to get the Bouchard script changed.

102   Ian MacDonald's thoughts on Mulroney and the intelligentsia are from his book, *Mulroney: The Making of the Prime Minister*.

102   Mulroney's classic opportunism: an interview with Peter White.

104   The anecdote on the appointment to Paris being so obvious is from an interview with Pierre-Marc Johnson.

107   Bouchard's comment on the impact of seeing Vancouver is from an interview with Adrienne Clarkson.

108   The scene at the Lévesque hideaway is from Bouchard's *On the Record*.

CHAPTER 9: THE AMBASSADOR

113   The faux pas during the toast at the embassy was described in an interview with Fred Bild and in Bouchard's autobiography.

115   In an interview, Fred Bild told the story of the liaisons

Bouchard had with the Péquistes and of how he chose to mis-interpret the embassy history to suit his political purposes.

116   Adrienne Clarkson's point that Bouchard rewrites history as he goes along to suit his political purposes was a view shared by many.

121   In an interview, Bombardier reported that Bouchard did not curb her movements anywhere.

122   de Belleval explained in an interview the sense of duty and obligation he and Bouchard shared.

123   Camille Guilbault told the story of Bouchard and younger women in an interview.

123   The episode with Jean-Louis Roy relating how Bouchard found the conditions for Meech to be far too weak is from Michel Vastel's book, *Bourassa* (Toronto: Macmillan Canada, 1991).

124   Norman Spector recounted how Bouchard did not want to hear about complaints from Quebeckers on the Meech con-ditions in an interview.

126   The high-water mark for Mulroney and Bouchard. From an interview with Ian MacDonald.

CHAPTER 10: A PSYCHIATRIC PERSPECTIVE

128   Bouchard's intellectual terms of reference: interview with John Ralston Saul.

129   "Islands of passion": interview with John Godfrey.

129   The references to Dr. Vivian Rakoff are from the two reports he submitted to Godfrey and from two subsequent interviews with him. Rakoff was at first hesitant to have his reports quot-ed, but finally gave consent. His study of Bouchard was from a distance. He never sat down and talked to him, but felt safe in drawing the conclusions in his studies from examining the wealth of material available on Bouchard.

132   The prime minister needs you: interview with Bernard Roy.

133   Transferring primal loyalties: interview with Ian MacDonald.

134   What does a secretary of state do?: interview with Ian MacDonald.

134   This was not the right appointment: interview with Bernard Roy.

135   Luc Lavoie related the story of being hired by Bouchard and Bouchard's reaction to the language dispute in Saskatchewan.

137   The story of Bouchard's by-election victory was compiled with the assistance of interviews with Pierre Gimaiel, Luc Lavoie, Benoît Bouchard, Ian MacDonald, Pierre Blais, Bernard Roy, Roger Banford and press reports. See also the accounts in Bouchard's autobiography and in Graham Fraser's *Playing for Keeps: The Making of the Prime Minister* (Toronto: McClelland & Stewart, 1989).

CHAPTER 11: THE FIRST BLACKMAIL

146   Account of Black's meeting with Mulroney is from Conrad Black, *A Life in Progress* (Toronto: Key Porter Books, 1993).

147   Fournier's relations with Bouchard: interview with Jean Fournier.

152   Protests to keep Bill 101 in force: from Lucien Bouchard's autobiography.

153   Luc Lavoie recounted the story of Lucien Bouchard's dismay over the federal reaction to the invocation of the notwithstanding clause.

153   For assessing the story of the relations between Lucien Bouchard and Brian Mulroney, there was perhaps no one better placed than Luc Lavoie. He worked for both men. He acted as a go-between and confidant for both. He was with one or both of them in the moments of highest drama. Even after their split, Lavoie somehow managed to stay on excellent terms with each of them. Lavoie was interviewed for the book over a five-hour lunch. The interview was followed by several telephone conversations.

157   In an interview, Roch Bouchard recounted how he felt "Mulroney lacked force in Ottawa." The influence on Lucien's thinking of Roch, Gérard and Alice Bouchard, while never a source of public conjecture, should not be underestimated. His family ties were most important and he was getting strong negative signals about Mulroney from all of them.

158   The prime minister wouldn't forget the retreat: from Bouchard's *On the Record*.

159   In an interview, Bernard Roy related the frustrations Bouchard faced while operating in Ottawa.

CHAPTER 12: THE ENVIRONMENTAL CENTRALIST

161   The episode of Gérard and the letter was puzzling and displayed his sensitivity over publicity on family matters. How could he have forgotten sending a letter to Lucien which touched off the biggest rift ever in their relations?

163   Bouchard's department invested with a veto power: *The Toronto Star*, February 1, 1989.

164   Mila Mulroney's memory of Audrey Best at the hairdresser: from Peter Newman's *The Canadian Revolution*.

165   Green's memories of working with Bouchard: from several interviews with Martin Green.

168   Patricia Dumas's recollections of working with Bouchard: from interviews with Patricia Dumas.

168   What Lucien wanted, Lucien would get: interview with Robert Charest.

170   Canada confronted with a "terrible, insidious danger": *The Guardian*, October 19, 1989.

172   Bouchard as a centralist on the environment: Amir Attaran, *The Globe and Mail*, Commentary page, October 3, 1996.

172   The most centralizing act ever adopted: interview with André Tremblay.

173   Bouchard's criticism of bilingualism: *La Presse*, November

19, 1989.

174   Trudeau shouldn't be criticized on bilingualism: Lysiane Gagnon, *La Presse*, November 21, 1989.

CHAPTER 13: "HE JUST EXPLODED"

176   On Bouchard being overworked like Guy Favreau, see Peter Newman's *The Distemper of Our Times: Canadian Politics in Transition* (Toronto: McClelland & Stewart, 1968).

176   The big thick goddam books: from an interview with Arthur Campeau.

176   For a further discussion of prime ministers and their relations with their close friends, see Graham Fraser's "Lucien and Brian," *The Globe and Mail*, May 18, 1991. Fraser's article also brought to light the behind-the-scenes rift between Bouchard and Stanley Hartt which may well have been a key factor in Bouchard's leaving.

180   Bouchard turning to the little phone beside him: from an interview with Pierre Blais.

184   Bouchard's remarkable about-face on Bill 178 is from *The Montreal Gazette*, February 1, 1990.

186   "It was just a job": from an interview with Fred Bild.

       Martin Green remembered Bouchard's temper tantrum in the Vancouver hotel room. His recall of the words Bouchard used while in full flight are to the best of his memory.

187   Lucien just exploded: an interview with Norman Spector.

188   Canada will have to choose between Newfoundland and Quebec: *La Presse*, April 7, 1990.

189   Raucous in the Commons: see *The Globe and Mail*, April 11, 1990, and *Le Droit*, April 11, 1990—"Prise de bec magistrale aux Communes."

190   "My honour! My self-esteem!": interview with journalist Graham Fraser, who was witness to the scene.

191   Bouchard gone mentally from Ottawa: interview with

Benoît Bouchard.

CHAPTER 14: THE HUBRIS COMPLEX

CHAPTER 15: DE GAULLE WAITING FOR THE CALL

209   Opening the future for his children: interview with Paul-André Gauthier.

211   Like Gretzky quitting the game after two periods: interview with Pierre Blais.

211   Quebec has stripped itself naked: for reports of his first speech after leaving government, see *The Montreal Gazette*, *The Globe and Mail* and *La Presse*, May 24, 1990.

213   Chrétien like an old ghost dragging its chains: *The Toronto Star*, May 28, 1990.

213   It was too painful for him: from an interview with Gérard Bouchard.

215   An agreement lacking honour and enthusiasm: Lucien Bouchard's column appeared in *Le Devoir*, June 12, 1990.

219   Too emotional for politics: interview with Nic Leblanc.

219   Tales from Paris: interview with Luc Plamondon.

220   English Canada will not yield unless there is a knife at its throat: see the chapter on Léon Dion in Jeffrey Simpson's *Faultlines*.

222   Bouchard left room with a great burst of laughter: *La Presse*, December 12, 1990.

223   Chrétien flattens man with vicious punch: see *Chrétien: The Will to Win*.

CHAPTER 16: THE POLITICS OF RESENTMENT

224   The politics of resentment: from Rakoff report for the Liberals.

226   The Bouchard comparison with Abbé Groulx: interviews with Jean-Claude Rivest and Graham Fraser. See also Jean-François Lisée's *The Trickster: Robert Bourassa and the Quebecers, 1990–1992* (Toronto: James Lorimer & Company, 1994).

227   The prickly relationship of François Gérin and Lucien
       Bouchard: for more detail see Manon Cornellier's *The Bloc*
       (Toronto: James Lorimer & Company, 1995).

228   The Bourassa government can't get out of it: *Le Devoir* and
       The Montreal Gazette, January 31, 1992.

229   Mulroney and Bouchard square off in the Commons: *The
       Globe and Mail*, March 12, 1997.

230   The Anglophones were let down by the premier: see Lysiane
       Gagnon's column, *La Presse*, June 13, 1991. Gagnon and a
       few other journalists picked up on Bouchard's reversal, but
       given the extent of his turnabout on a matter that had such
       impact, the story died surprisingly quickly.

231   Bouchard never bothered by contradiction: see Vastel's
       biography.

234   Spanish-Americans as a separate breed: from Paul Johnson's
       The Birth of the Modern: World Society, 1815–1830 (New York:
       HarperCollins, 1991).

235   Bourassa as Houdini: *The Montreal Gazette*, January 31,
       1992.

236   He was always taking the bus: from Manon Cornellier's *The
       Bloc*.

237   Authentic and intellectually brilliant: interview with André
       Tremblay.

238   On deriving inspiration from Churchill: interview with Eve-
       lyn Abitbol.

240   Bouchard is the one I brought to life: *The Globe and Mail*,
       September 10, 1992.

CHAPTER 17: THE CAMPAIGNER

241   All victims of the pursuit of images and clips: from Vastel's
       biography.

245   Bouchard was not well-schooled on economics. He had not
       studied the subject in depth at university and his experience

as a labour negotiator kept him far enough from the field. He sat on some corporate boards before entering politics, but his responsibilities in serving Mulroney did not include economic portfolios.

246   For a more detailed discussion of the Bloc's policy positions, see Cornellier's *The Bloc*.

246   Federalism cheating Quebec out of billions. For a more detailed description of Bouchard's complaints, see Rhéal Séguin's article, "Quebec loses out..." in *The Globe and Mail*, September 13, 1993.

247   The Sarah Scott affair: an interview with Sarah Scott. Her portrait of Bouchard appeared in *The Montreal Gazette* on October 16, 1993.

248   How dare you! How can you ask this! The words used in Bouchard's tantrum were recalled to the best of Scott's memory.

250   On Quebeckers' domination of top federal structure. One of the great mysteries of Canadian politics is why journalists and federalist politicians never picked up on this point. Quebeckers had what the United Nations termed the best country in the world. They also had, to a good extent, the run of it. It wasn't until the 1997 federal election campaign that an issue was made of it—and then in a rather divisive way—by the Reform Party's Preston Manning.

252   On Bouchard and the road of rationality: see André Pratte's column, *La Presse*, October 13, 1993.

253   Campbell's brief bubble began to burst: Bouchard's quotes throughout this section can be found in the press reports of the campaign in September and October of 1993.

255   Bouchard's debut in the Commons as Opposition leader: *The Montreal Gazette* and *The Toronto Star*, January 20, 1994.

CHAPTER 18: DEFYING THE ODDS

259   Jacques Godbout on France and the United States: from Ray Conlogue's *Impossible Nation: The Longing for Homeland in*

Canada and Quebec (Stratford, Ont.: Mercury Press, 1996).

260   On Bouchard's visit to the United States: see *The Globe and Mail* and *The Montreal Gazette*, March 3 and 4, 1994.

260   On Mulroney's visit as Opposition leader to Reagan: Lawrence Martin, *Pledge of Allegiance: The Americanization of Canada in the Mulroney Years* (Toronto: McClelland & Stewart, 1993).

261   Ralph Klein on Bouchard in the context of Louis Riel: *The Edmonton Journal*, May 27, 1994.

262   A fine example of the Quebec media's contrasting treatment of the Bouchard visit to France was Christian Rioux's article in *Le Devoir* "L'avantage de la glace…" on May 20, 1994.

263   Bouchard's dispute with Pierrette Venne: *Maclean's*, June 13, 1994. Bloc member Gilles Duceppe also commented on how he was the target of some of Bouchard's volcanic fits of temper. They were hardly pleasant, he said, but added that the leader had qualities which compensated for the character flaw.

263   On the dispute with Daniel Turp over partition: *Le Devoir* and *The Globe and Mail*, May 27, 1994.

264   Bouchard's control of his caucus: interview with Patty Torsney.

264   Bouchard on Ginn Publishing dispute: for insights on this and on how Bouchard ran the Bloc, see Don Gillmor's fine profile in *Saturday Night* magazine, "Lucien in the Sky with Diatribes," June 1994.

265   Bouchard's change in thinking on English Canada as the culprit in Meech Lake: *The Globe and Mail*, May 26, 1994.

267   Bouchard's trauma with flesh-eating disease: interviews included Gérard Bouchard, Roch Bouchard, Denis de Belleval, Luc Lavoie, Susan Delacourt, Luc Plamondon and Nic Leblanc. Noteworthy among the press reports was Barry Came's feature in *Maclean's*, "The Fight for His Life," December 12, 1994.

CHAPTER 19: UNDERMINING PARIZEAU

277   On the virage forced on Parizeau: see *Le Devoir, La Presse, The Globe and Mail* and *The Montreal Gazette*, April 10–15, 1995.

281   Child Simon rushed to hospital: interview with Luc Lavoie. While Lavoie didn't like the suggestion that Bouchard was an emotional time bomb, there were too many examples of volcanic behaviour on Bouchard's part to dismiss the description.

282   Bouchard's own people as the more guilty party. On his trip to Washington, Bouchard had granted that many French Canadians had run the country, but no one pressed him on it, or pointed out the hypocrisy in his blaming the other side.

282   On Chrétien's background: *Chrétien: The Will to Win.*

283   Bouchard following the tortuous path of the Quebec conscience. In Quebec this postulate was accepted with rare dissent. Applying it to other countries would suggest that any leader could swing from one party to another and back with impunity, excusing himself or herself with the explanation that he or she was simply incorporating the doubts of the population.

284   Mackenzie King on Franklin Roosevelt: Lawrence Martin, *The Presidents and The Prime Ministers: Washington and Ottawa Face to Face—The Myth of Bilateral Bliss, 1867–1982* (Toronto: Doubleday Canada, 1982).

284   The victim complex: an interview with Daniel Poliquin.

285   Bouchard as a reflection of an earlier time: an interview with Bill Fox.

285   de Gaulle on the man of action: Michel Venne in *Le Devoir*, January 14, 1996.

286   Wait until you see what Jean does to him in the next referendum: from interviews the author conducted for the biography of Jean Chrétien.

288   Quotations of Bouchard and others from the early stages of referendum campaign are from *Le Devoir, La Presse, The*

Globe and Mail and *The Toronto Star*.

CHAPTER 20: DEMONS EVERYWHERE

290   The job he had to do: interview with Denis de Belleval.

295   Slashing attacks on everyone. Journalist Benoît Aubin enu-
       merated the examples in a column on October 14, 1995,
       which was published in his *Chroniques de mauvaise humeur*
       (Montréal: Boréal, 1996).

296   Gérard Bouchard looks askance: an interview with Gérard
       Bouchard.

297   The temper flare-up with Fisher: from an interview with
       Tobias Fisher.

297   Initial polls show not much reaction: an interview with
       Eddie Goldenberg.

297   No contingency plan. Goldenberg went so far in an inter-
       view as to say that you can't have contingency plans in such
       campaigns. It seemed a strange comment from an adviser as
       politically seasoned as Goldenberg.

298   For Bouchard's fantastic same-day turnabout on the declara-
       tion of sovereignty, see article by Philippe Cantin, *La Presse*,
       October 19, 1995.

300   Chrétien breaks into tears at caucus meeting. The scene is
       based in good part on the description in Edward Greenspon
       and Anthony Wilson-Smith, *Double Vision: The Inside Story of
       the Liberals in Power* (Toronto: Doubleday Canada, 1996).

302   The grievance was that there was no grievance: an interview
       with Conrad Black.

302   Living in the best country in the world. de Belleval, becom-
       ing exasperated in an interview, went on to say, "OK, so
       we're stupid, but that's the way we are."

303   A bitterness from Bouchard never heard from anyone: inter-
       view with Jean-Claude Rivest.

304   The two Quebec journalists preparing a book on the refer-
       endum were Michel C. Auger and Michel David. They set
       their plans aside when Bouchard declined to grant them an

interview. Auger said he thought any suggestion that Bouchard purposely slowed down in the final few days was going too far. But he found it strange how the secessionists allowed the federalists to dominate the headlines in the last week and steal victory from what looked like certain defeat.

307   The media spin. The CBC lead the way on the verdict that the victory was a setback.

CHAPTER 21: DR. JEKYLL AND MR. HYDE

310   Jean Pelletier's letter to the editor was published in *La Presse*, December 18, 1995.

311   Bouchard's response to Chrétien: from Michel Vastel's biography.

311   The Chrétien declaration, "If Canada is divisible, Quebec is divisible too. It's the same logic," was delivered at a press conference in Vancouver on January 29, 1996. It was arguably the most significant statement he made in his first term in office.

313   Chrétien's sarcastic comment to Bouchard about being at Sussex Drive: from an interview with Chrétien spokesman Peter Donolo.

316   Bouchard came to Canada too late to understand: an interview with Sam Wakim.

316   Bouchard and the Massachusetts governor: *La Presse*, June 6 and 7, 1996. See also "PQ Policy flip-flops baffle backers," Rhéal Séguin, *The Globe and Mail*, June 6, 1996.

316   Bouchard respects Chrétien: Lysiane Gagnon in *The Globe and Mail*, June 15, 1996.

316   Never used the word betrayed: *The Ottawa Citizen*, February 4, 1996.

318   Rakoff's comments on Bouchard and the esthetic character disorder came in an interview following the filing of his reports.

319   Man refuses to shake Bouchard's hand: *La Presse*, February 14, 1996.

INDEX